WITHDRAWN

WILDE WRITINGS

CONTEXTUAL CONDITIONS

WILDE WRITINGS

CONTEXTUAL CONDITIONS

Edited by Joseph Bristow

Published by the University of Toronto Press in association with
the UCLA Center for Seventeenth- and Eighteenth-Century Studies
and the William Andrews Clark Memorial Library

©The Regents of the University of California 2003
Toronto Buffalo London
Printed in Canada

ISBN 0-8020-3532-9

Printed on acid-free paper

UCLA Clark Memorial Library Series

National Library of Canada Cataloguing in Publication

Main entry under title:

Wilde writings : contextual conditions / edited by Joseph Bristow.

(UCLA Clark Memorial Library series)
Includes bibliographical references and index.
ISBN 0-8020-3532-9

1. Wilde, Oscar, 1854–1900 – Criticism and interpretation.
I. Bristow, Joseph   II. William Andrews Clark Memorial Library
III. University of California, Los Angeles. Center for 17th- &
18th-Century Studies.   IV. Series.

PR5824.W54 2003   828′.809   C2002-902812-4

This book has been published with the help of a grant from the Center for
Seventeenth- and Eighteenth-Century Studies, UCLA.

University of Toronto Press acknowledges the financial support for its
publishing activities of the Government of Canada through the Book
Publishing Industry Development Program (BPIDP).

Contents

PART II: WILDE STAGES

PART III: WILDE CONTEXTS

PART IV: WILDE LEGACIES

List of Illustrations

Preface and Acknowledgments

Wilde Writings: Contextual Conditions brings together selected papers that were first delivered at the four conferences comprising the series "Oscar Wilde and the Culture of the Fin de Siècle" hosted by the William Andrews Clark Memorial Library, University of California, Los Angeles, in January to May 1999. During the academic year 1998–99 I held the Clark Professorship, and it was my privilege to arrange the programs for each conference in the series. I am especially grateful to the Center for Seventeenth- and Eighteenth-Century Studies for taking expert care of the many administrative tasks that had to be completed so that the conference series ran as smoothly as possible. The Center oversees all of the academic symposia held at the William Andrews Clark Memorial Library. In this regard, I would like to thank the staffs of the Center, particularly Nancy Connolly, Marina Romani, and Candis Snoddy. The director of the Center, Peter Reill, gave welcome support to the conference series; in addition, he warmly encouraged the publication of the present volume.

During the editorial process, the staffs of the University of California library system have been unfailingly helpful. In particular, my colleagues at the William Andrews Clark Memorial Library – Jennifer Schaffner, Carol A. Sommer, Suzanne Tatian, and Bruce Whiteman – generously shared their extensive knowledge of the largest Wilde archive in the world. On countless occasions they directed me toward materials that I would not otherwise have found. Marina Romani, Jennifer Schaffner, and Suzanne Tatian must be thanked for their help with processing a number of reprographic orders. Two research assistants, James Walter Caufield and Johanna M. Schwartz, undertook painstaking work in checking documentation, as well as making many helpful suggestions with regard to copyediting. The contributors responded generously to my various queries, and I remain grateful to them for their prompt feedback. Several people advised me on matters of copyright and permissions: Henny Finch (London Management), Diana Maltz, Merlin Holland, Elisabeth Molle (Musée D'Orsay), Ayala Sella (Art Resource), and Anna Taylor (Ashmolean Museum, University of Oxford). Craig Westwood at Fourth Estate kindly mailed me an advance copy of the British edition of *The Complete Letters of Oscar Wilde*, edited by Merlin Holland and Rupert Hart-Davis, published in 2000, thus ensuring that all references to Wilde's correspondence could be made to this definitive volume.

Wherever possible, contributors have provided in the main text the dates of the earliest performance or publication of primary works. One particular date is worthy of clarification. In the case of *Salomé*, the date appears as 1893, since the original French text was published in that year by the Librairie de l'Art Indépendant in Paris and by Elkin Mathews at John Lane in London. The play went into two weeks of rehearsals in June 1892, only to be refused permission for public performance by Edward F. Smyth-Pigott, Examiner of Plays for the Lord Chamberlain. The first English edition, translated by Lord Alfred Douglas and illustrated by Aubrey Beardsley, was published as *Salome* (without the final accent) in 1894 by Elkin Mathews and John Lane in London and by Copeland and Day in Boston. Throughout the volume, both *Salomé* and Salomé have been presented with the accent, since this is how both the title and the proper name appear in Wilde's original French text.

At the time of drawing this volume to a close, the uneven textual editing of Wilde's writings remains a matter of some concern to scholars. In the name of accuracy, contributors generally refer to the fourteen-volume edition of Wilde's *Collected Works*, edited by Robert Ross and published by Methuen in 1908. Contributors have also taken the opportunity to refer, where appropriate, to several modern editions that have greater authority. Such editions include the New Mermaid volumes of Wilde's Society dramas edited by Russell Jackson and Ian Small and the Norton Critical Edition of *The Picture of Dorian Gray* edited by Donald L. Lawler. Fortunately, the textual editing of Wilde's canon has already begun to improve with the recent appearance of the first volume in the Oxford English Texts edition published by Oxford University Press. In the present volume, the chapters by Josephine M. Guy, John Stokes, and

Ian Small derive from research undertaken in preparation for the Oxford English Texts edition, which promises to offer the most reliable resource in the study of Wilde's writings.

Since some of the materials discussed in *Wilde Writings* are not widely available outside of the William Andrews Clark Memorial Library, I have inserted call numbers. I trust this information will be useful to readers who intend to conduct research in the library's archives, especially in relation to its uncataloged materials.

A small part of the discussion in the introduction originates in my article, "Memorializing Wilde: An Explosive History," in the *Journal of Victorian Culture* 5 (2000), 311–22; permission to reprint has been granted by Edinburgh University Press. A short section of chapter 2 has previously appeared in Josephine M. Guy and Ian Small, *Oscar Wilde's Profession: Writing and the Culture Industry in the Late Nineteenth Century* (Oxford: Oxford University Press, 2000); permission to reprint has been granted by Oxford University Press. A number of copyright holders granted permission to reproduce illustrations in the volume. Figures 3 and 5 are copyright the Estate of Max Beerbohm, and appear by permission of London Management. Figure 8 appears courtesy of the Musée d'Orsay. Figures 8 and 9 appear by permission of Cassell & Co. Barnardos granted permission to reproduce figure 11. The William Andrews Clark Memorial Library permitted the reproduction of figures 1, 4, 13, 14, and 15. All efforts have been made to trace copyright holders. The publisher apologizes to any copyright holder who has not been acknowledged.

JEB
September 2001

WILDE WRITINGS

CONTEXTUAL CONDITIONS

Introduction

JOSEPH BRISTOW

Oscar Wilde! I wonder to how many of my readers the jingle of his name suggests anything at all? Yes, at one time, it was familiar to many and if we search back among the old volumes of Punch, *we shall find many a quip and crank out at its owner's expense. But time is a quick mover and many of us are fated to outlive our reputations and thus, though at one time Mr. Wilde, the old gentleman, of whom we are going to give our readers a brief account, was in his way quite a celebrity; today his star is set, his name obscured in this busy, changeful city.*

– Max Beerbohm, *A Peep into the Past* (1894)

I

Wilde Writings reveals how our knowledge of Oscar Wilde's diverse achievements – as a critic, dramatist, editor, journalist, and writer of fiction – has advanced considerably in recent years. Now, more than a century after his penurious demise on 30 November 1900, the "jingle of his name" (to quote his contemporary, Max Beerbohm) arouses an immense amount of scholarly interest. These days the academic world can confidently assert that it possesses greater understanding than ever before of a gifted man whose widely publicized successes and failures were often misrepresented both during his lifetime and in the years that followed his premature death at the age of forty-six. The thirteen studies brought together in this volume form part of a rapidly growing body of research that seeks to demystify the long history of gossip, rumor, and scandal that haunted both Wilde's professional existence and his posthumous reputation. Further, each chapter makes no apology for assum-

ing that Wilde's writings maintain a distinguished position in literary
history. During the past two decades his works – especially *The Picture of
Dorian Gray* (1890, 1891), the Society Comedies (1892–95), and *Salomé*
(1893) – have been taught extensively on college and university syllabi.
Yet, as other critics have been quick to point out, it took a remarkably
long time before students and teachers were willing to approach Wilde's
writings with some measure of seriousness. "For fifty years after his
death," writes Ian Small, "Wilde certainly did have a reputation, but it
was that of an infamous homosexual rather than a figure worthy of intellectual or academic attention."[1] *Wilde Writings* aims to provide an accurate account of some previously unexplored contextual conditions in
which Wilde forged his varied, rather uneven, career. But in order to
put the present volume in its own critical context, it is vital to understand why it is only of late that scholars can obtain a more focused perspective on Wilde's heterogeneous canon.

The major problem that confronts anyone wishing to research
Wilde's writings lies in how to negotiate the enduring legend of his
meteoric rise to stardom and his pitiful fall from grace. The sensational
facts form part of the familiar narrative that set a pattern for the rather
volatile manner in which Wilde's name would circulate excitedly in
modern culture. On 3 April 1895 Wilde appeared at the Old Bailey to
pursue a libel suit against the Marquess of Queensberry, the father of
Lord Alfred Douglas – a beautiful, temperamental aristocrat whose
noteworthy poetic talent would become evident while he was an undergraduate at Oxford. Douglas and Wilde had become intimate after they
met at Wilde's Chelsea home in June 1891. Wilde moved swiftly to this
hazardous action after receiving an offensive visiting card that the indig-
nant Queensberry left at Wilde's club. From what we can tell, the card
read: "To Oscar Wilde, Posing as Somdomite." While Queensberry's
memorable misspelling of his insult remains unquestionable, the near-
illegible handwriting suggests that he might have been labeling his
enemy a "Poseur." Like so many materials relating to Wilde, this
example proves somewhat hard to construe. In like manner, Wilde's
misguided decision to sue for defamation remains open to some speculation. His case, after all, failed miserably. Queensberry's defense garnered sufficient evidence to suggest that the plaintiff was indeed
sexually intimate with other men. As a consequence, Wilde had to put
his household belongings up for sale to cover expensive legal costs.
Thereafter, the Director of Prosecutions pursued two further trials that
resulted in the court sentencing Wilde on 25 May 1895 to twenty-four

months of imprisonment in solitary confinement with hard labor for committing acts of "gross indecency." The press, apart from one or two notable exceptions, vilified him.[2] Such was Wilde's downfall.

Wilde, it would appear, fell from great heights. His disgrace occurred not long after he seems to have reached the peak of his dramatic powers. In the weeks preceding the suit against him, two of his finest plays were diverting West End audiences. (Both productions came to an abrupt halt – An Ideal Husband on 27 April, The Importance of Being Earnest on 8 May – when the court proceedings destroyed Wilde's reputation.) An Ideal Husband opened at the Theatre Royal, Haymarket, on 3 January that year, while Earnest enjoyed a St Valentine's Day premiere at the fashionable St. James's Theatre. These Society Comedies, however, met with certain reservations among the more significant reviewers of the day. William Archer, a powerful critic who recognized Wilde as "as a writer, an écrivain, of the first rank,"[3] expressed misgivings about An Ideal Husband. In his view, this "very able and entertaining piece of work" suffered because several scenes were "overburdened with witticisms" of the kind that "threaten[ed] to become all trademark and no substance."[4] Another influential commentator, A.B. Walkley, similarly complained about the "cheapness" of the play's epigrammatic wit.[5] Walkley had already remarked on the "staleness of the incidents" dramatized in Lady Windermere's Fan (1892).[6] In some respects, the critical reception of Earnest was also unforgiving. An unsigned notice in The Theatre, which surveyed the London stage more thoroughly than most journals, contended that the play was "clumsily handled, the treatment unequal, the construction indifferent."[7] At the same time, Earnest seemed like a hodge-podge of different genres: "elements of farce, comedy, and burlesque are jumbled together with a fine disregard for consistency." Like many of his contemporaries, this anonymous reviewer disliked Wilde's stylistic handiwork, which on this view appealed to the limitations of an audience that seemed "unable or unwilling to distinguish between the tinsel glitter of sham epigram and the authentic sheen of true wit."

This somewhat negative commentary throws into question the degree to which Wilde commanded respect in a society that was prepared to fulminate against him when his so-called crime of gross indecency became public knowledge. Wilde's fortunes, like his reputation past and present, were mixed, and it is important not to exaggerate his dramatic success in the weeks before the trials. To be sure, he was making good money from his 1895 plays, yet opinion of them was not entirely favorable. Similar caution needs to be exercised when assessing what was in

many respects the depressing final phase of his career. After his release
from his brutalizing experience at Reading Gaol, Wilde left for France,
winding up some three and a half years later on his deathbed in the
Latin Quarter of Paris. Although certain unreliable sources led people
to believe that he died from syphilis, it was meningitis that actually killed
him.[8] He died in debt, with a handful of loyal friends tending him to the
last. As he knew only too well, so much scandal was eventually attached
to his name that he remained unmentionable in polite society. Yet in
1898 Wilde published what would quickly become his bestselling work.
The first six editions of *The Ballad of Reading Gaol* omitted any reference to Wilde, stating that the poem was the work of "C.3.3" (the number of his prison cell). There was, however, no doubt about his authorship. As modern scholarship has shown, Wilde probably earned more
money from this runaway success than he did from his other numerous
publications; seven thousand copies were sold within his lifetime.[9] Even
if Wilde could not be named in respectable company, he still commanded public attention. His humiliation, which led to his self-imposed
exile in Paris, participated in what became his last and greatest publishing triumph.

Wilde was not the only person to benefit financially, though not in
overwhelming amounts, during the years that followed the terrible
incarceration that weakened his spirit and broke his health. Shortly after
Wilde was buried, the actor-manager George Alexander, who held rights
to two of Wilde's dramas, put *Earnest* and *Lady Windermere's Fan* back on
the London stage in 1902 and 1904 respectively. Revivals of both plays
have regularly taken place ever since. At the same time, Wilde's devotees
poured their energies into the less profitable labor of trying to dignify
his literary reputation. But while the Society Comedies grew steadily in
popularity, the effort to establish Wilde's intellectual supremacy
remained by and large frustrated. In 1908 his literary executor, Robert
Ross, edited the handsome fourteen-volume *edition de luxe* of the *Collected
Works*. In the pages the *Academy*, the noted literary journal that he edited
from 1907 to 1910, Douglas warmly welcomed the white buckram-bound
edition, stating that "the failure of contemporary criticism to appreciate"
Wilde's genius remained "a lasting slur upon the intelligence of this
country."[10] Other reviewers, however, were largely unimpressed. In the
Times Literary Supplement, for instance, Harold Child commented that
that "the abiding taste left in the mind by the reading of these twelve
beautiful volumes is the taste of disappointment and disillusion."[11]
Observing that Wilde's "gaze was constantly fixed on himself," Child

stated that Wilde never learned "[i]ntrospection of the genuine kind." (303). Forever posing, Wilde eventually "grew into a Pierrot who liked to play the prophet" (303). In Child's ungenerous opinion, Wilde's critical essays reveal that he was simply "saying what other people ... said before him." (304). His talents, Child maintained, were much more suited to the theatre where Wilde's characteristic love of epigram – a "machine-made ... verbal jingle" (306–07) – none the less helped to produce a Society Drama that was "sparkling and exquisite." (306).

In 1914 Wilde's supporters redoubled their efforts to honor his achievements. In that year they unveiled an imposing monument to Wilde, completed two years before by the sculptor Jacob Epstein, in the Père Lachaise cemetery in Paris. At the same time, Stuart Mason's *Bibliography of Oscar Wilde* was greeted with applause. The *Library Association Record* acclaimed it as "the most comprehensive bibliography that exists in English."[12] The institutions of criticism, however, seldom took notice of Ross's great edition or Mason's extensive bibliographical research. The journal *Scrutiny* – which helped to strengthen the authority of English studies in British higher education – mentioned Wilde's name only once in the course of twenty-one years (1932–53): F.R. Leavis noted in passing that Wilde vulgarized Walter Pater's critical prose.[13] The entertainer, it seems, could never be a thinker. The commercial popularity of Wilde's drama in the 1930s, the decade when British television first broadcast *Earnest*, may well have masked what critics such as Richard Ellmann would much later uncover as the author's brilliant revision of Paterian thought in essays such as "The Critic as Artist" (1889).[14]

But there was another likely reason for the institutional reluctance to canonize Wilde in a period when stage and screen increasingly embraced him. Literary historians probably recoiled from the endless bickering and infighting that surrounded the popular books that fed a prurient public scandal-ridden accounts of his personal and professional life. In its assessment of "Oscar Wilde after Fifty Years," the *Times Literary Supplement* observed: "Passion, prejudice and hypocrisy have converged upon the name of Oscar Wilde, and continued to obscure and distort the story of his downfall."[15] Here the anonymous reviewer fixed the blame on Wilde's earliest biographers for society's rather mistaken image of him. The initial accounts of his career undoubtedly suffer from varying quantities of erroneous and improbable information. By and large, these inaccurate – at times reckless – narratives of Wilde's life draw on the unreliable memories, as well as fantasies, of people who either felt too close or not close enough to their subject's assumed notoriety.

In their nastiest form, the disputes over Wilde's legacy led Douglas, his sometime lover, and Ross, his greatest advocate, into infamous libel proceedings, as they engaged in legal struggles with each other for the best part of six acrimonious years over Wilde's controversial name. The bitter battles originated in Douglas' rather belated discovery of how roundly Wilde condemned him in the long prison letter that Ross would publish, in carefully abridged form, as *De Profundis* in 1905. This edition suppressed the many parts of the letter that inculpated Douglas for Wilde's imprisonment. On reading Arthur Ransome's *Oscar Wilde: A Critical Study* (1912) – the first attempt at a serious evaluation of Wilde – Douglas learned that the unpublished parts of Wilde's lengthy epistle referred to himself in most uncomplimentary terms. On this matter, Ross was Ransome's source. Deeply offended, the headstrong Douglas had no hesitation in pressing charges against Ransome, his publisher, and the distributor of the volume. The court proceedings of 1913 worsened Douglas' situation when he heard the defense read aloud the various passages from *De Profundis* that maligned him.

Douglas' enmity toward Ross, who officially took control of Wilde's literary estate in 1906, grew so deep that he put his name to a book that denounced his former lover. In a study titled *Oscar Wilde and Myself* (1914), Douglas led readers to believe that he felt that Wilde was "a person of careless and vicious life, whose talents were always carelessly and at times viciously employed."[16] "Such a man," the diatribe continued, "was almost, in the nature of things, bound to come to a miserable and degraded end." The book made various accusations about the derivative nature of Wilde's art. In particular, Wilde's essays were held in contempt: "he knew that the 'Decay of Lying' [1889], the 'Critic as Artist' and the 'Truth of Masks' [1888] were, in large measure, cribbed from Whistler" (229) – a viewpoint that does not entirely distort the truth. By 1925, however, Douglas began taking back these rancorous remarks, stating that Wilde's prison letter was the result of "wild delusions."[17] He chose instead to show that the contemptible Ross – "the High Priest of all the sodomites in London" – had made a fortune from exploiting the "cult" of Wilde (38). A few years later he suggested that *Oscar Wilde and Myself* was written in the name of self-preservation: it "presented a picture of what at that time I wished to be supposed to be" (210). Thereafter, he continued his recantation by emphasizing that his sometime coeditor, the puritanical T.W.F. Crosland, should be blamed for the earlier "cutting up" of Wilde.[18] By 1940, Douglas would reiterate that he treasured Wilde's memory "after an interval of turning against him."[19] But he added that as a Catholic (he converted to Rome in 1911) he "disapprove[d] deeply of homosexuality." (10–11). Not surprisingly, the *Times Literary Supplement* commented that no reliance could be placed upon Douglas' "uncorroborated word."

Yet in some respects Douglas proved somewhat more dependable than one of the biographers who for some time accepted Ross's version of Wilde. In this regard, Douglas recognized that Frank Harris had initially been misled by a number of tall tales. Like Ransome, Harris believed Ross's far-fetched story of how Wilde's corpse exploded soon after death. But to complicate matters, Harris himself was fanciful in the extreme. The *Times Literary Supplement* contended that Harris "never seems to have cared, or even to have known, whether or not what he was telling was the truth." In 1916 Harris' disreputable *Oscar Wilde: His Life and Confessions* appeared in the first of its many editions. As the title implies, the two lengthy volumes provide juicy exposés of Wilde's presumably more sinful moments. Not surprisingly, this so-called biography reads like a racy novel, with plenty of animated (but hardly authentic) passages of dialogue. Harris, who cannot resist the temptation to become the hero of the piece, pushes himself forward not only as Wilde's intimate ally but also as his savior. By the time Harris rushes breathless toward the trials of 1895, Wilde emerges as a desperately ruined man whose sufferings manage to evoke Harris' supposedly noble feelings of pity. Recalling how Wilde refused to flee the country after the second trial, Harris heightens the emotional pitch by stating that his "affection for Oscar Wilde date[d] from his confession ... that afternoon."[20] Having gained Wilde's "trust," "the barrier" between them was "thrown down." At this revelatory moment, Harris grew instantly aware of "the extraordinary femininity and gentle weakness of" Wilde's "nature." Such was his depth of pity that Harris refused to condemn Wilde for "that form of sexual indulgence" (I: 290–91). Harris' virtuous desire, he maintains, was to "protect and help him." None of this condescending nonsense about Wilde's apparently effeminate sexuality would warrant much attention were it not for the fact that Harris' biography became a cause célèbre, with sales that may have reached (if he is to be believed) forty thousand copies.[21]

The distortion of Wilde, however, predates by many years Douglas' and Harris' incoherent accounts. Their tendency in the 1910s and 1920s to paint such an eccentric picture of Wilde extends a tradition that was established quite soon after he graduated from Oxford in the late 1870s and bedeviled his career to the end. The innumerable cartoons, drawings, and paintings that mocked Wilde enjoyed a widespread influence on how the public came to perceive him. These images have left a lasting impression on how his name has been preserved in cultural memory. Mason's *Bibliography* was the first publication to gather up some of the better-known illustrations that made sport of Wilde. To this day, sketches of this variety feature on the covers of academic studies that seek to improve our understanding of Wilde's career.[22] In a climate where current scholarship seeks to adjust our view of Wilde, it remains instructive to inspect some of the drawings that made him appear more "aesthetic," arrogant, bloated, and voluptuous than he ever was. In almost every case, these illustrations – which have rarely been subjected to close examination – distort Wilde from such a diverse range of angles that they reveal uncertainty about the cultural meanings that could or should be attached to his name.

The extensive visual culture that Wilde's career engendered comes sharply into focus in at least three recent books: Jonathan Goodman's *The Wilde File* (1988), Merlin Holland's *The Wilde Album* (1997), and *The Wilde Years* (2000) edited by Tomoko Sato and Lionel Lambourne.[23] The numerous plates in these absorbing volumes remind us that at a comparatively young age Wilde made an impact seldom matched by his literary contemporaries. In the late 1870s and early 1880s, Wilde's rising status as the outlandish doyen of aestheticism roused the press to frenzy. The visual ridicule of Wilde dates roughly from 1880 when, at the age of twenty-five, he promoted himself as a fashionable young gentleman moving among the cultural elite of London. At social gatherings such as the avant-garde Grosvenor Gallery in New Bond Street, his quick-witted conversation, together with his dazzling couture, transformed this recent Oxford graduate into a national celebrity. Yet despite this rapid fame, Wilde failed to fulfil his ambitions to establish himself as a serious man of letters.

Even though by 1881 he had no less than forty poems accepted by various Irish and English magazines, Wilde did not manage to place a collection of them with a major company. When the minor publisher David Bogue produced Wilde's *Poems* in that year, commentators were hardly sparing in their criticism. "Aesthete of Aesthetes! / What's in a name? / The poet is WILDE, / But his poetry's tame," *Punch* remarked, this jeering quatrain appearing beneath a sketch where Wilde's face extrudes from a sunflower in a vase.[24] (This drawing counts among the many scornful cartoons of Wilde that *Punch* would publish over the years. The sunflower relates to the eccentric buttonhole that Wilde displayed at some public gatherings.) "Swinburne and Water" was the title that *Punch* gave to a later, derisory review.[25] "This," it stated, "is a volume of echoes." Such a judgment is unsurprising, given that a few of Wilde's works (principally "Charmides") derived from Swinburne's *Poems and Ballads* (1866), a volume that appealed to perverse eroticism in the name of championing the freedom of art above the strictures of morality. Wilde's Republican fervor also affiliated him with the strident anti-monarchical politics of Swinburne's *Songs before Sunrise* (1871). Reviewers promptly noted other conspicuous influences, such as Dante Gabriel Rossetti's *Poems* (1870). Yet in the ironically titled "Ave Imperatrix" (Benjamin Disraeli declared Queen Victoria Empress of India in January 1877), Wilde's forceful critique of British military conflict in Afghanistan appealed to the press in the United States. The *Century Magazine*, for example, regretted the "force of ridicule" that had set such "strong prejudice" against Wilde.[26] Even though the reviewer believed that there were "traces of weakness in plenty" throughout *Poems*, the magazine concluded that Wilde was "after all a poet of no mean calibre" (152). "Ave Imperatrix," the *Century* insisted, "outweigh[ed] a hundred cartoons of 'Punch'" (153). But in spite of the praise and blame that Wilde's *Poems* received, the book remained largely unread in 1881. (In any case, Bogue went into liquidation in August 1882, and interest in the collection only revived when Elkin Mathews and John Lane reprinted it a decade later.) Bogue sought to boost interest in the volume by putting it into five editions in the first year, in an attempt to give the impression that these reprints were meeting considerable demand. Sales, in fact, were modest. Plenty of people in Britain, however, had been forming pictures of what Wilde was supposed to embody, since it proved difficult to escape his irresistible iconicity.

It was in the years 1880 and 1881 that Wilde first caught the public's notice on a large scale. In Oxford, for example, Bowyer Nichols printed a striking illustration with the caption "Aesthetics v. Athletics: Torpid Week, 1881" (figure 1). This drawing concentrates attention on Wilde's legacy as a flamboyant proponent of "art for art's sake" while a student at Magdalen College, where he graduated with first class honours in Greats. In the same year as this drawing, Wilde's reputation became a source of debate when the Oxford Union Society voted 140 to 128 against accepting a presentation copy of *Poems*. (Wilde wrote the librarian of the union to protest the "coarse impertinence" of some of its members.[27]) Positioned in the midst of a field populated by marauding oarsmen (running in a state of raucous excitement), a wilting Wilde lan-

1 Bowyer Nichols, "Aesthetics v. Athletics," Oxford, 1881.

guidly raises his stick-like arms above his waist in despair, his slightly bent right knee barely supporting his feeble frame. The caricature, which suggests that his enormous head might topple from his body, reveals the pretentious aesthete – famed for his long hair and exuberant costume – aghast, uttering in despair: "This is indeed a form of death, and entirely incompatible with any belief in the immortality of the soul." The moral is clear. Here the Wildean desire to aestheticize the modern world is no match for the larger numbers of team-spirited men who know how, in Henry Newbolt's words, to "Play up! play up! and play the game!"[28] But, like so many drawings in this vein, Nichols' satire cannot emasculate Wilde as much as it might like. Although the drawing isolates Wilde's aestheticism as "a form of death," it lends a certain distinction to his eccentric masculinity, which makes a blunt contrast with the faceless uniformity of the hearty athletes. Even if "Torpid Week" is supposed to characterize Wilde's debility, it nonetheless hints that his polemical presence has, at least metaphorically, created a new fixture in the undergraduate schedule.

Elsewhere, other caricatures of the aesthetic Wilde undertake different methods that result in elevating his iconic presence in the very process of deriding him. In early 1881 the satirical British magazine *Entr'acte* published Arthur Bryan's "Mr. Oscar Wilde" (see *The Wilde Album*, 56). All the hallmarks of Wilde's increasingly familiar image – the flowing locks, the effete posture, the rather drowsy eyelids, and the limp wrist – are in place. Likewise, his supposedly affected manner of speech emerges in the legend beneath his name: "Quite Too Utterly Ecstatic." Yet Bryan presents Wilde with a certain dignity. Here Wilde's gaze stares back at the viewer in a manner that could scarcely be described as passive. By comparison, the British journal *Time* portrayed him as "The Bard of Beauty" in 1880. He is shown offering a sonnet to Ellen Terry and a triolet to Sarah Bernhardt, the famous actresses whose company he courted after he abandoned his ambitions to establish an academic career (see *The Wilde Album*, 58).[29] This cartoon certainly makes jibes at Wilde's wish to succeed with celebrities who might assist his career as an aspiring dramatist. For example, he hoped that Terry might star in his first play, *Vera*, which focuses on anarchist attacks on the Russian monarchy, but the role went to Mrs. Bernard Beere. The production was abandoned in December 1880, for reasons that remain open to dispute.[30] This image of the "The Bard of Beauty" stands alongside a poem of the same name (by "Oscuro Mild") that lampoons one of Wilde's lyrics. The poem that *Time* parodies is "The New Helen," which

Wilde dedicated to Lillie Langtry in admiration of her first appearance on the London stage as Kate Hardcastle in the 1881 production of Oliver Goldsmith's *She Stoops to Conquer.* "The New Helen," interestingly enough, originally appeared a year earlier in the opening volume of *Time.*[31] In sending up Wilde, therefore, the magazine was also partly performing an act of self-mockery.

A rather different representational process is at work in the famous cartoons of George Du Maurier, the leading illustrator of *Punch*, who recognized that Wilde presented one prominent aspect of the "Nincompoopiana" that in Du Maurier's view typified the Aesthetic Movement.[32] From the mid-1870s onward, when his satirical cast of aesthetic characters gradually took shape, a number of his drawings incorporated aspects of Wilde's demeanour, as well as his clothing. In "The Six-Mark Tea-Pot," for instance, Du Maurier portrays an Aesthetic Bridegroom (who sports Wilde's hairstyle) and an Aesthetic Bride (who resembles a Pre-Raphaelite model) contemplating the charms of this piece of blue and white china (figure 2).[33] (This type of Japanese china generated a craze in artistic circles after it appeared at the Great Exhibition at London in 1862.) The bridegroom, whose smoking jacket connotes a life of leisure, says to his beloved: "It is quite consummate, is it not!" "It is, indeed!" she exclaims. "Oh, Algernon, let us to live up to it." This exchange, while printed in October 1880, draws on what was already a staple part of the mythmaking that had gathered around Wilde. In the mid-1870s Dean Burgon delivered a sermon at the Oxford University Church that denounced the depraved morals of the brilliant undergraduate. Wilde had been rumored to declare that he "found it difficult to live up to the level of his blue china" that adorned his rooms at Magdalen.[34] Du Maurier, who knew the artistic world of London intimately, understood how Wilde followed in the wake of the established Pre-Raphaelite painter Dante Gabriel Rossetti, whose home at Chelsea was at one time filled with items of this type. In addition, by giving the bridegroom Swinburne's first name, Du Maurier suggested that Wilde's aestheticism owed much to a previous generation of artists and writers whose works had often been attacked for their presumed indulgence in sensuality.

The perception that Du Maurier detested all that Wilde represented came to public attention in one of Victorian culture's greatest subject paintings, *The Private View of the Royal Academy, 1881* by William Frith.[35] Here Frith presents a large number of important persons of the day; there are over forty faces in the well-dressed crowd, in various states of conversation or contemplation. The walls are equally crowded with ele-

2 George Du Maurier, "The Six-Mark Tea-Pot," *Punch*, 30 October 1880, 194.

gantly framed exhibits. But there is one figure that stands out in this populous scene. It is of course Wilde. Wearing a lofty top hat and a lavish buttonhole, Wilde could not contrast more starkly with the puny frame depicted by Bowyer Nichols. Here he towers above practically all of the other characters whose famous physiognomies shine out from the canvas. It might be said that Wilde dominates this carefully orchestrated painting, given the concentration of light that illuminates his complexion as he gazes upward, notebook in hand, at an exhibit placed above him on his left. What is more, several other people look at him from different positions. Situated to his right, Ellen Terry and her young son Edward Gordon Craig respectfully witness Wilde's scrutiny of the exhibits. By contrast, to Wilde's left stands Du Maurier, a man not known for smiling in public, giving Wilde the most hardened of stares.

As Frith pointed out, the painting seeks to "hit the folly of listening to self-elected critics in matters of taste, whether in dress or art."[36] In this regard, Wilde, "a well-known apostle of the beautiful," is the main culprit. Frith exposes how the upstart Wilde, whose earliest piece of journalism reviewed the opening of the Grosvenor Gallery in 1877, commanded unearned respect from vulnerable but influential parties such as Terry and her entourage. *The Private View* certainly draws a close correspondence between Wilde and the "aesthetic" women attending the opening of this prestigious exhibition in clothes whose "ugliness of form and oddity of colour" offend the eye. Where Wilde wears a florid lily on his lapel, one of his female acolytes toward the far left of the canvas dons a sunflower on her "aesthetic" dress. Since lilies and sunflowers were practically trademarks of Wilde's aestheticism, the painting implies that Wilde's promotion of this style was a distinctly feminizing one, a view certainly shared by Du Maurier.

The Private View made such an impression that Harry Furniss, the Irish illustrator who sometimes worked for *Punch*, produced a parody of it for the Christmas number of the *World* in 1882, and he would continue to caricature Wilde through the 1890s.[37] Where Frith's painting grants the viewer the privilege to survey each and every face upon the canvas, Furniss's drawing rearranges the assembled company to achieve the opposite effect. In this revision of *The Private View*, most of the distinguished persons stare back at the viewer, almost as if they realize that they are just about to be photographed. Rather than give Wilde pride of place, Furniss puts him on the left side of the drawing. With his left hand positioned behind his waist, Wilde leans forward to take a peek at a book that two women hold before them. Dressed in what appears to be a velvet frock coat, the clean-shaven Wilde, with his characteristically long hair, sticks out in a crowd composed mainly of bearded and mustachioed men. He remains, once again, proximate to the ladies not the gentlemen. But where Frith's painting bestows height and light upon Wilde, Furniss' has a different aim in mind. He darkens Wilde's complexion as if to suggest that the young aesthete belonged to a different race. His version of this scene discloses an evident problem in Frith's attempt to draw a critical picture of Wilde. By making Wilde the main center of attention at the Royal Academy, Frith conceded perhaps too much authority to the impostor whose opinions on art and artists were a source of irritation. Such speculations are complicated by the fact that the *World* had published several of Wilde's early poems.[38] The *World* therefore helped to advance the career that Furniss' drawing would prefer, literally, to denigrate in its pages.

These diversifying, not to say contradictory, images proliferated, not just in the press. One of the most popular satires of aestheticism was W.S. Gilbert and Arthur Sullivan's opera *Patience*, which played at the fashionable Savoy Theatre in 1881. Gilbert modeled the leading character Bunthorne partly on Wilde. Bunthorne, true to the Wilde myth, presents himself as "a judge of blue-and-white and other kinds of pottery."[39] But in Gilbert's libretto, Bunthorne's status as a lily-loving poet derives from the controversies that surrounded Pre-Raphaelitism in 1871 when Robert Buchanan launched an unscrupulous attack on the "mere animal sensations" evident in the apparent "fleshliness" of Rossetti's *Poems*.[40] It would also appear that Bunthorne's style was to some degree patterned on Swinburne.[41]

Wilde's name, however, became automatically associated with *Patience* when theater manager Richard D'Oyly Carte sought to wage a successful publicity campaign for its North American production. He turned to Wilde as spokesman for aestheticism, sealing a contract for a grueling ten-month schedule of lectures that stretched from coast to coast. No sooner had he landed in New York City than Wilde's manager ensured that he made his way to the studio of theatrical photographer Napoleon Sarony. Wilde adopted twenty-seven poses for the publicity photographs that presented him in the distinctive aesthetic dress that he had specially made in London.[42] In early 1882 it was possible to purchase the series of images in different sizes, and each shot confirmed for the American public what was already familiar to British viewers. Attired in silken hose, knee-breeches, a sumptuous velvet jacket, and a fur coat, Wilde stood before the camera. Within weeks advertisers would produce engravings of these images to promote such commodities as "aesthetic" ice cream and "aesthetic" wallpapers. In the process, Wilde was, in every sense, branded, as American newspapers drew on specific national icons to scoff at the pronouncements that he made in his lecture titled "The English Renaissance of Art." "Art," he rather grandly asserted, "cannot have any other claim but her own perfection."[43] Yet as time went by, he could not sustain his tour on this presentation alone. Since he needed more material, he prepared two additional lectures, including "The Irish Poets of '48." This highly politicized analysis, first delivered to a largely Irish-American audience at San Francisco in April 1882,[44] drew attention to his Irish nationalist heritage that would otherwise have remained invisible to those who persistently damned his love of art. (During his tour, Wilde reproved his manager for writing an article for the *New York World* that alluded to an unthinking illustration in the *Washington Post* that compared him to the "Wild Man of Borneo." "I regard all caricature and satire as absolutely beneath notice," he remarked bluntly.)[45]

Even when Wilde returned to England, marrying in 1884 and fathering two sons, the cartoonist's pen never strayed far from his career. But, as the next ten years rolled by, there was one caricaturist – a man who possessed a more informed understanding of his subject than most of his contemporaries – whose work began to reflect carefully on the rather unstable manner in which Wilde's image modulated before the public's gaze. The artist in question is the inimitable Max Beerbohm, who made his mark in 1894 when he was still an undergraduate. Beerbohm enjoyed social intimacy with the circle of young men whom Wilde befriended at Oxford in 1891. Although he remained connected with Wilde's associates during the early and mid-1890s, as his drawings show, Beerbohm hardly stood in awe of the figure whose features would preoccupy him for many years to come. The sheer diversity of these numerous caricatures suggests that Beerbohm found it impossible to contain the much-mocked Wilde in a single stereotype; time and again he represents Wilde in a range of styles. Given his acute consciousness of how caricature worked, Beerbohm occupied an excellent position from which to rethink how Wilde had undergone such massive transformations that the young aesthete of the early 1880s bore little resemblance to the older man who became renowned for his literary writings a decade later.

One of Beerbohm's earliest and most famous caricatures of Wilde, called "Personal Remarks," first appeared in the popular magazine *Pick-Me-Up* in September 1894 (figure 3). This striking drawing builds on the

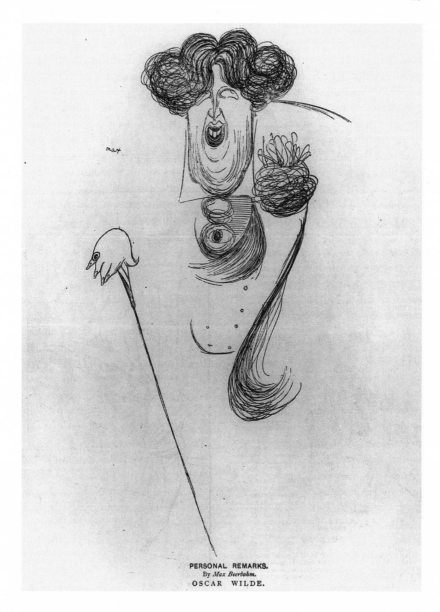

PERSONAL REMARKS.
By *Max Beerbohm*.
OSCAR WILDE.

3 Max Beerbohm, "Oscar Wilde: Personal Remarks," *Pick-Me-Up* 12 (1894), 392.

image of the increasingly corpulent Wilde depicted by Frank Hill in an unpleasant cartoon titled "A Voluptuary" that *Pick-Me-Up* published three months earlier. In "Personal Remarks" Beerbohm performs what he would later call "the delicious art of exaggerating, without fear or favour, the peculiarities of this or that human body, for the sake of exaggeration."[46] The exaggerations, which are by no means complimentary, remain all too plain to see. Here is Wilde, at the reasonably young age of thirty-nine, looking like a flatulent fop or a depraved dandy. His flounced tresses, his accentuated lips, and his diminutive hand with daintily manicured nails make a stark contrast with the expansive chins exploding over his tight shirt-collar. To be sure, Wilde's evening dress seeks to cut a dash – the buttonhole, the pointed cane, and the jeweled tiepin all say as much. But Beerbohm's caricature accomplishes what the finest examples of this genre often achieve; it shows how the pretensions of the human body, even when subjected to such close observation, maintain a compelling power over the viewer.

More sophisticated, however, is the undergraduate caricature that Beerbohm based on a well-known illustration appearing in the weekly magazine *Moonshine* in 1882. In the original (figure 4, perhaps attributable to Bryan), Wilde's long-haired and heavy-lidded features remain prominent in the oval portrait placed at the center of the page. Clad in the fur coat displayed in some of the Sarony photographs, his bust is wedged between a lily, on the one hand, and a sunflower, on the other. Around this portrait the caricaturist arranges a sequence of smaller vignettes. Readers witness Wilde in his aesthetic garb lecturing audiences in America where, it seems, "He is not a success." (Wilde's success or failure is debatable; he secured a good income from the tour.) In fact, there is a small accompanying image that shows Wilde's seasickness during his voyage across the Atlantic. In order to stress his physical frailty, the drawing reveals that Wilde cannot withstand "prime brisket of beef." "Would you like a bit of fat with it, sir?" a butcher asks Wilde. The caption beneath offers Wilde's pitiful response: "When there's no one looking – nature prompts." The insistence on Wilde's by now commonplace enfeeblement (he was over six feet tall and heavily built) looks pretty feeble in itself.

A decade later, Beerbohm critically revised this somewhat predictable cartoon from *Moonshine* by preserving its design but inserting sketches that update notable episodes in Wilde's developing career (figure 5). On this occasion, the three-quarter view of Wilde appears similarly languid but the rotund face shares the flabbiness that Beerbohm exagger-

4 "Days with Celebrities (32): Mr. Oscar Wilde," *Moonshine*, 28 January 1882, 37.

5   Max Beerbohm, "Oscar Wilde," *c.*1894, Ashmolean Museum,
University of Oxford

ated in "Personal Remarks." In this instance, however, Beerbohm's drawing style could not be more different. The rounder, thicker lines contrast with the severe angles that structure much of his *Pick-Me-Up* drawing. In the top left-hand corner Beerbohm copies *Moonshine* by presenting the seasick Wilde on the voyage to America. Beerbohm does the same by also depicting Wilde on his lecture tour. But by the time we reach the right-hand area of this clever caricature, we learn that Wilde's "style of dress has somewhat changed." Lower down Beerbohm represents an older, more respectable Wilde as "editor of 'The Woman's World,'" the pioneering journal that Wilde transformed into a highly intelligent forum of debate for educated women. Beerbohm perceptively shows Wilde torn between the contributors' competing demands to promote "fashion," on the one hand, and "women's rights," on the other hand. Thereafter, we witness Wilde's metaphorical fencing-match with Whistler that occupied much of the 1880s. (Whistler often felt that Wilde stole his best phrases. In 1890 Whistler declared, with some reason, that Wilde lifted "The Decay of Lying" from him.[47]) To the left, Beerbohm observes that Wilde is now what the press terms "an unrivalled raconteur." There follows a rather teasing picture that alludes to the polemical reception of *Dorian Gray* when the *Scots Observer* stated that Wilde was writing "for none but outlawed noblemen and perverted telegraph boys"[48] – an allusion to the homosexual scandal known as the Cleveland Street affair in 1889–90. In similar fashion, the *Daily Chronicle* felt that "the book ... will taint every young mind that comes into contact with it."[49] Beerbohm's drawing implies that such unpleasant commentary would seem to have amounted to a kick between Wilde's legs. Last but by no means least is a full-length sketch of Wilde from the rear, his left hand tucked beneath his capacious coat-tails, possibly implying that Wilde's main achievement has been to thrust his backside in our faces. This view of Wilde's broad bottom may have sexual connotations – it hints, obliquely, at sodomy. The more obvious reading, though, would suggest that the apparently ungainly Wilde, now in his late thirties, barely resembled the willowy aesthetic man of the moment that captivated *Moonshine.*

Beerbohm's remodeling of the cartoon in *Moonshine* remains significant because it accentuates the tremendous changes that Wilde's profession underwent from the early 1880s to the mid-1890s. Moreover, Beerbohm's drawing implies that this particular career has experienced such rapid transmutations that Wilde now looks old before his time. For some reason, Beerbohm never published this illustration. This is also the case with "A Peep into the Past," the amusing prose satire where Beerbohm treats the scarcely middle-aged Wilde as if he were an elderly writer whose early fame belongs to the dim and distant past. First printed in 1923, this hilarious short narrative – which enjoys poking fun as the "portly form" of the apparently "old gentleman" – was originally drafted for Henry Harland's *The Yellow Book*, the famous journal associated with literary Decadents that went on sale in the spring of 1894. It is well known that *The Yellow Book* proved inhospitable to Wilde; its resident artist, Aubrey Beardsley, had grown to dislike him deeply. It remains hard to tell if Beerbohm or Harland, as speculation suggests, refused to print the satire because the literary metropolis knew too much for comfort about Wilde's sexual indiscretions.[50] Beerbohm, it must be said, relished making a joke about "the constant succession of page boys, which so startles the neighbourhood" (11) around Tite Street, Chelsea, where Wilde established his family home in 1885. Most of the humor, however, derives from Beerbohm's witty perspective on Wilde as a somewhat superannuated figure whose "star is set" (9) and whose name for most readers is supposed to seem a matter of antiquarian interest. Beerbohm informs us that the fact that Wilde managed to put *Lady Windermere's Fan* on the London stage "fairly beat all records in senile enterprises" (13). But the more that Beerbohm offers examples of this kind the clearer it becomes that Wilde, even at this seemingly senile stage of his career, remains a prolific writer. (Between 1891 and 1894, Wilde published no less than nine books.[51])

"A Peep into the Past" impresses the idea that Wilde, even in his putatively declining years, had hardly retired from the world. "After early dinner," Beerbohm reports, "the time is passed pleasantly in reading Ruskin to his two youngsters, after that more literary work, a light supper, a glass of grog and bed-time. But not always rest!" (12). Beerbohm claims that he has learned from Wilde's good lady that the "old gentleman" can be found pacing around his home in the early hours of the morning "in parturition of that same joke" that he sketched for her at bedtime (12). Further, we hear that Wilde "has not yet abandoned his old intention of dramatizing Salome" (10), the protagonist of the Symbolist French-language play that the Lord Chamberlain's Office censored when it was in rehearsals during June 1892. What is more, Beerbohm reveals that "[o]nly last year an undergraduate journal called the *The Spirit Lamp* accepted a poem of his in which there were evidences that he has lost little of his old talent for versification" (10). (Under Douglas' editorship, *The Spirit Lamp* proved hospitable to literary writings on homoerotic themes. Wilde's sensual sonnet, "The New Remorse," counted among his three poetic contributions to it.[52]) Taken together, this humorous vignette proves not quite as disrespectful as it might at first appear. It obviously reveals how the grown-up writer, at the age of forty, no longer embodies the weakly aestheticism that amused the populace in the early 1880s. More to the point, it shows that Wilde – with his much-expanded girth – has matured at an almost unbelievable rate into a tireless writer.

II

A peep into the past of Wilde criticism reveals that it was only at the end of World War Two that scholarship truly began to appreciate Wilde's diverse authorial commitments. It was also at this time that readers could finally benefit from hindsight on the circumstances that sent him to jail. H. Montgomery Hyde's *The Trials of Oscar Wilde* (1948), the first volume of its kind to edit selections from the newspaper reports of Wilde's cross-examination, made a crucial intervention in what would become the nascent debate for homosexual law reform. This growing consensus for reform gradually led to the recommendations of the Wolfenden Report in 1957; yet ten years would pass before English and Welsh law partly over-turned the amendment that sent Wilde to jail. It was in this context that Peter Wildeblood's homosexual autobiography made a vital contribution to revising public perceptions of Wilde's imprisonment:

> I suppose that most people, if they were asked to define the crime of Oscar Wilde, would still imagine that he was an effeminate poseur who lusted after small boys, whereas in fact he was a married man with two children who was found guilty of homosexual acts committed in private with male prostitutes whom he certainly did not corrupt.[53]

The real harm, as Wildeblood sees it, lies in the Wilde legend: "the aura of secrecy and sordid glamour which still surrounds the case."

By 1954, when rather modest celebrations honored Wilde's name a century after his birth, Vyvyan Holland published his important mem-oirs that for the first time clarified Wilde's influence as a caring and much-missed father:

> Most small boys adore their fathers, and we adored ours. He was so tall and distinguished and, to our uncritical eyes, so handsome. There was nothing

about him of the monster that some people who never knew him and never
even saw him have tried to make him out to be. He was a real companion
to us, and we always looked forward eagerly to his frequent visits to our
nursery.[54]

Holland recounts how much time Wilde spent with his sons in the nursery. These treasured memories include Wilde taking his boys to the
Theatre Royal, Haymarket, in 1894 to see Herbert Beerbohm Tree in a
medley of stories for children called *Once upon a Time*. The image of
Wilde as a loving parent – a man who sang songs in Irish Gaelic to his
sons – helped to adjust our critical vision of a long-misinterpreted figure. (Then again, in the 1980s and 1990s, gay-affirmative critical writing
on Wilde would at times assume, as Christopher Lane observes, "that
Wilde's fatherhood requires no comment and had no bearing on Britain's queer history beyond its difficulty for Wilde's sons.")[55]

The most decisive shift in emphasis toward enlightened and sympathetic analyses of Wilde's oeuvre, however, occurred in 1962. In that
year Rupert Hart-Davis issued his magnificent edition of the *Letters*. This
remarkable 900-page volume for the first time printed documents that
had long lain in the vaults of archives or in the hands of private collectors. The *Letters* drew attention to the long item of correspondence that
Wilde wrote from prison to Douglas in early 1897. (Ross would later
name this letter *De Profundis*: Wilde's original title was "Epistola: In
Carcere et Vinculis.") By bringing much new material to light, Hart-
Davis illuminated a career that, while covering a relatively short period
of twenty-five years, proved remarkably varied and productive.

Richard Ellmann acknowledges that without the aid of the *Letters* it
would not have been possible for him to complete his highly acclaimed
biography of Wilde that appeared in 1987.[56] Ellmann's *Oscar Wilde*,
which remains the definitive biography, immediately commanded tremendous authority. Its huge success contributed enormously to Wilde's
growing academic respectability, paving the way for a new generation of
critics to consider Wilde's Irishness, his classical education, and his sexuality, as well his anticipation of postmodern aesthetics and his relations
with socialist politics. But no sooner had Ellmann published his book
than scholars observed that his immensely valuable research suffered
from numerous errors of fact, some of which were repeated from
already discredited sources.[57] The biography also managed to consoli-
date one of the less reputable aspects of the Wilde legend. "Homosexuality fired his mind," Ellmann at one point asserts. "It was the major

stage in the discovery of himself" (265). Ellmann's formulation suggests that male same-sex desire governed Wilde's each and every action from 1886: the year when Wilde, from what might be inferred, ceased conjugal relations with his spouse (283). There is no doubt that Wilde became actively involved in London's homosexual subculture during this period. Yet it remains questionable whether his sexual intimacy with other men finally uncovered his authentic self. Even more debatable is the teleology that Ellmann applies to Wilde's lifetime progress from his Dublin upbringing through his undergraduate years at Oxford to his long period of residence at London and thence to his final days at Paris. Ellmann divides Wilde's life into specific phases – "Beginnings," "Advances," "Exaltations," "Disgrace," and "Exile" – which endorse received wisdom about the writer's eventual victory and lightning defeat. Yet, slowly but surely, scholars have begun to see that the pattern of Wilde's accomplishments proved somewhat more erratic than the trajectory traced by Ellmann's great work might suggest.

This volume of essays reveals a man whose divergent kinds of literary labor do not follow some incremental pattern of assured development. Divided into four parts, *Wilde Writings* puts specific episodes in Oscar Wilde's professional career into a range of cultural, historical, political, and social contexts that disclose the miscellaneous nature of his output. Part I, "Wilde Writings," opens with John Stokes' exploration of the circumstances in which Wilde contributed articles to the *Dramatic Review* between 1885 and 1887. This chapter forms part of a growing body of scholarship that investigates how Wilde made much of his living in the 1880s through day-to-day work for the periodical press. Wilde's participation in the *Dramatic Review* remains significant because the journal arose at a time when distinguished critics, such as William Archer, urged the public to take drama more seriously as a literary form in its own right. Josephine M. Guy, in chapter 2, considers one of Wilde's most polemical essays, "The Soul of Man under Socialism" (1891), as an extended piece of journalism written to meet the specific editorial demands of Frank Harris at the *Fortnightly Review.* Guy maintains that once modern scholars look closely at the journalistic context of "The Soul of Man," it becomes difficult to uphold his essay as a coherent and progressive tract. She contends that Wilde's desire for socialist emancipation rests upon an appeal to a form of "Individualism" that can be traced to the campaigns waged by the right-wing Liberty and Property Defence League. The LPDL, Guy observes, actually opposed the activities of the reformist socialism promulgated by the Fabian Society, which some critics believe was a shaping influence on Wilde's essay. In an 1890 Fabian presentation on the controversial plays of Henrik Ibsen, for example, George Bernard Shaw, who knew Wilde's family reasonably well, would declare: "the way to socialism [is] through individualism."[58]

The third chapter, by Ian Small, takes a fresh approach to the textual status of *De Profundis*. He examines how scholars might characterize the various embodiments of this long letter. Small forces attention on the problems that arise when scholars use generic classifications such as autobiography, love-letter, or spiritual testimony to interpret such an idiosyncratic work. *De Profundis* remains an intriguing instance of how Wilde seems to have desired to make an intensely private epistle a form of public property, by ensuring that copies of it were typed up at a secretarial agency in London. Chapter 4, by Ellis Hanson, continues the discussion of *De Profundis* by showing how this letter represents pain and punishment, in a manner that is not quite as compromised – or abjectly masochistic – as other readers have sometimes believed. Taken together, these studies in Part I encourage us to think carefully about the contrasting conditions in which Wilde shaped his assorted writings for disparate audiences.

Part II, "Wilde Stages," looks at Wilde's somewhat belated success in the theatrical world from three different standpoints. In chapter 5, Kerry Powell analyzes Wilde's uneasy relations with the influential strands of purity feminism that inform "Mrs. Arbuthnot" (the early draft of *A Woman of No Importance* of 1893) and *An Ideal Husband.* Laurence Senelick, in chapter 6, situates Wilde's *The Importance of Being Earnest* in the context of the late-Victorian theater of homosexual blackmail, which came into focus when Marc-André Raffalovich and John Gray's *The Blackmailers* appeared at the Lyceum in 1893. The seventh chapter, by Peter Raby, explores in more detail than ever before the precise and rather difficult circumstances in which Wilde drafted *Earnest* while on vacation at Worthing during the summer of 1894. For the first time, Raby's discussion shows the amount of celebrity that Wilde enjoyed in this unostentatious Sussex seaside resort. Raby concentrates attention on the multiple personal and professional obligations that Wilde sought to fulfil while he juggled his schedule in order to accommodate the needs of his spouse, his sons, and his male lover while seeking, as he jovially informed Alexander, to pocket "bags of red gold."[59] ("I am so pressed for money, that I don't know what to do," he told the actor-manager, urging an advance for his new play.)

In Part III, "Wilde Contexts," Diana Maltz examines how Wilde's editorial labors made *The Woman's World* one of the main conduits for discussions of what she calls "aesthetic philanthropy." In recent years, researchers have acknowledged how Wilde reconstructed the journal from a fashion magazine into a forum that, in Stephanie Green's words, "invited debate over the legitimacy of women's voices in mainstream British society while featuring consumable icons of femininity such as fans, lace and feathers."[60] Maltz observes how Wilde proved highly responsive to the forms of "volunteerism" which public women such as Clementina Black and Octavia Hill had been undertaking among London's poor. Maltz's analysis certainly makes Wilde look altogether more active than the account that his assistant, Arthur Fish, would publish in 1913. (Wilde's editorial obligations, in Fish's eyes, made him "Pegasus in harness."[61] Fish states that Wilde's visits to the journal's office were remarkably brief.) By comparison, in chapter 9 Talia Schaffer throws light on a different aspect of Wilde's relations to women's cultural and political work. She discloses how much Wilde's wit owed to the popular novels of the female aesthete Ouida (Marie Louise de la Ramée), who rose to fame with *Held in Bondage* (1865).

Lisa Hamilton, in the tenth chapter, fixes attention on how the recent critical discussion of Wilde's central position in *fin-de-siècle* effeminacy has failed to engage with the presence of this phenomenon in novels by New Women during the 1890s. Hamilton asserts that the debate raging around Wilde's degeneracy at the time of the 1895 trials is attached to a much wider preoccupation among feminist thinkers regarding the perilous nature of those men whose effeminacy does not connote homosexuality but marks instead a form of heterosexually diseased masculinity. Hamilton's argument bears comparison with Powell's searching analysis of Wilde's relations with women who proved highly critical of marriage and the manner in which the sexual double standard operated within late-Victorian culture. In chapter 11, Stephen Arata contemplates another area of Wilde's thinking and writing – his appeal to the beauty of Jesus Christ – that has been somewhat obscured in the annals of criticism. Arata considers how Wilde's reflections on Jesus Christ participate in a concerted nineteenth-century tradition that sought to historicize the Lord, in the name of making him a fully humanized figure who could bear a symbolic relation to the contemporary age. At different points in his career Wilde found in Jesus Christ an image that was by turns inspiringly homoerotic, movingly compassionate, and politically rebellious. In other words, Christ was a figure whose cultural and spiritual meanings Wilde would reinterpret from the time of his earliest poems of the 1870s to his last long work of prose, *De Profundis.*

Wilde Writings concludes with two studies of Wilde's legacies. In chapter 12, Ann Ardis explores how the differing socialist politics of two turn-of-the-century journals, the *Clarion* and the *New Age*, drew extensively on Wilde's thought, while managing to avoid acknowledging his influence. For these socialists, it proved politically hazardous to explain why Wilde counted among the driving forces behind the aesthetic theories that they upheld in the name of human emancipation. The final chapter, by Xiaoyi Zhou, traces Wilde's legacy to socialism along an altogether different route. He shows what would happen to Wilde's aestheticism when it reached China in the 1920s. Since the early twentieth century Wilde's name has remained vital to the cultural and political consciousness of South East Asia. Xiaoyi Zhou draws attention to the absorption of *Salomé* into the bohemian theatrical world of Shanghai at the time of the May Fourth period – an era when Chinese intellectuals made calls for a decisive literary revolution. At the time, Xiaoyi Zhou suggests, many of the young writers who lauded Wilde's art failed to recognize how their appropriation of it remained deeply embedded in the capitalist structures that it might have appeared to contest. He reveals, however, that there was a growing awareness among some Chinese intellectuals that another Salomé – one embodying the spirit of liberation – might awaken the revolutionary energy that would finally be realized when Mao Zedong proclaimed the People's Republic of China on 1 October 1949.

III

Wilde Writings, then, adopts approaches to Wilde's shifting image from quite unexpected angles. In this spirit, I have chosen to end this introduction by saying a few words about a full-length portrait of Wilde held by the William Andrews Clark Memorial Library (figure 6). The first reproduction of this particular painting by American artist Harper Pennington appeared in Arthur Ransome's 1912 biography. At the time, Ross was the owner. In many respects, it was a treasured possession since the portrait, which hung on the walls of Wilde's Tite Street home, represented him in a manner that he would seem to have approved. In the most detailed analysis of Pennington's relations with Wilde, Sandra F. Siegel speculates that the portrait was a gift to Wilde. Moreover, the work paid homage to Whistler. Pennington, who was apprenticed to

6 Harper Pennington, "Portrait of Oscar Wilde," *c.*1884.

Whistler in the 1880s, drew on his master's characteristic style, evident in *Arrangement in Black: Portrait of Signor Pablo de Sarasate* (1884), among other works of this period. Even though Wilde's relations with Whistler grew increasingly vexed, Wilde for some time held Whistler's innovations in painting in high regard, as the poem "Impression du Matin" (1881) shows.

According to Siegel, this elegant portrait by Pennington may well have been based on an August 1883 photograph that Sarony's studio took of Wilde wearing a distinctive "Neronian" haircut. She proposes that this change in style shows how Wilde was "groping for a new perception of himself that differed from the one that had become familiar."[62] Pennington's work certainly presents a well-heeled gentleman who returns the viewer's gaze in a poised, assertive manner. There is a clear contrast with Sarony's rather unflattering photograph, in which Wilde's hair looks flattened and his face rotund. But it must be said that in order to create an adequate reproduction of Pennington's portrait – one that presents a fairly unfamiliar picture of Wilde – it has been necessary to lighten the image. In the original, the extensive use of black in the oils makes Wilde's figure and the background almost indistinct at points. In some ways, the technological labor that has brought Pennington's striking work more sharply into view serves as a reminder that the struggle to see Wilde clearly remains a matter of enduring concern to modern scholarship. Yet, as this volume attempts to show, academic research has been increasingly successful in providing new contexts for capturing aspects of Wilde's ever-changing image as he transforms before us in a variety of literary guises.

Notes

I am grateful to Malcolm Baker, Nicholas Frankel, Mark Samuels Lasner, and Sandra F. Siegel for the generosity with which they shared their expertise with me.

1 Ian Small, *Oscar Wilde Revalued: An Essay on New Materials and Methods of Research* (Greensboro, NC: ELT Press, 1993), 2.
2 Not all newspapers condemned Wilde outright. John Stokes has shown how the trials of 1895 occasioned the left-leaning *Reynolds' Newspaper* to provide a forum for readers' differing opinions on the topic of immorality in public schools and ancient universities; among the letters printed between 12 May

and 2 June is one from Christopher Sclater Millard (whose great bibliography of Wilde's work would appear under the pseudonym Stuart Mason in 1914) that stated that only *Reynolds'* and the *Daily Chronicle* had given "the poor wretch now in prison a fair hearing": Stokes, *Oscar Wilde: Myths, Miracles, and Imitations* (Cambridge: Cambridge University Press, 1996), 61.

3 William Archer, "'Mrs. Tanqueray' – and After?" in Archer, *The Theatrical "World" for 1893* (London: Walter Scott, 1894), 141, also printed in Karl Beckson, ed., *Oscar Wilde: The Critical Heritage* (London: Routledge and Kegan Paul, 1970), 149.

4 William Archer, "An Ideal Husband," in Archer, *The Theatrical "World" for 1895* (London: Walter Scott, 1896), 18.

5 "A.B.W." [A.B. Walkley,] Review of *An Ideal Husband, Speaker,* 12 January 1895, 43–4, reprinted in Beckson, ed., *Oscar Wilde: The Critical Heritage,* 181.

6 "A.B.W.," Review of *Lady Windermere's Fan, Speaker,* 27 February 1892, 257–58, reprinted in Beckson, ed., *Oscar Wilde: The Critical Heritage,* 120.

7 [Anonymous,] Review of *The Importance of Being Earnest, Theatre,* 1 March 1895, 169–70, reprinted in Beckson, ed., *Oscar Wilde: The Critical Heritage,* 200; further references appear on this page.

8 Merlin Holland explodes the longstanding myth that Wilde died of syphilis in "What Killed Oscar Wilde?" *Spectator,* 24–31 December 1988, 34–35. Holland claims that the originator of this erroneous story was Robert Harborough Sherard, whose earliest book on Wilde (*Oscar Wilde: The Story of an Unhappy Friendship*) was privately published in 1902. A helpful survey of the literature that discusses the cause of Wilde's death can be found in Ashley H. Robins and Sean L. Sellars, "Oscar Wilde's Terminal Illness: Reappraisal after a Century," *Lancet* 356 (2000), 1841–43.

9 Illuminating information about the publishing, marketing, sales, and economics of *The Ballad of Reading Gaol* is presented in Josephine M. Guy and Ian Small, *Oscar Wilde's Profession: Writing and the Culture Industry in the Late Nineteenth Century* (Oxford: Oxford University Press, 2000), 185–98.

10 "A.D." [Alfred Douglas,] "The Genius of Oscar Wilde," *Academy,* 11 July 1908, 35, reprinted in Beckson, ed., *Oscar Wilde: The Critical Heritage,* 308.

11 Review of Wilde, *Works, Times Literary Supplement,* 18 June 1907, 166, reprinted in Beckson, ed., *Oscar Wilde: The Critical Heritage,* 303; further references appear on this page.

12 "C.W.F.G." Review of Stuart Mason [Christopher Sclater Millard], *Bibliography of Oscar Wilde, Library Association Record* 16 (1914), 544–5. The reviewer, however, regards Mason's *Bibliography* an "outrageously ill-proportioned volume," while acknowledging that the work comprises the "greatest tribute to the memory and to the genius of Oscar Wilde."

13 F.R. Leavis, "Keats," *Scrutiny* 4 (1935–36), 390.
14 Many of Wilde's contemporaries recognized his debt to Pater's essays. Later, in 1914, Ernst Bendz made the first sustained attempt to show how Wilde "fuse[d] and transform[ed] ... by subtle magic of his own" "countless things that he borrowed from elsewhere" – notably the works of Arnold and Pater, *The Influence of Pater and Matthew Arnold in the Prose Writings of Oscar Wilde* (Gothenberg: Wettergren and Kerber, 1914), 19. Ellmann was arguably the first scholar to insist on recognizing the significance of Wilde's position in the history of nineteenth-century aesthetics, especially in relation to Arnold and Pater. See "The Critic as Artist as Wilde," in Ellmann, *Golden Codgers: Biographical Speculations* (London: Oxford University Press, 1973), 60–80.
15 [Anonymous,] "Oscar Wilde after Fifty Years," *Times Literary Supplement*, 24 November 1950, 1.
16 Lord Alfred Douglas, *Oscar Wilde and Myself* (London: John Long, 1914), 168–69; further page reference appears in parentheses.
17 Frank Harris and Lord Alfred Douglas, *New Preface to "The Life and Confessions of Oscar Wilde"* (London: Fortune Press, 1925), 36; further page reference appears in parentheses. Harris's *Oscar Wilde: His Life and Confessions* first appeared in 1916. Douglas' remarks in *New Preface* were incorporated in Harris, *Oscar Wilde: His Life and Confessions* (New York: Covici, Friede, 1930), xi–xxxiv.
18 Lord Alfred Douglas, *Without Apology* (London: Martin Secker, 1938), 58.
19 Lord Alfred Douglas, *Oscar Wilde: A Summing-Up* (London: Duckworth, 1940), 10; further page reference appears in parentheses.
20 Frank Harris, *Oscar Wilde: His Life and Confessions*, 2 vols. (New York: privately published, 1916), I: 290–91; further volume and page references appear in parentheses.
21 Douglas claims that Harris informed him of this figure: see Harris and Douglas, *New Preface*, 6. Harris' biography went into many editions until the 1970s.
22 William Rothenstein's *c.*1930 portrait of Wilde, owned by the William Andrews Clark Memorial Library, graces the cover of Ian Small, *Oscar Wilde – Recent Research: A Supplement to "Oscar Wilde Revalued"* (Greensboro, NC: ELT Press, 2000): Clark Wildeiana, Portfolio 14. The drawing attributed to Aubrey Beardsley, "Oscar Wilde at Work" (*c.*1891), which first appeared as the frontispiece to Mason's *Bibliography of Oscar Wilde*, features on the cover of Guy and Small, *Oscar Wilde's Profession*. In his annotated three-volume copy of the *Bibliography*, Mason has transcribed a letter from Ross dated 12 September 1913 that discusses the attribution of the drawing to Beardsley: see

Clark *PR 5822 A1 M64bi 1914a v.1, pages interleaved before and after frontispiece. This image also appears in C. Lewis Hind, ed., *The Uncollected Work of Aubrey Beardsley* (London: John Lane, 1925), plate 48; it is discussed in Linda Gertner Zatlin, "Wilde, Beardsley, and the Making of *Salome*," *Journal of Victorian Culture* 5 (2000), 344.

23 Jonathan Goodman, comp., *The Oscar Wilde File* (London: Allison and Busby, 1988); Merlin Holland, *The Wilde Album* (London: Fourth Estate, 1997); and Tomoko Sato and Lionel Lambourne, eds., *The Wilde Years: Oscar Wilde and the Art of His Time* (London: Barbican Centre and Philip Wilson, 2000). For an illuminating discussion of some of the caricatures that appear in these volumes, see Sandra F. Siegel, "Capital and Caricature: Working the Wilde Archive," unpublished paper presented at the William Andrews Clark Memorial Library, 22 January 1999.

24 "Punch's Fancy Portraits – No. 37," *Punch*, 25 June 1881, 298.

25 *Punch*, 23 July 1881, 26.

26 [Anonymous,] Review of Wilde, *Poems, Century Illustrated Monthly Magazine*, November 1881, 152; further page references appear in parentheses.

27 Wilde, "To the Librarian of the Oxford Union Society" (early November 1881), in Wilde, *The Complete Letters*, ed. Merlin Holland and Rupert Hart-Davis (London: Fourth Estate, 2000), 116. On the controversy surrounding the Oxford Union's rejection of Wilde's gift, see Sandra F. Siegel, "Wilde Gift and Oxford 'Coarse Impertinence,'" in Tagdh Foley and Séan Ryder, eds., *Ideology and Ireland in the Nineteenth Century* (Dublin: Four Courts Press, 1998), 67–78.

28 Henry Newbolt, "Vitaï Lampada," in Newbolt, *Selected Poems*, ed. Patric Dickinson (London: Hodder and Stoughton, 1981), 38–9. Newbolt's poem was written in June 1892 and was first collected in *Admirals All and Other Verses* (1897).

29 This caricature, by Alfred Thompson, appears alongside a poem, also titled "The Bard of Beauty" and signed "Oscuro Mild," that concludes: "O Swinburne! And O water! How ye mix, / To constitute the modern poet's song!": *Time* 3 (1880), 97.

30 There is some debate about whether or not the production was aborted in 1880 because its subject matter might offend the Russian monarchy. It may have been that lack of funds prevented the production from going ahead in that year: see Karl Beckson, *The Oscar Wilde Encyclopedia* (New York: AMS Press, 1998), 396–97.

31 Oscar Wilde, "The New Helen," *Time* 1 (1879), 400–02.

32 Du Maurier titled a number of his send-ups of the Aesthetic Movement in 1879 and 1880 "Nincompoopiana"; they are discussed in Leonée Ormond's

analysis of aestheticism: see *George Du Maurier* (London: Routledge and Kegan Paul, 1969), 243–307.

33 [George Du Maurier,] "The Six-Mark Tea-Pot," *Punch*, 30 October 1880, 194.

34 This anecdote is reported in Hesketh Pearson, *The Life of Oscar Wilde* (first published in 1946; reprinted Harmondsworth: Penguin Books, 1960), 42.

35 Frith's painting, together with a detail of the part of the work that features Wilde, appears in Lionel Lambourne, *Victorian Painting* (London: Phaidon, 1999), 24, 40.

36 W.P. Frith, *My Autobiography and Reminiscences* (New York: Harper and Brothers, 1888), 441; further references appear on this page.

37 Furniss made a point of mocking Wilde when *An Ideal Husband* and *The Importance of Being Earnest* premiered in London. In the main illustration to his article on "Oscar Wilde at the Haymarklet Theatre," Furniss portrays Wilde as an effeminized " ideal husband." Here a rather portly Wilde, attired in a dressing gown that features a sunflower design, bathes two squealing infants. In the background, Constance Wilde sits in a chair reading a book. She is smoking a cigarette in a mode that clearly alludes to the well-known poster for Sydney Grundy's play, *The New Woman* (1894). See *Lika Joko*, 12 January 1895, 211.

38 Wilde published seven poems in the *World*, including an early version of "Ave Imperatrix! A Poem on England": *World* 13 (1880), 12–13; see Mason, *Bibliography*, 225–34.

39 W.S. Gilbert and Arthur Sullivan, *Patience*, in *The Complete Annotated Gilbert and Sullivan*, ed. Ian Bradley (Oxford: Oxford University Press, 1996), 309.

40 Thomas Maitland [Robert Buchanan], "The Fleshly School of Poetry," *Contemporary Review* 17 (1871), 343. The notorious controversy that followed Buchanan's article, which surreptitiously employed a pseudonym in a journal that published signed articles, lasted for almost a decade.

41 William D. Jenkins, "Swinburne, Robert Buchanan, and W.S. Gilbert: The Pain that Was All but a Pleasure," *Studies in Philology* 69 (1972), 369–87.

42 Two of the photographs from the series taken at Sarony's studio are reproduced in this volume where Lisa Hamilton discusses how in 1905 Edgar Charles Beall appropriated these images as evidence of Wilde's sexual degeneracy (see pp. 240–41).

43 Wilde, "The English Renaissance of Art," in Wilde, *Collected Works*, ed. Robert Ross, 14 vols. (London: Methuen, 1908), XIV: 263.

44 The transcript of this lecture first appeared in Wilde, *Old Irish Poets and Poetry of the Nineteenth Century: A Lecture Delivered at Platt's Hall, San Francisco on Wednesday, April Fifth, 1882*, ed. Robert D. Pepper (San Francisco, CA: The

Book Club of California, 1972). Wilde's lecture covers the work of many of
the "men of forty-eight," including Thomas Davis, Charles Gavan Duffy,
Darcy McGee, Clarence Mangan, Samuel Ferguson, and John Francis Waller.
Wilde delivered "The Practical Application of the Principles of the Aesthetic
Theory to Exterior and Interior House Decoration, with Observations upon
Dress and Personal Ornaments" in New York City, 11 May 1882: see *Collected
Works*, XIV: 281–90.

45 Wilde, "To Colonel W.F. Morse" (late June 1882), in Wilde, *Complete Letters*,
174. The caricature of Wilde and the "Wilde Man of Borneo," which
appeared in the *Washington Post*, 22 January 1882, is reprinted in Mary
Warner Blanchard, *Oscar Wilde's America: Counterculture in the Gilded Age* (New
Haven, CT: Yale University Press, 1998), 32.

46 Max Beerbohm, "The Sprit of Caricature," *Pall Mall Magazine* 23 (1901), 121.

47 Whistler's claim that Wilde stole his ideas dates from the early 1880s. The
tension between them would come to head in January 1890 when Whistler
wrote a letter to the editor of *Truth* that Wilde was a "detected plagiarist":
James Whistler, "To the Editor of *Truth*" (early January 1890), in Wilde, *Complete Letters*, 419. Wilde's reply appears on the same page of *Complete Letters*.

48 [Anonymous,] Review of Wilde, *The Picture of Dorian Gray*, *Scots Observer*, 5
July 1890, 181, reprinted in Beckson, ed., *Oscar Wilde: The Critical Heritage*,
75.

49 [Anonymous,] Review of *The Picture of Dorian Gray*, *Daily Chronicle*, 30 June
1890, 7, reprinted in Beckson, ed., *Oscar Wilde: The Critical Heritage*, 73.

50 The unsigned Introduction to the first published edition of Beerbohm's
story states that it remains "impossible to say with certainty" if "A Peep into
the Past" was held back from *The Yellow Book* in 1894 "because of the impending Wilde scandal": Max Beerbohm, *A Peep into the Past* (n.p.: privately
printed, 1923), 3; further page references appear in parentheses.

51 The nine books are: *The Picture of Dorian Gray* (London: Ward, Lock, 1891);
Intentions (London: James R. Osgood, McIlvaine, 1891); *Lord Arthur Savile's
Crime and Other Stories* (London: James R. Osgood, McIvaine, 1891); *A House
of Pomegranates* (London: James R. Osgood, McIlvaine, 1891); *Salomé: Drame
en un acte* (Paris: Librarie de L'Art Indépendant; London: Elkin Mathews
and John Lane, 1893); *Lady Windermere's Fan: A Play about a Good Woman*
(London: Elkin Mathews and John Lane, 1893); *The Sphinx* (London: Elkin
Mathews and John Lane, 1894); *Salome: A Tragedy in One Act* (London: Elkin
Mathews and John Lane, 1894); *A Woman of No Importance* (London: John
Lane, 1892). This list excludes American editions and privately published
volumes.

52 Wilde, "The New Remorse," *The Spirit Lamp* 2 (1892), 97; "The House of

Judgment," *The Spirit Lamp* 3 (1893), 52–53; and "The Disciple," *The Spirit Lamp* 4 (1893), 49–50.

53 Peter Wildeblood, *Against the Law* (London: Weidenfeld and Nicolson, 1955), 5.

54 Vyvyan Holland, *Son of Oscar Wilde* (London: Rupert Hart-Davis, 1954), 52.

55 Christopher Lane, *The Burdens of Intimacy: Psychoanalysis and Victorian Masculinity* (Chicago: University of Chicago Press, 1999), 232. Lane's criticism is directed at two studies in particular: Neil Bartlett, *Who Was That Man? A Present for Mr. Oscar Wilde* (London: Serpent's Tail, 1988) and Alan Sinfield, *The Wilde Century: Effeminacy, Oscar Wilde, and the Queer Moment* (New York: Columbia University Press, 1994).

56 Richard Ellmann, *Oscar Wilde* (London: Hamish Hamilton, 1987), xi; further page references appear in parentheses.

57 The most comprehensive account of the errors in Ellmann's research is Horst Schroeder, *Additions and Corrections to Richard Ellmann's* Oscar Wilde (Braunschweig: privately printed, 1989).

58 George Bernard Shaw, "Fragments of a Fabian Lecture 1890," in J.L. Wisenthal, ed., *Shaw and Ibsen: Bernard Shaw's The Quintessence of Ibsenism, and Related Writings* (Toronto: University of Toronto Press, 1979), 88.

59 Wilde, "To George Alexander" (? July 1894,) in Wilde, *Complete Letters*, 597.

60 Stephanie Green, "Oscar Wilde's *The Woman's World*," *Victorian Periodicals Review* 30 (1997), 103. The reassessment of Wilde's editorial interventions in the journal began with Sandra F. Siegel's essay in Alvin Sullivan, ed., *British Literary Magazines: The Victorian and Edwardian Age, 1837–1913* (Westport, CT: Greenwood Press, 1984), 453–56.

61 Arthur Fish, "Oscar Wilde as Editor," *Harper's Weekly*, 4 October 1913, 18.

62 Sandra F. Siegel, "Wilde on Photographs: Four Unpublished Letters," *The Wildean* 17 (2000), 25.

PART I

WILDE WRITINGS

chapter one

Wilde's World: Oscar Wilde and Theatrical Journalism in the 1880s

JOHN STOKES

These days, despite the enormous popularity of Wilde's plays with scholars and theatergoers alike, the works still sit uneasily in a critical context that values above all formal experiment and radical politics, ideally in combination. Regenia Gagnier finds *Salomé* (1893) acceptable because she manages to link its aesthetic to that of Antonin Artaud.[1] Julia Prewitt Brown admires the comedies because the "excessive" qualities of Wilde's dandies remind her of the Monty Python television comedy series.[2] Other critics, however, remain perturbed by the conspicuous affluence of Wilde's theatrical style. Joseph Bristow asks what connection stage pictures built around "visual allure and social glamour" can have with a drama that, in other respects, might be considered "transgressive" in a reliably modern way.[3] And there are well-known political and moral trouble spots. Few can say for sure what Lord Goring (or his creator) intended with that late speech in *An Ideal Husband* (1895) about a man's life being "of more value than a woman's."[4] Yet it will always be hard to reconcile the sentiment with the idea of a playwright who many critics, following Katharine Worth's lead back in 1983, have wanted to compare with his contemporary, Henrik Ibsen.[5]

It is part of Wilde's fascination that we should have such difficulty in placing him. Although we make the best we can of his contemporaries such as Arthur Wing Pinero and Henry Arthur Jones, finding in their work interesting engagements with sexual mores and gender politics, in the end we accept their limitations and attribute their failings to the commercial restrictions of the time and the residual power of established dramatic structures. But Wilde is different: He is so various, so stylish in so many different ways, so thoroughly unpredictable, and so puzzlingly essential.

In this chapter, I suggest that Wilde's modernity lies less in his radical sympathies (his dislike of class hypocrisy, for example), less in his formal adventurousness (*The Importance of Being Earnest* as a forerunner of the Theater of the Absurd, and so on) than in his up-to-date appreciation of what a career in the theatre might offer an ambitious writer. And I want to link that to his professionalism – which is often a doubtful concept, since it suggests an indiscriminate, uninquiring approach to creative work. In Wilde's case, however, his modernity appears in his ability to grasp the theatrical wherever it is to be found. This gift, combined with the multiple potential of his immediate circumstances, made him, despite the initial playwriting failures such as *The Duchess of Padua* (1883), a figure to be reckoned with on the theatrical scene, as well as an early member of a new intellectual cadre that still has great cultural influence.

To demonstrate the point, I will concentrate first upon his relationship with a single periodical, the *Dramatic Review,* which ran from 1 February 1885 until 26 May 1894, before returning to the changing theatrical climate of which it was a symptom. Although Wilde only wrote some eight pieces for the *Dramatic Review,* and although these all appeared quite early on (between 14 March 1885 and 22 May 1886), they are significantly varied. They include notices of glamorous first nights at Henry Irving's Lyceum, the outdoor experiments of Wilde's friend E.W. Godwin, the Shelley Society's pioneer staging of *The Cenci* (1820), and undergraduate productions of Shakespeare at Oxford.[6] In addition, the *Dramatic Review* printed two of Wilde's poems, "The Harlot's House" (11 April 1885, 167) and his sonnet on the sale of Keats's letters (23 January 1886, 249), setting them on the page as Wilde had instructed with elegantly wide margins that drew attention to their distinctive poise. "If you would like a poem I will send you one," he had written to the editor about "The Harlot's House," "but I would ask you not to include any other poem in the number in which it appears, particularly no parody of any poet. Parodies are a legitimate form of art – and those in your paper I think exceedingly clever – but the art that appeals to laughter and the art that appeals to beauty are different things. Also a poem should be printed across the page: there should be no column lines."[7]

The self-confidence, the absolute trust in aesthetic value, is as astonishing as ever, especially given Wilde's immediate circumstances. He was just over thirty years old, the only books he had published were *Vera; or, the Nihilists* (1880) and *Poems* (1881), and the American sellouts were now behind him, though he was still giving public lectures on such subjects as dress reform. His career, if not in the doldrums, was as unfocused as it was always to be. In March 1885 he began regular reviewing, usually anonymously, for the *Pall Mall Gazette*, taking on whatever came to hand – from poetry to cookbooks, from three-volume novels to guides to etiquette, though curiously few books about the theater. Even so, and even though he had written no pieces for the stage himself since *Vera* and *The Duchess of Padua*, Wilde's interest in the theater had, if anything, grown. In May 1885 "Shakespeare and Stage Costume" – a bundle of archeological facts provided by Godwin, rounded off with some ideas about the importance of historical details originally put forward by Victor Hugo – appeared in the *Nineteenth Century*.[8] It was later to be known by the more portentous and characteristic title of "The Truth of Masks," though the argument remained largely the same. This was simply that, because Shakespeare had an extraordinary sensitivity to the power of architectural setting and of costume, any self-respecting theater producer should make every effort to strive for historical accuracy and to create with modern resources the stage pictures that Shakespeare's working conditions disallowed. Those days nobody had a more important role to play than the designer.

Wilde had always actively appreciated the talents of others; never one to consider spectatorship a purely passive pursuit, he was an assiduous theoretician. The *Dramatic Review* suited this mode well, since it was a journal designed for contributions from people with a creative interest in the field who were not necessarily practitioners while refusing to confine them to anonymity. For critics who thought of themselves as artists, here was an ideal home.

A number of continuing debates occupy the first year or so of the *Dramatic Review*, all of them of general concern as well as of particular interest to Wilde. What, for instance, is the precise role of archeology in the theater? This question draws contributions from William Archer as well as from Godwin himself, archeology's prime advocate.[9] Elsewhere there is some discussion of Ibsen, together with plentiful materials on such topics as the responsibilities of dramatic critics and the correct training for actors.

It is partly because of the level and range of intellectual inquiry and debate that the *Dramatic Review* needs to be distinguished from a longstanding professional weekly like *The Era*, which lasted for a century between 1838 and 1939. *The Era*'s function was similar to that of *The Stage* today, in that it was mainly of interest to theater workers concerned about employment. The *Dramatic Review* was also different from *The Theatre*, a relatively lavish periodical that began in 1877 and ran under Clement Scott's editorship between 1880 and 1897. *The Theatre* features cabinet photographs and gossip columns from Paris and London which are professional rather than personal. A compact monthly, *The Theatre* was clearly designed for preservation (leather-bound annual volumes still turn up in second-hand bookshops) and its judgments invariably reflect the conservative tastes of its editor. Scott is now best remembered for his splenetic attacks on the plays of Ibsen as they began to be staged in London in the early 1890s, but there is no denying his energy nor his cosmopolitan knowledge of theater history. A great deal of *The Theatre* was actually written by him and bears his initials; prolific and well connected, he was even on occasion to appear in the *Dramatic Review.*

When the first issue of the new publication appeared on 1 February 1885, its front cover listed current productions, among them Wilson Barrett's *Hamlet*, Mary Anderson's *Romeo and Juliet*, the Bancrofts' farewell performances in *Diplomacy*, Pinero's *The Rocket*, and Charles Hawtrey's *Private Secretary*.[10] The first inside page contained small box ads inserted by actors. These ads give dates of availability, addresses, experience, and specialties: "Juvenile, Heavies etc.," "Juveniles and Walking Gentlemen," and so on. A professional readership is anticipated, although a long unsigned editorial announces that "as all the arts meet in a dramatic representation, our subject matter must appeal more or less directly to all artists" (1 February 1885, 3).

This editorial tells us that the paper has been founded to serve a need for serious writing about drama at a time when there is endless tittle-tattle about theater people in society magazines but little comment on their art. It states that the *Dramatic Review* will not be covering sport because it is time to recognize that sport and theater are "incongruous interests." Readers are also informed that the articles will be "attested by the writer's signature (or by a steadily-maintained pseudonym) and must be taken as an expression of his or her individual opinion," and that many points of view will be covered, including "diametrically opposite ideas in parallel columns." The paper will thus permit or even encourage "divergent individuality." There will be coverage of provincial and Continental theater and of the amateur stage because "the actors of the future are often to be found among the amateurs of the present."

It is only when we reach page three that the implications of "divergent individuality" are made plain. Between pages three to six there are a number of signed articles, all of them deliberately provocative: "Managerial Instinct" by William Archer (3–4), followed by Sydney Grundy on F.C. Burnand (4–5), J.J. Blood on pantomime (5), and Clement Scott on how the archeology craze has interfered with the basic skills of the actor, including those of verse speaking (5–6).

On page six there are reviews (unsigned) of a comedy at the Vaudeville and of a translation of a French play at a Court matinée. Then comes "Notes by Ignotus," a whole page of theatrical reports and hearsay – who was with whom at which first night and the like – composed and compiled by the editor of the paper. Pages eight and nine give us subscription details (21*s.* 6*d.* per annum), and a lead article by one of Wilde's personal whipping boys, Harry Quilter, here sounding off about Lewis Wingfield's *As You Like It* at the St. James's, where the play is apparently over-encumbered by archeological paraphernalia. Then there are a couple of features by the journalist Robert Lowe and the playwright W.G. Wills, short notes from the Continent and the regions, and a satirical poem in the style of a music-hall song, "J.L.T. to F.C.B." This poem is attributed to "Ignotus" but pretends to be J.L. Toole's reply to F.C. Burnand's recent complaints of immorality in the acting profession; it is the kind of parody that Wilde thought would make an unsuitable companion for "The Harlot's House":

> Dear Friend of my bosom, how came you to do it?
> > To call the profession not quite *comme il faut?*
> To say that your daughters should not, if you know it,
> > Rub shoulders with Lottie and Tottie and Co.?
> The stage of to-day is a hot-bed of virtue,
> > As Irving and I have both lectured to show,
> And I do call it mean – though I don't want to hurt you –
> > For you to come fouling our nest, doncher know?

Finally, there are more small ads for actors and managers, including one for Mr. and Mrs. Hubert O'Grady, "The leading Legitimate Irish Comedians of the Day," touring their "Original Irish Dramas": "Emigration," "Eviction," and "The Gommoch."

As the introductory editorial justifiably claimed, there really was nothing on the market to compare with this new publication in its range of both subject and contributor. The items are of reasonable length (typi-

cally one thousand to fifteen hundred words) and they engage with the
actual topics of the moment, sometimes in a humorous way. Subsequent
issues were to include William Archer on "The Actor's Point of View"
(15 February 1885, 54–55), "Ibsen in England" (4 April 1885, 147), and
"The Realist's Dilemma" (26 September 1885, 69–70). Archer, who had
made an early name for himself with an attack on Irving entitled *The
Fashionable Tragedian* in 1877, was to become the leading progressive
critic of the day, the foremost champion and translator of Ibsen, a fervent if sometimes aesthetically naïve champion of realism; his pieces for
the *Dramatic Review* demonstrate this potential as well as his longstanding interest in the psychology of acting. George Bernard Shaw, here
mainly a music critic, was to write on both *Manon* and the "Qualifica-
tions of the Complete Actor" (19 September 1885, 64–65). There would
be extended notices of *The Mikado*, Pinero's *The Magistrate*, *Nora* (i.e. *A
Doll's House*) at the School of Dramatic Art (28 March 1885, 138),
together with appreciations of Modjeska (4 April 1885, 149), Jane
Hading (Clement Scott again, 13 June 1885, 307–08), and Lillie Langtry
(8 May 1886, 147). And yet, all the way through there would also be concerted attempts to keep in touch with the popular mainstream.

An unusual amount of attention was always given to presentation and
the overall consistency of layout. The combination of "divergent individuality" and collective debate mentioned in the editorial would be
emphasized even further in the second issue that came out on 8 February 1885. Now we find facsimile signatures of major contributors, Shaw,
Godwin, and Archer among them, appended to their articles. On Saturday 14 March 1885, Wilde's signature would appear below his article on
"Shakespeare on Scenery." (see figure 7). These signatures enhance the
notion of individuality because they are intended not simply to convey
some sense of authenticity (which could at best be an illusion since they
are mechanically reproduced), but of uniqueness. The signature guar-
antees that what we are about to read is indeed what William Archer
(for instance) thinks because there is, we would assume, only one
William Archer.

In fact, this is not always the case. Take the facsimile signature of that
well-known playwright, critic, and man about theatre-land "Alec Nelson," a frequent contributor to the *Dramatic Review*. There was actually
no such person, or rather we should say that it was not the only name
adopted by the person who wrote this particular article. Alec Nelson was
the pseudonym of Edward Aveling, the already notorious lover of
Eleanor Marx.[11] Aveling is sometimes described as having worked on

THE

DRAMATIC REVIEW.

A JOURNAL OF

THEATRICAL, MUSICAL, AND GENERAL CRITICISM.

VOL. 1, No. 7.]   LONDON, SATURDAY, MARCH 14, 1885.   PRICE 3D.

CONTENTS.

SHAKESPEARE ON SCENERY.

I HAVE often heard people wonder what Shakespeare would say, could he see Mr. Irving's production of his *Much Ado About Nothing*, or Mr. Wilson Barrett's setting of his *Hamlet*. Would he take pleasure in the glory of the scenery, and the marvel of the colour? Would he be interested in the cathedral of Messina, and the battlements of Elsinore? Or would he be indifferent, and say the play, and the play only, is the thing?

Speculations like these are always pleasurable, and in the present case happen to be profitable also. For it is not difficult to see what Shakespeare's attitude would be; not difficult, that is to say, if one reads Shakespeare himself, instead of reading merely what is written about him.

Speaking, for instance, directly as the manager of a London theatre, through the lips of the chorus in *Henry V.*, he complains of the smallness of the stage on which he has to produce the pageant of a big historical play, and of the want of scenery which obliges him to cut out many of its most picturesque incidents, apologises for the scanty number of supers who have to play the soldiers, and for the shabbiness of the properties, and finally expresses his regret at being unable to bring on real horses. In the *Midsummer Night's Dream*, again, he gives us a most amusing picture of the straits to which theatrical managers of his day were reduced by the want of proper scenery. In fact, it is impossible to read him without seeing that he is constantly protesting against the two special limitations of the Elizabethan stage, the lack of suitable scenery, and the fashion of men playing women's parts. Just as he protests against other difficulties with which managers of theatres have still to contend, such as actors who don't understand their words; actors who miss their cues; actors who overact their parts; actors who mouth; actors who gag; actors who play to the gallery; and amateur actors.

And, indeed, a great dramatist, like he was, could not but have felt very much hampered at being obliged continually to interrupt the progress of a play, in order to send on some one to explain to the audience that the scene was to be changed to a particular place, on the entrance of a particular character, and after his exit to somewhere else; that the stage was to represent the deck of a ship in a storm, or the interior of a Greek temple, or the streets of a certain town, to all of which inartistic devices Shakespeare is reduced, and for which he always amply apologises. Besides this clumsy method, Shakespeare had two other substitutes for scenery—the hanging out of a placard, and his descriptions. The first of these could hardly have satisfied his passion for picturesqueness and his feeling for beauty, and certainly did not satisfy the dramatic critics of his day. But as regards the descriptions, to those of us who look on Shakespeare not merely as a play-wright, but as a poet, and who enjoy reading him at home just as much as we enjoy seeing him acted, it may be a matter of congratulation that he had not at his command such skilled machinists as are now in use at the Princess's and at the Lyceum. For had Cleopatra's barge, for instance, been a structure of canvas and Dutch metal, it would probably have been painted over or broken up after the withdrawal of the piece, and, even had it survived to our own day, would, I am afraid, have become extremely shabby by this time. Whereas now the beaten gold of its poop is still bright, and the purple of its sails still beautiful; its silver oars are not tired of keeping time to the music of the flutes they follow, nor the Nereid's flower-soft hands of touching its silken tackle; the mermaid still lies at its helm, and still on its deck

stand the boys with their coloured fans. Yet lovely as all Shakespeare's descriptive passages are, a description is in its essence undramatic. Theatrical audiences are far more impressed by what they look at than by what they listen to; and the modern dramatist, in having the surroundings of his play visibly presented to the audience when the curtain rises, enjoys an advantage for which Shakespeare often expresses his desire. It is true that Shakespeare's descriptions are not what descriptions are in modern plays—accounts of what the audience can observe for themselves; they are the imaginative method by which he creates in the minds of the spectators the image of that which he desires them to see. Still the quality of the drama is action. It is always dangerous to pause for picturesqueness. And the introduction of self-explanatory scenery enables the modern method to be far more direct, while the loveliness of form and colour which it gives us, seems to me often to create an artistic temperament in the audience, and to produce that joy in beauty for beauty's sake, without which the great masterpieces of art can never be understood, to which, and to which only, are they ever revealed.

To talk of the passion of a play being hidden by the paint, and of sentiment being killed by scenery, is mere emptiness and folly of words. A noble play, nobly mounted, gives us double artistic pleasure. The eye as well as the ear is gratified, and the whole nature is made exquisitely receptive of the influence of imaginative work. And as regards a bad play, have we not all seen large audiences, lured by the loveliness of scenic effect, into listening to rhetoric posing as poetry, and to vulgarity doing duty for realism? Whether this be good or evil for the public I will not here discuss, but it is evident that the playwright, at any rate, never suffers.

Indeed, the artist who really has suffered through the modern mounting of plays is not the dramatist at all, but the scene painter proper. He is rapidly being displaced by the stage-carpenter. Now and then at Drury Lane I have seen beautiful old front cloths let down, as perfect as pictures some of them, and pure painter's work, and there are many which we all remember at other theatres, in front of which some dialogue was reduced to graceful dumb show through the hammer and tin-tacks behind. But as a rule the stage is overcrowded with enormous properties, which are not merely far more expensive and cumbersome than scene-painting, but far less beautiful, and far less true. Properties kill perspective. A painted door is more like a real door than a real door is itself, for the proper conditions of light and shade can be given to it; and the excessive use of built up structures always makes the stage too glaring, for as they have to be lit from behind, as well as from the front, the gas-jets become the absolute light of the scene, instead of the means merely by which we perceive the conditions of light and shadow which the painter has desired to show us.

So, instead of bemoaning the position of the playwright, it were better for the critics to exert whatever influence they may possess towards restoring the scene-painter to his proper position as an artist, and not allowing him to be built over by the property man, or hammered to death by the carpenter. I have never seen any reason myself why such artists as Mr. Beverley, Mr. Walter Hann, and Mr. Telbin should not be entitled to become Academicians. They have certainly as good a claim as have many of those R.A.'s whose total inability to paint we can see every May for a shilling.

And, lastly, let those critics, who would hold up for our admiration the simplicity of the Elizabethan stage, remember that they are lauding a condition of things against which Shakespeare himself, in the spirit of a true artist, always strongly protested.

Oscar Wilde

7   *The Dramatic Review: A Journal of Theatrical, Musical, and General Criticism*, 14 March 1885, 1.

the staff of the *Dramatic Review*.[12] There is also some evidence that he, an embittered man at the best of times, later complained that the journal had been boycotting him and that he was only allowed to contribute on the condition that he used a *nom de plume*.[13] Since he habitually used the name elsewhere, it is hard to know what exactly to read into that complaint. Moreover, it is true that the fighting editorial in the first issue had, as we have noted, conceded the use of "a steadily-maintained pseudonym" in its campaign to establish individuality.

The very first facsimile signature surely was authentic, at least in the sense that it was not a *nom de plume*. Although he had yet to make a name for himself as a playwright, it was thanks to the intervention of William Archer that "George Bernard Shaw" began contributing to the *Dramatic Review*.[14] Yet even Shaw, although he started with signed articles, later contributed anonymous paragraphs to the weekly music column or was cited as "a correspondent." There are instances of notices written by Shaw that actually appear under the "Ignotus" heading that the editor, Edwin Paget Palmer, usually employed.[15]

Apart from the facts that he was Irish and notorious for meanness, it has proved almost impossible to discover much about Paget Palmer, the driving force behind all this activity. This is a common problem for researchers of periodicals. Journalists, like actors, frequently leave little trace, and editors in particular can be shadowy figures, having a special, unique relationship with the prints that they control, both authoritative and invisible. (A figure such as W.T. Stead of the *Pall Mall Gazette* is really an exception.) Nonetheless, even if some portions might not have been composed by Paget Palmer, the columns attributed to "Ignotus" are frequently highly opinionated and, though often impertinent, are clearly intended to demonstrate intimate familiarity with prominent figures in the literary and theatrical world. Like Wilde, "Ignotus" wrote about the Oxford undergraduate productions and about Lady Archibald Campbell's "Pastoral Players." He did not hesitate to disagree with his own contributors, taking on Godwin himself on the subject of archeology (12 September 1885, 52), and expressing an irreverent impatience with the aristocratic posturing of Lady Archibald:

> In my humble opinion, the whole thing was a piece of exquisite tomfoolery. If I were asked to tell the outer world my own impression of the affair, it would doubtless be in a critical sense vague and unsatisfactory, for I could only see Lady Archibald Campbell, in green tights, striking stained-glass attitudes under a tree, and anon, all the love-sick maidens from

Patience disporting themselves to fiddle-de-de-music, in company with creatures disguised in tow and red ochre, but whom it could be seen by the programme were shepherds, suffering more or less from temporary insanity.
(1 August 1885, 4)

Paget Palmer never had an easy relationship with his contributors, and he
would sometimes turn down pieces. "The money minus the publication
is less than I bargained for," Shaw (anxious for exposure) complained in
1885 when Paget Palmer spiked a piece on a Bach Choir concert but paid
him a guinea nonetheless.[16] Shaw returned the money: "If you give
cheques for nothing, you will ruin yourself as an editor. If I write articles
merely for money, I will ruin myself as an artist."[17] In April 1886, upset at
the way he had been treated, Shaw wrote to Paget Palmer "advising him
to do his own musical criticism,"[18] and wrote very little for the paper after
that point. Normally, Shaw sent in regular accounts. Paget Palmer's rates
seem to have varied: Shaw got a guinea an article for the *Dramatic Review*
(at about the same time he received £2 7s 6d for three articles for the
Pall Mall Gazette); Wilde's piece on "Shakespeare on Scenery" made its
author exactly twice that amount (see *Complete Letters*, 256–57).

For a while during the mid-1880s, Paget Palmer was well informed in
addition to being well connected. Yet by the end of 1886 the more interesting names were beginning to fade at the same time as the number of
posed portrait photographs and gossip items were increasing. By 1887
"Alec Nelson" still features, along with puffs for his plays, but, given that
Aveling's personal reputation and his financial dealings were equally
dubious, this is hardly a sign of intellectual or economic health. "Ignotus" broadened his scope to take in dog training and the management
of gambling clubs, and regrettably revealed an anti-Semitic streak that
seems exceptional even by the standards of the day. Already the *Dramatic
Review* had become much more hostile to theatrical innovation. Despite
contributions from J.T. Grein, founder of the Independent Theatre,
"Ignotus" remarks that he "would be very sorry to find a work like *A
Doll's House* becoming popular" (22 June 1889, 339), and in 1891 there
is a negative review of *Hedda Gabler* and an attack on Zola (9 May 1891,
229–30). It is difficult to know how much of this reactionary response
derived directly from Paget Palmer himself. But the fact that he seems
to have managed to keep one foot in the door for a while is made clear
by the publisher's need to insert a formal announcement in the issue of
10 October 1891. This stated categorically that the ex-editor no longer
had any connection with the paper (10 October 1891, 405).

The subsequent three years are directionless. There are attacks on
Salomé (2 July 1892, 421), *Lady Windermere's Fan* (5 November 1892,
710), and *Widowers' Houses* (17 December 1892, 806), tepid references
to George Alexander (19 November 1892, 743), and criticism of
Eleanor Marx (24 December 1892, 822). At the same time, there is
some enthusiasm for *A Woman of No Importance* (22 April 1893, 248) and
An Enemy of the People (17 June 1893, 376), and *The Second Mrs. Tanqueray*
is much approved of (3 June 1893, 342). The amount of music-hall
coverage increases and in general the *Dramatic Review* becomes, until
its final collapse, much more like *The Era*, a trade magazine, mainly
of interest to those directly involved in the day-to-day business of the
theater. Who was responsible for these opinions and decisions, it is
impossible now to say.

It is at this point that, were this to be a study only of journalistic practice, one would point out the obvious lessons. Newspapers are always
collective (not necessarily unanimous) texts; they are the daily or weekly
proof that the very notion of a purely individual author is a construct,
imposing the idea of an integrated literary voice where, in reality, there
is none. Newspapers are better understood as dialogical, as an orchestra-
tion of contrived voices that, whether by accident or design, interact
with one another.

When speaking of newspapers and periodicals, as with some other literary texts such as popular fiction, it is therefore correct to stress production and consumption rather than creation and response because a
"production" is so obviously what they are and "consumption" so obviously what they invite. It is better even to think of the words "Oscar
Wilde" as they are attached to, say, a piece in the *Dramatic Review* as part
of this process of production, as a label rather than a source – as a kind
of brand-name, in other words. No wonder facsimile signatures that
guaranteed a recognizable style seemed such a good idea to Paget
Palmer as he set out to capture or create a new market of literate
theatergoers in the 1880s.

But I want to make a theatrical claim about the *Dramatic Review* too, specifically about Wilde's place within its milieu. He obviously had a direct
connection with Paget Palmer (what other editor would have published
Wilde's poems so carefully?). He was at home with many of the other contributors. He knew some of them personally and with a few he was in
active agreement, the most obvious example being Godwin. In fact,
Wilde was a reasonably typical contributor to the *Dramatic Review* in that
he was mainly interested in reform of the status quo. Toward Henry Irv-

ing, whose repertoire since he had taken up tenancy at the Lyceum in 1878 had become increasingly predictable with a reliance on Shakespearean spectacle and modern costume drama, Wilde felt a certain ambivalence. Nevertheless he was prepared to be more effusive than Archer and less critical than Shaw. Irving had the resources for the pictorial theater that Wilde enjoyed and the acting talent – he had, above all, Ellen Terry, the object of much adulation among Wilde and his friends – but he did not always use his assets to their best effect. Unlike *The Theatre*, where Clement Scott paid monthly homage, the contributors to the *Dramatic Review* have a slightly admonitory attitude to the Lyceum. Modern plays, too, said Wilde, could benefit from the "exquisite" production values maintained at the Lyceum (6 June 1886, 278),[19] a respectful, even sycophantic, complaint about the absence of exciting new commissions.

In its early days, the *Dramatic Review* brought together a whole range of the theatrically concerned people, as interested in enhancing standards of acting, design, and costume, as they were in changing intellectual attitudes, even as the Ibsen campaign got under way. It is hard to know what to call them. This group was not exactly a clique because it was too diverse. Nor, as we have seen, did it comprise an avant-garde. It had no precise "agenda," to use a favorite word of today, though another recently popular term, a "network," might be more fitting.

The main commitment that Wilde shared with his fellow contributors was to theatrical presentation. He had an unwavering concern with surface, with how things should look and sound in performance. There is an aesthetic, or at least a set of theatrical assumptions, visible in Wilde's *Dramatic Review* pieces. It can be summarized as follows: Drama is a visual as well as verbal art. "[T]heatrical audiences are far more impressed by what they look at than by what they listen to" (14 March 1885, 1; *Reviews*, 8), and therefore productions should always look as good, as "beautiful," as possible. When the play is ancient one should aim to inspire in the audience the kind of mixture of nostalgia and sensory excitement that Walter Pater (not cited but clearly present in Wilde's cadences) derived from Renaissance paintings:

> For in plays of this kind [i.e., *Henry IV*], plays which deal with bygone times, there is always this peculiar charm, that they combine in one exquisite presentation the passions that are living with the picturesqueness that is dead. And when we have the modern spirit given to us in an antique form, the very remoteness of that form can be made a method of increased realism. (23 May 1885, 265; *Reviews*, 26)

But pictorial demands should not be allowed to interrupt dramatic impetus because that would interfere with the spectators' capacity to create a sense of the real out of what they perceive in front of them. For Wilde, the primary vehicle in this process is the actor whose visibly moving and breathing body brings the imagined past to unquestionable life: "For while we look to the dramatist to give romance to realism, we ask of the actor to give realism to romance" (23 May 1885, 265; *Reviews*, 26). Differences between genres are a factor here, requiring different attitudes on the part of the performer, a point captured neatly in "An audience looks a tragedian, but a comedian looks at his audience" (23 May 1885, 265; *Reviews*, 24). Differences between genders are also subject to conventions. Although Shakespeare was constrained by his dependence on boy actors, the Player Queen in *Hamlet* should still come on stage in male costume to show the reality of the Elizabethan theater (9 May 1885, 227; *Reviews*, 20). Even Lady Archibald Campbell's intriguing but misleadingly cross-dressed Orlando needs her low voice and the "strange beauty of her movements" to compensate for "the possible absence of robustness" in her interpretation (6 June 1885, 296; *Reviews*, 35).

Reform in the theater means drawing upon other arts, other disciplines: "On the stage, literature returns to life and archaeology becomes art" (20 February 1886, 35; *Reviews*, 46). There are endless variations on this sub-Wagnerian formula. Over the centuries modern theater has developed ever improving methods, and Wilde is both generous and seemingly knowledgeable about the importance of carefully placed gas jets and well-painted backcloths. Consequently, we should always strive to overcome the limitations of Shakespeare's theater (which the dramatist himself complained about) and have no truck with misguided attempts to recreate the Globe (14 March 1885, 1; *Reviews*, 10). At the same time, we should respect, learn from, and even try to recreate the successfully spectacular theater of the past: the Greek theater, for example, which John Todhunter and Godwin had invoked with their *Helena in Troas* in 1886 at Hengler's Circus. Proof of the value of authenticity (i.e., Godwin's "archeology") lies, as ever, in the contribution it makes to effect.

And that is about the extent of it. There is no mention of audience composition, outright gender confusion, women's rights, or class satire: those "modern" topics that interest us today, that we look for and usually find in the plays that Wilde, together with one or two other contributors (most obviously Shaw), wrote in the 1890s. What we have instead is a broad-based enthusiasm for many kinds of theater based on the appreciation of harmonious visual and aural impressions.

This enthusiasm extends to performers. The *Dramatic Review* gave Wilde a chance to puff some sympathetic young actors as well as the established figures. There is plenty of praise, for example, for George Alexander's "brilliant performance" as Laertes, rather more in fact than the role would normally attract:

> Mr. Alexander has a most effective presence, a charming voice, and a capacity for wearing lovely costumes with ease and elegance ... the performance was most spirited and gave great pleasure to every one. Mr. Alexander is an artist from whom much will be expected, and I have no doubt he will give us much that is fine and noble. He seems to have all the qualifications for a good actor. (9 May 1885, 227; *Reviews*, 19)

And Beerbohm Tree does equally well as Paris in *Helena in Troas*:

> Ease and elegance characterised every movement he made, and his voice was extremely effective. Mr. Tree is the perfect Proteus of actors. He can wear the dress of any century and the appearance of any age, and has the marvellous capacity of absorbing his personality into the character he is creating. To have method without mannerisms is given to only a few, but among the few is Mr. Tree. (22 May 1886, 161; *Reviews*, 71)

It should then have come as no great surprise that by the 1890s these should have been the two actors (by that time actor-managers) with whom Wilde was to have the most successful, if sometimes touchy, professional relationships. Accomplished actors such as Alexander, Wilde wrote in "The Truth of Masks," "can move with ease and elegance in the attire of any century."[20] Like Wilde himself, they were versatile time-travelers.

Another actor and fellow contributor to the *Dramatic Review*, whom Wilde often picked out for praise, was Hermann Vezin (1829–1910), who played Jacques in Godwin's production of *As You Like It*, the lead role in *The Cenci*, and Priam in *Helena in Troas*. Vezin is an especially significant figure in the theatre of the late nineteenth century. Having worked with Charles Kean, Samuel Phelps and Charles Fechter, John Hare and the Kendalls, and having achieved a standing that fell just short of the first rank (he replaced Irving as Macbeth when the star fell ill), he devoted much of his later life to teaching elocution. (His wife coached, among others, Eleanor Marx.) Diction was Vezin's specialty, as well as deportment. "With Mr. Vezin," wrote Wilde, "grace of gesture is an unconscious result – not a conscious effort. It has become nature, because it was once art" (22 May 1886, 161; *Reviews*, 71), a neatly circular formula that brings together both aesthetic result and intellectual intention and sets a standard of conduct, both on and off the stage, to which all good Wildeans should aspire. Vezin was an actor-scholar, clearly a favorite of Paget Palmer as well as of Wilde. His series of tributes, "My Masters," on great performers of the past – Kean, Rachel, Phelps, Fechter – ran week in week out in the *Dramatic Review* throughout 1885. He was even allowed to include a piece about what he did during his holiday on the Isle of Wight (29 August 1885, 38).

There were other connections at work in the *Dramatic Review*. While announcing that "Mr. Oscar Wilde has promised me his impressions of the affair next week, so I will only say a few words about it," "Ignotus" himself went down to Oxford to see the undergraduate *Henry IV* in May 1885. He was not entirely impressed by what he saw:

> Anything more comical than Mr. Lang's delivery of the prologue I never heard. I couldn't help finding excuses for the deplorable ignorance of the elementary principles of elocution manifested by nearly all the performers, when listening to the droning of this pedagogue. Nevertheless there were many things to be pleased at. The stage management was excellent. Mr. Mackinnon as Prince Henry, Mr. Gilbert Coleridge as Falstaff, and Mr. Mitchell-Innes as Poins were above the average amateur standard, while it was Mr. A. Bourchier of Christ Church as Hotspur really astonished me. This young man might be a great actor with time and study. His voice is almost perfectly under control, and he is "intense" enough for Tite Street. He was the life and soul of the performance. (16 May 1885, 248)

Wilde, Tite Street's "intense" resident, was to think a great deal more of the production, probably because he could appreciate the advances that had been made by theatrically inclined dons and undergraduates since he had left the university some half-a-dozen years earlier.[21] *Henry IV* had a prologue specially written by George Curzon and spoken by Cosmo Gordon Lang, a future Archbishop of Canterbury. The audience included the Bishop of Oxford, the Deans of Westminster and Christchurch, and Benjamin Jowett, now Vice-Chancellor. Wilde attended the dinner after the performance and made what "Ignotus" described as an "amazing" speech (23 May 1885, 264), though there appears to be no record of it. Wilde's review has some of the pomposity and superiority of a senior alumnus. But he makes a point of generously naming names, as he did when he returned to Oxford in February 1886 to review a student production of *Twelfth Night*, performed by express permission of Jowett, who was again in attendance.

Some of these Oxford men (the women seem to have been aristocratic debutantes specially imported for the occasion), on coming down, were to join the professional theatre, and some of them were to continue working far into the twentieth century when Wilde was long gone, if never quite forgotten. Arthur Bourchier, for example, lived until 1927. Educated at Eton, he had a protracted Oxford career not graduating until 1889, and was a founder of the Oxford University Dramatic Society (OUDS). After Oxford, Bourchier worked for Lillie Langtry and Augustin Daly before becoming an actor-manager himself. Other founder members of OUDS, such as Alan Mackinnon, also went on to follow professional careers. Frank Benson played Clytemnestra when the *Agamemnon* was performed in the Balliol College Hall in 1881 – a production to which Wilde claimed to have made an administrative contribution.[22] After a short spell with Irving, Benson was in 1883 to create his own company of cricketing thespians. On the same theatrical occasion, Rennell Rodd, then a would-be poet and the particular object of Wilde's admiration, painted the scenery. He later became a diplomat. W.L. Courtney, who played the Watchman in the same production, stayed on at Oxford and held a fellowship at New College between 1876 and 1890. He invited Irving to lecture at the university in 1886, wrote unsuccessful plays as well as respectable works of philosophy and a great deal of journalism, including an item for *The Woman's World*, which Wilde edited from 1887 to 1889. In 1890 Courtney became dramatic critic and literary editor of the *Daily Telegraph*, a post he held until 1925, adding the editorship of the *Fortnightly Review* in 1894.

These men set a precedent for what has become a common pattern in modern British theater: the Oxbridge graduate who moves into show business and the media. They were the prototypes for the Kenneth Tynan generation at Oxford in the 1950s, for the graduates of the Cambridge Footlights in the same period, through to someone like Stephen Fry today. Like it or loathe it, the Oxbridge presence and influence in the English theater can hardly be denied. Nor, for that matter, can the air of the high-spiritedness, "ardour" and "gladness," as Wilde called it (23 May 1885, 264; *Reviews* 23), that these graduates have usually brought to their activities.

Such connections strongly affected theatrical styles as well, by strengthening the curious interdependence of amateur and professional. We might remember the edict of "Ignotus" in the first issue of the *Dramatic Review* that "the actors of the future are to be found among the amateurs of the present." It is one of the more explicable ironies of theater history that as the acting profession became more and more professionalized, in the modern sense of organized unions, minimum rates, teaching academies and so on, the performance ideal remained "amateur," in the sense of appearing relaxed, natural, and instinctive, superficially free of commercial or careerist taint. Like British sport, the English theater for long suffered the class-bound fantasy that there are "gentlemen" and "players."

Elitist, charming, and stylish (in spite of its periodic fits of guilt and moral anxiety), as well as indiscriminate in its enthusiasms: these qualities characterize a continuous element in British cultural tradition. Had he experienced the long and successful career in the theatre that he confidently expected and would have enjoyed immensely, Wilde, despite his Irishness and (with due discretion) his homosexuality, would have continued working with men and women who, like himself, had their tastes molded in the 1880s. This was his formative experience, a matrix of gathering forces, primed to capture the West End just a few years later, in the early 1890s. It was a networking world that had direct links with what was to become known in the 1950s as the Establishment and yet was not exactly of it. It was a world that had access to aristocratic patrons, to the ancient universities, even to the Church. It was, and would have remained, Wilde's world – style over substance, theatrical to the end. It is still, to a degree, our world too.

Notes

1 Regenia Gagnier, *Idylls of the Marketplace: Oscar Wilde and the Victorian Public* (Stanford, CA: Stanford University Press, 1986), 109.

2 Julia Prewitt Brown, *Cosmopolitan Criticism: Oscar Wilde's Philosophy of Art* (Charlottesville, VA: University Press of Virginia, 1997), 87.

3 Joseph Bristow, "Dowdies and Dandies: Oscar Wilde's Refashioning of Society Comedy," *Modern Drama* 37 (1994), 54, 56.

4 Wilde, *An Ideal Husband*, ed. Ian Small, in *Two Society Comedies*, ed. Russell Jackson and Small (London: Ernest Benn, 1983), 264.

5 In fact, the connection was made at the time by the likes of Clement Scott, as Katharine Worth observes: see Worth, *Oscar Wilde* (London: Macmillan, 1983), 18–19.

6 "*Hamlet* at the Lyceum," 9 May 1885, 227; "*Olivia* at the Lyceum," 30 May

1885, 278; "*As You Like It* at Coombe House," 6 June 1885, 296–97; "*The Cenci*," 15 May 1886, 151; "*Henry the Fourth* at Oxford," 23 May 1885, 264–65; and "*Twelfth Night* at Oxford." Further page references to contributions to the *Dramatic Review* appear in parentheses. Some of Wilde's contributions to this journal are reprinted in Wilde, *Collected Works*, ed. Robert Ross, 14 vols. (London: Methuen, 1908); volume, title, and page numbers also appear in parentheses.

7 Oscar Wilde, "To Edwin Palmer" (March-April 1885), in *The Complete Letters of Oscar Wilde*, eds. Merlin Holland and Rupert Hart-Davis (London: Fourth Estate, 2000), 256–7.

8 "Oscar Wilde," "Shakespeare and Stage Costume," *Nineteenth Century* 17 (1885), 800–18.

9 Godwin wrote seven articles for the *Dramatic Review* that appeared under the heading "Archaeology on the Stage": 8 February 1885, 19–20; 22 February 1885, 53; 7 March 1885, 84–5; 5 September 1885, 42; 19 September 1885, 60–1; 10 October 1885, 92–93; and 24 October 1885, 112–13. For more on Godwin, see John Stokes, *Resistible Theatres: Enterprise and Experiment in the Late Nineteenth Century* (London: Paul Elek, 1972), 33–68.

10 The first day of publication was a Sunday, a day of the week specifically chosen because of its convenience for members of the theatrical profession, though the idea was probably uneconomic and the custom was not to be maintained for long. For most of its subsequent life the paper appeared on a Saturday.

11 For an account of Aveling's career, see William Greenslade, "Revisiting Edward Aveling," in John Stokes, ed., *Eleanor Marx (1855–1898): Life – Work – Contacts* (Aldershot: Ashgate Publishing, 2000), 41–51.

12 George Bernard Shaw, diary entry for 9 February 1885, in Shaw, *Diaries 1885–1897*, ed. Stanley Weintraub, 2 vols. (University Park, PA: Pennsylvania State University Press, 1986), I: 59.

13 Chushichi Tsuzuki, *The Life of Eleanor Marx 1855–1898: A Socialist Tragedy* (Oxford: Clarendon Press, 1967), 162, and Shaw, diary entry for 12 February 1885, in *Diaries*, I:60.

14 Shaw, "Preliminary Notes for 1885 Diary," in Shaw, *Diaries*, 53.

15 See Dan H. Laurence, *Bernard Shaw, A Bibliography*, 2 vols. (Oxford: Clarendon Press, 1983), II: 526.

16 Bernard Shaw, "To Edwin Paget Palmer," 26 February 1885, in Shaw, *Collected Letters 1874–1897*, ed. Dan H. Laurence, 4 vols. (London: Max Reinhardt, 1965–88), I: 119.

17 Shaw, "Letter to Edwin Paget Palmer," 2 March 1885, in Shaw, *Letters*, I: 121; see also Shaw, diary entry for 2 March 1885, in Shaw, *Diaries*, I: 66.

18 Shaw, Diary Entry for 22 April 1886, in Shaw, *Diaries*, I: 163.
19 This quotation appears in Oscar Wilde, *Reviews* (London: Methuen, 1908), 32; further page references appear in parentheses.
20 Wilde, "The Truth of Masks," in *Intentions, Works*, VIII: 267.
21 For the history of these and other productions, see Humphrey Carpenter, *OUDS. A Centenary History of the Oxford University Dramatic Society: 1885–1985* (Oxford: Oxford University Press, 1985), and Alan Mackinnon, *The Oxford Amateurs: A Short History of Theatricals at the University* (London: Chapman and Hall, 1910).
22 See Richard Ellmann, *Oscar Wilde* (London: Hamish Hamilton, 1987), 101–02.

chapter two

"The Soul of Man under Socialism": A (Con)Textual History

JOSEPHINE M. GUY

I

Work by textual critics on Oscar Wilde's writing practices has produced a number of observations now so accepted that they have ossified into truisms. They are that Wilde's works exist in several versions, that he was a thorough reviser, and that he frequently resorted to plagiarism. There is, however, less agreement about how to interpret these observations, and some difficult questions persist: Is there development in Wilde's rewriting? Do different versions of the same work necessarily indicate artistic seriousness? What is the precise relationship between works and versions? And what is the line between creative borrowing and mere copying, between plagiarism and topicality? These are still contested areas. At the same time, there is a basic assumption underlying recent accounts of Wilde that knowledge about the "facts" of his writing practices leads to a more secure sense of his achievements: once we know how his works were written, we will be better able to establish their value. It is now common wisdom to assume that Wilde's drafts and rewritings are the seal of what Peter Raby calls his "artistic seriousness."[1]

This use of textual scholarship to define the literary value of a work is unusual. Normally, textual scholarship proceeds from a judgment about a writer's worth: thus scholars edit works precisely because those works are considered canonical. It is rare that textual scholarship produces *prima facie* grounds for allowing a writer into the canon. In the case of Wilde, it is because there has been so little agreement about his literary achievements that textual scholarship has assumed an explicitly evaluative function. Textual editing of course is never wholly value-neutral.

But with Wilde the question of value is particularly prominent. We can glimpse this anxiety over valuing Wilde's work in the tendency to incorporate every fragment of his writing into some larger creative "synthesis," a term used by Philip E. Smith II and Michael S. Helfand to argue for a coherence underlying the jottings in Wilde's undergraduate notebooks. Similarly, Sos Eltis's account of the Society Comedies imposes a creative teleology in which Wilde's every revision works toward the realization of a radical politics.[2]

Clearly, the evaluative use of editorial work on Wilde remains open to question. The emphasis placed on coherence and development has led to a view of his oeuvre where individual works comment upon one another in ways that make them appear as part of some larger design. Thus critics have sometimes attributed intentions to one work on the basis of its alleged similarity to another, one written at a different time and under different circumstances. It is not at all obvious, however, that Wilde's revisions actually answer to this pattern.[3] The relationship between the assumptions underlying textual scholarship and theorizations of a writer's literary creativity is complex. Nevertheless we can grasp some of the issues involved by looking at what initially seems a very different problem: namely, how we value a work when we know (and can know) next to nothing about its textual history. "The Soul of Man under Socialism" is such a work.

In comparison to the poems, plays, *The Picture of Dorian Gray* (1890, 1891), and *Intentions* (1891), there seems very little for the text-editor of "The Soul of Man under Socialism" (1891) to do. There is no known extant manuscript, no corrected typescript, and no printer's proof.[4] In addition, there is little information to be gleaned from Wilde's correspondence. Our knowledge of the essay's composition, and of Wilde's attitude towards it, is therefore sketchy.

The essay exists in several versions, only one of which has any claim to authority. The earliest version, titled "The Soul of Man under Socialism," was printed in February 1891 in the *Fortnightly Review*, edited by Frank Harris. The only evidence of Wilde's further interest in the piece occurs in a letter, which Rupert Hart-Davis dates in the summer of 1891, to Jules Cantel concerning its possible inclusion in a French translation of Wilde's volume *Intentions* (published in May 1891). This translation did not appear until 1914.[5] Later in 1891, "The Soul of Man" was reprinted twice in the United States. It appeared in March in the American Humboldt Library of Science Series, together with essays by the anarchist William C. Owen and William Morris. The second reprint was in the April edition of the *Eclectic Magazine*, whose editorial rationale was to reproduce material from British periodicals.[6] Several of Wilde's works had already been reprinted there, including "The Decay of Lying" (1889), "The Portrait of Mr. W. H." (1889), and his anonymous translation of Ivan Turgenev's story, "A Fire at Sea," for *Macmillan's Magazine* (1886). There is no evidence that Wilde had any involvement in these republications. Moreover, given the general conditions governing American reprints of British periodical material at the time, any such involvement would have been extremely unlikely. Certainly, there is no evidence that he gave his permission for the two reprints. Three years later, in May 1895, the essay was republished in Britain as a book entitled *The Soul of Man* by Arthur Lee Humphreys, a friend of both Oscar and Constance Wilde.

Richard Ellmann suggests that the initial arrangement with Humphreys was made in the summer of 1894, at the same time as Constance Wilde was planning, again with Humphreys, an anthology of Wilde's aphorisms titled *Oscariana*, which was privately printed in January 1895.[7] We do not know whether the idea to reprint "The Soul of Man" came from Humphreys, Constance, or indeed from Wilde himself. Biographers of Constance have emphasized her close involvement in *Oscariana*; in Ann Clark Amor's terms, it was "truly her personal project."[8] They make no reference, however, to a similar concern with "The Soul of Man." Strong evidence that Wilde had little interest in the project comes from a letter concerning the proofs of the earlier *Fortnightly* version of the essay. Wilde complains about "an error of setting" in which a paragraph "is out of place" (*Complete Letters*, 462).[9] Despite the fact that Wilde asked for it to be corrected "at once," the correction was not made, either because the letter arrived too late, or because the revision was too difficult or expensive. More important, the paragraph remains misplaced in the 1895 book edition, which suggests that on this occasion, and unlike *Oscariana*, Wilde did not see proofs; or, equally significantly, that if he did, he no longer cared about his piece.

The most plausible reason for Wilde's agreeing to the republication of "The Soul of Man" was financial. By the late summer of 1894 Wilde was deeply in debt: he was casting about for projects that would produce what he described to George Alexander and Charles Spurrier Mason as "bags of red gold" (*Complete Letters*, 597).[10] Wilde certainly saw *Oscariana* as a way of earning money, and he suggested to Humphreys in November 1894 that it should be sold at five shillings (with a more expensive version at a guinea) rather than the price originally mooted by Humphreys, that of 2*s*. 6*d* (*Complete Letters*, 623–4).[11] The modest success of *Oscariana* (two hundred copies were reprinted in May 1895) may have encouraged the book version of "The Soul of Man." Only a cautious fifty copies, however, were printed and the format suggests a cheap price. The use of "brown paper wrappers" for *The Soul of Man* is further evidence that Humphreys was in sole charge of the volume. Wilde had always concerned himself with the material aspects of book production. In his review of a collection of ballads called *Low Down* in 1886 he referred disparagingly to the "cover of brown paper like the covers of Mr. Whistler's brochures," and when Humphreys originally suggested "paper covers" for *Oscariana*, Wilde complained that he did not want a "'railway bookstall' book."[12] The cheap and limited edition of *The Soul of Man* was thus uncharacteristic: it undercut the whole purpose of book publication as Wilde typically saw it, which was to earn both money and cultural capital. Two of Wilde's most recent books had been the five-guinea Bodley Head edition of *The Sphinx* (published in June 1894) and the 15*s*. edition of *A Woman of No Importance* (published in October 1894).

The substantive variants between the periodical and book version of the essay involve only one omitted word. Changes to accidentals are more common, but they are principally of one sort: the omission (again in the book version) of the frequent use of italics to emphasize phrases and aphorisms. This decision may have been a matter of the housestyle of the printers that Humphreys used, the Chiswick Press, or it may have been designed to make the work appear more serious. A reviewer of the *Fortnightly* version associated the frequent italicization with a playful intention to be provocative for its own sake – to "startle and excite talk" (see Mason, *Bibliography*, 73). There is no evidence that Wilde was responsible for these minor changes, and, considering the speed with which his personal life was moving toward crisis in the spring of 1895, his apparent lack of interest is hardly surprising. The timing of the republication of what was in part a defense of freedom may have been an attempt by Humphreys (or Constance) to justify Wilde's behavior, scandalous details of which Queensberry's defense was putting under scrutiny at the Old Bailey. Commercial motives cannot have been uppermost, for Humphreys could not have anticipated making money from such a tiny print-run. It is also significant that Humphreys did not reprint *The Soul of Man* until well after Wilde's death. The first new edition appeared in 1907, with a second impression in 1909; another edition, with a preface by Robert Ross, Wilde's literary executor, appeared in 1912. According to Mason, the text was virtually identical to the 1895 book, although Humphreys produced it in both 1*s.* and 2*s.* editions. Finally, Humphreys also included "The Soul of Man" in a selection of Wilde's aphorisms and epigrams published in 1904 under the "head-line" of Sebastian Melmoth (the pseudonym Wilde adopted after leaving prison) in the Belles Lettres Series of his Royal Library (see Mason, *Bibliography*, 405–7, 558).[13]

The only other version of the "The Soul of Man" with any claim to authority is that edited by Ross himself. He printed it together with the essays in *Intentions* as volume 8 of the first collected edition, published by Methuen in 1908. Ross faithfully reproduced the *Fortnightly* version. Significantly, he did not reorder the misplaced paragraph, which suggests that he did not have access either to a manuscript of the essay or to any other documents by Wilde relating to it. (It was usual in nineteenth-century periodical printing practice for compositors to discard copy once they had finished with it. When Wilde did republish occasional pieces, he often worked from the periodical texts.) Given these details, choices about copytext seem simple. The only version that we know with certainty had Wilde's full authority was that in the *Fortnightly*. It seems, then, that there is very little work for the modern editor of "The Soul of Man" to do. Yet it is this paucity of textual information that remains interesting because it has had important consequences for how we identify and therefore value Wilde's essay.

II

"The Soul of Man" is usually bracketed with those works of Wilde that literary historians have judged to be "serious": the plays, the fiction, and the criticism. Yet there is no evidence that "The Soul of Man" was subject to the kind of textual work – namely, revision and redrafting – that scholars have discussed in order to demonstrate Wilde's artistic seriousness. On the contrary, the textual condition of "The Soul of Man" is much closer to that of Wilde's uncollected journalism. It suggests a piece that was written simply for an occasion. Moreover, the uncollected journalism has generated much less interest among critics and literary historians. John Stokes has commented on how the conventions of professional journalism constrained Wilde, hampering the development of "the famous style" that would "become a badge of personality." Despite his attempt to revalue the early journalism by pointing out the "progressive" nature of Wilde's opinions, Stokes nevertheless reaches a conven-

tional conclusion: the transgressive Wilde did not fully emerge until the
1890s when he was able to "choose titles and adopt attitudes that no professional [journalist] could possibly permit."[14]

As Stokes's reasoning demonstrates, the assumption that seriousness
can be equated with rewriting has typically been conflated with another
argument: namely, that there is a distinction in the nineteenth century
between the value placed upon a book and that of the disposable nature
of popular periodical publication, particularly those cheap papers such
as the *Pall Mall Gazette* to which Wilde regularly contributed during the
1880s. In other words, in this view Wilde's serious critical works are
those pieces that he revised in order to re-present in book form. It is
easy to see why modern scholars tend to categorize "The Soul of Man"
as a serious work – as "art" rather than journalism. The essay was written
some time in the autumn or winter of 1890, when Wilde was purport-
edly making that transition from journalist to serious artist, and then
republished as a book in 1895 at the very height of his career. The mere
existence of the book version seems to have been sufficient to confer
status upon it. Yet when we recall that there is no evidence that Wilde
had anything more than a token involvement in the book publication –
certainly not in the way that he did for the essays reproduced in *Intentions* (which were substantially revised) or the proposed book version of
"The Portrait of Mr. W. H." – the grounds for categorizing the work as
serious look less secure.[15] How, *as a piece of text*, is "The Soul of Man" to
be distinguished from Wilde's uncollected journalism? And how valid
are those attributions of value and seriousness that derive their authority from theories about Wilde's habit of revision?

It is notable that in recent revaluations of Wilde's oeuvre, "The Soul
of Man" has attracted little attention. In 1990, Isobel Murray argued for
the essay's "classic" status by categorizing it with what she termed
Wilde's "prison writings." According to Murray, it is only when read in
the context of later works (that is, anachronistically) that the seriousness
of "The Soul of Man" can properly be appreciated.[16] Lawrence Danson's
1997 study is even more telling. He wryly notes of "The Soul of Man"
that "it is wise, it is good, it is quotable, but it can also be breezily incon-
sequential or demonstrably wrong."[17] Danson's uncertainty relates
directly to his observation that the textual history of "The Soul of Man"
constitutes a "problematic exception" (11). In contrast to the essays in
Intentions, there is no evidence of the process of polishing associated
with Wilde's revision of his journalism into art.

Danson's and Murray's defensiveness discloses an anxiety: the value that they find in "The Soul of Man" comes from its association with works whose achievements seem more secure. For Murray, grouping "The Soul of Man" with the prison writings gives it a political identity and therefore a seriousness of intention. By comparison, for Danson the fact that "The Soul of Man" could have been included in *Intentions* suggests Wilde conceived and valued it in the same way as "The Critic as Artist" or "The Decay of Lying." The limitation of these explanations, however, is that they tell us nothing about Wilde's actual intentions when he wrote the essay. More bizarrely, they assume that we cannot understand the intentions behind one work – "The Soul of Man" – until we know those behind others.

What happens if we limit ourselves to the few facts which we do possess about the composition of "The Soul of Man"? The first evidence that the essay was neither intended by Wilde, nor initially interpreted by its contemporary readers, as serious political polemic comes from the *Fortnightly* itself. When Harris took over the editorship of this famous organ of radicalism in 1886, the quality of contributions and the circulation had suffered a sharp decline. Young and relatively inexperienced, Harris was hired to rescue the ailing *Review.* That he doubled the circulation in a year was largely a result of changes to its tone and style. John Morley's earlier vision of the *Fortnightly*, which he edited from 1867 to 1882, was as a forum for serious debate about current affairs. Under Harris's direction this gave way to a concentration on creative and critical literature. What little political analysis that did remain was both more extreme and more marginal. Harris would eventually resign his editorship after repeated quarrels with the publisher (Chapman and Hall) over the extent of the literary material and the promotion of causes such as anarchism.[18] Wilde, then, represented exactly the kind of writer whom Harris wanted for his restyled *Review*: someone who was clever, provocative, and, above all, entertaining. It was as a critic and personality, not as a political theorist, that Wilde attracted Harris.

Harris had already published Wilde's "Pen, Pencil, and Poison" in the *Fortnightly* in January 1889. A year later, he solicited another piece, asking for an essay that sounds very like "The Soul of Man." He specified "an Article on Literature or any Social Subject as paradoxical as you please," to be finished "within 8 days."[19] It seems that at this point Wilde was too busy to respond. Harris's stress on speed and entertainment, however, strongly indicates that he was not looking to Wilde for a studied piece. Later that year, he wrote again to Wilde expressing admiration for the "Critic as Artist," which had appeared in the *Nineteenth*

Century in the summer and autumn of 1890: "I've done you wrong in my thoughts these many years, of course, ignorantly, but now, at last, I'll try to atone. You're certain, I think, to be a *chef-de-file* (if I may use Balzac's coinage without offence) of the generation now growing to manhood in England."[20]

The timing and nature of Harris' compliment may have flattered Wilde into finally producing the piece. It might also have encouraged Wilde to rework some of those ideas in "The Critic as Artist" that Harris admired, for the general drift of the apologia for artistic freedom and the diatribe against public opinion and the press, which take up a significant proportion of "The Soul of Man," would have been familiar to readers of the *Nineteenth Century*. What appears to be new is what Harris would have called the "social subject": the reevaluation of charity that begins the essay and the argument about the relative merits of Socialism and Individualism (as Wilde presented these terms in his essay) that frames and politicizes the discussion of the artist. But how original is this material? More important, in what ways can we describe it as serious?

Arguments for Wilde's originality typically employ a process of contextualization where the aim is to discover his sources or influences, and so the nature of his contribution to contemporary debates – whether Wilde's opinions rise above what Stokes has termed the "generally acceptable" (77). In the case of "The Soul of Man," critics have drawn attention to Wilde's allusions to the work of figures such as Prince Kropotkin, George Bernard Shaw, Sidney Webb, William Morris, Chuang Tsu (a translation of whose work Wilde had reviewed in 1890) and Ralph Waldo Emerson, as well as, to a lesser extent, Herbert Spencer, Charles Darwin, Ernest Renan, Friedrich Engels, Honoré de Balzac, John Ruskin, Walter Pater, Matthew Arnold, and Edmund Burke.[21] It is an impressive list and seems to indicate intellectual seriousness on Wilde's part. At the same time, its eclecticism amounts to little more than name-dropping; Wilde offers no sustained engagement with these writers' positions. How could he? How would it be possible in a short article to synthesize the views of Morris and Burke? It is worth remembering that any contextualization undertaken by a modern critic is selective. Unlike the textual data about a work's composition (which are finite, in the sense that they are limited to the availability of manuscripts, typescripts and so on), contextual information is constrained only by a prior definition of relevance. In this respect, it is interesting to see how little consideration has been given to the journalistic context of "The Soul of Man." Its relationship with contemporary periodical literature, and thus to what is local and topical, has been marginalized, despite the fact that what we know about the textual history of the essay places it unequivocally within the domain of journalism. The resolve to find seriousness in "The Soul of Man" seems to have determined what is to count as relevant context.

For modern readers, Wilde's perverse rejection of charity as degrading, and his attempt to reconcile such diametrically opposed doctrines as Socialism and Individualism, seem typical of his iconoclasm – of the paradoxical mode of argument that has traditionally been taken to characterize his originality. Yet, if we look at Wilde's essay in the context of contemporary journalism, these paradoxes appear far from new. There were precedents for them in the periodical press. Drawing attention to the ways in which Wilde's essay engages with a journalistic discourse does not deny that there are allusions to Chuang Tsu, Emerson, Morris, or Darwin. But it does suggest that they exist alongside another much more obvious range of contemporary reference, one that locates the value of the essay very differently from that which Murray and Danson claim.

III

Wilde opens the "The Soul of Man" with a witty attack on charity, claiming that it "creates a multitude of sins." Philanthropy was to become a frequent butt of Wilde's humor. "The Soul of Man," however, threatens to develop the joke into something like a reasoned argument: philanthropic benevolence prevents an understanding of the real cause of poverty, the existence of private property. Such a proposition was certainly contentious, but it was not particularly novel. As the *Nineteenth Century*'s readers would remember, two months earlier, in December 1890, a similar position had been argued by the Reverend Hugh Price Hughes in a debate with Cardinal Manning and Hermann Alder over what was termed "Irresponsible Wealth." The occasion was the publication in the *Nineteenth Century* in November 1890 of a long essay by W.E. Gladstone praising the best-selling "Gospel of Wealth" essays by the famous American philanthropist, Andrew Carnegie.[22] Carnegie controversially defended the principle of private property, while condemning what he saw as the evils of excessive wealth. He argued that the rich should voluntarily bind themselves to donate a proportion of their profits for philanthropy. According to Philip Magnus, Gladstone dragged Carnegie's name into conversation as early as February 1890 during a ten-day visit to All Souls, Oxford, when he spoke at the Union Society.[23] By the time his essay appeared in the *Nineteenth Century*, it was merely rehearsing views that had already been widely discussed.

The responses to Gladstone's piece by Manning and Alder endorsed his appeal to the rich in Britain to follow Carnegie's example. Wilde may have had Manning and Alder in mind when he suggested in "The Soul of Man" that the idea that "property has duties" had been said "so often and so tediously that, at last, the church has begun to say it."[24] In contrast to Manning and Alder, Hughes's essay was much less enthusiastic. He claimed that millionaires were fundamentally "unnatural" and that Carnegie himself, although "personally a most estimable and generous man," was nevertheless "an anti-Christian phenomenon, a social monstrosity, and a grave political peril." In a "really Christian country," Hughes argued, "a millionaire would be an economic impossibility. Jesus Christ distinctly prohibited the accumulation of wealth." Hughes continued:

> In London we are living on the verge of a volcano ... Never has there been
> so vast a multitude of half-starved men, within sight of boundless wealth,
> and outside the control of the Christian church ... Lazarus is no longer
> lying on the door-step of Dives, in the quiescence of sullen despair, licked
> by the dogs. He is standing upright at the corner of the street, vehemently
> gesticulating, and his burning words are sinking deep into the hearts of a
> large crowd of hungry-looking men. (891, 895–96)

The drift of this passage is strikingly similar to Wilde's condescending outburst in "The Soul of Man" that "a poor man who is ungrateful, unthrifty, discontented, and rebellious is probably a real personality" (295). Another echo of Hughes in Wilde's essay concerns Wilde's ironic sympathy for the rich; owning property, Wilde argues, involves "endless claims upon one, endless attention to business, endless bother ... In the interest of the rich we must get rid of it" (294). Hughes had offered similarly caustic sympathy for Carnegie's plight, suggesting that "[i]f a man is so unfortunate as to have enormous wealth he cannot do better than act upon Mr. Carnegie's distributive principles" (879). In support of his position, Hughes quoted a long passage from Spencer's "most interesting and instructive" *Study of Sociology* (1873), which he interpreted as evidence of an antagonism to "class-bias." More precisely, Hughes saw Spencer's "plea for a natural social condition" as the antithesis to "the unrestricted competition ... which Mr. Carnegie regards with so much complacency" (894). This was not the only interpretation of Spencer's political theory in the late 1880s (his work was more usually appropriated by vehement free traders); yet it is one very similar to Wilde's invocation in "The Soul of Man" of Spencer's "law of evolution," which he, too, uses to authorize an egalitarian, anti-competitive utopia.

These similarities between Hughes's and Wilde's attacks on charity do not indicate plagiarism, a term that is simply inappropriate to the self-referring nature of nineteenth-century journalism. Further, there are significant differences of tone between the essays; where Hughes remains carefully poised between politeness and contempt, Wilde is openly mocking. Wilde, however, may have taken inspiration from Hughes's polemic in the knowledge that readers would recognize the allusion: Wilde participates in a continuing debate whose terms of reference were well known. I am suggesting, then, that "The Soul of Man" did not depend primarily upon the novelty of its argument; rather, as with any journalism, it rehearsed positions already familiar, but recast them in provocatively witty ways – ways that would exhibit Wilde's own distinctive personality. Thus the "contrariness" that Stokes identifies with the mature Wilde may be little more than a pose (28) – more a journalist's attempt to keep up with fashion, than an original mode of criticism.

This sense that the value of Wilde's argument resides principally in its style is reinforced when we look at the context for his discussion of Socialism and Individualism. As far back as 1965 J.D. Thomas observed that the difficulty of the essay "is that it is a treatise on Individualism" (83). Subsequent literary historians have been slow in taking up this hint, concentrating instead on Wilde's debts to works such as the *Fabian Essays in Socialism* (1889), in the belief, as Danson puts it, that Socialism "was all around" Wilde.[25] But so too was Individualism. The modern critical reluctance to attend to the significance of late nineteenth-century Individualism seems to derive from a perception that the subject is too protean.[26] Scholars, however, have drawn this conclusion because they have failed to differentiate adequately between two distinct uses of the term. Capitalized (as in Wilde's essay), Individualism denoted a specific politics, a usage which should not be confused with individualism spelt with a small "i" that referred (in most cases pejoratively) to the methodological atomism that underlay much nineteenth-century social thought, and that was often interpreted as a justification for egotism.[27] The political Individualism that Wilde engages with in "The Soul of Man" would have been as familiar to his contemporary readers as Socialism. For the modern critic, though, understanding these different political formations has been unavoidably shaped by perceptions of their relevance to the twentieth century. Socialism (particularly of the Fabian variety) has enjoyed a long pedigree in Britain, and has been considered indispensable to understanding the history of the Labour Party. Individualism, by contrast, was short-lived. Emerging in the early 1880s, to all intents and purposes it was a spent force by 1910. As a consequence, its politics has generally been considered irrelevant and its propagandists consigned to what Edward J. Bristow terms the dustheap of history.[28] Little wonder, then, that literary critics have been reluctant to investigate Wilde's interest in political Individualism, for it appears to threaten his reputation as a serious thinker.

Like late nineteenth-century Socialists, the Individualists were not a cohesive group. Nevertheless they did have some fundamental positions in common that conferred on them, publicly at least, a distinctive political identity.[29] Their central platform was a rigorous anti-statism that entailed an opposition to many of the traditional functions of government, including collectivist legislation. In terms of late nineteenth-century politics, this meant that Individualists opposed not only socialists, but also what was termed the "New Radicalism." New Radicalism represented a transformation of Millite liberalism (and its doctrine of negative liberty) into a program for a strong interventionist state (or positive liberty). The most trenchant theorist of New Radicalism was T.H. Green; it had received wider publicity, however, through the *Fortnightly Review* that had published "The Radical Programme" in instalments from 1883 to 1885. The most visible evidence of New Radicalism was the reforming governments of the late decades of the nineteenth century, particularly Gladstone's second ministry (1880–85). The Individualists typically justified their anti-statism in terms of Spencer's "Law of Equal Freedom": "every man may claim the fullest liberty to exercise his faculties compatible with the possession of like liberty by every other man."[30] Thus Individualists assumed a negative definition of liberty; they defined freedom as the absence of physical or legal constraints (the market was not generally seen as a constraint). Likewise they assumed that liberty and government were antithetical terms. Wilde recasts this law in "The Soul of Man" where he claims that "Individualism ... converts the abolition of legal restraint into a form of freedom that will help the full development of personality" (300).

In the popular mind, the Individualists' antipathy to the state often made them indistinguishable from anarchists. At the same time, as M.W.

Taylor points out, their hostility to any kind of social reform meant that in practice their policies were conservative, advocating the preservation of the political status quo. Individualists typically drew upon Spencerian notions of social evolution – the idea that society was a delicate organism evolving through processes of increasing differentiation toward a structure of such complexity that it was beyond comprehension and should not be interfered with. Individualists used this concept to justify the preservation of existing institutions, particularly those relating to property rights and the unequal distribution of wealth. Their wonderfully tautologous defense held that the very existence of those institutions demonstrated that they themselves were "natural," the result of a process of complex growth. Individualists also tended to oppose democracy on the ground that it undermined property rights by enfranchising the working classes and promoting class-based legislation. Echoes of this hostility to democracy recur throughout "The Soul of Man," although for slightly different reasons: for Wilde, democracy represents a "bludgeoning of the people by the people for the people" (301). On more specific matters, most Individualists united in proposing the abolition of state education and state religion; state inspection of factories, mines, railways, and ships; state regulation of labor; government ownership of postal and telegraph services; and finally, and for Wilde perhaps most important, state interference with the stage and other forms of entertainment.[31]

One of the best gauges of Individualism's political influence in the late nineteenth century is provided by the campaigning activities of the Liberty and Property Defence League. The LPDL was a highly successful political pressure group founded in 1882 by Lord Elcho (later Earl of Wemyss), and supported at various times by all of the main ideologues of Individualism. As the name implies, the LPDL's aim was to defend the rights of property and promote laissez-faire doctrines. It funded two journals – *Jus* (1887–88) and the *Liberty Review* (1892–1909) – as well as circulating in the 1880s and 1890s what Bristow has calculated as "thousands of leaflets and pamphlets" of "anti-socialist barrage" (775). The LPDL was also active in Parliament; its supporters claimed to have "opposed 368 bills with 'more or less success' by 1891" (768). In 1889 the LPDL combined with the Personal Rights Association to organize a series of events to counter the influence of the best-selling *Fabian Essays in Socialism*. These ranged from public lectures, to widely reported debates between leading Socialists and Individualists, to anti-socialist lantern-shows and what were termed the "liberty missionaries" who propagandized Individualist policies from the saddles of tandem tricycles in London parks (775). In 1891 the Individualists produced a more formal response to the *Fabian Essays* when they published their own collection entitled *A Plea for Liberty*, introduced by Spencer.

In the late 1880s and early 1890s the Individualists thus enjoyed a high public profile, none more so than their most flamboyant and iconoclastic propagandist, Auberon Herbert. Herbert's conversion to Individualism came about after his discovery in the mid-1870s of the work of Spencer. He subsequently abandoned his parliamentary career, devoting the rest of his life to a zealous campaign against all forms of state intervention. Herbert's extreme views first came to general public notice in 1884 through the *Fortnightly Review* which published what would become his best-known work, "A Politician in Trouble about His Soul," which outlined his hostility to a coercive state.[32] In May 1890 Herbert founded his own journal, *Free Life*.[33] The subtitle, "Organ of Voluntary Taxation and the Voluntary State," gives a flavor of its content; Herbert used it to propagandize what he termed voluntaryism, an extreme Individualist creed that centered on an idiosyncratic scheme for voluntary taxation. Many of his fellow Individualists ridiculed the idea, seeing it as wholly impractical.

There can be little doubt that Wilde knew of Herbert. From late 1888–89 Herbert had orchestrated, largely through the pages of the *Nineteenth Century*, a vigorous campaign against state interference with education. Wilde, writing for the same journal, could not have missed the debate; his recurring jokes from this period about the value of a gentleman's education seem a direct reference to the controversy that Herbert had instigated.[34] In "The Soul of Man" the influence of Herbert is more directly evident in Wilde's advocacy of "*voluntary associations*" (296) and his claim that "the State is to be a voluntary association" (302). The argument is made in the context of a typical Individualist critique of the authoritarian elements of Socialism. Herbert's journal, *Free Life*, had been in circulation for around nine months when "The Soul of Man" appeared; moreover, Herbert himself had first come to prominence in the pages of the *Fortnightly*.[35] Contemporary readers of Wilde's essay could hardly have missed the connection. The difficulty, however, is to know what exactly they would have made of it, and what indeed Wilde may have intended by aligning himself with such a controversial polemicist.

Herbert was hardly a serious figure. He certainly did not possess the same stature as some of the other Individualists, such as Wordsworth

Donisthorpe, a Tory barrister and mine-owner, or J.H. Levy, a professor at Birkbeck College. Both these men enjoyed substantial reputations, so much so that even their opponents respected their work. Donisthorpe, for example, earned praise from figures as diverse as the economist John Elliott Cairnes, T.H. Huxley, and the political scientist, W.S. McKechnie. Levy won testimonials from influential socialists such as Shaw and E. Belfort Bax. By contrast, Herbert's voluntaryism was on the intellectual fringe of Individualism. While Wilde's general attraction to the Individualist critiques of authoritarianism and an interventionist state is easy to understand, his appropriation of Herbert's views is less expected: it sits uneasily with an attempt to style Wilde as a serious thinker. The tactic can be explained, though, as a journalist's ambition to be topical and to entertain. So the explicit allusion to Herbert (as opposed to other, more serious Individualists) maximizes opportunities to outrage but at the obvious risk of trivializing the issues involved.

There is ample evidence that in the late nineteenth century there *was* a serious debate about the politics of the Individualists. A glance at any of the heavyweight periodicals of the time reveals numerous and varied contributions about Individualism. The dense and sometimes turgid prose of Donisthorpe in the *Westminster Review* contrasts strikingly with the popular *ex-cathedra* qualities of T.H. Huxley's writing in the *Nineteenth Century*, which is different again from the careful philosophical distinctions drawn by Thomas Whittaker in an essay on "Individualism and State-Action" that appeared in *Mind*.[36] When we look at "The Soul of Man" in relation to this wider debate, it becomes obvious that Wilde was highly selective in the way that he presented his argument. He overlooked the serious issues under discussion – such as the distinction between philosophical and psychological individualism that interested Whittaker, or the practicalities of limiting the role of the state which occupied Donisthorpe, or the more general problem of deriving principles of justice from a theory of natural rights – in favor of the more sensationalist aspects of Individualism, such as Herbert's voluntary state. Such an observation does not necessarily devalue Wilde's essay; he does, after all, acknowledge that his argument is "utopian" (303). But it does require a re-characterization of his motives. "The Soul of Man" therefore needs to be seen for what it was designed to be – entertainment. An essay designed to entertain does not have to answer to the same criteria of coherence, integrity, and originality that we usually expect from a serious work.

Wilde's discussion of Individualism of course goes beyond casual references to voluntaryism. "The Soul of Man" repeatedly endorses the Individualists' general antipathy toward the state, including that implicit in what Huxley called "regimental socialism" (847). Similarly, Wilde reiterates the Individualists' claim that their politics were the result of a process of evolution, invoking the father of evolutionary Individualism, Spencer: "Individualism," Wilde argues, "*comes naturally and inevitably out of man.*" He continues: "It is the point to which all development tends. It is the differentiation to which all organisms grow. It is the perfection that is inherent in every mode of life, and toward which every mode of life quickens ... *Evolution is the law of life, and there is no evolution except toward individualism*" (*Fortnightly*, 316). To be sure, critics have noted Wilde's use of Spencer in "The Soul of Man." But its political implications have been overlooked, despite the fact that the Individualists' appropriation of Spencer explicitly politicized his work.[37]

Spencerian Individualism was fundamentally conservative. Moreover, when aligned with Darwinian biology it appeared to normalize the inequities of industrial competition as simply the "survival of the fittest." As one Individualist, M.D. O'Brien, put it: "Industrial struggle is at once both the condition and opportunity of the really efficient man, and the more there is of it the more will efficiency flourish and inefficiency come to grief ... in this great battle of life, somebody must lose; somebody must go to the wall."[38] It was exactly this kind of argument that permitted the Individualists to attack philanthropy. From that perspective, charity (like all social legislation) represented an inappropriate interference in the evolutionary process. Significantly, however, Spencer himself had never gone this far. Despite coining the phrase "survival of the fittest," his use of Darwin was inconsistent.

Spencer conceptualized his theory of evolutionary development, which Wilde alludes to, in *First Principles* (1862) as the cornerstone to the larger project of his *Synthetic Philosophy*. That is, Spencer's definition of evolution as increasing structural differentiation was not derived originally from biological processes, although Spencer did attempt to affiliate contemporary biological accounts (including Darwin's) to his general theory. It was only in Spencer's later and more political works, such as *The Study of Sociology* (1873) and *Men versus the State* (1884), that Darwinian language became explicit.[39] And it was these works, particularly *Men versus the State*, that inspired his Individualist followers. One reason for Spencer's ambivalent attitude toward Darwin concerned Spencer's rejection of the idea that individual competition was the sole motor for evolution (exactly the issue highlighted by Hugh Price

Hughes in his response to the Carnegie-Gladstone debate). Spencer was aware that his theory of social evolution seemed to disregard individual suffering. He therefore insisted on the role played by cooperation, arguing that altruism was an innate element of human character which, although an essential component of evolution, was not itself subject to environmental pressure. As Taylor argues, "Spencer's ideal ... was not a society of self-interested individuals, but one in which people voluntarily formed organizations for mutual assistance" (94). The Individualist followers of Spencer (particularly Herbert) found his theory of altruism useful, because it seemed to answer the criticism that the politics of Individualism benefited only a narrow interest group. At the same time, such a position was undermined by the Individualists' parallel commitment to social Darwinism: a model of society based on voluntaryism was not easily reconciled with the idea of a competitive, self-interested struggle in which the "weak go to the wall" (see Taylor, *Men versus the State,* 85–97).[40] The Individualists' Darwinian reading of Spencer thus exacerbated contradictions that were latent in his own work.

Wilde's deployment of Spencer in "The Soul of Man" suggests that he may have glimpsed this problem, and was using it in order to critique the Individualists' defense of privilege. So the Spencerian "law" of evolution that Wilde invokes appears to be stripped of its Darwinian connotations. At one point Wilde complains about "the modern stress of competition" in which "sympathy is naturally rare" (317). At the same time, this complaint consorts oddly with Wilde's comment that Darwin is "a great man of science" (293). This in turn echoes an earlier remark in "The Critic as Artist": "the nineteenth century is a turning point in history simply on account of the work of two men, Darwin and Renan."[41] Wilde's rejection of competition is contrasted with the altruism which he sees developing naturally under Individualism, and which, he argues, "will be absolutely unselfish," allowing man to "realise sympathy and exercise it freely and spontaneously" (316–17). Wilde also argues (again *pace* Spencer) that altruism is innate: "What a man really has, is what is in him. What is outside of him should be a matter of no importance" (297). Finally, Wilde refigures (but certainly does not resolve) the Individualist paradox that the exercise of altruism can actually be detrimental because it perpetuates undesirable elements of society and thus interferes with the evolutionary process. For Wilde, the problem with contemporary altruism is not the aid it gives to the destitute or "unfit" but rather the opposite. It helps the rich by perpetuating private property – that is, the very system that Individualists had tried to legitimate though their interpretation of Spencerian evolution. "Socialism, Communism, or whatever one chooses to call it," Wilde argues, "by converting private property into public wealth, and substituting co-operation for competition, will restore society to its proper condition of a thoroughly healthy organism" (293).

It is precisely this marriage of a Socialist critique of private property with an Individualist attack on authority that represents the central paradox that has impressed Wilde's modern critics. The use of Socialism to critique Individualism in order to reach a higher form of Individualism which neither traditional Socialists nor traditional Individualists would recognize, certainly looks very Wildean in its reversals. How coherent, though, is this strategy? The recuperation of Spencerian evolution from Darwinian biology hardly makes for a convincing explanation of the socialistic transformation of private property into public wealth (and therefore of competition into cooperation). If evolution holds true as a "theory of life" (to use Wilde's term), then it means that the private property which has harmed "true" Individualism must also be the product of evolution and thus in some sense natural. More precisely, Wilde makes no attempt to explain how evolutionary "differentiation" will lead to the abolition of private property. This is a striking omission when we consider that the Individualists saw the same evolutionary mechanisms leading to the exact opposite situation, the preservation of existing institutions. At one point, Wilde hints at the agency of individuals – at the role that "agitators" play in bringing about social change. But it is exactly this kind of human agency which a law of evolution disallows. Wilde invokes quite incompatible notions of social change without registering their contradictions. He also fails to resolve the contradiction inherent in the Individualists' theory of altruism: how a system of private property could have evolved in the first instance if altruism is indeed innate and thus not subject to evolutionary pressure.

These problems are produced by Wilde's unexpected appropriation of nature to authorize his concept of Individualism. Only a few months earlier, in "The Critic as Artist," he had launched sustained attacks on the whole concept of the natural and on the formative relationship between art and life. In an ironic contrast, in "The Soul of Man," he claims that "under Individualism people will be quite natural and absolutely unselfish" (316). Moreover, he further states "the true personality of man ... will grow naturally and simply, flower-like, or as a tree grows"; and then declares that Individualism *comes naturally and inevitably out of man* (298). The use of the term "natural" derives of course from Wilde's appropriation of evolutionary theory. This is a tactic that was in turn enforced by his (and the Individualists') anti-authoritarianism. By substituting for human agency a concept of natural necessity, evolution seemed to avoid the coercion associated with contemporary politics, whether by the government, revolutionary or militant Socialism, or Fabian arguments about the role of a reforming state. In this respect, "The Soul of Man," far from being a political essay, is its very antithesis, for it dissolves the grounds of both political debate and political action. For all its paradoxes and reversals, Wilde's essay shares the same fundamental conservatism of not only Spencer but also those high Tory, landowning Individualists. Wilde's opposition to private property does not distance him from Individualist politics as much as he might have wished.[42]

IV

It might be objected that my explanation has been over-elaborate, and that my stress on logic and consistency of argument runs counter to the spirit of Wilde's witty prose. But this, in a sense, is exactly the issue, for my contextualization has been designed to show that Wilde's essay is not serious: that its paradoxes and reversals cannot bear the weight of detailed analysis. If contrariness, as Stokes hints, is Wilde's metier, then we should resist pressing his work for synthesis or closure. Stokes's other claim about Wilde's artistry was that his opinions rose above the "generally acceptable" – that they were, in some sense, original. I have questioned this claim, too, by showing Wilde's dependence on, and relationship with, elements of contemporary journalistic debate. There is, however, one final and compelling piece of evidence on the topic of Wilde's purported originality, for it turns out that even his marriage of a Socialist critique of private property with an Individualist attack on authority was not new. An almost identical attempt to reconcile these politics had appeared less than two years earlier in the May 1889 number of the *Contemporary Review.* Moreover, the writer was someone well known to readers of the *Fortnightly Review* and probably to Wilde himself: Grant Allen.

Allen was a prolific writer. His reputation derived initially from his publications in the late 1870s on physiological aesthetics. In the 1880s and 1890s, however, he reached a much wider audience through his fiction and journalism. He produced numerous novels and short stories, as well as contributing many articles on popular scientific and social topics for a variety of periodicals. The occasion of his essay, "Individualism and

Socialism," was the discussion of a pamphlet that Allen had received
from the LPDL. He claimed that the notion of liberty that it promoted
was merely a defense of privilege. More particularly, the land-owning
Earl of Wemyss represented to Allen an affront to what he termed "true"
or "thorough-going" Individualism, which he defined in a manner
remarkably similar to Wilde:

> Individualism ... is only logically and consistently possible if it starts with
> the postulate that all men must, to begin with, have free and equal access
> to the common gifts and energies of Nature – soil, water, air, sunshine; and
> to the common stock of raw material – stone, wood, coal, metal ... An Indi-
> vidualist is a man who recognizes without stint the full, free, and equal
> right of every citizen to the unimpeded use of all his energies, activities and
> faculties, provided only he does not thereby encroach upon the equal and
> correlative right of every other citizen.[43]

Allen went on to claim that none of these conditions obtained in Britain
where the law protected landowners whom he called "the squatting and
tabooing class" (732). Significantly, Allen was careful to distinguish his
understanding of Individualism from certain kinds of Socialism. He was
prepared to concede that Socialism shared with Individualism "a strong
sense of the injustice and wickedness of the existing system," and an
ambition to promote "a more equitable distribution of the goods of life
among those who do most to produce and defend them." He nevertheless dissented strongly from "much that the Socialists proclaim as their
end and aim" – that is, from what he termed the "*deus ex machina*" role
that Socialism gave to the state (738). Wilde, of course, called this
"authoritarian Socialism."

Allen's tactic of combining an Individualist anti-statism with a Socialist critique of private property is virtually identical to that of Wilde in
"The Soul of Man." The real difference concerns the tone of their arguments. Wilde's vision of the future is self-consciously and wittily utopian,
brought about by the mysterious law of evolution. Allen, by contrast, is
more concerned with practical politics, such as campaigning for the
abolition of monopolies and privileges. To these ends, Allen claims, the
"so-called Socialists and the real Individualists can work in harness side
by side most amicably" (739). It is impossible to establish with certainty
whether Wilde had read Allen's essay. There is, however, an interesting
exchange of letters between the two men that immediately followed the
publication of "The Soul of Man."

"The Soul of Man" appeared in the *Fortnightly Review* in the same issue as Allen's essay on "The Celt in English Art." On reading it, Wilde wrote to Allen expressing his "real delight" in the article; he went on to propose that Allen join him for a celebratory "Celtic Dinner." Allen read Wilde's piece, and in a letter that crossed in the post he commended Wilde on his "noble and beautiful essay." "I would have written every line of it myself," Allen commented, "if only I had known how" (*Complete Letters*, 469–70). There may be something a little disingenuous in Allen's response because, in a sense, he had written some of Wilde's essay. At the very least Allen may have given Wilde the idea about how to reconcile Individualism and Socialism. Likewise, the effusiveness of Wilde's praise might disguise embarrassment.

V

I have shown that in the context of contemporary journalism the "social subject" of "The Soul of Man" starts to looks less like a serious discussion about freedom and authority and more like a provocative (but occasional) contribution to local controversies about the values of those who called themselves Individualists. The political reference of Wilde's essay, and the humor derived from it, is thus much more topical than critics have realized, and it is precisely this topicality which may explain Wilde's relative lack of interest in the essay after 1891, and why also modern critics have struggled with its paradoxes. Late nineteenth-century readers would certainly have found much that they recognized: the attack on charity, authoritarianism, and militant Socialism; the advocacy of voluntaryism; and the redefinition of Individualism through a Socialist critique of private property. None of these arguments was new. Nor were Wilde's comments on the role of the artist; they too had already been rehearsed, although in different ways, in "The Critic as Artist." If divorced from its local reference, then Wilde's reconciliation of the politics of Socialism and Individualism will appear perverse – a paradox, but an empty one. As a result, modern scholars run the risk of judging the essay as a failed or compromised work of art.

But I would like to view "The Soul of Man," in keeping with its textual condition, as an exemplary piece of occasional journalism. It is distinguished by the quality of the urbane wit that flatters the 1890s readers into thinking that they (and indeed Wilde himself) understand more than is in fact the case. The paradoxes and reversals are provocative but not profound: rather than a higher, deconstructive mode of criticism they are the self-conscious display of the skilful journalist, a display designed to attract and startle the fickle magazine buyer. In this respect, the tone of Wilde's essay is uncannily reminiscent of the cynicism of Jasper Milvain in Gissing's *New Grub Street* (1891): "I shall write for the upper middle-class of intellect," he explains to his sisters, "the people who like to feel that what they are reading has some special cleverness, but who can't distinguish between stones and paste."[44] This conclusion may seem to disparage Wilde's talent, until we remember that it is Wilde whom we continue to read today, while those more earnest figures – Allen, Donisthorpe and Herbert – remain on the "dustheap."

Notes

1 Peter Raby, "Wilde's Comedies of Society," in Peter Raby, ed., *The Cambridge Companion to Oscar Wilde* (Cambridge: Cambridge University Press, 1997), 143.

2 See Philip E. Smith II and Michael S. Helfand, eds., *Oscar Wilde's Oxford Notebooks* (Oxford: Oxford University Press, 1989), vii; and Sos Eltis, *Revising Wilde: Society and Subversion in the Plays of Oscar Wilde* (Oxford: Oxford University Press, 1996).

3 Arranging versions of Wilde's works into a chronological narrative of development is complicated by a number of factors. First, revisions were undertaken for a variety of reasons, which often conflicted with each other: a "purist" concern with refinement – the polishing of individual lexical items – coexists with a pragmatic, "cut-and-paste" mentality in which the need to expand material led to the incorporation of whole blocks of text which had their origins in other works. Secondly, Wilde often reincorporated material discarded from early drafts into later ones, and moved material between different works. Finally, works were revised in order to re-present (and resell) them to a different kind of reader: Wilde created different versions to perform different functions. In none of these cases is a concern with the integrity of the work paramount. These issues are discussed in Josephine M. Guy and Ian Small, *Oscar Wilde's Profession: Writing and the Culture Industry in the Late Nineteenth Century* (Oxford: Oxford University Press, 2000).

4 A corrected autograph manuscript of "The Soul of Man under Socialism" was advertised in April 1920 as part of the Stetson sale; purchased by Maggs, it was exposed as a forgery by Fabian Lloyd. Intriguingly, two letters from Robert Ross to the publisher Grant Richards, held at the William Andrews Clark Memorial Library, reveal that some years earlier, in the summer of

1912, Richards was enlisting Ross's help to dispose of what Ross terms "the manuscript of 'The Soul of Man'" through a dealer called Robson. This may be a reference to the Lloyd forgery. See the William Andrews Clark Memorial Library, uncataloged MSS. ALS, Robert Ross to Grant Richards, 16 August 1911; TLS Robert Ross to Grant Richards, 24 July 1912.

5 Wilde, *The Complete Letters of Oscar Wilde*, ed. Merlin Holland and Rupert Hart-Davis (London: Fourth estate, 2000), 487; further page references appear in parentheses.

6 See the *Eclectic Magazine* 52 (1891), 465–83; and "The Soul of Man under Socialism, the Socialist Ideal – Art and the Coming Solidarity. By Oscar Wilde, William Morris, W. C. Owen," *The Humboldt Library of Science* 147 (1891). The Humboldt Library of Science was a periodical dedicated to publishing what its advertising termed "the foremost scientific writers of the age." The number containing the essays by Wilde, Morris, and Owen was reissued in January 1892.

7 Richard Ellmann, *Oscar Wilde* (London: Hamish Hamilton, 1987), 401.

8 Anne Clark Amor, *Mrs. Oscar Wilde* (London: Sidgwick and Jackson, 1983), 152.

9 This letter is discussed by Horst Schroeder, "A Printing Error in 'The Soul of Man Under Socialism,'" *Notes and Queries* n.s. 43 (1996), 49–51.

10 In another letter ("To Charles Spurrier Mason," August 1894), Wilde comments that the new play will bring him "a lot of red gold": *Complete Letters*, 603.

11 The expensive edition was never produced in Wilde's lifetime. Mason notes that some copies of such an edition were advertised for sale in 1903 but not by Humphreys: see Stuart Mason [Christopher Millard], *Bibliography of Oscar Wilde* (London: T. Werner Laurie, 1914), 555–56; further page references appear in parentheses.

12 Wilde, *Collected Works*, 14 vols., *Reviews*, ed. Robert Ross (London: Methuen, 1908), XIII: 90; and Wilde, "To Arthur L. Humphreys," late November 1894, *Complete Letters*, 623–24.

13 In addition, 250 copies of a pirated version of *The Soul of Man* (following the *Fortnightly* in the accidentals) was published in 1904.

14 Stokes, "Wilde the Journalist," in Raby, ed., *The Cambridge Companion to Oscar Wilde*, 69, 77, and 78; further page references appear in parentheses. For a more recent attempt to revalue Wilde's journalism, see Catherine Ksinan, "Wilde as Editor of *Woman's World*: Fighting a Stale Slumber in Certitudes," *English Literature in Transition* 41 (1998), 408–26.

15 The only surviving 105-page manuscript of the enlarged version of "The Portrait of Mr. W. H.," held at the Rosenbach Library, consists partly of full

manuscript pages and partly of sheets from *Blackwood's Edinburgh Magazine*
with manuscript corrections and editions. It should be noted that it is
unclear whether the manuscript represents finished work. Its discoverer,
Mitchell Kennerley, claimed that it had been given to Frederick Chapman,
an officer manager of John Lane, to prepare for the printer. Horst
Schroeder, however, has cast doubt on Kennerley's account of the manuscript's provenance, and it seems more likely that it represents merely a
working draft; see Schroeder, *Oscar Wilde, "The Portrait of Mr. W. H" – Its Composition, Publication and Reception* (Braunschweig: Technische Universität
Carolo-Wilhelmina zu Braunschweig, 1984), 36–39.

16 Oscar Wilde, *The Soul of Man and Prison Writings*, ed. Isobel Murray (Oxford:
Oxford University Press, 1990), xi.

17 Lawrence Danson, *Wilde's Intentions: The Artist in His Criticism* (Oxford: Clarendon Press, 1997), 152; further page reference appears in parentheses.

18 See Walter E. Houghton, ed., *The Wellesley Index to Victorian Periodicals 1824–
1900*, 5 vols. (London: Routledge, 1966–87), II, where it is claimed that Harris's editorship represented "an open flaunting of accepted standards of literary taste and political discussion" (181).

19 Frank Harris, "To Oscar Wilde," 10 February 1890, in Ian Small, *Oscar Wilde
Revalued: An Essay and New Materials and Methods of Research* (Greensboro, NC:
ELT Press, 1993), 79.

20 Frank Harris, "To Oscar Wilde," offered as item no. 1139 in Maggs Catalogue
(1951), quoted in Ellmann, *Oscar Wilde*, 309.

21 See, for example, Danson, *Wilde's Intentions*, and Wilde, *The Soul of Man and
Prison Writings*, ed. Murray; both draw on J.D. Thomas's "'The Soul of Man
under Socialism': An Essay in Context," *Rice University Studies* 51 (1965), 83–
95; further page references appear in parentheses.

22 See W.E. Gladstone, "Mr. Carnegie's 'Gospel of Wealth': A Review and A Recommendation," *Nineteenth Century* 28 (1890), 677–93; and Henry Edward
[Manning], Card. Archbishop, Hermann Alder, Hugh Price Hughes, "Irresponsible Wealth," *Nineteenth Century* 28 (1890), 876–900; further page reference appears in parentheses. The two essays that made up Carnegie's
"Gospel of Wealth" originally appeared in the *North American Review* and
were reprinted in the *Pall Mall Gazette* (for which Wilde reviewed regularly
from 1884 to 1890). Carnegie's reply, "The Advantages of Poverty," appeared
in the *Nineteenth Century* 29 (1891), 367–85. Carnegie singled out in particular the criticism of Hugh Price Hughes. Interestingly, the piece was reproduced the following month in the same issue of the *Eclectic Magazine* as the
reprint of Wilde's "The Soul of Man under Socialism."

23 Philip Magnus, *Gladstone: A Biography* (London: John Murray, 1954), 384.

24 Wilde, "The Soul of Man under Socialism," *Fortnightly Review* n.s. 49 (1891), 294; further page references appear in parentheses.

25 The implication of Danson's comment is similar to A.E. Dyson's claim that we can "take [Wilde's] socialism for granted": *The Crazy Fabric: Essays in Irony*, (New York: St Martin's Press, 1973), 148. It is worth noting that in the mid-twentieth century it was fashionable to identify Wilde's position with anarchism; see, for example, George Woodcock, *Anarchism* (Cleveland, OH: World Publishing, 1962), 33–34, 305, 448.

26 Danson, quoting Steven Lukes's comments about the term's qualities, implies that it is too intractable to be worth worrying about: see *Wilde's Intentions*, 161; and Lukes, *Individualism* (Oxford: Blackwell, 1973).

27 The account of individualism which follows is indebted to M.W. Taylor, *Men versus the State: Herbert Spencer and Late Victorian Individualism* (Oxford: Clarendon Press, 1992); further page references appear in parentheses. For reasons of space, I have had to simplify Taylor's argument. It is important, though, to emphasize the distinction that he draws between the political individualism of the 1880s and the methodological individualism that underwrote the doctrines of the Manchester School or Philosophic Radicals in the earlier decades of the century. It was this latter kind of individualism that was transformed in the 1880s into what was termed "New Radicalism" or "New Liberalism."

28 Edward J. Bristow, "The Liberty and Property Defence League and Individualism," *Historical Journal* 18 (1975), 770; further page references appear in parentheses.

29 Taylor distinguishes between two broad kinds of Individualists: the "belligerent," non-university polemicists, who tended to argue (like Spencer) from a priori methodological atomism; and the "empiricists" who claimed that "experience" should define the limits to state intervention. Although the latter group had a more lasting political influence, serving on numbers of royal commissions, it was the former and more extreme group – figures such as Wordsworth Donisthorpe and Auberon Herbert – who were the intellectual leaders and who attracted the strongest publicity. See *Men versus the State*, 16–31.

30 Herbert Spencer, *Social Statics* (1850), quoted in Taylor, *Men versus the State*, 3.

31 See Bristow, "The Liberty and Property Defence League and Individualism," and Norbert C. Soldon, "Individualist Periodicals: The Crisis of Late Victorian Liberalism," *Victorian Periodicals Newsletter* 6 (1973), 22.

32 Herbert's piece was serialized in the *Fortnightly Review* in six parts from March 1883 until March 1884. See "A Politician in Trouble about His Soul. Part I," n.s. 33 (1883), 315–34; "Parts II and III," n.s. 33 (1883), 667–90; "Part

IV," n.s. 34 (1883), 354–76; "Part V," n.s. 34 (1883), 806–23; and "Part VI," n.s. 34 (1884), 354–76.

33 The first issues appeared under the cover of George Lane Fox's *Political World*, a journal established in July 1888 which folded in August 1890. By May 1890 *Free Life* became an autonomous publication. It continued under Herbert's editorship until August 1901; the price in the 1890s was 1*d.*, suggesting a large intended readership.

34 See Josephine M. Guy, "Self-Plagiarism, Creativity and Craftsmanship in Oscar Wilde," *English Literature in Transition* 41 (1998), 6–23. There is some evidence that Wilde might have known Herbert earlier than this, for in the mid-1880s both men were invited to speak to the Tyneside Sunday Lecture Society. (I am grateful to Peter Raby for this information.)

35 It is worth noting that Herbert continued to contribute to the *Fortnightly* in the late 1880s and early 1890s; indeed a piece by him appeared in the issue immediately preceding that of Wilde's "The Soul of Man under Socialism." See Herbert, "'The Rake's Progress' in Irish Politics," *Fortnightly Review* n.s. 49 (1891), 126–42.

36 See Donisthorpe, "The Basis of Individualism," *Westminster Review* 70 (1886), 118–56; T.H. Huxley, "Government: Anarchy or Regimentation," *Nineteenth Century* 27 (1890), 843–66; and Thomas Whittaker, "Individualism and State-Action," *Mind* 49 (1888), 52–62.

37 See, for example, Smith and Helfand, *Oscar Wilde's Oxford Notebooks*, 80–86. Their narrow focus on the evidence from Wilde's undergraduate notebooks leads them to concentrate on the biological aspects of Spencer's sociology, with the result that they have little to say about Spencer's politics and his (and Wilde's) complex relationship with Individualist pressure groups.

38 M.D. O'Brien, *The Natural Right to Freedom* (London: Williams and Norgate, 1893), 323–4, quoted in Taylor, *Men versus the State*, 89.

39 Even then, Spencer was keen to distance himself from Darwin. For example, in a footnote to "The Study of Sociology. XIV. Preparation in Biology," in the *Contemporary Review* 22 (1873), he states: "Probably most readers will conclude that ... I am simply carrying out the views of Mr. Darwin in their applications to the human race. Under the circumstances, perhaps, I shall be excused for pointing out that the same beliefs, otherwise expressed, are contained in Chapters XXV and XXVIII of *Social Statics*, published in December, 1850" (339–40).

40 Taylor suggests that the contradiction worked in two ways: on the one hand, the endorsement of selfishness implicit in a Darwinian struggle for survival might actually retard the altruistic impulse; on the other hand, the active promotion of altruism might prolong the survival of the unfit (in Victorian

terms, the undeserving poor). It is perhaps worth noting that the dilemma of how altruism can evolve when the motor of evolution is self-interest continues to occupy modern evolutionary biologists.

41 Wilde, *Collected Works*, 14 vols., VIII: 222.

42 Criticism of Individualist politics by New Radicals was widespread, particularly the contradictions implicit in their use of social Darwinism. Wilde was certainly aware of this body of work for he had reviewed David George Ritchie's *Darwinism and Politics* (1889) in *The Woman's World*. Ritchie, an Oxford philosopher, Fabian, and supporter of New Radicalism was a trenchant critic of Spencer. In 1889 Wilde commented that he wanted to see "a reconciliation of Socialism with Science," but that he had found Ritchie's book "very slight and amateurish" (Wilde, "To Mrs. R.B. Cunninghame Graham," *c.* 30 June 1889, in *Complete Letters*, 403–04).

43 Grant Allen, "Individualism and Socialism," *Contemporary Review* 54 (1889), 738 and 731–2; further page references appear in parentheses.

44 Gissing, *New Grub Street* (Harmondsworth: Penguin, 1987), 43–44.

chapter three

Love-Letter, Spiritual Autobiography, or Prison Writing? Identity and Value in *De Profundis*

IAN SMALL

I

For at least a generation, most critical interpretations of Oscar Wilde's works, whether they have acknowledged it or not, have depended on an expressive aesthetic which is authenticated by a particular reading of his life. The best-known instance of this practice was Richard Ellmann's 1987 biography, which explained Wilde's creativity in relation to his sexuality. Ellmann famously asserted that "[h]omosexuality fired [Wilde's] mind," and went on to link what he called Wilde's "annus mirabilis" (1891) with the meeting with Lord Alfred Douglas.[1] Later critics, such as Christopher Craft, Richard Dellamora, Jonathan Dollimore, and Alan Sinfield, presented more subtle readings of the works, but the expressive paradigm predicated of the oeuvre remained fundamentally the same.[2] More recently an interest in Wilde's identity as an Irishman has allowed critics such as Davis Coakley, Declan Kiberd, Jerusha McCormack, Richard Pine, and Sandra Siegel to see a different politics in his writing.[3] So, for example, in Kiberd's view *The Importance of Being Earnest* (1895) "becomes ... a parable of Anglo-Irish relations and a pointer to their resolution"; or in McCormack's argument the Russian Prince Paul in *Vera; or, The Nihilists* (1880) is "an honorary Irishman."[4]

A third group of critics has identified Wilde as a European intellectual, engaging with an eclectic tradition of philosophical thought that goes back to Immanuel Kant and Friedrich Schiller and which includes Herbert Spencer, G.W.F. Hegel, Friedrich Nietzsche, and Søren Kierkegaard. Philip E. Smith II and Michael S. Helfand, and later Julia Prewitt Brown, have traced a nexus of intellectual concerns in Wilde's undergraduate notes which they see animating the rest of his oeuvre. For Smith and Helfand, "Wilde's aestheticism ... is shown by the notebooks to be based on a carefully reasoned philosophical and political stance, a synthesis of Hegelian idealism and Spencerian evolutionary theory which fundamentally shaped his criticism and fiction."[5] Brown describes a different set of intellectual interests, characterized not in terms of a search for synthesis, but as "a paradoxical interrelatedness of opposites."[6] Nevertheless, like Smith and Helfand, she employs a methodological strategy which in effect erases crucial distinctions between works, and which therefore ignores the specificities of their textual conditions. For example, the textual condition of the undergraduate notebooks, presumably never intended to be read by any one other than Wilde, is wholly different from that of "The Decay of Lying" (commissioned by the *Nineteenth Century* in 1885). Both of these are different again from the work known as *De Profundis*, written in part as a semi-private letter. Yet Brown can see all three pieces in terms of a continuing engagement with the idea of a "cosmopolitan criticism," in which Wilde's writings are linked with a tradition which embraces Kierkegaard and Kant, and later Theodor Adorno and Walter Benjamin. This tendency to elide the obvious material differences between Wilde's writings – the different forms in which they were published, their different markets or readerships, the different functions or purposes they had for his career – is common to nearly all of those interpretations tied to a reading of the life.

Why has attending to these political, sexual, and intellectual currents so diverted the attention of critics from the material conditions of textual production? It is of course true that, compared with writers such as Charles Dickens and Thomas Hardy, much less information about the textual condition of Wilde's oeuvre has been readily available to the critic. It is also true that Wilde's bankruptcy in 1895 dispersed some vital documents, a situation which, when taken with the number of different publishers for whom he worked, may have led to a perception that information about his writing has been irretrievably lost. Relevant archives, however, do survive. In collections such as the William Andrews Clark Library, in the records of the Bodley Head, or in the Macmillan archive, there is abundant information about the day-to-day details of Wilde's publishing activities. Moreover, there has been some significant textual work undertaken on individual elements of the oeuvre, particularly on the poems and on the society comedies.[7] So why has this information been routinely ignored? One answer might be that the highly politicized

Wildean persona through which the works are now typically read must inevitably exclude the pragmatic, quotidian, and often tedious details of a writer's life in the last two decades of the nineteenth century.

This accusation of myopia or bias is a serious one, and it would require more than a single chapter to substantiate it. More precisely, it would be necessary to show systematically how knowledge of the contemporary material elements of literary production affects issues of modern interpretation. Such an injunction is of course the burden of much recent writing on the sociology of texts, particularly by Jerome J. McGann.[8] Text sociologists and theorists do not claim that an understanding of the conditions of production and consumption of a literary work will result in a single authoritative interpretation; but they do assert that it will make certain kinds of readings very difficult to sustain. For example, the modern reading of Wilde's dramatic works as political satire is not easy to reconcile with the awkward fact, transparent in the *Letters*, that in 1891 he was much more interested in selling to theater managers *The Duchess of Padua* (a play privately printed in 1883 and which modern critics see as something of an embarrassment) than he was in finishing the allegedly subversive *Lady Windermere's Fan* (1892), for which he had received a commission. Similarly, the gay and anti-colonial subtexts recently detected in *The Importance of Being Earnest* sit uncomfortably with what we know of Wilde's reasons for writing it (which were explicitly financial) and his difficulties in placing it.[9] The dimensions of this problem – namely, the relationship between issues of interpretation and information about a work's materiality – are perhaps best seen by taking what is the hardest case in Wilde's oeuvre, by examining the textual condition that is both the most complicated and the most often misrepresented, that of *De Profundis*.

Most critics would view *De Profundis* as the exception in the oeuvre: composed under uniquely difficult conditions, apparently written as a single continuous piece of prose, and never published in Wilde's lifetime, it seems to be a totally different animal from the performed or published works. Never fully private, but never until 1962 fully public; the central piece of evidence read out in court in a libel case, yet kept out of public view by that self-same legal system; a letter, and yet also a literary work – these overfamiliar facts about its textual condition seem to set *De Profundis* apart. Paradoxically, however, the apparent uniqueness of *De Profundis* seems to have liberated critics into doing whatever they want with Wilde's text, as if the intricacies of its textual condition are registered only to be dismissed.

When critics refer to *De Profundis* they usually have in mind the manuscript written by Wilde in prison, now housed in the British Library, and published in 1962 by Rupert Hart-Davis.[10] The title *De Profundis*, taken from Psalm 130, was in fact chosen by Robert Ross and was initially used for a substantially shortened and heavily edited version of the manuscript that he published as a new literary work by Wilde in 1905. Significantly, Hart-Davis does not confuse these two different documents. The text which he reproduces in the *Letters* is explicitly edited, identified, and annotated as part of Wilde's correspondence – a circumstance acknowledged by Ellmann, for whom it is simply a love letter, one of the greatest ever written (484). As I have indicated, however, other critics, by using the title *De Profundis* to refer to the Hart-Davis text, have obscured its epistolary status, treating it as just another piece of critical prose. Certainly they use Hart-Davis' text in ways very different from Wilde's other correspondence. For example, it is frequently included in anthologies of Wilde's published works as if it possessed a simple and unproblematic literary identity. In other words, many critics have wished to incorporate the prison manuscript into the body of Wilde's "serious" and public writing, despite the fact that the text they use is the one that its modern editor identifies as a letter. This change of identity is particularly obvious in Isobel Murray's anthology of Wilde's writings entitled *The Soul of Man, and Prison Writings* (1990), where she reproduces Hart-Davis' text from the *Letters* but renames it *De Profundis*, apparently in order to give it the same kind of identity as the published work, *The Soul of Man*.[11] (In order to avoid confusion I will refer to the document in the British Library and reproduced by Hart-Davis in 1962 simply as "the prison manuscript"; I use *De Profundis*, followed by the appropriate date, to refer to the work(s) of that name which Ross edited.)

The use of Wilde's other letters is always to document local details of his life. Hart-Davis' text of the prison manuscript, by contrast, typically takes on a kind of universality in which its summarizing (or what we might call "über") qualities are more significant than any local reference. So the usual literary reading of it is what Brown calls "a theologically imbued autobiography" (xviii). How often have we seen appropriations of Wilde's famous claim – that he "was a man who stood in symbolic relations to the art and culture of my age" (*Letters*, 466; *Complete Letters*, 729) – used as a template to interpret the rest of the life and oeuvre? That said, critics have differed strikingly in the kinds of connections that they have drawn between the prison manuscript, Wilde's life, and the rest of his work. For numerous scholars its status as expressive autobiography does not prevent it from simultaneously continuing a political discussion about the nature of freedom and individualism begun in embryo in earlier works, such as the Oxford notebooks (dating from 1874–8) and "The Soul of Man under Socialism" (1891).[12] For other critics, such as Dollimore, that summation points in a very different direction. He sees the prison manuscript representing a capitulation to bourgeois values which signals Wilde's abandonment of his oppositional sexual politics.[13] In all these cases, though, the meaning of the prison manuscript is defined in terms of its relationship with, and the way it comments on, the rest of the oeuvre. This is a paradoxical situation when we recall that most commentators would also acknowledge that the textual condition of the prison manuscript is unique.

We might ask why this paradox is so rarely noticed. Why are none of the other letters, especially the other personal letters to Douglas, assimilated to the oeuvre in the same way? Textually, what entitles us to treat the prison manuscript as a special case? Nobody, to my knowledge, has ever tried to answer this question, even though they assume in their criticism that it can be answered. It is significant that where critics do pay attention to the work's textual condition, they tend to single out only those aspects that suit their particular readings; less convenient details are quietly ignored. We know that the salutation of Wilde's letter was to Lord Alfred Douglas ("Dear Bosie"); but Wilde also wished to have his letter copied, not once but twice; and he instructed Robert Ross and More Adey to read it prior to sending it to Douglas. To see the work principally as a love-letter, as Ellmann does, is clearly incompatible with these details. Likewise, the letter's semi-private nature also undermines the claims made for its expressive, autobiographical, and redemptive functions. If the writing of the prison manuscript was only, or primarily, a form of catharsis, then once more Wilde's desire to have it copied, together with the possibility of revising it at a later date, makes little sense. Finally, to treat the work as an important piece of political writing is not easily aligned with its very restricted circulation. We might legitimately ask what could be political about a document which initially had such a small audience, and which was also a love-letter? All of this is to say that the relationship between the identity, intention, status, and textual condition of the prison manuscript is very complex, yet its full ramifications have never been properly explored nor appreciated. This is an unfortunate situation because it turns out that a very good case can be made for treating the prison manuscript as a draft of a literary work as well as a letter. Here it will be helpful to begin by rehearsing all the known details about its original composition.

II

It is generally agreed that Wilde wrote his prison manuscript between January and March 1897 in prison at Reading, although this information appears to derive only from Hart-Davis' conjectural dating, which he does not explain.[14] Interestingly, Ross describes the manuscript as being written "at intervals during the last six months of the author's imprisonment," suggesting that Wilde began it in late 1896.[15] The then governor of Reading Gaol, Major J. O. Nelson, testified that "each sheet [of the manuscript] was numbered before being issued and withdrawn each evening at locking."[16] Hart-Davis, however, disputes this testimony and suggests that the surviving manuscript is, in part at least, a fair copy. Individual folios are not free-standing as one might have expected them to be; for example, only two of the sheets finish at the end of a sentence. In other words, Hart-Davis implies that Wilde must have had access to more writing materials, and must have composed more drafts, than the prison authorities were prepared to admit. If the governor's account were true, it would suggest a unique work in Wilde's oeuvre, because we now know that Wilde was often a conscientious reviser. Wilde's other compositional practices suggest that his works *never* came to him fully formed, or fully thought out. The physical act of writing to a large extent coincided with – or perhaps was – the creative process itself, and common sense suggests that this would have always been the case, even though in prison he might have had more time to think before putting pen to paper.

We may not know when the work was begun, but we do know with certainty that the text was finished by 1 April 1897, because on that day Wilde wrote to Ross telling him to expect the manuscript in the post.[17] In fact, the manuscript was retained by the prison authorities until Wilde's release on 18 May and was not given to Ross until 20 May when Wilde met him in Dieppe. Hart-Davis suggests that Wilde's letter to Ross of 1 April may also have been withheld because a second letter dated 6 April repeats much of the information of the first, particularly that concerning Wilde's divorce settlement.[18] Nevertheless, in his 1908 edition of Wilde's collected works Ross testifies that he received the original letter (*Collected Works*, XI: xiii). Moreover, given the importance that Wilde obviously attached to his manuscript, it is hard to believe that he and Ross would not have discussed its contents when they met seven weeks later.

Apart from appointing Ross as Wilde's literary executor, the letter contains the only detailed account of Wilde's intentions toward the manuscript. In brief, Wilde gave Ross three sets of instructions. First, he was to read, along with More Adey ("whom I always include with you"), the manuscript (*Letters*, 512; *Complete Letters*, 780). From the very beginning, then, Wilde envisaged a readership larger than the individual to whom the letter was addressed. Secondly, Wilde instructed Ross to keep the manuscript in his possession but have a "carefully" typed copy made for the author (*Letters*, 512; *Complete Letters*, 780). Wilde suggested that Ross should use Mrs. Marshall's Typewriting Office in the Strand, one of the two agencies that he or his managers habitually employed for preparing copies of the Society comedies. Indeed, Wilde stipulated that it should be typed on "good paper such as is used for plays"; he also stipulated that "a wide rubricated margin should be left for corrections" (*Letters*, 513; *Complete Letters*, 781). The term "rubricated" is interesting. It is typically used to refer to marginal commentaries, glosses, or corrections made in red to liturgical works. Wilde's manuscripts reveal that he made habitual marginal glosses and corrections to his own typescripts, often in colored ink or pencil. The detailed instruction about the margin points to an intention to revise, change, or rework the typescript of the letter at a later date, and presumably for some other audience or purpose.

Wilde's comments suggest that the manuscript was a letter (and finished as such), but it is important to remember that Wilde gave instruction that the manuscript, not the typescript, be given to Douglas. The manuscript was also, and simultaneously, the draft for some possible future work (which could hardly be another letter and obviously not to the same person). These instructions immediately controvert the common assumption that the manuscript represents Wilde's final interest in or thoughts about his work. The fact that Wilde died three years later, and apparently without making the projected corrections, does not undermine the argument that when writing the manuscript in prison he seemed to have an intention to carry on working from it on his release. Put simply, there is evidence that the letter was never *just a letter*; whatever else it might have become on revision, the text could not have been the same as that letter which Wilde instructed Ross to send to Douglas.

To return to Wilde's instructions to Ross in his letter of 1 April: his second injunction was that after Ross had verified the typed copy, he was to send the manuscript to Douglas via Adey. Importantly, Wilde indicated that Douglas should not be told that a copy had been taken unless he complained "of injustice in the letter or misrepresentation" – which of course he later did (*Letters*, 514; *Complete Letters*, 782). At the same time, Wilde's comment to Ross that he hoped "someone will let him [Douglas] know that the letter is one that he thoroughly deserves" demonstrates that Wilde intended that Douglas should know that his letter had been read by others. It might be worth commenting here that the manuscript held in the British Library is in places corrected. No one to my knowledge has ever noted the oddity of Wilde wanting to send a heavily corrected letter to anyone. It is often assumed that Ross alone made the decision to send the typed copy, and not the manuscript, to Douglas; but, as Maureen Borland has hinted, this decision could well have been made with Wilde's consent.[19] Although Ross's action was not in keeping with Wilde's instruction in his letter of 1 April 1897, we cannot discount the possibility that Wilde later changed his mind. There was a considerable – and, for Wilde, a worrying – delay in the preparation of the typescript. Wilde wrote from Berneval to Ross on 15 June asking why he had not heard about the "type-writer [that is, typist], or my letter" (*Letters*, 609; *Complete Letters*, 897). On 20 July 1897 he wrote to Ross telling him he did not like the idea of "the type-written manuscript" being sent to William Dixon (*Letters*, 624; *Complete Letters*, 914). (Dixon had offered his services to Wilde as a typist as early as May.) The term "type-written manuscript" is perplexing; it may refer to an existing typed copy that Dixon might use as the basis of a further copy. Vyvyan Holland, however, suggests that there was only ever one typed copy and a carbon.

It is this sort of conflicting evidence that makes the reconstruction of the textual history of Wilde's prison manuscript so difficult. We cannot be absolutely sure about how many copies were made or when. We do know for certain that by 15 June Wilde had not received a copy, and that Ross had been with Wilde in Normandy from 20 to 27 May 1897 with the manuscript to hand. It is almost inevitable that the two men discussed the manuscript during this period; some or all of the differences between it and the typescript may have been the result of decisions taken then. That is to say, Wilde may have cooperated with Ross in the preparation of the text for the edited and typed copy eventually sent to Douglas. Such a scenario goes some way to explaining why the decision was later made to send a typescript, and not the manuscript, to Douglas. If this narrative is correct, then it is arguable that Holland's 1949 text, which he says was produced from the carbon copy of the typescript sent to Douglas, has Wilde's authority.[20] The question that we ought to ask ourselves is the following: Is it likely that, at a time when Wilde was obsessed with Douglas, and when Ross saw a substantial and new piece of writing for the first time, it would have been entirely ignored for a week? Ironically, the manuscript itself records the intellectual productivity of Wilde's time spent with Ross, that "The Decay of Lying" (1889) grew out of a single dinner with him. Moreover, Borland describes how, during Wilde's imprisonment and the weeks immediately following it, when Douglas was neglectful, Wilde came increasingly to rely on Ross.

So what we have, then, is a letter which was perhaps to form the basis of another work – a letter which itself was semi-public, in that it was Wilde's intention that it should be read by several people. The phenomenon of the semi-public letter, one that a writer intends to be read by a select group, remains complex but there are numerous examples. It seems, for instance, that Lord Chesterfield's letters to his son, or those of Alexander Pope, although they are addressed to specific recipients, were nonetheless written with an eye to eventual publication. A more pertinent analogy for the case of Wilde is the personal letter, again written to an individual correspondent but intended for circulation among family or friends. Matthew Arnold's letters, and his family's sense that they were a collective family property, represent such examples. In these cases, the letter was not fully public, in the manner of Wilde's prison letters to the *Daily Chronicle*; but nor was it fully private, in the sense that it was written in the knowledge and with the expectation that it would be read by more than one individual. In this sense, semi-public letters are very different from the private love-letter written for a unique recipient. We typically predicate qualities such as sincerity, honesty, and intimacy only on the assumption that a letter is intended for one particular reader. These qualities are important if we read Wilde's manuscript as expressive or autobiographical.

The problem with the manuscript is that none of these categories adequately describes it because it contains aspects of all of them. On the one hand, the personal nature of some of the material, and Wilde's claim that it would be a lesson to Douglas, strongly supports Ellmann's reading of it as a love-letter. On the other hand, such intimate letters are not usually intended to be read *in advance* by other people, particularly when one such reader – that is, Ross – is a former lover, and therefore not likely to be sympathetic. Indeed, by some lights, this action would constitute a form of betrayal, and thus undermine the kinds of claim made for it by Ellmann. This circumstance certainly compromises Ellmann's assumptions about honesty and intimacy. In any case, love-letters are rarely copied in advance of their delivery. And, if copied, they are seldom retained in a form that allows for later correction or revision. If the text were simply a love-letter, then for whom would these later putative corrections be made? Wilde's instruction to Ross that the letter be read in advance; his stipulation that it be copied both for his own use and (here I am anticipating slightly) also for posterity; and the fact that he was reserving the possibility of revising it at a later date – all of these details suggest that Wilde had a complex set of intentions toward his text. These varying intentions as a consequence point to difficulties in attributing a simple or single identity to the manuscript.

Let us turn once again to Wilde's letter and his instructions to Ross. To complicate matters, Wilde made a third set of stipulations. He suggested that Ross should have a second typewritten copy made (presumably from the first, because the manuscript by this time, had Wilde's plan been put into practice, would have been dispatched to Douglas). The first copy, with the wide rubricated margins, was for Wilde; the second one was to be retained by Ross, because he was to be Wilde's executor and should "have complete control over my plays, books and papers" (*Letters*, 512; *Complete Letters*, 780). In addition, Wilde also asked Ross to arrange for two typed copies of an abridgement of the text to be made. These would include material from folio 9 to folio 14 of the manuscript. These extracts were to be, in Wilde's words, "welded" by Ross with anything else "you may extract that is good and nice in intention, such as the first page of sheet 15" (*Letters*, 513; *Complete Letters*, 782). These typed copies were then to be sent to a woman whom Wilde identifies as the "Lady of Wimbledon" (Adela Schuster), and Frankie Forbes-Robertson, who could in turn permit her brother Eric to read it.

At this point the problems of textual identity of Wilde's manuscript become even more intractable, for Wilde seems to have in mind a substantially different work from the prison manuscript. The abridgement is not the letter, but nor is it the possible future emended work derived from the typescript of the letter. If this abridgement had been made (or indeed was made, but is now lost), it would be highly unlikely that either Schuster or Forbes-Robertson would have been told that they had received a truncated version of a longer manuscript. Wilde describes this projected abridgement as if it would be a different work intended for a different audience. It was "a sort of message or letter I send them – the only one, of course, I dare send"; it would contain "something of what is happening to my soul ... but merely in the spiritual consciousness that is separate from the actual occupations of the body" (*Letters*, 513; *Complete Letters*, 782). For the textual scholar, it is important to register the fact that Wilde delegates responsibility for constructing this "other" truncated text to Ross. Equally important is Wilde's sense that he must present his account of himself in different ways for different individuals. The "soul" revealed to the "public," represented by Adela Schuster and the Forbes-Robertsons, will be very different from that revealed to Douglas, Ross, and Adey. The idea of Wilde contriving his self-image for different publics should again caution us against reading the letter simply as sincerely expressive.

Wilde's instructions to Ross were detailed. Nevertheless, they were not carried out precisely. Ross may have had two typescript copies made. He may have sent one of them to Douglas (who claimed to have begun reading it but then to have destroyed it). However, Ross did keep the other typescript (or carbon) copy for himself, together with the original manuscript. After Wilde's death, Ross proceeded to implement the second of Wilde's instructions – using his own judgment, along with Wilde's suggestions, to make what was effectively a new work from an abridgement of the letter. Published in 1905, Ross entitled this abridged work *De Profundis*. In the 1905 text, all personal references to Douglas (and thus to its origins as a "private" love-letter) were omitted. Ross revised and slightly expanded this text for his edition of Wilde's works in 1908.

Ross's account of the genesis of the 1905 and 1908 texts are given in the dedication to the 1908 edition; he describes how he had been put under pressure by Max Meyerfield to fulfil a prior agreement to send Meyerfield extracts of the letter for German publication. Fulfilling this request, Ross claimed, made him realize the importance of a simultaneous English publication of the same extracts. He states that he sent the whole manuscript to Methuen, who, to his surprise and with the encouragement of their reader, E.V. Lucas, accepted it. Ross also remarks that "a very distinguished man of letters who acted as their reader" (i.e. Lucas) had a hand in the editorial work ("A Prefatory Dedication," XI: x).[21] Modern critics often take this collaboration as a reason to question the text's authority; they see it as a bowdlerized version of the manuscript. In the same dedication, however, Ross also clearly notes that he was preparing "the portions" of the letter "in accordance with the writer's wishes" ("A Prefatory Dedication," XI: vii). These wishes were those which Wilde set out in his letter of 1 April 1897, because Ross's 1905 edition corresponds quite closely to the abridgment that Wilde suggested should be made.

A second strand to understanding Ross's 1905 edition of *De Profundis* is to see it as a repackaging of a sanitized Wilde, as a sort of flag for the collected edition. Some contemporary reviewers of the 1905 edition did indeed see it as an attempt to recuperate Wilde; and some were very suspicious, questioning its sincerity. Similarly, modern critics tend to see it as inauthentic precisely because it is incomplete; that is, they see it as a poor, corrupt version of the authentic letter in which a cautious Ross mutes Wilde's voice. By contrast, however, I would like to suggest that while Ross is certainly repackaging Wilde, it is in a way in which Wilde (in principle at least) had authorized. In this sense, Ross's *De Profundis* is Wilde's, at least in large part. For this reason, I would suggest that Ross's 1905 text has authority but as a different work from the manuscript. A hypothetical third work is the essay that Wilde might have produced from the typescript with the rubricated margin. This hypothetical text of course does not exist, but the fact that Wilde had it in mind is important because it feeds into what Wilde intended for his manuscript. The fact that he conceived of other uses for the manuscript – uses that could not possibly be further letters, and that must in some sense constitute other works – helps to provide authority for the Ross edition. It reminds us that we have grounds for seeing it as Wilde's work, and not simply that of Ross and Lucas.

My general contention, then, is that we should understand the textual history of *De Profundis* not in terms of versions of a single work, but in terms of the production of a number of separate works: a letter (A1); an intended revision of the typescript of that letter which would inevitably change its identity (?A2); and a further work (or works) derived from an abridgment of the letter (A3). The stemma can be schematized as follows:

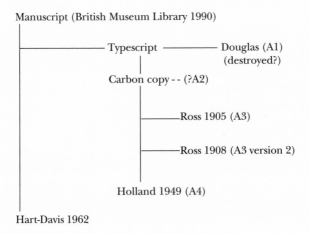

Manuscript (British Museum Library 1990)

Typescript ———— Douglas (A1)
(destroyed?)

Carbon copy - - (?A2)

Ross 1905 (A3)

Ross 1908 (A3 version 2)

Holland 1949 (A4)

Hart-Davis 1962

The consequence of this textual history is rather strange. Critics who wish to identify the prison manuscript as a letter have a difficulty, for the document that Douglas might have received was the typescript (A1). Evidence that this typescript was quite different from the manuscript comes from Holland's 1949 edition (A4) that was derived from the carbon copy of the typescript perhaps sent to Douglas. Critics who wish to identify a literary work called *De Profundis* have a choice of text. Ross's 1905 edition (A3) has some authority on the grounds that it was an abridgment of the manuscript which Wilde partly authorized for limited public consumption. The 1949 Holland text (A4) also has some authority because it is derived from the typed version for which Wilde so anxiously waited and which he might have worked up for publication. Ironically, the manuscript that is held in the British Library has the least authority to be considered a literary work: the view of it most consistent with the extant evidence is that it is a *draft* for both a future literary work and for a letter. In this argument, the text of the manuscript in the British Library properly belongs neither in an edition of the letters nor in an edition of Wilde's literary works but in the apparatus of that edition.[22]

Notes

1 See Richard Ellmann, *Oscar Wilde* (London: Hamish Hamilton, 1987), 265 and 290; further page reference appears in parentheses.

2 See Christopher Craft, *Another Kind of Love: Male Homosexual Desire in English Discourse, 1850–1920* (Berkeley, CA: University of California Press, 1994); Richard Dellamora, *Masculine Desire: The Politics of Victorian Aestheticism* (Chapel Hill: University of North Carolina Press, 1990); Jonathan Dollimore, "Different Desires: Subjectivity and Transgression in Wilde and Gide," *Textual Practice* 1 (1987), 48–67; Jonathan Dollimore, *Sexual Dissidence: Augustine to Wilde, Freud to Foucault* (Oxford: Clarendon Press, 1991); and Alan Sinfield, *The Wilde Century: Effeminacy, Oscar Wilde and the Queer Moment* (London: Cassell, 1994).

3 See Davis Coakley, *Oscar Wilde: The Importance of Being Irish* (Dublin: Town House, 1994); Declan Kiberd, "Oscar Wilde: The Resurgence of Lying," in Peter Raby, ed., *The Cambridge Companion to Oscar Wilde* (Cambridge: Cambridge University Press, 1997), 276–94; Declan Kiberd, *Inventing Ireland: The Literature of the Modern Nation* (London: Jonathan Cape, 1995); Jerusha McCormack, ed., *Wilde the Irishman* (New Haven, CT: Yale University Press, 1998); Richard Pine, *The Thief of Reason: Oscar Wilde and Modern Ireland* (Dub-

lin: Gill and Macmillan, 1995); and Sandra Siegel, "Oscar Wilde's Gift and Oxford's 'Coarse Impertinence,'" in Tadhg Foley and Seán Ryder, eds., *Ideology and Ireland in the Nineteenth Century* (Dublin: Four Courts Press, 1998), 69–78.

4 Declan Kiberd, "Oscar Wilde: The Artist as Irishman," 17, and McCormack, "Oscar as Aesthete and Anarchist," in McCormack, ed., *Wilde the Irishman*, 88.

5 See Philip E. Smith II and Michael S. Helfand, eds., *Oscar Wilde's Oxford Notebooks: A Portrait of the Mind in the Making* (New York: Oxford University Press, 1989), vii.

6 Julia Prewitt Brown, *Cosmopolitan Criticism: Oscar Wilde's Philosophy of Art* (Charlottesville, VA: University Press of Virginia, 1997), xv; further page reference appears in parentheses.

7 The most significant recent editorial work has been on the poems and on *The Importance of Being Earnest*. See Bobby Fong and Karl Beckson, eds., *The Complete Works of Oscar Wilde, Volume 1: Poems and Poems in Prose* (Oxford: Oxford University Press, 2000); and Joseph Donohue (with Ruth Berggren), ed., *Oscar Wilde's* The Importance of Being Earnest*: The First Production* (Gerrards Cross: Colin Smythe, 1995) (further page reference appears in parentheses).

8 See, for example, Jerome J. McGann, *The Textual Condition* (Princeton, NJ: Princeton University Press, 1991).

9 Contrary to received wisdom, most authoritatively endorsed by Ellmann, Donohue makes it clear that *The Importance of Being Earnest* was subject to complex negotiations between Wilde and Alexander.

10 See Wilde, "To Alfred Douglas," (? January–March 1897) in Wilde, *Letters*, ed. Rupert Hart-Davis (London: Hart-Davis, 1962), 423–511; further page references appear in parentheses. Hart-Davis' 1962 edition of the *Letters* was expanded and updated by his co-editor, Merlin Holland, in Wilde, *The Complete Letters*, ed. Holland and Hart-Davis (London: Fourth Estate, 2000); page references to this more recent edition also appear in parentheses.

11 See Wilde, *The Soul of Man, and Prison Writings*, ed. Isobel Murray (Oxford: Oxford University Press, 1990), v.

12 See, for example, Wilde, *The Soul of Man*, ed. Murray; Bruce Bashford, "Oscar Wilde as Theorist: The Case of *De Profundis*," *English Literature in Transition*, 28 (1985), 395–406; William E. Buckler, "Oscar Wilde's Aesthetic of the Self: Art as Imaginative Self-Realization in *De Profundis*," *Biography* 12 (1989), 95–115; Jerome H. Buckley, *The Turning Key: Autobiography and the Subjective Impulse since 1800* (Cambridge, MA: Harvard University Press, 1984); Avrom Fleishman, *Figures of Autobiography: The Language of Self-Writing in Victorian and Modern England* (Berkeley: University of California Press,

1983); and Rodney Shewan, *Oscar Wilde: Art and Egotism* (London: Macmillan, 1977).

13 See Dollimore, "Different Desires," especially 54–57, and 61–63.

14 See Wilde, *Letters*, ed. Hart-Davis, 423 n2. Merlin Holland, while noting that Hart-Davis "meticulously edited" Wilde's correspondence in the 1962 *Letters*, points out that editors must contend with the fact that "Wilde seldom dated his letters." He adds: "It might be thought that the extensive Wilde literature would answer most dating problems, but exactitude was not the leading quality of Wilde's early biographers" (*Complete Letters*, ed. Holland and Hart-Davis, xv, xvii).

15 Robert Ross, "A Prefatory Dedication to Dr. Max Meyerfield," in Wilde, *Collected Works*, ed. Robert Ross, 14 vols. (London: Methuen, 1908), XI: xiii; further volume and page reference appears in parentheses.

16 Cited by Hart-Davis in Wilde, *Letters*, ed. Hart-Davis, 424 n2, and Wilde, *Complete Letters*, ed. Holland and Hart-Davis, 683 n1.

17 See Wilde, "To Robert Ross," 1 April 1897, *Letters*, ed. Hart-Davis, 512–17, and *Complete Letters*, ed. Holland and Hart-Davis, 780–86. (Ross printed an edited part of this letter in his 1908 edition of Wilde, *Collected Works*, XI: 12–19.)

18 See Hart-Davis's comment in Wilde, *Letters*, ed. Hart-Davis, 512 n1, and in *Complete Letters*, ed. Holland and Hart-Davis, 780 n1.

19 Maureen Borland, *Wilde's Devoted Friend: A Life of Robert Ross, 1869–1918* (Oxford: Lennard Publishing, 1990), 93–103.

20 Oscar Wilde, *De Profundis: Being the First Complete and Accurate Version of "Epistola: In Carcere et Vinculis," the Last Prose Work of Oscar Wilde*, ed. Vyvyan Holland (London: Methuen, 1949), 11.

21 See also Borland, *Wilde's Devoted Friend*, 94.

22 It is possible to trace a line of corrections and substitutions from the 1949 edition (i.e., the nearest surviving approximation of the typescript) through the 1905 and 1908 editions; this suggests that the text from which Ross habitually worked was the typescript and not the manuscript, and that Holland's copy-text was the same as Ross's. The William Andrews Clark Memorial Library, University of California, Los Angeles, has two other typescripts of *De Profundis*: one bears the working title of the Augustin-Hawke typescript; and another, presumably made to establish American copyright, refers back to the second American (1909) edition.

chapter four

Wilde's Exquisite Pain

ELLIS HANSON

When I read Oscar Wilde's prison writings, not to mention his letters from his self-imposed exile on the Continent, I am struck by how excruciating they are – and how pleasurable. His very pain is made exquisite to me. It is exquisite not because I would have wished upon him the same cruelty that he suffered at the hands of his more homophobic contemporaries. Rather, Wilde invites us to rethink suffering itself and its relation to writing, desire, and the very philosophy of aestheticism through which he defined himself as an artist. In criticism about Wilde, the pain of his imprisonment, his public humiliation, his exile, and his early death are often conceptualized in the language of either masochism or martyrdom, two characterizations that complement each other exceptionally well in his case. The discussion of masochism is usually psychoanalytic in its impetus, emphasizing his unconscious motives in submitting to the abuse of both Lord Alfred Douglas and the public trials that he was doomed to lose. The discussion of his martyrdom offers a far more political conception of Wilde self-consciously presenting himself as an unjustly condemned defender of emotional and artistic freedom, the first saint of gayness *avant le lettre*, and the first saint of aestheticism, though he was always afraid that his miraculously blossoming staff would turn into an umbrella or something equally ridiculous. Wilde said much, particularly in his later letters, to support both views, which are not necessarily opposed to each other. In reconsidering such criticism, I am struck by the psychologizing imperative by which his suffering is largely of biographical interest. Such studies cite his writing only as a further sign of the progress of his resplendently aggrieved personality. In approaches of this kind, critics remain preoccupied with the moral character of the man, the politics or the pathology of his conduct, rather than his development as an artist and an intellectual. Faced with these limiting perspectives, we might pose some different questions. What is the significance of his suffering for his art, indeed for our understanding of aestheticism itself as a movement? How does Wilde's suffering become emblematic of his relationship to art?

Suffering in art is inevitably a pleasure. Whenever aestheticism is praised or assaulted along political and psychological lines, it is generally for its conception of pleasure and pain in relation to art. Is it hedonistic? Does it sacrifice politics to personal pleasure? Does it trivialize pain by aestheticizing it? Are its pleasures and pains perverse or narcissistic, is its sensuality effeminate? The question of the formal expression of suffering in Wilde's work – the essentially aesthetic problem of representing suffering in literature – has rarely been considered, even though this exquisite pain (what has been called masochism or martyrdom) may be seen as a figure for aesthetic experience itself. Queer theory has certainly done much to politicize and psychologize Wilde in the past decade, especially with respect to homosexuality. But here I would like to emphasize the formal dimension of its method. By queer theory, I mean the analysis of sexuality as rhetoric, as a language with a variety of formal rules and narrative structures. Queer theory helps us to recognize the erotic dimension of a formalist approach through which we can conceive of Wilde's exquisite suffering not as a personal malady nor merely as a political predicament, but more specifically as an aesthetic innovation peculiar to the tradition in which he wrote.

In the comic and epigrammatic universe of *The Importance of Being Earnest* (1895), suffering is never to be taken seriously except as a joke, and even in the conduct of his life, Wilde's appetite for pleasure garnered him a reputation for hedonism. Nevertheless, Wilde was, in his own way, a connoisseur of suffering. He characterized his prison sentence as a turning point in his understanding, the moment when suffering acquired a very personal significance for him as a mode of aesthetic and erotic pleasure that he claimed he did not fully comprehend even when he wrote of the sadism of his Salomé or the broken heart of his Happy Prince. In the prison letter to Douglas that he wrote in 1897 (first published in expurgated form under the title *De Profundis* in 1905), Wilde looks back at his career before his arrest and remarks upon a certain incompleteness in his oeuvre. He detects a tendency to limit himself to "the sungilt side of the garden" but then reveals that the "other half of the garden had its secrets for me also."[1]

Where the word *secret* in Wilde's work generally hints at transgression, sexual and otherwise, here it takes on all the gravity of a religious mystery, though I would add that its Edenic allusion is no less ripe with erotic significance. The apple that he has to offer us is made of ashes, but the peculiar gift of wisdom – this knowledge of the significance of sorrow – which he seeks to bestow on Douglas is also a lesson of love for each other that dared finally to speak its name. Wilde's secret here is not merely that he loves a man but that he is suffering for him as well, and the suffering is exquisite. Wilde refers to himself as "maimed, marred, and incomplete" (733), and he maps the more melancholy precincts of the garden, those from which he once recoiled in fear as if from a thing as unspeakable as his own desire:

> Failure, disgrace, poverty, sorrow, despair, suffering, tears even, the broken words that come from the lips of pain, remorse that makes one walk in thorns, conscience that condemns, self-abasement that punishes, the misery that puts ashes on its head, the anguish that chooses sackcloth for its raiment and into its own drink puts gall – all these were things of which I was afraid. (*Complete Letters*, 739)

Here a transgressive desire becomes sorrow, and sorrow becomes art. His sorrows are legion. As his sentence progresses (if it can be said to progress), his broken words emerge into broken rituals with characteristic gestures, isolated and mechanical, that they are doomed to repeat. They become archetypes of suffering arranged in grim procession as though they were figures in a biblical allegory or Dante's inferno. They become performative gestures as yet without agency, and they await the animating genius of the aesthete who will inhabit them and require for his pain a certain perfection of form. As with all Wilde's secrets, the charm is in the telling, the slow and suspenseful unraveling of a mystery – even a religious mystery – that proves to be less a secret than a paradox that is readily observable. This paradox is already known, if not quite comprehended, in a long literary tradition that his letter traces from Christ through Dante to himself.

In *De Profundis*, Wilde sees himself within a Christian tradition of martyrdom, though arguably it is martyrdom at a loss for a god apart from the spirituality of beauty. He speaks of Christ as the first great romantic, and he himself would seem to be one of the last. Wilde arrives relatively late in romantic literature's cult of its own agonies, a tendency at once aesthetic, erotic, and spiritual that represents melancholia, self-sacrifice, suffering, and suicide as various shades of martyrdom in the worship of love or beauty for its own sake. Wilde represents the Decadence of this tradition, a status he shares with a number of other artists he mentions in *De Profundis*. He names Charles Baudelaire, Alphonse de Lamartine, and Paul Verlaine, though he might also have spoken of Algernon Charles Swinburne, Leopold von Sacher-Masoch, Richard Wagner, Walter Pater, J.-K. Huysmans, Rachilde, and Octave Mirbeau. Pleasure in pain is essential to this later Decadent aesthetic, in which the intensity of romantic agony is tempered with the irony and perversity of aestheticism. Wilde is a fine representative of a literary moment, swiftly disappearing in his own time, in which it was still possible to think of pleasure in pain as a radical aesthetic practice rather than as a sexual perversion or a sexual identity. In speaking of his exquisite pain, I hope to offer an analysis that is not so much historical or psychological as formal. Wilde gave a peculiar aesthetic form to his pain, and it is only in that form, that appeal to the aesthetic, that he found significance for it.

I would use the term *masochism* were it not for the fact that I must first free it from its pathological nuances, not to mention its curious banality. I do not wish to contribute here to the myriad studies of "masochism" by scholars who are content to deploy the usual psychoanalytic clichés on the subject and debate the distinction between moral masochism and perverse masochism. Nor do I wish to decide whether masochism is an erotic appeal to the pre-oedipal mother or to the pre-oedipal father. What we call masochism, however, seems to me too various in its structure and its deployments to justify the formulae that are deemed to be universal in such theories. Even within the aesthetic tradition that I have mentioned, Sacher-Masoch's pleasure in pain is not the same as Pater's or Wilde's, though they share certain precepts about art. My approach is similar to the newer and more historical critiques, John Noyes's most notable among them, by which "masochism" derives its form and meanings from its social context, though my argument here is not primarily historical.[2] I turn to theorists such as Michel Foucault and Gilles Deleuze for the aesthetic dimension of their work on masochism in order to view Wilde's conception of pain as a radical artistic practice. My intention is not to pathologize, minoritize, or even rigorously historicize Wilde's exquisite pain. Instead, I wish to aestheticize it, examining its rhetoric as a sexual aesthetic through which he resisted the pathologizing imperatives of modern psychology and the minoritizing imperatives of modern identity politics that would embrace the term *masochism* in the century that followed.

In the history of sexuality, there is an ugly moment that occurred in 1886, when the Austrian sexologist Richard von Krafft-Ebing published *Psychopathia Sexualis*. Without any consultation with the author, Krafft-Ebing split Sacher-Masoch's name in two and coined the word *masochism* to define a pathological, degenerate, and perverse sexual appetite for pain and humiliation. In one stroke, he turned romance into medical history and a famous aesthete into a notorious case study in perversion. Sacher-Masoch's novel *Venus in Furs* (1870) ceased to be art, ceased to be aestheticism, and became instead sexology. In fact, there is virtually no criticism about this novel that is not an exercise in etiology or a study of the psychological or historical function of the masochistic "perversion." Needless to say, Sacher-Masoch's admirers were not pleased, but Krafft-Ebing was impervious to any criticism of his medicalizing sleight of hand. In a later edition of his magnum opus, he speaks to the point without apology:

> I refute the accusation that I have coupled the name of a revered author with a perversion of the sexual instinct, which has been made against me by some admirers of the author and by some critics of my book. As a man Sacher-Masoch cannot lose anything in the estimation of his cultured fellow-beings simply because he was afflicted with an anomaly of his sexual feelings. As an author he suffered severe injury so far as the influence and intrinsic merit of his work is concerned, for so long and whenever he eliminated his perversion from his literary efforts he was a gifted writer, and as such would have achieved real greatness had he been actuated by normally sexual feelings.[3]

Here it is difficult to see how Krafft-Ebing is refuting the accusation rather than, say, reveling in it. Despite this literary opinion, Sacher-Masoch's reputation, insofar as he still has one, is based almost entirely on *Venus in Furs*. It remains one of the most widely read German novels of the nineteenth century, not the least because the popular usage of the word *masochism* has made it an erotic touchstone. A modern reader, arriving at this novel after more than a century of psychological theorization on sexual perversions, might reasonably be surprised to discover that Sacher-Masoch never looked to a physician to supply him with "normally sexual feelings," whatever those are. Nor did he feel incapacitated as a writer by his sexual "anomaly" (quite the opposite). Such medical categories are wholly absent from his novel, in which he describes his submissive alter ego, Severin, as a "supersensualist." Drawing on the language of a romantic aesthete or libertine, he proclaims proudly that his sensibilities – whether they appear aesthetic, erotic, or spiritual – are simply more receptive and refined than those of other people.

Like Sacher-Masoch, Wilde found himself in much the same crossfire of self-definition, especially after his trials, when he became the world's most famous homosexual or sodomite, even though we have no account of his ever using such words to describe himself. The term *homosexuality* entered the English language along with *masochism* in the first translation of *Psychopathia Sexualis*. According to Alfred Douglas, Wilde read the book while he was writing *Salomé* (1893).[4] Wilde also appears in pseudoscientific studies such as Marc-André Raffalovich's *Uranisme et Unisexualité* (1896) and Max Nordau's *Entartung* (1892), which Wilde read in the French translation, *Dégénérescence* (1894). In these books his name is attached to newfangled sexual pathologies as a high-cultural guarantor of their definitional power. After his trials, Wilde the prophet of beauty became a popular *exemplum gratis* of degeneracy and vice, even by men such as Douglas (later in his life) and Raffalovich, who were ever in danger of being tarred with the same brush. Nordau was especially thorough in his pathologizing of contemporary aestheticism and naturalism, and he had much the same dismissive diagnosis for Baudelaire, Verlaine, Henrik Ibsen, Emile Zola, and many other writers we now think of as the literary geniuses of the age.

While in prison, Wilde tried to use the language of perversion to his advantage. He wrote a letter of petition to the Home Secretary in an effort to stimulate pity for his condition and to acquire some books. In this letter he cynically confesses that he suffers from "loathsome modes of erotomania," "revolting passions," "monstrous sexual perversion," "sensual monomanias," "morbid passions, and obscene fancies," and "sexual insanity" (*Complete Letters*, 658), to list a few of his choicer phrases. His vocabulary, a jumble of moral and medical pejoratives, is a highly calculated parody of the popular and scientific sexual jargon of the age. To the uninitiated he seems a model of supplication and self-castigation, but to those familiar with his ironic style and his sexual opinions, he is clearly playing an insincere game with language. He argues that forms of sexual madness "are diseases to be cured by a physician, rather than crimes to be punished by a judge" (656). Here he presents an argument familiar to readers of the *Psychopathia Sexualis*, in which Krafft-Ebing is understandably eager to extend his authority by replacing legal and religious definitions of sexuality with medical ones.[5]

Wilde's irony is particularly deft, however, in that he uses pathological language self-consciously as a reverse discourse. Aware that Krafft-Ebing, Nordau, and Cesare Lombroso relied on great writers to illustrate their pathological sexual categories, he tries to convince the Home Secretary that "erotomania" is a symptom of literary genius (though, as he points out to Douglas in *De Profundis*, he knew perfectly well that not all literary geniuses are so blessed):

> In the works of eminent men of science such as Lombroso and Nordau, to take merely two instances out of many, this is specially insisted on with reference to the intimate connection between madness and the literary and artistic temperament, Professor Nordau in his book "Dégénérescence" published in 1894 having devoted an entire chapter to the petitioner as a specially typical example of this fatal law. (656)

Wilde is paying himself a compliment here, and he later argues that he should be given books in order to rescue him from his brooding on his obscene fancies. Once he was out of prison, however, the masquerade of ironic pathos was no longer necessary, and he was his old epigrammatic self in ridiculing the sexology of his time, not to mention his cameo appearances among its many case studies. In 1897, the year of his release, he wrote to the notoriously naughty publisher Leonard Smithers, "I am now simply an ordinary pauper of a rather low order: the fact that I am also a pathological problem in the eyes of German scientists is only interesting to German scientists: and even in their works I am tabulated, and come under the law of *averages*!" (606). If he was perverse, in other words, it was only because he was extraordinary, and no scientific quantification of the Teutonic variety was equal to his genius. At this point in his life, he seemed especially eager to reject the definitional power of a sexual science that he deemed vulgar and inaccurate. A month before his letter to Smithers, he had written to the poet Ernest Dowson and quipped, "Psychology is in its infancy, as a science. I hope, in the interests of Art, it will always remain so" (*Complete Letters*, 969).

Wilde offers us a rich occasion to define sexual experience in largely aesthetic terms. He offers us art as a counter-discourse to the pathologizing imperative of psychology and psychoanalysis in the past century. He speaks of artists who took not a degenerate but an exquisite pleasure in pain. Although since the 1980s gay studies has done much to rescue Wilde's homosexuality, not to mention his literary reputation, from decades of homophobic readings, his fascinating sexual and aesthetic deployment of pain has all but escaped remark except among psychoanalytic critics. The result may be interesting only to German scientists, but I am amazed that a century after Krafft-Ebing and Nordau were translated into English, psychological criticism still seeks to pathologize Wilde's sexuality. I do not suppose that all psychoanalytic criticism is necessarily pathologizing in its intentions, but it is a fair generalization within studies of Wilde.

Janine Chasseguet-Smirgel's *Creativity and Perversion* (1985) might be taken as paradigmatic of modern regrettable trends in psychoanalysis. She deems herself radical in her view of perversion as a revolutionary shortcut through the oedipal conflict. For her, Wildean aestheticism is a function of the sublimation of anal-sadistic drives by which the artist, through an alchemical sleight of hand, seeks to plate his feces with gold: "anality is not so much changed by the idealization process as it is merely covered with a coating of glittering jewels."[6] Jonathan Dollimore, who justly regards this reading as "quite possibly the nadir of psychoanalytic criticism," points out that in her view "the creative-anarchic challenge of the perverse is collapsed or reduced to an exclusively psychosexual subversion."[7] I would agree and add that it is curiously essentialist, in that all perversion abides by the same compulsion. The formula is so mechanical, ahistorical, and impersonal that it cannot distinguish how or why Wilde's writing might be different from that of other aesthetes we might deem perverse. The reading is entirely driven by the dictates of the theory. Where there is a fire, she smells smoke, and where there are elegant homosexuals, she smells the dirty secret of anality they must, by their very nature, be trying to hide. What more could there be to say? Freudianism rarely gets this simplistic in its literary applications, but Chasseguet-Smirgel was outdone recently by Melissa Knox, whose exercise in psychobiography, *Oscar Wilde: A Long and Lovely Suicide* (1994), is a critical howler. Knox tackles once again the inexhaustibly fascinating question of the etiology of homosexuality and masochism. She is quick to repeat the standard Freudian line on Wilde as though she had coined it herself: "Oscar's anality is visible in his style and choices of subject matter; many of his works show a preoccupation with smell, particularly perfumes."[8] She adds, "Wilde's preoccupation with gold, silver, and precious stones in *Dorian Gray* and *Salome* is another expression of anal interests" (23).

Knox's just-so story about the incestuous origins of Wilde's homosexual masochism is nothing if not elaborate, and it has all the sensational revelation of secrets, one veil at a time, that typifies Freudian Gothic. Knox assumes that the Marquess of Queensberry was paranoid because he complained that supporters of Wilde attacked him. According to this logic, if Queensberry was paranoid, then he must also be repressing powerful homosexual desires (because that is how it works in Freud). Likewise, if Queensberry was a repressed homosexual, then he must of course have been immensely attractive to Wilde, and maybe he was really what Wilde was looking for, after all. Scarcely pausing for breath, Knox concludes that Wilde entertained masochistic fantasies of playing Sporus to Queensberry's Nero. And, what is more, she means it. In a Wildean context, such shameless improbability is endearing, but Knox comes off sounding like "The Portrait of Mr. W. H." (1887) run amok. In her view, Wilde remains so self-conscious that she is hard-pressed to find an unconscious mystery worth elucidating. She feels that she has found one in his masochism, and she claims that Wilde's refusal to escape arrest and run to France is utterly irrational and can only be explained by his unconscious appetite for self-destruction. She then ignores his decidedly conscious and perfectly reasonable explanation of his refusal to flee: namely, that one ought to be a martyr in the defense of great ideas and emotions, that running to Europe with his tail between his legs would have been cowardly, a betrayal of his love, and an admission of guilt. From Knox's perspective, his gesture ceases to be admirable and becomes merely deluded, pathological, and perverse – and we are called upon to forgive him. Thus she ends her book on an oddly moralistic and patronizing note: "But although he did not receive forgiveness, and indeed his life was not forgivable, we have to forgive him because of all he has given us" (136).[9]

Putting aside the question of who should forgive whom, I would prefer to offer an account of the self-conscious artistry of Wilde's eroticized suffering as chivalry – as romance. In *The Romantic Agony* (1933), Mario Praz demonstrates with encyclopedic thoroughness the prevalence of homoerotic and masochistic themes in Decadent texts, even where the sexuality of their authors may have been ostensibly neither.[10] I would add that these two sexualities, along with fetishism, are the key erotic metaphors for aestheticism itself. They are sex as art. The queer sexualities in these texts are so busy figuring art that they are rarely recognizable as something real people actually did in the nineteenth century – hence the frequent but misguided dismissal of Decadent writing as prurient fantasy inattentive to the realities of sexual oppression. Perhaps the best example of this queerness as meditation on art occurs in Swinburne's Lesbian lyric "Anactoria" (1866), in which Sappho's cruel passion for her lover – "I would find grievous ways to have thee slain"[11] – becomes the basis for their immortality through poetry. All experience is aesthetically transformed when her song of love is sung, when desire is brutally and exquisitely murdered into meter, such that wherever her rhythms are read, "Memories shall mix and metaphors of me" (I: 64). As Yopie Prins has argued, Swinburne sings a lesbian and masochistic sublime through his sensual engagement with the poetic rhythms of Sappho, and she writes of this line, "Sappho reveals herself to be a power that structures the entire world: the lightning that blinds, the thunder that deafens, the water that shudders, and the 'immeasurable tremor of all the sea' all repeat the rhythms of the tortured and torturing Sapphic body."[12] This poem, though very different in style and tone from *De Profundis*, lends to aestheticism a certain sexual sensibility that Wilde appreciates as well. This exquisitely homoerotic suffering is all perversity and paradox, presented as sterile pleasure. It is a painful receptivity, theatricality, fantasy, an endless aggravation of desire, a wild self-assertion against tradition and within tradition, a reversal of gender roles, and a rendering irrelevant of all that is familial, marital, heterosexual, and temporal. It is, in short, an aesthetic experience, one that defies any aim but pleasure in the beautiful – pleasure that can be so intense that it becomes indistinguishable from pain.

The exquisite pain of aestheticism finds its postmodern echo in queer theory. Foucault was never more Wildean than when he addressed the aesthetics of sexuality by discussing gay culture and sadomasochism in an interview in the gay magazine *The Advocate*. In "Sex, Power, and the Politics of Identity" (1984), he poses a theory of sexual creativity as an alternative to psychological theorization on etiology: "What I meant was that I think what the gay movement needs now is much more the art of life than a science or scientific knowledge (or pseudoscientific knowledge) of what sexuality is."[13] This "art of life," vaguely described here under the pressures of an interview, is more clearly articulated in the later volumes of his *History of Sexuality*. But here he is called upon to elaborate on sexuality as "a kind of creation, a creative enterprise," adding that the "practice of S&M is the creation of pleasure, and there is an identity with that creation. And that's why S&M is really a subculture. It's a process of invention" (165, 169–70). His keynote is always creativity:

> Sexuality is something that we ourselves create – it's our own creation, and much more than the discovery of a secret side of our desire. We have to understand that with our desires, through our desires, go new forms of relationships, new forms of love, new forms of creation. Sex is not a fatality: it's a possibility for creative life. ("Sex, Power," 163)

Foucault's choice of leatherfolk is far from arbitrary. It seems to work better for his argument than gay sexuality of a more vanilla flavor – though both enjoyed even in his time a profound association with art and artistic creativity in that they had to be self-consciously and arduously constructed and maintained within a largely hostile social milieu. In other words, their social institutions and vocabularies were not already at hand, not already ubiquitous, and so one had to create the concept of the sexuality and the sexual culture as if one were generating a new vernacular.

For Foucault no less than for the aesthetes of the previous century, the cultures of eroticized pain, like the cultures of desire between men, serve as metaphors for aesthetic creativity itself. They represent sex as art. Those people who are condemned as perverts within more scientific (or pseudoscientific) rhetoric become instead aesthetic innovators, and the emphasis of the critical inquiry shifts from defining a putative pathology to expanding the range of human expression. Here Foucault's language is not without a touch of romance, given that its creative geniuses work against the grain of convention and, insofar as it is possible, invent the form of their own pleasures. We should not be surprised, then, that Foucault's epigrammatic style in this interview should make him sound at times like Wilde, who also had considerable faith in the power of individual artists to rewrite their own lives. At a time when psychological discourse on sexuality is stereotyped and repetitive – not to mention ideologically suspect – it becomes as much an ethical imperative as an aesthetic one to develop a formal analysis that seeks to multiply the possibilities for pleasure in a culture typified by sexual oppression and prejudice. Like Wilde, Foucault is the critic as artist as sexual innovator.

It is within this tradition that I also see the value of Gilles Deleuze's theoretical work on masochism. To articulate a more strictly literary, aesthetic approach to Wilde's eroticization of pain, I take as a model Deleuze's essay *Coldness and Cruelty* (1967), which is in part a formal study of masochism in *Venus in Furs*. It also happens to be a rather Freudian attack on Freud, in which he draws on an anthropological paradigm to define the cruel mother figures that he claims dominate Sacher-Masoch's imagination. But more original, I think, is Deleuze's ability to speak of eroticism in terms of rhetoric and narrative, speaking of myth, irony, humor, contractual relations, a pedagogical imperative, bisexual triangulation, suspension, and frozen temporality as Severin fantasizes Wanda's whip posed eternally over his shuddering body. "There is," Deleuze writes, "a fundamental aesthetic or plastic element in the art of Masoch," and he distinguishes between sadism and masochism primarily in formal terms, suggesting that the work of Sacher-Masoch, with its elaborate investment in fantasy and contractual relations, is "formal and dramatic" in a way that the work of Sade is not: "there is an aestheticism in masochism, while sadism is hostile to the aesthetic attitude."[14] The analysis of sexuality becomes for Deleuze the formal analysis of rhetoric, which strikes me as a fair description of queer theory. We might consider Wilde's work, particularly his letters, along the same lines. There are five characteristics of Wilde's literary deployment of exquisite pain that I would like to examine, five ways in which he valorizes eroticized suffering as a way of figuring aesthetic experience itself: paradox as perversity; romance as artifice; timelessness and monumentality; aggravated sensitivity; and ironic failure.

In a much-quoted epigram that neatly conjoined the intellectual with the emotional and the aesthetic with the erotic, Wilde remarks in *De Profundis*, "What the paradox was to me in the sphere of thought, perversity became to me in the sphere of passion" (*Complete Letters*, 730). By perversity, he does not mean "perversion" in the sense of an unconscious deviance, but rather a self-conscious aesthetic tendency to go against the grain, a tendency that he attributes not to any psychological peculiarity of his own, but rather to what is most distinctive of the age. He writes, "I was so typical a child of my age that in my perversity, and for that perversity's sake, I turned the good things of my life to evil, and the evil things of my life to good" (732–33). This evocation of perversity for perversity's sake resonates with the great motto of aestheticism, "art for art's sake," and indicates Wilde's belief that there is a perversity that might be enjoyed for the sheer perfection of its form when beautifully realized. We need not read far in *De Profundis* to find that this perversity is often sexual, as we find Wilde famously "feasting with panthers" (758) in the sexual underworld to which he gravitated. He discovered in such delectably dangerous company a moral and sexual perversity that he valorized in primarily aesthetic terms. His aestheticism entails a radical series of displacements in valuation, a rejection of more traditional standards of judgment that are essentially moral (good versus evil), rational (reasonable versus insane), political (just versus unjust), physical (pleasure versus pain), commercial (profitable versus useless), or medical (healthy versus pathological). All experience is judged perversely by a standard of beauty, such that a number of paradoxes ensue: beautiful flowers of evil; cruelty that is aesthetically just; an insane desire that seems reasonable and healthy because it is true to itself; and of course a profound suffering that becomes, through art, a sublime pleasure. Wilde found it effortless to slip from the language of pain to that of romance and back again in a marvelous paradox by which self-destruction was romantic and pain exquisite.

In a rather flirtatious letter dated 1885 to an admirer, H.C. Marillier, Wilde praises the addressee for his love of the impossible, which he remarks upon in English, Greek, and French – "*l'amour de l'impossible* (how do men name it?)." How do they indeed? Naming the desire in this letter is a problem never quite resolved. Its homoeroticism is indistinguishable from the agonies of its aestheticism:

> Some day you will find, even as I have found, that there is no such thing as a romantic experience; there are romantic memories, and there is the desire of romance – that is all. Our most fiery moments of ecstasy are merely shadows of what somewhere else we have felt, or of what we long some day to feel. So at least it seems to me. And, strangely enough, what comes of all this is a curious mixture of ardour and of indifference. I myself would sacrifice everything for a new experience, and I know there is no such thing as a new experience at all. I think I would more readily die for what I do not believe in than for what I hold to be true. I would go to the stake for a sensation and be a sceptic to the last! Only one thing remains infinitely fascinating to me, the mystery of moods. To be a master of these moods is exquisite, to be mastered by them more exquisite still. Sometimes I think that the artistic life is a long and lovely suicide, and am not sorry that it is so.
>
> And much of this I fancy you yourself have felt: much also remains for you to feel. There is an unknown land full of strange flowers and subtle perfumes, a land of which it is joy of all joys to dream, a land where all things are perfect and poisonous. (*Complete Letters*, 272)

This passage is constructed of one epigrammatic paradox after another: fantasy made reality, passion made skeptical, pain made pleasure, mastery made submission, suicide made creative, the unknown made vivid, and the perfect made poisonous. It is a very self-conscious musing about the past and the future as an idealization, a romance, a beautiful lie. It is a pastiche of Baudelaire's invitation to the voyage where all is grace and measure – and perfection, poison, and pleasure. It is about the explosion of the present, of the self, of the real, in favor of an artificial world, an anywhere out of the world, where, as in *Venus in Furs*, reality can be

remade as a theatrical *mise-en-scène* conceived in one's own ideal image.
Is an unconscious conflict required for "you yourself" to have felt it, or
just an aesthetic sensibility that seeks to transcend the dullness of the
past with the romance of memory? Romance becomes a fantasy of the
self that is also a disavowal of the self through the very artistic creativity
that brings one's sensibility into being. The paradox and the perversity
is to make life imitate art, to perfect the poisonous romance that will kill
life into art, a certain exquisiteness of mood that we master through a
calculated submission.

Romance for Wilde is the artful lie, the elaborate fantasy that makes
one, perversely, the true author of one's own life. Yet it is a Decadent
romance, one that recognizes a necessary violence towards the real,
which is defined not by its materiality but by its dullness, its aesthetic
imperfection. Romance at its best is sublimely violent, perfection of
form at any cost, while realism is merely a bore. For this reason, Wilde is
obliged to distinguish between exquisite pain and mere cruelty. Exquisite pain is romance, whereas the more mundane cruelty is merely a stupid form of realism – it is simply what happens. In a letter to the editor,
Wilde dutifully attempted to explain this distinction to the readers of
the *Daily Chronicle* shortly after his release from prison in 1897:

> People nowadays do not understand what cruelty is. They regard it as a sort
> of terrible mediæval passion, and connect it with the race of men like
> Eccelino da Romano, and others, to whom the deliberate infliction of pain
> gave a real madness of pleasure. But men of the stamp of Eccelino are
> merely abnormal types of perverted individualism. Ordinary cruelty is sim-
> ply stupidity. It is the entire want of imagination. It is the result in our days
> of stereotyped systems of hard-and-fast rules, and of stupidity. (*Complete
> Letters*, 848)

On the face of it, this passage reads at first like a dismissal of Eccelino,
but phrases such as "terrible mediæval passion" and "real madness of
pleasure" should tip us off to Wilde's sympathies. "Abnormal types of
perverted individualism" may sound like a pathologizing slight since its
language is indeed lifted from the likes of Nordau and Lombroso. But,
then, we recall that the abnormal, the perverse, and the individual were
three of Wilde's most passionate ideals, and when those words were
applied to him by German scientists, he generally translated the insult
into an admission of his own literary genius. Eccelino stands in for Sade
or Gilles de Rais, the artists of cruelty who captured the Decadent imag-

ination through the aesthetic effort of a deliberate, refined, and self-destructive infliction of pain. In *De Profundis* Wilde speaks of being positioned uncomfortably between "Gilles de Retz and the Marquis de Sade" in the public imagination, but then he says he finds a more stimulating companionship in these disreputable figures than in the improving moral pabulum popular in his own day: "Nor have I any doubt but that the leper of mediævalism, and the author of *Justine*, will prove better company than *Sandford and Merton*" (719). Eccelino, whatever his moral failings, is the stuff of legend, cruelty as art rather than cruelty as the dull and degrading grind of the British prison system – or for that matter, the pious moralism of Thomas Day's *Sandford and Merton* (3 vols., 1783–89) – that seeks to discipline out of existence the very individualism that the romanticized criminal comes to represent for Wilde.

Through the phrase "stereotyped systems," Wilde distinguishes between the violence of art that ennobles the spirit and the ideologically insidious violence of the penal bureaucracy that produces nothing put a dumb degradation. The distinction of course is a perilous one, especially if one happens to be one of the children tortured and murdered by Gilles de Rais. It could be argued that aestheticizing violence does not redeem it but rather distracts us from a far more important moral and political endeavor to end it. Needless to say, Wilde made such a moral and political endeavor in his efforts at prison reform. But for him there was still the problem of meaning in the violence that he experienced, indeed the violence that is all but inevitable in even the most charmed of lives. He also shifts the focus to his own pain, from Sade to something more like Sacher-Masoch, since the comparison between himself and Gilles de Rais is patently absurd. For Wilde, even the moral and political imperative to relieve suffering must also have an aesthetic dimension to be effective, to impress itself on the sensibilities of others by appealing to more than just intellect or conscience. Further, there remains the problem of the violence already committed and the capacity of the sufferer to survive psychologically as well as physically. Art gave Wilde the necessary solace of meaning and dignity in suffering and, without excusing the injustices done him, allowed him to sublate his pain into something more beautiful that, ironically, celebrated the very love for which he was condemned.

The trick is to become the author of the narrative of one's own suffering, and this is by no means easy. In *De Profundis*, Wilde writes,

I remember as I was sitting in the dock on the occasion of my last trial listening to Lockwood's appalling denunciation of me – like a thing out of Tacitus, like a passage in Dante, like one of Savonarola's indictments of the Popes at Rome – and being sickened with horror at what I heard. Suddenly it occurred to me, *"How splendid it would be, if I was saying all this about myself!"* (*Complete Letters*, 769)

Throughout the letter, there is ordinary pain, the dumb suffering inflicted upon Wilde. But, then, there is also exquisite pain, the brilliant tragedy of his soul to which only an artist, preferably himself, can sign his name. Note the distressing moment of envy when he is left to admire the artistry of his own accusers, when he is even so thrilled by their denunciation that they seem to trigger in him a reflex to literary history. Why, then, abandon such artistry to the enemy and the sadist? Why not be oneself the inheritor of a tradition of unparalleled vituperation, rather than being merely the victim of it? There is pain but, more important, there is the story that is told of one's own pain, the narrative context and significance it is given, the splendid and edifying iconography of suffering. The shift from sadism to masochism is an essential move from victim to author: the self-conscious serving up of one's own soul for sublime sacrifice. Authorial power in the hands of the victim can prove not only a political and moral triumph but also an aesthetic one. If I get to tell the story of my pain, then I might get to cast myself in the lead role of Saint John the Baptist or even in the role of Christ, the man of sorrows himself. Even before he wrote *De Profundis*, Wilde was writing letters to friends from prison in which he seemed to be authorizing some Christian melodrama of his own fall and his canonization as "Saint Oscar of Oxford, poet and martyr," casting Douglas and others as disciples in supporting roles. In 1896 he wrote a letter to Robert Ross in which, through metaphor, he cleverly turns his life into a staging of *Salomé*. He begins the letter with a bit of business about royalties from the play and seems at first not to appreciate his own irony in the turn of phrase, "I brought out *Salome* at my own expense" (*Complete Letters*, 668). But then he goes on to elaborate on the self-immolating figures of speech in a manner that could hardly be unconscious: "[S]uch passions are False Gods that *will* have victims at all costs" (671). "The refusal to commute my sentence has been like a blow from a leaden sword" (669). "I admit I lost my head" (670). Once again, he seems to be play-acting roles from his own script, not merely discussing *Salomé* but enacting it, with himself as the saint center stage. From the Precursor he moves deftly in *De Profundis* to an impersonation of the Messiah himself:

To the artist, expression is the only mode under which he can conceive life at all. To him what is dumb is dead. But to Christ it was not so. With a width and wonder of imagination, that fills one almost with awe, he took the entire world of the inarticulate, the voiceless world of pain, as his kingdom, and made of himself its eternal mouthpiece. Those of whom I have spoken, who are dumb under oppression and "whose silence is heard only of God," he chose as his brothers. He sought to become eyes to the blind, ears to the deaf, and a cry on the lips of those whose tongue had been tied. (*Complete Letters*, 746)

Implicit in this peroration about Christ's humble followers is an allegory of Wilde's own relationship to the sexually oppressed whose public symbol he became, not to mention those suffering under the penal system he sought to reform. The paradoxical tension between voice and voicelessness, form and obliteration, and representation and oppression politicizes Wilde's identification with Christ even as it aestheticizes it. Ironically, he is using the Christian reference to give voice to a suffering that dare not speak its name, the victimization of homophobia, a suffering that Christian authorities among a great many others were wont to inflict with impunity. Christ represents a profound and historically revolutionary act of love and self-sacrifice, but before its moral and political force can be felt, his image must exercise a certain aesthetic force. For this reason, Wilde construes Christ as a romantic artist whose significance he insistently defines in terms of artistic beauty:

And feeling, with the artistic nature of one to whom Sorrow and Suffering were modes through which he could realise his conception of the Beautiful, that an idea is of no value till it becomes incarnate and is made an image, he makes of himself the image of the Man of Sorrows, and as such has fascinated and dominated Art as no Greek god ever succeeded in doing. (*Complete Letters*, 740)

As always, Christianity in Wilde is the last hope of paganism, the last influential remnants of an ancient Greek sensibility. Christ is regarded not only because he is good but also because he is beautiful, because he has given exquisite form to an idea. The true artist of pain knows the pleasure of giving articulation to abjection that is otherwise without voice. In this new mythic archetype for the romantic artist, Wilde discovers in Christianity a masochistic ideal, the exquisiteness of his own pain when he himself has the pleasure of giving it a refined aesthetic form that has all the power of myth.

This mythic dimension, a timeless repeatability of Christ's gestures, lends to Wilde's suffering a monumental quality that is evident also in Sacher-Masoch's *Venus in Furs*. Deleuze speaks of the moments of frozen time or suspension in Sacher-Masoch, those instances in the narrative when Wanda strikes a terrible pose of ferocity with her whip in the air. It is the perfect moment of expectation, one that is past innocence but precedes trauma. This is the eminently repeatable image in which masochism is ideally aestheticized as a form of anticipation, of waiting for pain, before a mythic or monumental figure who stands somehow outside time and outside history – a pure fetish who is subject only to the rules of art. Wanda is Venus, Judith, Aspasia, and Catherine the Great. Like Pater's Mona Lisa, she seems to transcend history by accumulating it – occupying every age and summing up all powerful women, legendary and historical – through a single stylized gesture, the poised whip, that emblematizes the painful pleasures of suspense. For Wilde, Christ fills much the same monumental role as Wanda. But rather than wielding a whip poised in the air, he is always already lashed and crucified, the eternally beatific bottom with thorns long set like gems in his flesh. His passion is limited to a few characteristic and endlessly iterable gestures of humiliation ritualized for us as though every retelling were for us to pass through the Stations of the Cross again. Although all time dates forward or backward from the hour of his birth, the moment of his passion is curiously outside time, defying history by accumulating it and shaping it.

In his famous account of his humiliation on the train platform at Clapham Junction, Wilde re-enacts the degradation of Christ. Modern-day crowds jeer at the prisoner in his uniform, and he draws on the language of trauma to speak of that hour as it repeats itself month after month, such that he cries every day at the same moment. It is a frozen moment outside time, monumental in its biblical allusion and endlessly repeatable as a traumatic nightmare. The event itself was stupid cruelty, but Wilde's account recontextualizes the scene and assigns it a new significance, a new narrative structure, by which he can flog himself anew with his own hand. His humiliation becomes a form of exhibitionism, an ironic reversal that desire plays on oppression. If the humiliation were dumb, it would have no resonance beyond its own moment. In *De Profundis*, art makes suffering expand in the space of time and history as generously as in the space of the imagination:

I have passed through every possible mood of suffering. Better than Wordsworth himself I know what Wordsworth meant when he said:

Suffering is permanent, obscure, and dark
And has the nature of Infinity.
But while there were times when I rejoiced in the idea that my sufferings
were to be endless, I could not bear them to be without meaning. (*Complete Letters*, 730)

When he discovers meaning in the endlessness of suffering, then his humiliation becomes his "treasure": "As I found it, I want to keep it" (730). Wilde discovers aesthetic intensity most movingly only with his experience of sorrow, which he deems an essential artistic accomplishment. The intensity of suffering and the intensity of aesthetic experience seem to be much the same thing, or at any rate they are mutually dependent on each other, and they provide an occasion to elaborate on his aggravated sensitivity as an aesthete. He tells Douglas, "You have yet to learn that Prosperity, Pleasure and Success may be rough of grain and common in fibre, but that Sorrow is the most sensitive of all created things" (722). He adds, "There is nothing that stirs in the whole world of thought or motion to which sorrow does not vibrate in terrible if exquisite pulsation" (722). In true decadent fashion, that Paterian pulsation is never adequately exquisite without also being devastating, and the more subtly one reverberates to its horror, the better. Sorrow, therefore, is privileged among aesthetic intensities: "I now see that sorrow, being the supreme emotion of which man is capable, is at once the type and test of all great Art" (737).

Besides Christ, the mythic figure who best aestheticizes this exquisite pulsation is Marsyas, the Greek faun who conspired with Pan to challenge Apollo as the god of music. He challenged Apollo's lyre with his own pipes, and lost. As punishment, Apollo flayed him alive in one of his less than gentle, albeit rivetingly homoerotic, moods. In fact, Marsyas is in hot competition with Saint Sebastian as the favorite classical emblem of gay male masochism. He turns up in *Venus in Furs* at one of its queerest moments, when Severin is looking forward with convincing trepidation to the jealous torment of being whipped by his mistress's virile lover, Alexis Papadapolis, better known as "the Greek." "But Apollo whipped all poetry from me," Severin cries out, poetically.[15] The most intense moment of failure becomes paradoxically the most artful moment of triumph, indeed the most memorable line in the book. What Severin calls his cure is ironically the climax of his desire at its most perverse. Wilde exercises Marsyas to much the same purpose, and he further makes Marsyas the very symbol of modernity in art, slipping smoothly as ever from the painful to the aesthetic:

> When Marsyas was "torn from the scabbard of his limbs" ... to use one of
> Dante's most terrible, most Tacitean phrases – he had no more song, the
> Greeks said. Apollo had been victor. The lyre had vanquished the reed. But
> perhaps the Greeks were mistaken. I hear in much modern Art the cry of
> Marsyas. It is bitter in Baudelaire, sweet and plaintive in Lamartine, mystic
> in Verlaine. (*Complete Letters*, 755–56)

He hears it also in Chopin, Burne-Jones, and Arnold's *Empedocles*.
Dante and Tacitus once again provide him with a serviceable turn of
phrase about cruelty that lives up to his aspirations for art. Through
Marsyas we hear in poetry the intense, even pleasurable, high screech of
a man submitting to his own flaying as the symbol of a peculiarly human
predicament. Whatever the intensity of beauty in this cry of Marsyas, it is
founded, like the story of Christ's passion, on failure. Marsyas lost the
competition. He is punished and humiliated, a failed artist turned grotesque. His beauty is a function of his failure. At the heart of masochism's melodramatic scenes of suffering is a failure, a mockery, an
ironically disavowed knowledge that one's tragedy is always in danger of
becoming a grotesque comedy.

In the same way, *De Profundis* is a masterpiece of irony, an absurdist
tragedy, and Wilde appears to know it. It is too rich in paradox and too
sublime a song for the subject it treats and the selfish man, Lord Alfred
Douglas, to whom it is addressed. On the last page of the letter, Wilde
even refers to his own failure. His letter, he says, shows us quite clearly
"its aspirations and its failure to realise those aspirations" (780), primarily because it gives vent to the very feelings of bitterness and scorn
that it strains to disavow. Certainly, there were plenty of readers eager to
flay the author, but not for the crimes for which he seeks to flay himself.
Shortly after the Marsyas passage comes the scene at Clapham Junction
where Wilde most fears that tragedy will become a grotesque comedy:
"Everything about my tragedy has been hideous, mean, repellent, lacking in style. Our very dress makes us grotesques. We are the zanies of
sorrow. We are clowns whose hearts are broken. We are specially
designed to appeal to the sense of humour" (756). Nevertheless, there is
nothing hideous, mean, repellent, or lacking in style in his account of
his suffering, which makes something beautiful of his own status as grotesque, his own triumph in aestheticizing his failure to love and his failure to be understood.

The passage resonates with a letter he wrote after leaving prison, an
open letter to a newspaper about a prisoner named Prince who was

driven mad by the wardens and then punished with flogging for behaving like the lunatic he had become. In his letter of 27 May 1897 to the *Daily Chronicle*, Wilde gives us another Marsyas in place of himself at Clapham Junction:

> It was my last Sunday in prison, a perfectly lovely day, the finest day we had had the whole year, and there, in the beautiful sunlight, walked this poor creature – made once in the image of God – grinning like an ape, and making with his hands the most fantastic gestures, as though he was playing in the air on some invisible stringed instrument, or arranging and dealing counters in some curious game ... The hideous and deliberate grace of his gestures made him like an antic. He was a living grotesque. (*Complete Letters*, 853)

He is an antic, a comic figure, a grotesque, as Wilde described himself on the platform of the train station. He is also Christ as one of the zanies of sorrow, a Prince among men, made once in the image of God and choosing the Sabbath for his performance. What I find most touching is that invisible stringed instrument – not pipes but the lyre of Apollo himself, a lyre purely of the imagination willed into being by the aesthetic demands of trauma – and on it this Prince of Sorrows plays his mad music with a deliberate grace like that deliberate infliction of pain that Wilde ascribes to Eccelino da Romano. Both are seen as artists of exquisite pain in part through their failure, their imprisonment – for, after all, Decadence is an aesthetic of failure, a romance rendered all the more compelling by our suspicion that its aesthetic aspiration, to burn always with a hard gem-like flame, is impossible and perhaps even dangerous to achieve in a fallen world. Wilde presents us with dreams from which he is continually waking us. The aesthetic effort is all the more romantic for being rather hopeless.

And so I leave you with one final passage from Wilde, from a letter written in September 1897 to Reginald Turner from Naples where he was living once again with Douglas, like some emperor in exile, and annoying all his friends for taking up again with the man who they believed had ruined him. It would seem to me that British homophobia ruined Wilde, not any man he loved, and here he makes a certain distressing irony evident. Having defended his desire before the British public, he was now defending it to his dearest friends, who ought to have known better. The letter is one of the most exquisitely painful he ever wrote. He plays the music of his heart breaking, which he regards as preferable to the dreary monotone of a world without love and without creativity. It is a cry of Marsyas that has taught me much about Wilde's extraordinary capacity for love in the face of all that had failed in his life, all that was improbable, and all that was simply against the law: "Much that you say in your letter is right, but still you leave out of consideration the great love I have for Bosie. I love him, and have always loved him. He ruined my life, and for that very reason I seem forced to love him more: and I think that now I shall do lovely work" (948). Here we collide immediately with his paradox, that a life ruined might also be an artistic inspiration, a *vita nuova*, to cite his reference to Dante – the beginning of a life newly devoted to doing lovely work. These letters are the only proof of that lovely work. His suffering finds him plucking at an invisible lyre in the air despite himself. He refuses the widespread contention that Douglas is his enemy, and he turns his pain once again into something exquisite, inspired by and created for a man who may well be unworthy or perhaps even incapable of hearing its refined music. As the passage continues, he speaks of Douglas in a manner that sounds like an elaborate act of self-delusion, referring to him as a great poet and a faithful lover (though, as Wilde says, Douglas certainly did love him more than he was capable of loving anyone else). Finally, however, it is the note of tragedy that makes Wilde's love seem not deluded but self-consciously romantic, another work of exquisite artistry. Wisely, he celebrates love not because it is requited or deserved, but because, in its most generous if most painful incarnation, it has no need of being either. He writes to Reginald Turner,

> So when people say how dreadful of me to return to Bosie, do say *no* – say that I love him, that he is a poet, and that, after all, whatever my life may have been ethically, it has always been *romantic*, and Bosie is my romance. My romance is a tragedy of course, but it is none the less a romance, and he loves me very dearly, more than he loves or can love anyone else, and without him my life was dreary. (*Complete Letters*, 948)

Notes

1 Oscar Wilde, *The Complete Letters of Oscar Wilde*, ed. Merlin Holland and Rupert Hart-Davis (London: Fourth Estate, 2000), 739, 740; further page references appear in parentheses.
2 John K. Noyes, *The Mastery of Submission: Inventions of Masochism* (Ithaca, NY: Cornell University Press, 1997).

3 Richard von Krafft-Ebing, *Psychopathia Sexualis*, trans. F.J. Rebman, twelfth edition (New York: Medical Arts Agency, 1906), 132–33.

4 Cited from Douglas's testimony for the defense in Maud Allan's libel trial in 1918 against Noel Pemberton-Billing. By this time in his life Douglas was insistently homophobic, and he regarded Krafft-Ebing's book as pornographic, an opinion he claimed to adopt from the medical authorities at the *Lancet*; see Philip Hoare, *Oscar Wilde's Last Stand: Decadence, Conspiracy, and the Most Outrageous Trial of the Century* (New York: Arcade, 1998), 152.

5 See, for example, his list of reasons for the repeal of certain German vice laws regarding sexual offenses between men: Krafft-Ebing, *Psychopathia Sexualis*, 578–80.

6 Janine Chasseguet-Smirgel, *Creativity and Perversion* (London: Free Association, 1985), 98.

7 Jonathan Dollimore, *Sexual Dissidence: Augustine to Wilde, Freud to Foucault* (Oxford: Clarendon Press, 1991), 199–200.

8 Melissa Knox, *Oscar Wilde: A Long and Lovely Suicide* (New Haven, CT: Yale University Press, 1994), 22; further page reference appears in parentheses.

9 A few pages earlier, Knox writes: "Like a saint, he had been dying for the sins of others, the nameless homosexuals of his age" (131). Here Knox makes it abundantly clear for what sin she thinks Wilde is to be forgiven, though usually, when he is canonized a saint, the sin he is said to have died for is homophobia, not homosexuality.

10 Mario Praz, *The Romantic Agony*, trans. Angus Davidson (London: Oxford University Press, 1933).

11 Algernon Charles Swinburne, "Anactoria," in Swinburne, *Poems*, 6 vols. (London: Chatto and Windus, 1904), I: 58; further page reference appears in parentheses.

12 Yopie Prins, *Victorian Sappho* (Princeton, NJ: Princeton University Press, 1999), 132.

13 Michel Foucault, "Sex, Power, and the Politics of Identity," in Foucault, *Essential Works of Michel Foucault, 1954–1984, vol. 1: Ethics: Subjectivity and Truth*, ed. Paul Rabinow (New York: New Press, 1997), 163; further page references appear in parentheses. The interview was conducted in June 1982 and published in *The Advocate*, 7 August 1984.

14 Gilles Deleuze, *Coldness and Cruelty* (1967), in *Masochism: An Interpretation of Coldness and Cruelty*, trans. Jean McNeil (New York: George Braziller, 1971), 61, 95, 115.

15 Leopold von Sacher-Masoch, *Venus in Furs* (1870), in *Masochism*, 226.

PART II

WILDE STAGES

chapter five

Wilde Man: Masculinity, Feminism, and
A Woman of No Importance

KERRY POWELL

I

Feminism in the later Victorian period was defined to a large extent by a puritanical morality which, as historian Barbara Caine points out, requires far more attention than it has yet received.[1] This surprising moralistic strain in the emerging women's movement – surprising in its reach and intensity – helps to account for the troubled relationships between *fin-de-siècle* feminists on the one hand, and many progressive men (including Oscar Wilde) on the other. Wilde's opposition to the enforcement of traditional codes of gender made him the natural ally of late-Victorian feminists, but his vehement opposition to their reconfiguration of masculinity made him their adversary. As a journalist, novelist, playwright, and criminal, Wilde's career was to some extent shaped in reaction to what feminism was (or was becoming) in one of its most significant forms, in the latter decades of the nineteenth century.

Wilde and some militant feminists of his time, however, were united in their common recognition that traditional conceptions of gender were regulatory fictions, not the expression of a universally "true" manhood or womanhood or core personal identity. In this regard, Wilde and certain late-Victorian feminists anticipated the crucial insights of twentieth-century gender theorists such as Judith Butler and Joan Riviere – in particular, the idea that gender is not a manifestation of biological sex but a ritualized drama (or "masquerade," in Riviere's phrase), through which the body takes on cultural meaning and typically serves the purposes of entrenched social power.[2] For Wilde and these early feminists, as for performance theorists of a later time, there is no expressive, essential reality behind the enactment of gender, although there certainly seems to be, owing to the ritualized and socially enforced gestures, speeches, and acts that go into the performance. For "those who fail to do their gender right," as Butler points out, the consequences can be catastrophic – as they would be finally for Wilde – even if there is no right or wrong except within the framework of the ritual drama of gender itself.[3] At the same time, however, recognizing, as both Wilde and some feminists did, the performativity of gender created an opening to attack and reconstruct the categories of gender that were sanctioned by custom and authority. Wilde and these militant feminists agreed in particular on the need for a radical critique of normative masculinity. They clashed, however, in their prescriptions of what should replace it.

II

Wilde's trials were one of many *fin-de-siècle* dramas centering on new ideas of male virtue and morality and, as Joseph Bristow has argued, the trials became a defining moment in the late-Victorian reconstruction of masculinity.[4] Wilde's trials were a product of the Criminal Law Amendment Bill of 1885, one part of which singled out the so-called "gross indecency" of men and targeted masculine vice for punishment. By contrast, the Contagious Diseases Acts (often abbreviated as the CD Acts) introduced in 1862 empowered police and magistrates to confine suspected prostitutes in lock hospitals for forced treatment in order to control the spread of syphilis and other sexually transmitted diseases among military men, although the men themselves were not subject to any such surveillance. Feminists, led by Josephine Butler and her Ladies' National Association, pointed out that these acts "so far as women are concerned ... remove every guarantee of personal security which the law has established and held sacred, and put their reputation, their freedom, and their persons absolutely in the power of the police." The CD Acts therefore punished only women, leaving unpunished, in the words of an LNA manifesto, "the sex who are the main cause, both of the vice and its dreaded consequences; and we consider that liability to arrest, forced medical treatment, and (where this is resisted) imprisonment with hard labour, to which these Acts subject women, are punishments of the most degrading kind."[5] In her memoir, Butler argues that the CD Acts aimed at not just "the enslavement of women" in general but a class of women in particular, "the daughters of the people" (*Personal Reminis-*

cences, 73). It was working poor women who, unable to survive otherwise, swelled the ranks of prostitutes in the Victorian era, as Butler knew
(and which historian Judith Walkowitz has more recently documented).[6] Prostitutes were thus vulnerable to oppression on the
grounds of class as well as of gender.

Victorian feminism, however, was far from monolithic. The opposition to the CD Acts, led by Josephine Butler and her allies in the Ladies'
National Association, was not shared by all leaders of the Victorian
women's movement. Emily Davies and Frances Cobbe, for example, represented a type of feminism devoted single-mindedly to emancipation
(which Butler also supported), critiquing women's oppression from the
perspective of a political and economic liberalism deeply influenced by
John Stuart Mill. More cautious than Josephine Butler, and more deco-
rous, they remained silent on issues of state-regulated prostitution and
the social control of women's bodies. Among the most prominent of
Victorian feminists was Millicent Fawcett, a moderate and pragmatist
who at first kept silent about the CD Acts, opposing them but choosing
to focus her efforts on the campaign for women's suffrage. By the
mid-1880s, however, Fawcett was increasingly concerned with the sexual oppression of women and had become a founding member of
the National Vigilance Association. Like Butler and Ellice Hopkins
(founder of the militant White Cross Army), she now combined an
advocacy for women's suffrage with the NVA's campaign for social
purity. "The more I dwell upon the details of Josephine Butler's life and
work," Fawcett would write in this later phase of her own career, "the
more I become convinced that she should take the rank of the most distinguished Englishwoman of the nineteenth century."[7] Butler, Fawcett,
Hopkins, and their numerous allies sought to end the double standard
and the sexual exploitation of women by insisting upon purity for men
as well as women and raising the level of morality in every sphere of life.

In literature these ideas were circulated by the most widely read feminist novel of the *fin de siècle*, *The Heavenly Twins* (1893) by Sarah Grand.
In one strand of the book's complicated narrative, a bride discovers that
her husband has had sexual relationships before their marriage, making
him a "moral leper" with whom she will tolerate no intimacy, physical or
emotional. Their marriage is never consummated. *The Heavenly Twins*
was an instant and huge success, and more than any other text it created
an awareness of what seemed to some men the most problematic
demand of the developing women's movement. Grand expressed that
demand in her own voice in a magazine article that appeared shortly

after the publication of *The Heavenly Twins*. "Man morally is in his infancy," she wrote in 1894. "There have been times when there was a doubt as to whether he was to be raised or woman was to be lowered, but we have turned that corner at last; and now woman holds out a strong hand to the child-man and insists ... upon helping him up."[8] Disagreement among women on the subject of male purity was turned into ridicule on occasion by men who had little sympathy with feminism in the first place. For example, in Sydney Grundy's hit play *The New Woman* (1894), a young woman named Enid Bethune, sounding like a member of the Ladies' National Association or White Cross Army, proposes that "a man, reeking with infamy, ought not to be allowed to marry a pure young girl." "Certainly not!" responds Victoria Vivash, a feminist of a very different order – "*she* ought to reek with infamy as well."[9] But *The Woman Who Did*, as Grant Allen phrased it in the title of his notorious novel of 1895, was comparatively rare among late-Victorian feminists and often the creation of wishful-thinking men like Allen. It was *The Woman Who Didn't*, as Victoria Cross entitled her fictional rejoinder to *The Woman Who Did*, which registered more accurately the tone of late-Victorian feminism.[10] There were exceptions like George Egerton, who celebrated female sexuality in her fiction of the 1890s, and Mona Caird, whose novels and journalistic writing advocated free love. But for most of those in the organized women's movement, the cause had little to do with loosening the sexual restraints placed upon women and everything to do with raising the standard of conduct for men.

Butler and her allies focused their attacks on the belief that men were naturally corrupt and unchaste and that regulated, legalized prostitution was necessary in order to gratify inevitable male lust. The campaigns against the CD Acts and for social purity therefore were founded upon the assumption that this view of masculinity as a naturalized category of gender was fraudulent. It was exposed as what performance theorists today would call a regulatory fiction rather than an expression of biological or any other kind of fact. In attempting to demolish this construction of masculinity and replace it with another, Victorian feminists on the side of social purity were implicitly, and sometimes explicitly, recognizing the performativity of gender in their "great crusade" against the sexual control of women by men. In Butler's view, for example, the Contagious Diseases Acts had brought into existence a "diabolical triple power" of doctors, magistrates, and police whose purpose was to place certain women under surveillance and enforce their degradation as embodiments of the Victorian nightmare of feminine evil and uncontained sexuality.[11] These women, Butler recognized, were "maddened, hardened and stamped underfoot by men," actually defined into being by medical and legal authority. The "tortured and fiendish" womanhood of Victorian prostitutes was, for Butler, therefore, nothing more nor less than the creation of men "[b]owing down before the unrestrained dictates of their own lusts" – lusts which they falsely imagined to be natural and unchangeable, determined by their masculine gender (*Personal Reminiscences*, 134).

Josephine Butler and like-minded feminists refocused their energies after the repeal of the CD Acts in a campaign against vice in general, "against the tacit permission – the indisputable right, as some have learned to regard it – granted to men to be impure at all."[12] This enthusiasm for the purification of society as a whole became a powerful force in the wake of W.T. Stead's journalistic exposure of child prostitution in England. Stead's revelations appeared in a series of articles in the *Pall Mall Gazette* in 1885, the same year that the Criminal Law Amendment Bill was enacted with criminal penalties for men found guilty of "gross indecency." It remains unclear how many feminists were involved in these social purity campaigns, but the number was enormous. They involved not only members of the National Vigilance Association but also the Social Purity Alliance (which preceded it), the White Cross Army, the Ladies' National Association, and the newly emergent Women's Liberal Association (an offshoot of the Liberal Party). The new moral fervor transcended any single organization, although the NVA became perhaps its most radical exponent by harassing prostitutes as well as their clients and by fiercely opposing birth control and "impure" literature. Eventually Butler would resign from that organization, so great was its clash with her own liberal principles. But her devotion to the cause of social purity would be undiminished. Butler saw the campaign against the CD Acts and the agitation for social purity as being joined by what she called "the central principle" of the feminist crusade – an insistence upon the purity of all members of society, men as well as women – as the only way to end the double standard of morality and the sexual control of women by men (*Sursum Corda*, 12). The campaign for social purity, like the campaign against the CD Acts, challenged the received idea that the male gender is naturally corrupt and "impure," seeking to replace it with a new performance of masculinity that would be governed by the same high standard of conduct that was applied to women.

Once the CD Acts were repealed, the controversy around them continued even as the focus of militant feminists began to shift to the cause of purity in all areas of life. Efforts were made to reinstate the CD Acts in the 1890s, efforts fiercely opposed by feminists, and in the meantime opposition was aroused against regulated prostitution in various parts of the empire and against proposals to introduce it in others. Even before the repeal of the CD Acts, however, the rhetoric of the movement was deeply colored by its adherence to a single standard of purity for both men and women and, crucially, by a recognition that dominant readings of gender in no way expressed a "true" masculinity or femininity. Butler, in a polemic of 1882 entitled *The Hour before the Dawn: An Appeal to Men*, advocates what she describes as "two radical principles – namely, the sacredness of the home, and the duty of men to live and to suffer women to live in purity." Butler excoriates the CD Acts and the "unequal standard of morality for the sexes," which is for her the ultimate cause of prostitution, as contrary to every principle of justice and right. "The law of personal purity obliges men and women equally to rule their lives by their highest spiritual ideal," Butler proclaims, quoting the manifesto of the Social Purity Alliance. The idea that "unchastity is a 'necessity' for man" is false to the core, not the warrant of a natural and immutable masculinity but rather "man's invention, for his own base convenience."[13] In *Sursum Corda*, her address to the Ladies' National Association in 1891, Butler attacks the eminent historian and social critic W.E.H. Lecky for his romanticized description of the prostitute as the "priestess of humanity," charged with the mournful office of bearing the sins of men and thus preserving the purity of English homes. "What beautiful language, what subtle arguments," exclaims Butler, "have men brought, in all ages, to the support of the recognised indulgence of their own selfish interests and degraded passions!" (*Sursum Corda*, 19–20).[14] Embedded in these pronouncements is the same insight that would produce theories of performative gender a century later. In understanding the Victorian idea of masculinity as a fabrication manufactured and sustained to further the interests of men, Josephine Butler anticipates Judith Butler's assertions a century later that the gendered body is brought into being by gestures and enactments that create the illusion of an organizing gender core, an illusion "discursively maintained for the purposes of the regulation of sexuality" (136). Although her much earlier observations are not generalized to the level that a theory of gender would require, Josephine Butler nevertheless argues for a reconfiguration of gender that would both reveal its performativity and destabilize masculinity as a naturalized category of identity.

In the early years of the CD Acts Butler visited the garrison towns where they were in effect and personally met many "Queen's women," as the prostitutes called themselves, as well as soldiers who were quartered in those places. One of the men, recalls Butler in the pamphlet *Truth before Everything*, explained the behavior of himself and his fellow soldiers as the result, not of their own nature, but of the expectations of those above them. "Oh Ma'am," the soldier told Butler, "*they expect us to be bad, and we are bad.*" After italicizing the young soldier's comment, Butler drove the point home herself:

> "They – the authorities – expect us to be bad." That boy expressed the whole truth concerning the effect of this degrading State institution, in those few simple words. Why should not the authorities give a trial to the plan of *expecting* these soldiers to be *good*?[15]

With these words Butler rejected the idea that the CD Acts could be justified by appealing to the gendered nature of men as inevitably corrupt, thus requiring the sacrifice of a whole class of women. As suggested by the comments of the boy soldier, Butler emphasizes that the sordid behavior of some men is nothing more than the acting out of a script that has been written by "the authorities" to enforce their view of what men are and should be. It is a performative event rather than the outward manifestation of "real" masculinity that would justify the policing and "enslavement of women" brought about by the CD Acts. Masculinity as her contemporaries understood it, inevitably sensual and corrupt, was thus exposed by Butler as a ritual social drama that furthered the self-seeking agenda of men themselves. By the same token, and crucially, the *new* masculinity that Butler advocated was also performative in nature, rather than expressive of an internal gendered identity. In asking the question "Why should not the authorities give a trial to the plan of *expecting* these soldiers to be *good*?" Butler in effect concedes that her script for a purified masculinity is just that – a masquerade, not the manifestation in practice of an essential masculine nature or even the result of a humanist individual choice by which a particular man would determine for himself what it meant to be *male*.

Rhetorically as well as ideologically, these developments marked a significant historical moment. The term "masculinity" was becoming a signifier whose content was in doubt, or at least contested by opposing parties with regard to what the concept, and gender itself, could be said to mean, if anything, in and of itself. The terms "purity," "puritan," and

"puritanism" had also become battlegrounds. On one side Josephine
Butler asserted: "It is a beautiful word that of Purity." Yet she worried
that because of its political cachet many societies had begun to use that
name without fully endorsing the program of feminist social purity. In
Truth before Everything, for example, she writes that some groups oppose
"impure" literature and yet support the state regulation of vice. While
on the one hand, even her foes appropriated the term "purity" to work
at cross-purposes with feminists such as herself, on the other hand,
there were enemies passionately eager "to get rid of this 'damnable
Puritanism' which is so irksome to them." For this latter group the
hated term "purity" was beginning to stand for the revisionary gender
categories that a radical feminism was promoting. "Nothing, they
know," writes Butler, "would so rapidly and forcibly conduce towards
their liberation from this oppressive yoke [of "purity"] than that the
State should itself proclaim ... that free fleshly indulgence is necessary
for man, and therefore not to be blamed, but rather to be facilitated"
(*Truth before Everything*, 22). Around the word "purity" the cultural
battle-lines were drawn, putting under severe strain the true/false oppositions of old ways of thinking.

III

"You are unjust to women in England," an assertive young American
tells her hosts at a country house in Wilde's hit play of 1893, *A Woman of
No Importance*, "and till you count what is a shame in a woman to be an
infamy in a man, you will always be unjust." Her feminism, like Josephine Butler's, challenges the double standard by applying the same
morality to men that had always been expected of women. When the
name of Lord Henry Weston comes up in conversation, "a man with a
hideous smile and a hideous past," Hester Worsley insists that her com-
panions bear in mind the outcast women whose ruin is due to him. Not
that his female victims deserve a better fate – "let all women who have
sinned be punished," she says – but they should not be the only ones to
suffer. "If a man and woman have sinned," she says, "let them both go
forth into the desert ... let them both be branded ... don't punish the
one and let the other go free. Don't have one law for men and another
for women." As it is, however, immoral men are welcomed in the highest
society and the best company; "no dinner party," Hester regrets, is complete without them, while everyone ostracizes the woman that has
"sinned."[16]

Hester's complaint about the way in which guilty men are welcomed into the best homes was a prominent theme of feminist discourse at the time. In *The Hour before the Dawn*, for example, Josephine Butler laments that a profligate man is "received in society and entrusted with moral and social responsibilities, while the lapse of a woman of the humbler classes ... is made the portal for her of a life of misery and shame" (64). Elsewhere Butler expresses regret that the male "black sheep" can enter almost anyone's drawing-room "with as fair an exterior as that of any other man." This unequal state of affairs, she reflects, is to a large degree the fault of women themselves, "guilty before God in their weak indulgence to men whom they know to be vicious, and in their cowardly shrinking from the task of discrimination" (*Sursum Corda*, 34, 36). All the women in *A Woman of No Importance*, with the exception of Hester Worsley and Mrs. Arbuthnot, shrink from the "task of discrimination" in exactly the way that Butler complains of. When Hester complains in Act II that Lord Henry Weston is welcome at everyone's dinner parties even though "he has wrecked innocent lives, poisoned lives that were pure,"[17] Lady Hunstanton objects by way of reply that "he is really such good company." Lady Caroline Pontefract, embarrassing Hester with the disclosure that Lord Henry Weston is her brother, concedes that he is "infamous, absolutely infamous" but suggests that his moral failings can be overlooked because "he has one of the best cooks in London" (55).

Most of Hester Worsley's declarations at this early point in the play could have been spoken by Josephine Butler and her allies in the Ladies' National Association, campaigning for the abolition of the CD Acts and regulated prostitution. Wilde's character insists upon the moral accountability of men in a manner not unlike Butler's exhortation to "fallen" men in a pamphlet published by the Social Purity Alliance in 1882:

> You who have sinned grossly or habitually can never be the same in earthly relations as those who have escaped the deeper pollutions. You are wounded for life; ... you will be, even when restored by God, sorrowful men, burdened with bitter memories, weakened through the wearing of heavy chains ... You can never become what you were, – *never what you were*." (*The Hour before the Dawn*, 8–10)

But Wilde's characterization of the feminism of social purity slides into caricature when he has Mrs. Arbuthnot remark that not only should men and women be "punished" in the same way, but "the children, if there are children, in the same way also." Hester agrees: "Yes, it is right that the sins of the parents should be visited on the children ... It is God's law" (A Woman of No Importance, 88). Although the syphilis epidemic certainly transmitted the sins of the parents to their children, the primitive and retributive morality expressed by Hester and Mrs. Arbuthnot was far from typical of fin-de-siècle feminism. Josephine Butler, instead of condemning prostitutes themselves, took up their grievances against police and medical authority out of "principles of freedom and of respect for the individual man and woman."[18] In Butler's view, society's condemnation of the woman who has sinned is extreme; it "drives such an one out of bounds, sets its hell-hounds on the track, and makes recovery all but impossible" (The Hour before the Dawn, 64). As Millicent Fawcett points out, Butler not only sympathized with prostitutes but also invited them into her home as honored guests (151). From this perspective, Hester Worsley appears quite out of harmony with the feminism that she espouses when she exclaims: "I don't complain of their punishment. Let all women who have sinned be punished." (In the first surviving draft Wilde wrote "banished" rather than "punished").[19] As for "fallen" men, Butler's attitude was condemnatory, for she saw that the syphilis epidemic stemmed from their undisciplined behavior: "they disperse plagues and death wherever they move by the very infection of their breath" (The Hour before the Dawn, 26–27). Yet Butler's reaction to the crime and punishment of Wilde as an individual man would be more sympathetic than judgmental. "I am so sorry for Oscar Wilde," she wrote shortly after his criminal trial and conviction. "I pray for him constantly – that God will tell him that He does not despise him."[20]

Lord Illingworth in A Woman of No Importance is presented as an obvious target of the moral-purity type of feminist – "a bad man," as Mrs. Arbuthnot charges (92), and of course one who is indispensable at dinner parties and widely admired. He is conceited about having so many bad qualities, mocks the idea of moral uprightness and purity which had become the agenda of many feminists, and remarks flippantly at one point that "it is better to be beautiful than to be good."[21] Wilde himself surely agreed with Illingworth on these matters but Lord Illingworth does not have it all his own way in this drama. In the end it is the character known as "the Puritan," the doctrinaire purity feminist Hester Worsley, who comes out best, if somewhat chastened and changed. By the final curtain she has had to modify her views on the punishment of sin, and Mrs. Arbuthnot has taught her the value of at least some flexibility where moral codes are concerned. In essence Wilde is formulating new ratios between, on the one hand, the Puritan morality of many Victorian feminists and, on the other hand, his tendency to the amoral aestheticism embodied in Lord Illingworth.

This reading of the play is borne out by early manuscript drafts of *A Woman of No Importance* – manuscripts that in the absence of a complete scholarly edition have not figured extensively in criticism of the play. It seems certain that Wilde was writing within the general context of contemporary feminism from the beginning. In his autograph manuscript titled *Mrs. Arbuthnot* (the earliest known draft of the play), the liberal politician Mr. Kelvil is inserted early into Act I to deliver the opinions that remain in subsequent versions of the play, notably his enthusiasm for the increasing involvement of women in politics and his approval of the moral dimension that they have brought to political discourse. "The growing influence of women is the most reassuring thing in our political life," he remarks in the autograph manuscript, adding approvingly: "women are always on the side of morality."[22] By contrast, this earliest version of *A Woman of No Importance* introduces Lord Illingworth as the adversary of Kelvil's point of view. Illingworth is himself amoral, uninterested in women's growing influence in politics, and skeptical about the very existence of women like Hester Worsley (called Mabel in this first draft) and the purity feminists on whom she is modeled. "I don't believe in the existence of Puritan women," Lord Illingworth discloses to Mrs. Allonby. "There is not a woman in the world who would not be charmed if one kissed her."[23] But as Wilde revised the play he sharpened its referencing of the social purity movement in certain respects even as he softened the play's hostile and at times inaccurate attitude toward it in other revisions. For example, not until the comparatively late draft that was submitted to the Lord Chamberlain for licensing of the play did Wilde include this exchange between Lady Stutfield and Mr. Kelvil, the liberal MP who is an outspoken advocate of women's rights and purity – a man on the same side of the political fence as the National Vigilance Association and Ellice Hopkins's White Cross Army:

LADY STUTFIELD: And what have you been writing on this morning, Mr. Kelvil?

MR. KELVIL: On the usual subject, Lady Stutfield, on Purity.

LADY STUTFIELD: That must be such a very, very interesting thing to write about.

MR. KELVIL: It is the one subject of really national importance now-a-days, Lady Stutfield.[24]

Kelvil, noting that he plans to address his constituents on the subject of purity, then reflects: "I find that the poorer classes of this country display a marked desire for a higher ethical standard." In this observation Kelvil follows the lead of purity feminism in its sense of its own growing solidarity with the working class to counter the resistance often displayed by those of higher rank. Struggling against opposition from powerful and well-placed men and women, Josephine Butler was surprised to find how readily the working class was "carried up to the highest standard in judging of a moral question, and how almost universally they acknowledged the authority of the ethical truths which we endeavoured to put before them." Boiler-fitters, engine-makers, and the like "perfectly understood the message, and acted upon it with intelligence" (*Personal Reminiscences*, 31–32). Nor was their role, as Butler saw it, a subservient one. Working men themselves organized meetings, initiated plans of action which they often headed up, launched petitions to Parliament, and entered into dialogue with politicians standing for election – liberal politicians like Kelvil in Wilde's play, who finds the ethical sense of the poorer classes especially congenial to the politics of purity.

Early drafts of *A Woman of No Importance* include some harsh attacks on Hester's puritanism which were later deleted from the play: for example, a passage in which Lord Illingworth argues stridently that the "real enemy of modern life ... is Puritanism, and the Puritan spirit."[25] Also dropped from later versions was a passage in which Lord Illingworth vows to cure his son of his new-found puritan views: "It doesn't run in our family to take the Puritan side of things."[26] The final drafts also soften Hester's rhetoric of strict moral purity, deleting, for example, her Butler-like description of Lord Henry Weston as "a man who has wrecked innocent lives, and poisoned lives that were pure." In early versions Gerald Arbuthnot adopts the vocabulary of purity feminism to denounce his father, Lord Illingworth, as not only "infamous" but also "foul" and "polluted." These lines were also deleted by Wilde, thus lowering the rhetorical temperature of the play and moderating the polemical tension between his own position on masculinity and that of the militant feminists whom he was engaging in dialogue in *A Woman of No Importance*. Of course, Hester's own puritanism is mocked in the finished text of the play but less vehemently than in earlier versions. For example, Mrs. Allonby in the final, published version of the play can still say of the young American woman that "[s]he is a Puritan" (35) but Wilde drops her sneering follow-up from earlier drafts: "an out-and-out Puritan – the worst I ever met."[27]

To a large extent Wilde moderates his play's conflict with the radical feminism of social purity through changes that he gradually incorporates in the character of Lord Illingworth, who becomes much less aggressively bad and less confrontational in his conduct towards Hester Worsley and Mrs. Arbuthnot. By cutting some of his more strident condemnations of puritan women, Wilde prepares for the moment in Act IV when Illingworth recognizes that the social purity feminist Hester Worsley is a "fin-de-siècle person" whose critique of marriage as an institution has surprising affinities with his own views. Also deleted from the final text of the play is Illingworth's shrill denunciation of good women in answer to Aleck Arbuthnot (as Gerald was called in early drafts), who has just asked him, "there are good women in society, aren't there?" "Oh, lots of them. One doesn't meet them at dinner. At least one shouldn't. Good women are invariably ignorant women. Ignorance is the price a woman pays for being good." In typescript Wilde crossed out this passage, and on the verso page wrote out by hand a new version. Aleck's question about whether there are good women in society remains the same but now Illingworth says simply: "Far too many. Goodness is an admirable thing, I dare say, but it is certainly not becoming." Although the point being made is similar in both versions, the latter concedes something to puritan women ("goodness is an admirable thing") and otherwise states its case less aggressively than before.[28]

Wilde again ratcheted down the conflict between Lord Illingworth and Mrs. Arbuthnot as he rewrote the fourth act. The play still concludes melodramatically in the final version when Mrs. Arbuthnot strikes Lord Illingworth across the face with his own glove, then refers to him as "a man of no importance," just as she had in the earliest surviving drafts of *A Woman of No Importance*. As before, Mrs. Arbuthnot has only moments ago turned down Lord Illingworth's proposal of marriage and, stung by her rejection, he has lashed back with the remark that "It's been an amusing experience to have met amongst people of one's own rank, and treated quite seriously too, one's mistress and one's ..." At this point, when Lord Illingworth is about to call his own son a bastard, the slap occurs in all versions of the play, but what happens next changed significantly as Wilde rewrote the ending. In an early typescript Lord Illingworth responds to Mrs. Arbuthnot's slap in the face with an insulting speech that draws attention to her own past: "You are the woman whom I did the honour of asking to be my wife. How foolish the wisest of us are at times. But some day your son may call you by a worse name. He has my blood in his veins as well as yours."

In the revised version of the scene this mean-spirited attack is crossed
out by Wilde. Indeed, Lord Illingworth says nothing at all. But on the
verso page of the typescript Wilde has written just this: "Lord Illingworth starts. He controls himself, and goes to window and looks out at
his son. Sighs, and leaves the room."[29] Not remorse, exactly, but regret
at least, along with an apparent recognition that his mode of life has
cost him something and that the puritan feminism that he has mocked
may have something to say to him after all. Gone is the bitter, confrontational attack on Mrs. Arbuthnot with which Lord Illingworth had
originally concluded. This difference made for a notable effect in performance. When Beerbohm Tree (as Lord Illingworth) acted this scene
in its revised form at the Haymarket Theatre, a critic was struck by the
fact that "there was just a look of mingled love and remorse in Mr. Tree's
expressive face as he made his exit."[30]

At the beginning of the play, Lord Illingworth declared: "I don't
believe in the existence of Puritan women." But now their reality has
been brought home to him with a slap in the face and the loss of the son
he loves: he has an altered understanding of puritan women. The puritan women in the play have changed too. Hard at first (exaggeratedly
so) by comparison to real-life models such as Josephine Butler and Millicent Fawcett, they have learned to soften the demands of their austere
morality in recognition, as Hester says, that "God's only law is love."
Although *A Woman of No Importance* began in its earliest drafts as a
rhetorical and ideological confrontation with an emerging and radical
feminist movement, it developed in its final version into a search for
common ground – a hybridized performance of gender which, if not
fully realized in the text of the play, lies just over the horizon, beyond
the final curtain. The marriage of Hester Worsley and Gerald Arbuthnot
will reconfigure traditional understandings of gender, a goal of puritan
women and Lord Illingworth alike. In doing so it will presumably work
against the excesses of the feminism of social purity, on the one hand,
and of Wildean aestheticism (embodied in Lord Illingworth), on the
other hand.

In *A Woman of No Importance*, therefore, Wilde was making concilia-
tory gestures toward the advocates of purity even as he was resisting
them, and in return the play was received with satisfaction in some quar-
ters where a positive reaction to Wilde could not have been expected.
One religious journal, for example, remarked in its review that "a living
sermon is being preached nightly at the Haymarket."[31] In a remarkable
interview, Sir Edward Russell, the leading advocate of social purity, edi-

tor of the Liverpool *Daily Post*, and well-known drama critic, confided to a reporter over tea that he was heartened by a "the gospel of a new purity" in a few modern plays, "a purity that the churches have not dared to teach." The churches, Russell explained, were concerned mainly with "technical morality – the morality of the letter of the Ten Commandments," so that, for example, "they bless all marriages – even the most shameful" and "do not dare – even if they cared – to demand any of the things that really go to make marriage lovely and wedlock pure." Immediately the interviewer thought of the new play by Wilde, and asked: "But the representation of such states of society as that shown in 'A Woman of No Importance' – do you consider it beneficial?" The purity crusader hesitated, unsure how to respond. "I scarcely know," Russell confessed, then weighed in with the view that perhaps Wilde was on the side of purity after all. "Mr. Wilde satirises the society which he represents, and out of it there grows that wonderful tragedy with its magnificent lesson. Yes, the daring of the play justifies itself, and we are the better for seeing it."[32]

IV

A year or so later Wilde began writing *The Importance of Being Earnest* around the idea that one becomes what one performs. "Why should there be one law for men, and another for women," asks Jack Worthing, embracing the unmarried, puritanical woman writer Miss Prism, whom he now believes, mistakenly, to be his mother.[33] Jack's comment implies a rescripting of gendered identity, revised to make it less prescriptive, more fluid and performative, and it is not long until this appropriately fatherless and motherless character becomes a new man himself – the man he has pretended to be in his ritualized performances as E(a)rnest. At the final curtain, he can announce his discovery of the importance of *being* E(a)rnest, though not within the usual Victorian construction of masculinity. Even though this type of manhood enforced an outward performance of conscientiously "earnest" behavior, it none the less concealed (as Josephine Butler and the purity feminists never wearied of pointing out) a corruption believed to be an unchangeable dimension of masculine identity. Jack Worthing – imaginative, androgynous, unearnest – exhibits a manhood that negotiates its path between traditional understandings of masculinity, on one side, and a new feminist reading of the male, on the other. This pleasure-seeking new man would never be converted by Josephine Butler's *The Hour before the Dawn*, and yet his opposition to a traditional and absolutist codification of masculinity, along with his now single-minded devotion to Gwendolen Moncrieff, gives him something important in common with the militant feminists of the *fin de siècle*.

Only a few months after *Earnest* opened its brief run at the St. James's Theatre, Wilde, looking defeated and tired, was defending himself in court against charges of gross indecency, lying repeatedly about his relations with a string of young prostitutes. His testimony would end catastrophically, in conviction and imprisonment under a new law that among other things enforced upon men the purity that many feminists of the time were demanding. Amid the arid exchanges between Wilde and the prosecutor, however, there came an exceptional moment when Wilde was himself again – or rather a moment when he was able to imagine a self that he might become, even if he had not yet done so. Cross-examining Wilde, counsel Charles Gill asked him, "What is the 'Love that dare not speak its name'?" referring to a poem by Wilde's lover Alfred Douglas. Wilde replied with a spontaneous and lyrical speech that elicited a burst of applause from the crowded courtroom and was widely reported in the press:

> The "Love that dare not speak its name" in this century is such a great affection of an elder for a younger man as there was between David and Jonathan, such as Plato made the very basis of his philosophy, and such as you find in the sonnets of Michaelangelo and Shakespeare. It is that deep, spiritual affection that is as pure as it is perfect.[34]

Pure? Perfect? In Wilde's plays "purity" and "perfection" were qualities that were almost always deemed inappropriate for a man. When Lady Chiltern, member of the Women's Liberal Association with Josephine Butler, cries out to Sir Robert Chiltern in *An Ideal Husband*, "you were to me ... a thing pure, noble, honest, without stain," her husband replies, somewhat petulantly: "There was your mistake. There was your error."[35] Cecil Graham makes the same point more stylishly in *Lady Windermere's Fan*: "[W]hat on earth should we men do going about with purity and innocence?"[36]

And yet Wilde sometimes took a second look at the radical feminism of social purity. He did so in *A Woman of No Importance*, and in his criminal trial he tried to imagine a manhood that was "pure" and "perfect," unconstrained by existing scripts for the performance of masculinity. That was also the project of many late Victorian feminists, including Josephine

Butler. But as Jacques Derrida has argued in "Signature Event Context," there could never be a performative statement without a "a general iterability" or "citationality" behind it, just as every sign, whether spoken or written, is always cited, placed implicitly between quotation marks.[37] Part of Wilde's own performance of masculinity, as it developed in his trials, certainly involved citations from the past – Plato, Shakespeare, and so on. At the same time, the gendered body that Wilde was trying to imagine was implicated as well in the social rituals of the present, those *"perpetual spirals of power and pleasure,"* to use Michel Foucault's terminology, which by establishing new discourses of regulative sexuality also produced new categories of gender, or as Foucault puts it, "determined the sexual mosaic." That is to say, the power embodied in the recently enacted Criminal Law Amendment Bill searched out and brought to light the suddenly illegal sexual activities of Wilde. But in doing so the bill also provided Wilde with what Foucault calls "the pleasure that kindles at having to evade this power" and the opportunity to step forward and declare himself and what he was, or could become.[38] In the dock, and before that in his plays, Wilde was trying to imagine a new performance of gender, a new masculinity, and in that brave and disastrous undertaking his citation of the radical feminism of the *fin de siècle* was crucial.

Notes

1 This essay is an attempt, in part, to provide an improved understanding of the subject. I would like to thank the staffs of the William Andrews Clark Memorial Library, University of California, Los Angeles, the Fawcett Library at London Guildhall University, and the British Library, without whose extraordinary cooperation this chapter would have been inconceivable. Barbara Caine's *Victorian Feminists* (Oxford: Oxford University Press, 1992), especially 238–59, her chapter on the 1890s, has been a valuable resource; further page reference appears in parentheses. Michael Foldy in *The Trials of Oscar Wilde: Deviance, Morality, and Late-Victorian Society* (New Haven, CT: Yale University Press, 1997) offers useful insights into the social purity movement as a whole, although his focus is quite different from mine.

2 Joan Riviere, "Womanliness as a Masquerade," in Victor Burgin, James Donald, and Cora Kaplan, eds., *Formations of Fantasy* (London: Methuen, 1986), 38.

3 Judith Butler, *Gender Trouble: Feminism and the Subversion of Identity* (New York: Routledge, 1990), 140.

4 Joseph Bristow, "Wilde, *Dorian Gray*, and Gross Indecency," in Bristow, ed., *Sexual Sameness: Textual Differences in Lesbian and Gay Writing* (London: Routledge, 1992), 44–63.

5 "Women's Protest," quoted by Josephine Butler in *Personal Reminiscences of a Great Crusade* (London: Marshall, 1896), 18; further page references appear in parentheses.

6 Judith Walkowitz, *Prostitution and Victorian Society: Women, Class, and the State* (Cambridge: Cambridge University Press, 1980).

7 Millicent Fawcett and E.M. Turner, *Josephine Butler: Her Work and Principles and Their Meaning for the Twentieth Century* (London: Association for Moral and Social Hygiene, 1927), 1; further page reference appears in parentheses.

8 Sarah Grand, *The Heavenly Twins* (New York: Cassell, 1893) and "The New Aspect of the Woman Question," *North American Review*, 158 (1894), 270–76.

9 Sydney Grundy, *The New Woman: An Original Comedy, in Four Acts* (London: Chiswick, 1894), 28.

10 Victoria Cross, *The Woman Who Didn't* (London: Lane, 1895); Grant Allen, *The Woman Who Did* (Boston: Roberts, 1895).

11 Josephine Butler, "Letter to the Members of the Ladies National Association," quoted in Caine, *Victorian Feminists*, 182.

12 Josephine Butler, *Sursum Corda: Annual Address to the Ladies' National Association* (Liverpool: Brakell, 1871); further page references appear in parentheses.

13 Josephine Butler, *The Hour before the Dawn: An Appeal to Men*, second edition (London: Trübner, 1882), 63–65, 71.

14 Josephine Butler makes a similar point using similar language in *Social Purity: An Address Given to Students at Cambridge*, second edition (London: Dwyer, 1881), 20. One of Lecky's most widely read books, with many editions in the late nineteenth and early twentieth centuries, was *A History of European Morals from Augustus to Charlemagne* (London: Longmans, Green, 1869).

15 Josephine Butler, *Truth before Everything* (London: Dyer, n.d.), 20; further page reference appears in parentheses.

16 Oscar Wilde, *A Woman of No Importance*, ed. Ian Small, in *Two Society Comedies*, ed. Small and Russell Jackson (London: Benn, 1983), 53; further page references appear in parentheses.

17 This social purity rhetoric was written into the first surviving draft of the play, now in the British Library, but was deleted in later versions, including the first edition, one of many significant alterations of this kind.

18 Josephine Butler, "Women and Politics: Extract from a Speech at a Meeting of the Portsmouth Women's Liberal Association, 1888," a pamphlet among the Butler Papers in the Fawcett Library, London Guildhall University.

19 Quoted from Wilde's autograph manuscript in the British Library, entitled *Mrs. Arbuthnot*, and from Jackson's edition of the play, 53.

20 Letter from Josephine Butler to Stanley Butler, 4 June 1895, manuscript in Fawcett Library.

21 "It is better to be beautiful than good" was deleted from the published play.

22 Quoted from the manuscript in the British Library, Act I, 18.

23 Manuscript in the British Library, Act I, 41.

24 Quoted from the licensing manuscript of *A Woman of No Importance* in the British Library.

25 Wilde inserted this speech in his own handwriting on the verso of page 3, Act III, in an early typed draft of the play in the British Library. The typescript was apparently derived from the earliest known manuscript of the play.

26 This remark is crossed out in a typescript entitled *Mrs. Arbuthnot*, in the William Andrews Clark Memorial Library, University of California, Los Angeles, which appears to mark an intermediate stage of the composition of the play, falling somewhere between the early autograph manuscript and the licensing version (Act 4, TS, 14).

27 These lines are crossed out in the typescript *Mrs. Arbuthnot* in the Clark Library (Act 1, TS, 16).

28 Quoted from the Clark Library typescript of *Mrs. Arbuthnot* (handwritten across Act 3, TS, 4).

29 Quoted from the Clark Library typescript of *Mrs. Arbuthnot*. In the first edition, Wilde adds a few additional words but preserves the subdued reaction by Lord Illingworth (crossed out on Act 4, TS, 19; handwritten on same page).

30 Quoted from a review of *A Woman of No Importance* in *Gentlewoman* magazine from a file of press clippings in the William Andrews Clark Memorial Library, University of California, Los Angeles. The article is titled " 'A Woman of No Importance' at the Haymarket," 24 April 1893.

31 *Illustrated Church News*, 27 April 1893, quoted from a clipping in the Clark Library.

32 Quoted from a clipping from the *Westminster Budget* in the William Andrews Clark Memorial Library, University of California, Los Angeles, Wildeana Box 2.15.C, 1893.

33 Wilde, *The Importance of Being Earnest*, ed. Russell Jackson (London: Benn, 1980), 101.

34 Quoted by Richard Ellmann, *Oscar Wilde* (London: Hamish Hamilton, 1987), 435. Accounts in contemporary newspapers are substantially the same.

35 Wilde, *An Ideal Husband*, ed. Jackson, in *Two Society Comedies*, 210.

36 Wilde, *Lady Windermere's Fan*, ed. Ian Small (London: Benn, 1980), 65–66.

37 Jacques Derrida, "Signature Event Context," in *Margins of Philosophy*, trans. Alan Bass (Chicago: University of Chicago Press, 1982), 309–30.

38 Michel Foucault, *The History of Sexuality Volume 1: An Introduction*, trans. Robert Hurley (New York: Pantheon, 1978), 45–49.

chapter six

Wilde, and How to Be Modern:
or, Bags of Red Gold

PETER RABY

This chapter examines some of the circumstances surrounding the writing of *The Importance of Being Earnest* (1895), and how these may have affected the nature of that text. For the first time in his playwriting career, and no doubt driven by financial pressure, Wilde trailed a draft scenario before a manager, in a letter to George Alexander during the summer of 1894. Clearly, his long letter was following up a previous conversation: "There really is nothing more to tell you about the comedy beyond what I told you already. I mean that the real charm of the play, if it is to have charm, must be in the dialogue. The plot is slight, but, I think, adequate."[1] Wilde proceeded to tell Alexander a great deal about the comedy, including an extremely detailed description of the "slight" plot; "everything ends happily," he concluded:

> *Result* Curtain
> Author called
> Cigarette called
> Manager called
> Royalties for a year for author.
> Manager credited with writing the play. He consoles himself with bags of
>   red gold.
> Fireworks (*Complete Letters*, 596–97)

This stated intention to complete a play in a particular timeframe is a significant factor in the pattern of Wilde's movements and moods during August, September, and October 1894, when he was working on successive drafts. There are unfilled gaps in the narrative of Wilde's life at this period, in spite of the fact that these months have been subjected to extensive commentary. Understandably, the events of the 1895 trials will soon dominate, and will cast their own shadow retrospectively on the summer of 1894 (the evidence concerning Alphonse Conway,[2] for example, or Wilde's own impassioned and bitter account of his Sussex tribulations with Douglas in *De Profundis*). There are difficulties in sequencing and dating several of the letters. There are unsolved problems in deciding precisely when Wilde was in Worthing, and when he visited London, or Brighton. One factor, however, emerges clearly: Wilde was not working on this play in secret, and he was much more expansive and buoyant about it than seems to have been the case with his previous dramas. This impression may of course be an accident of survival in terms of correspondence. But he was not in the habit of saying much about his plays during the actual writing process, except to fob off his expectant actor-managers. "I can't get a grip of the play yet: I can't get my people real," he told Alexander about *Lady Windermere's Fan* in February 1891. "I am very sorry, but artistic work can't be done unless one is in the mood; certainly my work can't. Sometimes I spend months over a thing, and don't do any good; at other times I write a thing in a fortnight" (*Complete Letters*, 463). Of *A Woman of No Importance* (1893), he informed Beerbohm Tree in September in 1892 that he had written two acts: "I am very pleased with it so far" (*Complete Letters*, 535). But other comments are largely concerned with practicalities about rights. With *Earnest*, he seems totally and openly confident, and free. He was in the mood. And so he wrote to Alexander:

> Well, I think an amusing thing with lots of fun and wit might be made. If you think so, too, and care to have the refusal of it – do let me know – and send me £150. If, when the play is finished, you think it too slight – not serious enough – of course you can have the £150 back – I want to go away and write it – and it could be ready in October – as I have nothing else to do – and Palmer is anxious to have a play from me for the States "with no real serious interest" – just a comedy. (*Complete Letters*, 597)[3]

There are all kinds of teases and evasions in this letter. Perhaps the least reliable statement is "of course you can have the £150 back," closely followed by "I have nothing else to do." Wilde makes one thing clear: the projected play is something quite different from anything he has attempted before. But he does not commit himself on the nature of that difference. Nor, significantly, does he claim that he could accomplish this one in a week, or even three, the amount of time he predicted it would take to beat the Pineros and the Joneses with *Lady Windermere's Fan*.[4] A play "with no real serious interest," full of fun and wit, may take longer: a tougher assignment than being serious. He rewrote and revised *Earnest* extensively, both pre- and post-production.

Wilde was fully as conscious and sensitive as George Bernard Shaw about his status as a playwright. Within the continuing debate about the state of modern British drama in the 1890s (for example, the *Pall Mall Magazine*'s 1893 question, "Is the Theatre Growing Less Popular?"),[5] William Archer had recently thrown down the gauntlet. In the *Fortnightly Review* of 1 May 1894, he states in his article "Some Recent Plays":

> One simple and significant fact is sufficient, if not to excite alarm, at least to give us pause. It is this: *during the past six months not a single serious play has been produced with success.* Under the term "serious play" I include everything that is not farce, burlesque, or Adelphi melodrama; so that, in other words, every play of the smallest artistic pretension produced between October 1st, 1893, and April 15th, 1894, has been a more or less flagrant failure.[6]

Archer went further. Since May 1893, only two "serious" plays had met with any success. Both the date and the choice of plays would have been irritating to Wilde. The date excluded *A Woman of No Importance*. It allowed Archer to cite Arthur Wing Pinero's *The Second Mrs. Tanqueray* (1893) and Sydney Grundy's *Sowing the Wind* (1893) as the two successes. While he thought *Sowing the Wind* "pretty and sympathetic," it was none the less a "comparatively trivial" piece of work (601). The omission of *A Woman of No Importance* was probably a deliberate act on Archer's part. In "Plays and Acting of the Season" (*Fortnightly Review,* August 1893), Archer's summary was casually dismissive: "Were it not for *The Second Mrs. Tanqueray*, the season, however delightful, must have left behind it a certain sense of humiliation. Against a whole regiment of foreign masterpieces, we should have had nothing of our own worth bringing into the field except one single scene in *A Woman of No Importance*."[7] Archer's attitude to Wilde was ambivalent. He recognized Wilde's class but always hinted at some reservation. In his review of *A Woman of No Importance*, Archer had written: "The one essential fact about Mr. Oscar Wilde's dramatic work is that it must be taken on the very highest plane of modern English drama, and furthermore, that it stands alone on that plane. In intellectual calibre, artistic competence –

ay, and in dramatic instinct to boot – Mr. Wilde has no rival among his fellow-workers for the stage."[8]

This remark prompted Wilde to write to Archer in April 1893, saying with what pleasure he had read his "luminous, brilliant criticism" of his play; there were of course points where he differed, but "I love our modes of difference" (*Complete Letters*, 561). Archer, naturally enough, took Wilde's side in the matter of *Salomé* (1893) and the Lord Chamberlain's refusal to grant it a licence. In the *Fortnightly Review* retrospective, Archer had also praised one play of Wilde's, *Lady Windermere's Fan* – "one of the two thoroughly well-written, or really *written*, plays of our time."[9] (The other play that Archer favored was W.E. Henley and Robert Louis Stevenson's *Beau Austin* [1884]). But, in a possibly annoying and distinctly condescending comparison between Wilde and J.M. Barrie, Archer offered his advice as to how these two might achieve "serious art on the higher plane" ("The Drama in the Doldrums," 167). "A play," he wrote, "is neither to be improvised like a comic song nor to be inlaid like a sonnet-sequence" (160). Mr. Wilde would therefore have to conquer his "fatal fastidiousness, not to say indolence" (160). Only then, ran the argument through the series of articles, would he achieve, like Pinero, a play of European merit.

Provoked by Archer, Wilde rose to the challenge: to write a play devoid of "real interest," lacking in apparent seriousness, very much *fin-de-siècle*, but resolutely refusing to engage with contemporary issues. The mode was deliberately a mode of difference. Archer, in 1892, had championed Pinero's *The Profligate* (1889) as the kind of play that would make audiences take British drama seriously. Wilde's new play would contain a battery of harmless profligates.

Wilde had many reference points for his play, and no model. Russell Jackson has pointed out some of the standard ingredients that *Earnest* lacks: no raisonneur, no idealistic young woman (each an element that Archer might have expected in a play to be taken seriously).[10] More surprisingly, the play featured no real decadence. Kerry Powell and Joseph Donohue have ingeniously and convincingly identified numerous analogies and parallels in contemporary and recent Victorian drama, including farce.[11] Wilde, as his September 1894 letter to Alexander indicates, was well aware of his unusual take on the material: the dialogue was "sheer comedy" ("the best I have ever written"), the idea farcical (*Complete Letters*, 610). It could not be made part of a repertoire of serious or classical pieces, "except for fun" – "as Irving plays Jeremy Diddler to show the Bostonians how versatile he is, and how a man who can realise

Hamlet for us, can yet hold his own with the best of fantastic farce-play-ers" (*Complete Letters*, 610).

Wilde was both flattering and tempting Alexander by the comparison. But the reference to James Kenney's *Raising the Wind* (1803), appropriate enough in Wilde's desperately straitened circumstances, highlights one more strand of farcical comedy which Wilde was exploiting. The heiress-hunting, penniless young man's excursion to the country is a staple of eighteenth-century comedy, and Jeremy Diddler (quite as hungry as Algernon Moncrieff but not nearly so well dressed) is a particularly shameless representative of the type. There are a number of correspondences between the plays. These include Diddler's embarrassing lack of relations, his captivation of a blue-stocking, fiction-loving garden wench, Peggy Plainway, and the rapid reversal of his status when it is suddenly revealed that he has "the trifling collateral recommendation of ten thousand pounds" in his pocket.[12] Perhaps the most striking echo is Peggy's dismay, when she discovers that her wooer is not, as she had fondly supposed at Bath, "the all-accomplished Mortimer" (15), but bears a name with little music, and no vibrations:

PEGGY: And isn't that your name, then?
DIDDLER: No, my dear, my legitimate appellation is Mr Diddler.
PEGGY: What? and am I to have a lover of the name of Diddler? (46)

But these, and other motifs, are the mere building blocks for Wilde's construction. The architecture is his.

Wilde wrote *Earnest* during (or around) a family summer holiday at Worthing, and the seaside resort and its locality has given a number of names to the text. Apart from the overwhelmingly dull and respectable John Worthing himself, there is the champagne-quaffing Lord Shore-ham, and the play's one-time working-title, "Lady Lancing." But *Earnest* owes rather more than names to the context in which Wilde wrote it. It is a holiday play, a stylish excursion, and an elegant and deliberate relax-ation from the serious: a delicate act of imagination flowering exotically within the ritual of the annual exodus from London. Worthing was a mildly surprising venue for the Wildes' summer holiday. The Sussex town first became fashionable when Princess Amelia stayed there for a sea-bathing cure, at what was thought to be a safe distance from the more rackety pleasures of the Prince Regent at Brighton. A thirty-minute train journey from Brighton, and only two hours from Victoria, it had a quieter, less raffish ambience than its smarter neighbor. Wor-

thing was marketed strongly in the 1890s as "The Madeira of England" –
the nearest point to the sea from St Paul's cathedral, with a death rate of
only eleven to the thousand.

This particular advertising campaign – "Worthing for complete restoration to health unrivalled in the United Kingdom" – suffered a sharp
setback in 1893, when the best efforts of the Sanitary Committee failed
dismally, and 188 people died of typhoid. The resulting loss of popularity may have been the reason Constance Wilde could take 5 The Espla-
nade for 10 guineas a week. This was something of a squash for the
family, in addition to the maid, the horrid Swiss governess, the cook, the
cook's little boy, and Arthur the valet. Besides, there was no separate
writing room for Wilde. But Worthing, with its sands, was a much more
suitable place for a family holiday than crowded, pebbly, and ostenta-
tious Brighton. While the local paper could not boast quite the sono-
rous roll-call of the well-connected who were announced as staying at
the Grand or the Metropole Hotels in Brighton, the Worthing Visitors'
List contained enough titles to create the impression of a fashionable
masquerade. On Monday, 13 August, at the close of a glorious summer
day, the *Worthing Gazette* reported: "the long line of houses on the front"
had "suddenly passed into the possession of the customary number of
summer visitors, who were to be seen on the balconies or at the open
windows."[13] Meanwhile, "on the opposite side the extensive promenade
was thronged with people," to be entertained by the Rhine Band, or
"the whimsicalities of the Royal Olympians," or "the agreeable vocal performances of the unknown noblemen in black dominoes and unim-
peachable evening dress." Not quite Dieppe, perhaps, but a gesture in
its direction.

Wilde, these summer months, was juggling his several lives. The an-
guished account of the October episode with Douglas, the Bunburying-
in-earnest and the farcical interludes in lodgings and in expensive
Brighton hotels, recounted blow for blow in *De Profundis*, overlays the
summer idyll with a dark, retrospective narrative. But for all the occasional tension created by Douglas' visits – wished for yet at the same
time unwelcome – there is evidence that there was a good deal of family
happiness. Constance wrote to her brother on 31 August that her son
Cyril had gone out with his father in a boat and that Oscar had given
her a plot for a book she was planning.[14] Vyvyan Holland's recollections
of his childhood may embrace Worthing: "Perhaps my father was at his
best with us at the seaside. He was a powerful swimmer; he also thoroughly enjoyed sailing and fishing ... I preferred helping my father to

build sand-castles, an art in which he excelled."[15] These were traditional pleasures of an English seaside-holiday, even in the stormy summer of 1894. "I am away by the seaside," Wilde wrote to William Rothenstein, "bathing and sailing and amusing myself" (*Complete Letters*, 601). Amusing himself included playwriting. As Ada Leverson recalled: "There had been rumours for weeks that at Worthing Oscar was writing a farce, and how each day he wrote a part of it and each evening he read it to the Elect – his wife, children and a few friends"[16] – a series of previews.

There was, too, inevitably, a second kind of private holiday going on, a sub-text of sailing and bathing in the company of Conway, interspersed with the doomed attempts to reconcile Douglas' visits with family life. Douglas and Worthing did not go together, as Wilde feared, and would discover only too painfully. But playwriting on holiday does not seem to have been a problem, judging by Wilde's relaxed comments to Douglas: "My play is really very funny: I am quite delighted with it. But it is not shaped yet. It lies in Sibylline leaves about the room, and Arthur has twice made a chaos of it by 'tidying up.' The result, however, was rather dramatic" (*Complete Letters*, 602). The shaping progressed rapidly. In six weeks or so, the first draft was ready to be typed by Mrs. Marshall's agency. Wilde, having taken his new comic mode to that state of readiness, was ready to construct another modern play. He scribbled off the tragic love scenario to Alexander, which eventually became *Mr. and Mrs. Daventry*. Worthing was proving a highly productive interlude.

Meanwhile, the public framework of entertainment in Worthing continued, and in this respect Wilde, less predictably, participated. He may have been longing to go to Paris, where, as he told Douglas, "they say one wears flannels and straw hats and dines in the Bois" (*Complete Letters*, 594), or to Dieppe. But he decided to play the role of the well-known artist on holiday, and patronize the local events.

Brighton and Worthing catered for a London clientele. Once the London season was over, society could for a time enjoy out-of-town pleasures with the minimum of disruption and inconvenience: Goodwood Races and Cowes Regatta were within easy reach. Using the fast and frequent rail service, the London theater companies could manage the journey to the South Coast comfortably. During that summer, in Sussex, Wilde could have seen Cissie Loftus, Max Beerbohm's muse, at the Pavilion, as well as the "terribly old-fashioned" *The Foundling* (1894), a seaside farce actually set in Brighton, at the Theatre Royal, Brighton. In Worthing, there was the D'Oyly Carte's *Utopia Ltd* (1893); Brandon Thomas's *Charley's Aunt* (1892) was also playing. Again, in Brighton, there was a production of Grundy's *The New Woman* (1894) with Rose LeClercq, the first Lady Bracknell, as the dragonish Lady Wargrave.

Wilde's presence in Worthing intrigued the Brighton papers. They used the opening of *The New Woman* to drop his name, claiming that his "latest mots" were discussed in the foyer of the Theatre Royal, and commenting that during his stay at Worthing "he had of course been made a very public character."[17] On 22 August the *Worthing Gazette* reported him "busily flitting about" in a small rowing boat on the town's annual Lifeboat Day.[18] On 7 September he and someone the paper styled "Lord William Douglas," together with the Mayor, were the patrons of a concert given by the Olympian Quartet in the Assembly Rooms – a group described by Wilde in his letters as "the vagabond singers of the sands" (*Complete Letters*, 608). Eight days later Wilde has moved even more center stage, presiding over the Worthing "Venetian" Water Carnival, and distributing the prizes. The event was reported, with different glosses, in the Worthing, Brighton, and national papers. This carnival, which took place on the evening of Saturday, September 15, was a kind of grand climax to the holiday season. The pier was illuminated with Japanese lanterns and bracket lamps, and decorated with a device, in colored lights, that declared "Go it Worthing!" Mr. Wright's Band performed on a steam launch, and the Pier Band played in the Pavilion. Colored fire burned, fireworks were discharged, and the centerpiece was a "Procession of Illuminated Boats."[19]

Wilde made the end-of-evening speech, and distributed the prizes. As this speech has not been reported since 1894, it is worth quoting at some length. It reveals Wilde, for once, not having to strive unduly for effect. He began by congratulating Worthing on "the extremely beautiful scene that evening."[20] He thought, however, there was one thing that marred the regatta. There was a sailing boat, not belonging to Worthing, but coming from some wicked, tasteless spot, bearing a huge advertisement of a patent pill. He hoped that boat would never be allowed to enter Worthing again. (Much laughter – it was presumably a Brighton boat.) He considered that such a charming town would become one of the first watering places on the South Coast. It had beautiful surroundings and lovely long walks, which he recommended to other people but did not take himself. (More laughter) ("No gentleman ever takes exercise," in the four-act version of *Earnest*.)[21] Alluding to the "EXCELLENT WATER SUPPLY," he said he was told that the total abstainers who visited Worthing were so struck with the purity and excellence of its water that they wished everybody to drink nothing else. (Laughter)

Then, in a finale that seems to fit effortlessly with the tone of the play he has by this moment completed, he concluded:

> Above all things, he was delighted to observe in Worthing one of the most important things, having regard to the fashion of the age – the faculty of offering pleasure. To his mind few things were so important as a capacity for being amused, feeling pleasure, and giving it to others. He held that whenever a person was happy he was good, although, perhaps, when he was good he was not always happy. (Laughter). There was no excuse for anyone not being happy in such surroundings. This was his first visit, but it would certainly not be his last. (Applause).

Clearly that Saturday evening Wilde was at his most charming. He talked as though he were answering a reporter's question: "Mr. Wilde, what brings you to Worthing?" "Oh, pleasure, pleasure! What else should bring one anywhere?" The first draft of his play was complete; it was a moment of achievement to celebrate. Wilde received a vote of thanks in the Worthing Pier Pavilion from Captain Fraser, and was praised in the Worthing press for his "good-nature." The Brighton *Society*, a touch more sophisticated in its angle, commented that "there was a good deal more in the same vein of semi-cynical banter with which the author of 'The Decay of the Art of Lying' [*sic*] has made us rather agreeably familiar."[22] Pleasure was mutual; and fireworks were arcing in the night sky over the sea.

In London, the very same day, Robert Hichens' *The Green Carnation* was published: a malicious squib, tied to Wilde's coat-tails, and smartly brushed aside. But Hichens' satire had hit his mark, with the conversation of Lord Reggie and Amarinth so blatantly echoing that of Douglas and Wilde: "there is an art even in missing a train, Reggie."[23] The holiday was coming to an end. Constance Wilde returned to London. Wilde's children went back to school. Wilde, revising his play, entered upon one of his most tortuous episodes with Douglas, with the scene shifting to the Grand Hotel, and the lobby of the Metropole, foreshadowing T.S. Eliot's Mr. Eugenides in "The Fire Sermon" section of *The Waste Land* (1922). Wilde seemed on the point of distancing himself from Douglas when he read of the tragic death of Douglas' eldest brother, Viscount Drumlanrig; exasperation turned to sympathy, and the tragic mode was sealed. Derision on Clapham Junction platform, as Wilde waited for the train to take him to jail, would soon replace the applause of Worthing Pier.

Out of these circumstances emerges *Earnest*, unharmed by its complex textual history, revised, reduced, trimmed for performance, retouched for publication, but still holding the sense of holiday and exquisitely shaped enjoyment. Wilde, surrounded on the south coast by Victorian farce and seaside entertainment, created a farcical comedy of elegance and decorum, as urbane and economical as an Aubrey Beardsley caricature. By embracing the trivial, he contrived to capture the texture of late-Victorian society, transforming its relentless observation of convention into a comic but unnerving masquerade, through which the characters pursue their ideals of form and style, manipulating circumstances to fulfil their desires. By substituting fiction – or imagination, or invention, or lying – for fact, he effortlessly called into question the whole fabric of society, without having to raise a single real or serious issue. His fable, told in such wonderfully musical and expansive phrasing, has a completeness that defies reality, holding it at bay while the holiday mood prevails. For the serious, Ibsenite William Archer, thirsting for plays of European significance, Wilde offers a trivial comedy.

I do not believe that in this play Wilde was specifically working out either his sexuality or his Irishness, or his ambivalent status as an artist, although the nature of his new form of drama created room for those meanings. The dramatic world he fashioned looked and sounded sufficiently like contemporary society to be mistaken for it. The clothes were up to the minute. The politics, or the political references, struck the contemporary note. The names had the right ring about them. There is probably not much more to be said about the names, which have been exhaustively treated by many commentators. But the more one reads in the newspapers and documents of the 1890s, the more one is struck by Wilde's uncanny gift of selection in this area. In the Court section of Kelly's Directory (1891) are four Cardews, six Fairfaxes, eight assorted Moncrieffs, and even three Markbys; but, needless to add, no one by the dull, solid name of Worthing. Closer to the point of composition, in the weekly guest lists of the Grand Hotel and the Metropole, Brighton, for August 1894, Wilde's own name appears, along with those of Mrs. Daubeny and Mrs. Bunbury. Meanwhile, featuring in almost every issue of the *Brighton Guardian and Hove Recorder*, as part of the staple crime report, was the Deputy Stipendiary Magistrate of the Brighton Bench, Mr. R.C.S. Bunbury.

In *Earnest*, Wilde caricatured social life, birth, baptism, betrothal, marriage, and death as glittering farce. The fireworks dazzled, intricate patterns of pleasure. Wilde, at Alexander's insistence, removed most of the darker shadows that touched the play, most notably the arrest of Algernon for debt. But even so, the text remains highly charged, ready to develop in many directions. It is the women, and principally Lady Bracknell, who carry the most lethal armory. Lady Bracknell delivers the cruelest line in the play: "Is this Miss Prism a female of repellent aspect, remotely connected with education?" (97). She also captures the exquisite hypersensitivity of public decorum in her remark to Gwendolen: "Come, dear, we have already missed five, if not six, trains. To miss any more might expose us to comment on the platform" (96) – a sequence of thought both bafflingly absurd and at the same time convincing. There was, after all, little privacy for the fashionable, or would-be fashionable, in late-Victorian England.

It is that sort of apparently random detail that anchors *Earnest* to social life. It also forms a bridge between Wilde and the English drama of the 1950s and 1960s. Wilde's explosion of English social life was conducted through language, through his ability to replicate and distort the infinitely nuanced weapons of conversation. He creates, in Eugene Ionesco's phrase, a "false" language – artificial, theatrical, entertaining, but not quite "real."[24] Tom Stoppard, Joe Orton, and Harold Pinter, each in different ways outsiders, deploy comparable skills in selection and imitation of English speech patterns, creating an illusion of Englishness that they undermine even as they construct it. It is no accident that Wilde serves as a common reference point for later twentieth-century comedy: Orton's *What the Butler Saw* (1969), Stoppard's *Travesties* (1974), or, more recently, Mark Ravenhill's *Handbag* (1998). In *Look Back in Anger* (1957), John Osborne, with eye and ear sharply attuned to his theater audience, has Jimmy Porter exclaim (in response to Helena's "I think you're a very tiresome young man"): "Oh dear! Oh dear! My wife's friends! Pass Lady Bracknell the cucumber sandwiches"[25]: class warfare in a single sentence. Archer, who arguably provoked Wilde into his new mode of writing, had the grace (unlike Shaw) to capitulate before it: "What can a poor critic do with a play which raises no principle, whether of art or of morals, creates its own canons and conventions, and is nothing but an absolutely wilful expression of an irresistibly witty personality?"[26] Archer accepted *Earnest* temporarily, but he was a serial revisionist, and in *The Old Drama and the New* was briskly dismissive. Of the first three "serious comedies," he wrote that Wilde treated the art of the dramatist "with contemptuous insincerity."[27] "[T]here was no real substance in his work," he added (304); "one feels that in his heart he despised the stories he was telling." Even of *Earnest*, which he calls a "delightful piece of original humour," he comments that in the last act it "degenerates into rather poor farce."

To argue against Archer and Shaw, I would say that it is Wilde's embracing of farce, and of insincerity, in this play that gave him new freedom. One moment of dialogue in the original scenario strikes a *fin-de-siècle*, modern note. The guardian, Bertram Ashton, is on his knees proposing when the "Duchess" enters: "Mamma, this is no place for you" (461). In the manuscript notebook in the Clark Library, this has been expanded into the following exchange:

> GWEN: Leave the room, Mamma. This is no place for you.
> DUCHESS: Mr. Worthing rise from this semi-recumbent posture – it is most unbefitting.[28]

The child orders her mother from the room. The mother blocks the proposal not on grounds of suitability, but of style. And, significantly, the traditional image of comic unity, the proposal, is here placed near the beginning of the play, relegating it to a mere gesture, while its counterpoint, the "wicked" double life, is never illustrated, only suggested.

A century on, critics are still teased by Wilde, though we have the excuse of a hundred or so years of stage life to continue to provoke us; and Wilde's play has become part of the universally recognized classic repertoire, a final riposte to Archer. With all its artifice, *Earnest* concludes with a spectacular set piece of pleasure and affirmation, in which the self-created John Worthing christens himself to his own immense satisfaction. This is Wilde's image of unity, of harmony, of family life: the importance that being Ernest brings him; the knowledge of who he is, of who his parents were (and you could not get much more serious than an Indian army general); a brother, who will also be a kind of son-in-law, as the husband of his ward; an aunt, welcome or unwelcome as the case may be; and a bride who is also his first cousin. As Richard Pine has described him: "Wilde himself was the superbly undramatic dramatist because he too could not understand why he continued to put before his audiences the archetypally wounded family."[29]

Wilde was trapped between the *fin-de-siècle* drawing-rooms of Mayfair and the idea of the happy English home, between "chicken to the sound of flutes" in the Metropole, and building castles on Worthing sands. V.S. Pritchett called Samuel Butler's novel *The Way of All Flesh* (1903), featuring that other Ernest (Ernest Pontifex), "one of the time-bombs of literature": "One thinks of it lying in Butler's desk at Clifford's Inn for thirty years, waiting to blow up the Victorian family and with it the whole great pillared and balustraded edifice of the Victorian novel."[30] Wilde's farcical fable, quite as explosive, is transmitted through the travesty of family relations, each individual spinning off into the world of his or her desires. And in the farcical third act that baffled Archer, Wilde conjures a fictional unity, by means of the magical black bag, and the secret formula in the Faustian book of the Army Lists: a theatrical coup so blatant that for a moment, blinded by the pyrotechnics, you do not notice the flaws in Ernest's coming home. The self-christening certainly triumphs – although, as the four-act version indicates, a more thorough re-birth may be appropriate. We can see this idea in Lady Bracknell's advice to Dr. Chasuble to have Miss Prism baptized without delay: "To be born again would be of considerable advantage to her" (127). A hundred years on, we see the cracks more clearly, as the play's holiday gaiety evaporates.

It is interesting to place *Earnest* beside the second great English comedy to be written in Worthing: Harold Pinter's *The Homecoming* (1965), another fable of brothers, which also concludes with the vivid, but this time silent, theatrical image of a wounded family; or to see Wilde's play as foreshadowing an image from that earlier Pinter seaside comedy of menace, *The Birthday Party* (1958) – where Stanley, the concert pianist, a broken artist, returns ever so quietly to London, the party over.

Earnest, like *An Ideal Husband*, carries the indicator: "Time: The Present." But while *An Ideal Husband* has specific social and political resonance for the later twentieth century, Wilde's farce escapes more easily to take its place within the international repertory of the twentieth and the twenty-first centuries. In terms of mood and tone, there is very little distance between it and the work of Pinter; Lady Bracknell prompts Mrs. Rafi in Edward Bond's *The Sea* (1973) or Lady Croom in Tom Stoppard's *Arcadia* (1993). Wilde strikes the postmodern note. By avoiding so-called serious issues, he creates a new kind of comedy, in which his characters, impatient with society, invent themselves on the other side of the looking glass. From Worthing, a burst of fireworks; and for a moment, the actors make you forget the darkness that follows.

Notes

1 Oscar Wilde, "To George Alexander," ? July 1894, Wilde, *The Complete Letters*, ed. Merlin Holland and Rupert Hart-Davis (London: Fourth Estate, 2000),

595; further page references appear in parentheses. This letter was mislaid for many years. It appears in Wilde, *Letters*, ed. Hart-Davis (London: Rupert Hart-Davis, 1962), 359; this fragment was reprinted from A.E.W. Mason, *Sir George Alexander and the St. James's Theatre* (London: Macmillan, 1935), 74. A typescript of the whole letter is in the William Andrews Clark Memorial Library; see Peter Raby, "The Making of *The Importance of Being Earnest*," *Times Literary Supplement*, 20 December 1991, 13. The manuscript letter was sold at Sotheby's, New York, on 7 December 1999, for $70,000, which must put it in the running for the most valuable scenario ever written. See also Peter Raby, "The Origins of *The Importance of Being Earnest*," *Modern Drama* 37 (1994), 139–47; and Ian Small, *Oscar Wilde Revalued: An Essay and New Materials and Methods of Research* (Greensboro, NC: ELT Press, 1993), 65–68; further page reference appears in parentheses.

2 Alphonse Conway was a newspaper boy whom Wilde met on the beach at Worthing. He was cited by Queensberry as part of his Plea of Justification in the libel action. See Wilde, "To Lord Alfred Douglas," 13 August 1894, in Wilde, *Complete Letters*, 602.

3 One of the later complications with Alexander over *The Importance of Being Earnest* involved American rights. Alexander was interested in the possibility of touring the new comedy, or farce, in the United States; Wilde argued that it would be an unsuitable vehicle for a "romantic actor of modern and costume pieces"; more pertinently, he hoped "to make at least £3000 in the States with this piece, so what sum could I ask you for, with reference to double rights?" ("To George Alexander," ? September 1894, *Complete Letters*, 610).

4 Remark attributed to Wilde by Frank Harris, *Oscar Wilde, His Life and Confessions*, 2 vols. (New York: privately printed, 1916), I, 139.

5 William Archer, "Is the Theatre Growing Less Popular?" *Pall Mall Magazine* 1 (1893), 353.

6 William Archer, "Some Recent Plays," *Fortnightly Review* n.s. 56 (1894), 600; further page references appear in parentheses.

7 William Archer, "Plays and Acting of the Season," *Fortnightly Review*, n.s. 54 (1893), 255.

8 Archer's review of *A Woman of No Importance* appears in the *World*, 26 April 1893, and is reprinted in *The Theatrical "World" for 1893* (London: Walter Scott, 1894), 105.

9 William Archer, "The Drama in the Doldrums," *Fortnightly Review*, n.s. 52 (1892), 161; further page references appear in parentheses.

10 Russell Jackson, "The Importance of Being Earnest," in Peter Raby, ed., *The Cambridge Companion to Oscar Wilde* (Cambridge: Cambridge University Press, 1997), 161–77.

11 Kerry Powell, *Oscar Wilde and the Theatre of the 1890s* (Cambridge: Cambridge University Press, 1990); and *Oscar Wilde's* The Importance of Being Earnest: *A Reconstructive Critical Edition of the Text of the First Production, St. James's Theatre, London, 1895*, ed. Joseph Donohue and Ruth Berggren (Gerrards Cross: Colin Smythe, 1995). Powell suggests that Wilde might have seen *The Foundling* (1894) on a visit to London, while he was in the process of writing *The Importance of Being Earnest* (108–10). Wilde could more simply, and economically, have seen it in Brighton; but what is really striking is the way in which Wilde effortlessly assimilates and transforms popular material and motifs.

12 James Kenney, *Raising the Wind: A Farce in Two Acts*, second edition (New York: D. Longworth, 1804), 45; further page references appear in parentheses.

13 *Worthing Gazette*, 15 August 1894, 6. For the social background and development of Worthing, see D. Robert Elleray, *Worthing: Aspects of Change* (Chichester: Phillimore, 1985). Ten guineas may have been less than the cost of a Brighton house but it was a considerable sum for Wilde, who was overdrawn at the bank. A visit to Alexander at the Garrick Club produced enough money to enable him to pay the rent, and Cyril's school fees.

14 Autograph letter, Constance Wilde to Otho Lloyd, 31 August 1894, Merlin Holland Collection.

15 Vyvyan Holland, *Son of Oscar Wilde* (London: Rupert Hart-Davis, 1954), 54–55.

16 Ada Leverson, *Letters to the Sphinx from Oscar Wilde and Reminiscences of the Author* (London: Duckworth, 1930), 28.

17 *Brighton Society*, 15 September 1894, 5.

18 *Worthing Gazette*, 22 August 1894, 5.

19 See *Worthing Gazette*, 19 September 1894, 3. Wilde's role as "patron of aquatic enterprises" was also picked up in the London *Globe*: "At Worthing, last evening, he presented the prizes for the best decorated boat at a Venetian fete, and made the highly original observation that anything as pretty he had never seen before. It was not brilliant, but then no one expects the great wit to say brilliant things in the provinces." "Captious criticism, this," commented the writer of "Local Notes" in the *Worthing Gazette*: "The writer should rather have given Mr. Wilde praise for his good-nature" (19 September 1894, 5).

20 *Worthing Gazette*, 19 September 1894, 3.

21 Oscar Wilde, *The Importance of Being Earnest: A Trivial Comedy for Serious People*, ed. Russell Jackson (London: Benn, 1980) 110; further page references appear in parentheses.

22 *Brighton Society*, 15 September 1894, 5.

23 [Robert Hichens,] *The Green Carnation*. The Pioneer Series (London: Heinemann, 1894), 211.

24 Eugene Ionesco, *The Joke's on Us, Arena*, BBC2 Television, 1989.

25 John Osborne, *Look Back in Anger* (London: Faber, 1957), 50–51.

26 William Archer, *World*, 20 February 1895, reprinted in *The Theatrical "World"
for 1895* (London: Walter Scott, 1896), 57.

27 William Archer, *The Old Drama and the New* (Boston: Small, Maynard and
Company, 1923), 303–04; further page references appear in parentheses.

28 "*A Woman of No Importance, The Importance of Being Earnest*: MS Notes of Aphorisms and Short Speeches for Use in These Two Plays," AMS Notebook, 1894,
Clark Library.

29 Richard Pine, *The Thief of Reason: Oscar Wilde and Modern Ireland* (Dublin: Gill
and Macmillan, 1995), 271.

30 V.S.Pritchett, "A Victorian Son," in Pritchett, *The Living Novel* (London:
Chatto and Windus, 1946), 102.

chapter seven

Master Wood's Profession: Wilde and the Subculture of Homosexual Blackmail in the Victorian Theatre

LAURENCE SENELICK

I

In 1987, when Richard Ellmann's monumental life of Oscar Wilde appeared to great acclaim, some readers were beguiled not so much by a biographical revelation or critical *aperçu*, but by a picture. At the end of a sheaf of more or less familiar illustrations came a photograph of a fleshy figure in the garb of an Oriental houri, stretching out her arms to a shaggy head on a platter. The caption read laconically: "Wilde in costume as Salomé."[1] The only other information provided was an attribution to the Guillot de Saix Collection, by way of the well-known Roger-Viollet, a French photographic agency that provides an archival service.

As a collector of theatrical imagery with a special interest in nineteenth-century photographs, I was instantly suspicious. Why had so incendiary a picture never been seen before? Why was there no mention of it or its provenance in the copious text, or for that matter in any of Wilde's letters or the reminiscences of his contemporaries? Why was the caption so unforthcoming about the photographer or the circumstances? A perusal of Norman Page's day-by-day chronology of Wilde's life reveals no surreptitious trips to a studio.[2] It would have been no casual matter for Wilde to break from his routines, find a costumier to provide an odalisque outfit that would both suggest the unproduced *Salomé* and accommodate his ample figure, set up an appointment with a photographer capable both of recording the transvestitic stunt and keeping his mouth shut, and then, presumably with the help of an experienced dresser, adopt a series of attitudes. At elaborate sessions such as this, photographers usually took a full range of poses: Why had only this one survived? And, more significantly, what was the impulse behind this masquerade, especially if the photographs were not circulated, even clandestinely?

Fishy as this alleged portrait might seem to anyone familiar with the vagaries of pictorial documentation and the ease with which photographs can be manipulated, students of the word fell over themselves to add this *pièce judiciaire* to their dock briefs. In *Sexual Anarchy* (1990), her study of gender and culture at the *fin de siècle*, Elaine Showalter reproduced the picture with the additional invention that it had "been taken in Paris"; she must have assumed (erroneously) that no English photographer would have dared.[3] Showalter, however, was dubious enough to dub the picture a "mystery" and avoided basing her assumptions upon it.

Not so Marjorie Garber. In *Vested Interests* (1992), her attempt to demonstrate that the transvestite stands at the crux of all civilization, she praised the image as "not a send-up but a radical reading that tells the truth ... by playing with the possibility of regendering the gaze." Garber was so eager to establish the female role of Salomé, written with Sarah Bernhardt in mind, as a site for cross-dressing that she made the photograph the centerpiece of an extended but essentially inapposite discussion. Her conclusion was: "Thus: Wilde the author, Wilde the libertine, Wilde the homosexual, as Salomé. The transvestite Wilde is yet another version of the 'to seem' that replaces the 'to have' in Lacan's trajectory of desire."[4] That is a lot of intellectual baggage to transport on so rattletrap a conveyance.

While American cultural critics were making a meal of the image, the first person to call it spinach was a Wilde expert, John Stokes, who noted a similarity between the costume and that of the actress Leonora Sengera in a German photograph in the same collection. Stokes concluded that she remained an enigma.[5] No wonder: he had got the name wrong. It was a German scholar at Braunschweig who, following up a hunch that the Salomé in question was not Wilde's but Richard Strauss's, tried to track down the soprano Leonore Sengern. In the course of his investigations, however, he turned up in the 1907 volume of the German theatre journal *Bühne und Welt* pictures of yet another soprano, Alice Guszalewicz, as Salomé: same features, same costume, same embonpoint as in the Ellmann photograph.

The tale of how this studio portrait of a *zaftik* Hungarian diva came first into the de Saix collection, then was copied by Madame Roger-Viollet and eventually misidentified as Wilde in drag in the magazine *Le*

Monde in 1987; how Ellmann rejoiced at the discovery but could not personally verify it, and how after his death his less cautious publishers rushed to include it as a "scoop" – all this has all been recounted by Wilde's grandson Merlin Holland in the *Times Literary Supplement* in July 1994.[6]

It makes for a cautionary fable about leaping to conclusions in matters of iconography. But that is not the only reason I have gone into such detail about this particular image. The salient issue is why the picture, even when discredited by specialists, would not be relinquished by the cultural critics who had so eagerly embraced it. Confronted with what she called the "admittedly unwelcome" facts, Showalter continued to hedge, insisting that her homoerotic reading of *Salomé* was based on more than the photograph. Garber airily dismissed those facts as irrelevant to her reasoning, and suggested that those who insisted on the picture's inauthenticity were suffering anxiety about gay male identity.[7] The picture was too perfect to lose, for, as Garber had declared, it incarnated a welcome concept of Wilde the homosexual and libertine: everyone knows that gay men do drag as naturally as straight men do golf, so it should come as no surprise that Wilde wrote *Salomé* as an opportunity to get himself up as a nautch-girl. In Alan Sinfield's words, "[I]t is part of the modern stereotype of the gay man that he should want to dress as a woman, especially a fatally gorgeous one. Our cultures observe the Wilde they expect and want to see."[8]

At first glance, it seems a natural error to fall into: throughout his life, Wilde was noted for his dressing-up. To trace the languid aesthete in velvet knee breeches and shoulder-length locks to the beringed dandy with artificially waved hair – to pass from the lily to the green carnation – is to trace the trajectory of Wilde's self-making. His constant insistence on surface, his writing on dress, both male and female, his close attention to personal appearance are all aspects of his credo of the profundity of the superficial.

But that is precisely why his cross-dressing is improbable: it would have been so loaded a statement, so blatant a message, that it would have been conceived only with much forethought and followed up with much fanfare. A personality as exhibitionistic as Wilde's would not go to all that trouble and then bury the advertisement. And during his trials, when the prosecution was questioning hotel chambermaids about the stains on his bedsheets and pressing his renters about whether they wore female attire, such damning evidence as these photographs would surely have been produced.

In characterizing a Victorian sodomite, Showalter, Garber, and others were applying anachronistic assumptions. The defining attribute of a middle-class male homosexual in Europe at the turn of the last century was not an addiction to drag but a susceptibility to blackmail.

II

Blackmail was perfected in the nineteenth century. Although the word itself is a good old Tudor one, the special sense "to extort money under threat of revealing a discreditable secret" does not appear in print before the 1890s. It replaced the earlier word "delation," the act of denouncing citizens to the government; the new word shows that the impeachment had shifted from state service to private enterprise. Before personal blackmail can be effective, one needs a modicum of social mobility with its accompanying standards of etiquette and morality; the individual must be at risk of losing reputation, position or influence in the eyes of society at large. An accusation of base birth, for instance, can be injurious only in a society that prizes pedigree above all, and can harm only an individual seeking to move in a higher sphere than that of his origins.

Social position or the perception of social position teetered insecurely on paper foundations. The Victorian blackmailer's prime weapon, the purloined letter or the mislaid missive, was a recurring prop in the well-made play: Sardou's archetypal 1860 comedy *Les Pattes de mouche* (*A Scrap of Paper*) proliferated into sheaves of tell-tale correspondence in which the happiness of the heroes is inscribed. Rare was the society drama whose intrigue's unraveling did not depend upon the recovery of an indiscreet note.[9]

The prominence of blackmail as a *fin-de-siècle* plot motor is known to modern readers less through drama than through two adventures of Sherlock Holmes, "A Scandal in Bohemia" (1892) and the more scabrous "Charles Augustus Milverton" (1904). The theater and prose fiction, however, were alike in treating women and royalty being blackmailed for past indiscretions or adulteries. "True crime" paints a different picture. Police memoirs connect the first detailed accounts of blackmail with male homosexuality. Even in France, where homosexual acts were not illegal per se, blackmail was a lucrative business. Inspector Canler of the Sûreté enumerated "fear of scandal, fear of infamy, disgrace at depravity divulged" as sufficient motives for putting up and shutting up; he pointed out that few men were so insouciant as to go to the police and confess they were vile wretches in order to denounce someone else as a viler wretch.[10]

Where legislation criminalized sexual relations between males, the victim of extortion was in greater jeopardy. In England, from 1781 to 1828, evidence of both penetration and emission had to be proved before a man could be convicted of buggery, a capital offense; in consequence of this, most judges were cautious to convict. The Offences against the Person Act of 1828 repealed the need to demonstrate emission, but the death penalty was not abolished until 1861 when it was altered to penal servitude for life. At that time, the requirement to prove penetration was re-enacted. The supplementary Criminal Law Amendment Act of 1885, known as the Labouchère amendment after its deviser, made the commission of "any act of gross indecency" between males, not amounting to buggery, whether in private or public, subject to up to two years' imprisonment with or without hard labor.[11]

Although the Labouchère amendment had as its chief aim to prevent public indecency and the corruption of minors, it was so general in its phrasing, especially in stipulating the guilt of "any male person" "in public or private," that it immediately broadened the scope of the blackmailer's targets. These laws put the blackmailer in a privileged condition, for even if he were to be convicted of extortion, he was allowed to testify in court against his victim. Male prostitutes or merely attr⟩⟨tive young hoodlums were adept at enticing respectable clients into compromising situations and then soliciting money or valuables under threat of exposure. In the case of a closer relationship, inculpating correspondence may have been abstracted and held for ransom. Often the demand would come in the form of a letter stipulating the sum of money to be paid if the victim's name and conduct were not to be disclosed to the police, the newspapers or, occasionally, the victim's family. Less frequently cash or jewelry might be mulcted on the spot, under threats of violence or scandal.[12]

No voices were raised against the Labouchère amendment at the time of its passage. In contrast, the infamous §175 of the imperial penal code in Germany (1871), also known as a blackmailer's charter, was quickly assailed as unjust; attempts at law reform emphasized that it enforced the victimization of the homosexual, driven by innate and ineluctable impulses. In France, however, cartoons and popular journalism laid the blame at the homosexual's own door by promulgating two unsavory stereotypes: a depraved old gentleman, so jaded in his appetites that he seeks forbidden fruit, thus putting himself at the mercy of an effeminate youth or sturdy prole, who proffers the apple of Sodom. In *Teleny* (1893), the pornographic novel once attributed to Wilde, this typology is obvious in the episode where the narrator first discovers the existence of "tearoom" sex. Lurking outside a Parisian *pissoir,* he surreptitiously observes "an old, wiry, simpering man as shrivelled as a frost-bitten pippin" link up with "a workman – a strong and sturdy fellow ... a brawny man, with massive features; clearly, a fine specimen of a male."[13] In this standard scenario, the old gentleman is bourgeois, outwardly respectable and moneyed; the youth is plebeian and on the make: money, rather than mutual attraction, is the bond between them. Blackmail is in the offing.

This typology did more than emphasize the generation gap between the parties in the homosexual bargain by highlighting it as a "refinement" for worn-out voluptuaries. By insisting on the cash nexus between buyer and seller, it demonstrated how homosexuality crosses class lines. Syphilis had already intruded into the nineteenth-century consciousness as no respecter of persons, violating the middle-class family through its fathers' and sons' traffic with women of the lower orders. Homosexuality was seen to go even further in that direction. It was, declared a correspondent to a scientific journal in 1904, "the *only* vice which suppresses castes. The respectable man and the ruffian are equals – and talk to one another naturally, live together despite differences in upbringing. This vice achieves what charity cannot, equality among classes. Is this not sufficiently strange and unnerving?"[14] In this light, blackmail might be construed, not as persecution of a minority but as an emblem of the unsettling Masonic compact between homosexuals.

III

Blackmail had played no part in Wilde's life until he met Lord Alfred Douglas. Ellmann puts it neatly: "The love affair began under the threat of blackmail and under this threat it flourished" (384). Douglas was being blackmailed over an indiscreet letter and wrote to Wilde in the spring of 1892 craving help; Wilde put him in touch with his solicitor George Lewis who exchanged £100 for the incriminating document. On the basis of this arm's-length complicity, the writer and the lordling soon became lovers. It was Douglas who introduced Wilde to the world of rent-boys, working-class hustlers who benefited most from extortion, and Wilde took up the role of generous sugar daddy with gusto. He was apparently stimulated and excited by his proximity to blackmailers; his famous line about "feasting with panthers" allegorizes not indulging in illicit sex but rubbing elbows with extortionists who drop their aitches. (The panther in question was Robert Clibborn, a particularly hardened young hustler, who was later sentenced to seven years' penal servitude for blackmail.) To quote Ellmann again: "The gang – for Wood, Allen, Clibborn, and others constituted a gang – had obviously marked Wilde for prolonged milking. It was as tricky a game for them as for him, since there were heavier penalties for blackmail than for indecency. Their running such risks fascinated Wilde. Clibborn and Allen, in particular, he admired for waging 'an infamous war against life'" (434).[15]

One young poet who had fallen under Wilde's spell was John Moray Stuart-Young, a poorly educated boy from a Manchester slum. Stuart-Young purports that in June 1894 he and Wilde met for the first time at a dinner at the Savoy.

> There was present, besides myself and Wilde, a young man of about twenty, whom he introduced as "Freddy" Atkins. He seemed to be somewhat embarrassed by our conversation, for with my serious precociousness I insisted upon discussing Art and literature. Wilde must have found me vastly amusing, and I was in the Seventh Heaven of delight. I recall one remark with the poignancy of regret: "You are quite refreshing, Jack. If I only had a boy of your calibre near me oftener, I might be a better man."
>
> His conversation was brilliant and epigrammatic in the extreme. He was a wonderful talker, and even before such a mean audience as myself and "Freddy" Atkins (whom I afterwards learned was a youth with a yearning for music-hall life) he exerted him to please and interest.[16]

The three later went to the Haymarket to see *Lady Windermere's Fan*, Wilde holding Stuart-Young's hand all through it, and then walked about the streets. When Atkins returned home, Wilde accompanied fifteen-year-old Stuart-Young to the railway station. It was an innocent enough evening, with a clear distinction made between those aspirants to Parnassus whom Wilde chatted up and those cruder proles he bedded.

Stuart-Young's memoir of meetings with Wilde and the letters he printed in his tribute *Osrac, the Self-Sufficient*, issued by the Hermes Press in 1905, have been dismissed as "fibs and fictions," and a "tissue of lies,"[17] although even his harshest critic admits that some of his assertions are possible. Even though the self-congratulatory passage I have quoted is probably a fabrication, it indicates the way in which the imagination of Wilde's homosexual admirers and epigones cherished the confrontation of exquisite sensibility with rough trade. By 1905, Stuart-Young, obsessed with Wilde and fully apprised of the trial testimony, is drawn to invent his scenario: Wilde the dramatist staging a meeting between an impressionable, artistic teenager and a Cockney renter. That Stuart-Young should select Atkins for his mythic opposite is an indication that, even if he did not have first-hand experience of the sodomitic demi-monde, he was well read in its lore.

Freddy Atkins, a billiard-marker and part-time variety singer whom Wilde had taken to Paris the year before Stuart-Young's alleged dinner, made a career of blackmailing the gentlemen he escorted to his home. He later gave some of the most damning testimony against Wilde at his trial. The anonymous editor of *The Shame of Oscar Wilde*, privately printed in Paris in 1906, was to describe Atkins as "the lowest and most contemptible" of Wilde's sodomitical associates. He was apparently a well-known figure in the West End, haunting the louche promenades of music halls in make-up and corsets, often derided by his female competition. According to one well-informed source:

> He was an infallible judge of the class of man he wished to meet and rarely made a mistake. He would follow a likely subject about, stumble against him as though by accident and make an elaborate apology in mincing, female tones. Once in conversation with his "mark," he speedily contrived to make the latter aware that he did not object to certain proposals. He invariably permitted the beastly act before attempting blackmail, partly because it afforded him a stronger hold over his "victim" and partly because he rejoiced in the disgusting thing for its own sake.[18]

This was the individual whom Wilde in the witness box, even after Atkins had blackened his name, described as "bright and amusing."

Blackmail offered Wilde a challenge: he was flouting not only good society by his sexual indiscretions. He was also refusing to play by the subculture's rules and to tremble before threats of extortion. It becomes a recurrent trope in his correspondence. He writes to Alfred Douglas in March 1893, "I would sooner be rented all day [i.e. be blackmailed by every renter in London] than have you bitter, unjust, hating."[19] Later, in *De Profundis* (written in 1897), he would castigate Douglas for attempting emotional blackmail by posting compromising open postcards and public telegrams, a method Wilde says he should have left to Alfred Wood. It was the seventeen-year-old Wood who had stolen letters from Wilde's coat; when Wilde refused to pay the required ransom, Wood gave him back the letters, except for one which was to prove fatal at his trial. This was a missive of January 1893 containing the sentence, "I know Hyacinthus, whom Apollo loved so madly, was you in Greek days" (*Complete Letters*, 544). Both Wilde and Douglas were to confide in Pierre Louÿs that they were worried that Wood had withheld the letter for purposes of eventual blackmail. They were right.

In *De Profundis* Wilde chronicled the history of that letter for Douglas, incidentally illustrating how private lives were made public spectacles:

> It passes from you into the hands of a loathsome companion: from him to a gang of blackmailers; copies of it are sent about London to my friends, and to the manager of the theatre where my work is being performed ... Society is thrilled with the absurd rumours that I have had to pay a huge sum of money for having written an infamous letter to you: this forms the basis of your father's worst attack: I produce the original letter myself in Court to show what it really is; it is denounced by your father's Counsel as a revolting and insidious attempt to corrupt Innocence: ultimately it forms part of a criminal charge ... That is the result of writing you a charming letter. (*Complete Letters*, 702)

What Wilde has charted here is a contamination seeping throughout all strata of society that the nineteenth century usually configured as the syphilis contracted from prostitutes and borne into the bosom of the family or that Dickens, more cautiously, allegorized as an all-pervading smallpox in *Bleak House* (1853).

There were other incriminating missives which Wilde attempted to buy back and which eventually came into the hands of the Marquess of Queensberry; trial testimony reveals that Wilde paid £15 (more likely £35) for one letter and a bribe to Wood to go to America. It is evident that over time Wilde's bravado evaporated and, rather than the intrepid tamer of panthers, he dwindled into the ordinary punter at the mercy of a gang.

IV

Given these realities, it should not be surprising that the first English play to delineate a homoerotic relationship in a reasonably overt manner is entitled *The Blackmailers* (1894). What may cause surprise is that the blackmailers of the title are homosexual members of high society; and the surprise grows on learning that the equation of homosexuality and extortion is made not by some bulwark of entrenched morality, but by John Gray and Marc-André Raffalovich.

Gray, a minor poet who occasionally signed himself "Dorian," had been a close friend of Wilde's for a time; Wilde had defrayed the expenses of Gray's first book of poems. Raffalovich, a Russian-Jewish dilettante of flamboyant manner, saw himself as a rival of Wilde; it has been suggested that he and Gray began playwriting to emulate Wilde's recent success as a dramatist. The two men lived together first in London, then in Edinburgh. Gray had converted to Roman Catholicism in 1890; Raffalovich was to follow suit six years later. After Gray took orders, they both seem to have devoted their lives to expiating the sins of their youth. Raffalovich attacked his past homosexual practices with special animus in an article on "L'Affaire Oscar Wilde" contributed to the 1896 volume *Uranisme et Unisexualité*, published in a series edited by the criminologist Alexandre Lacassagne. As a prolific writer on "uranism and unisexuality" in European scientific journals, Raffalovich made the argument that "uranistes" were like anyone else and could play a valuable part in society once they "renounce sexual sensualities, and devote themselves to a celibacy which will not be sterile."[20] In his view, homosexual celibacy would be the equivalent of heterosexual marriage.

The Blackmailers received a single matinée performance at the Prince of Wales Theatre on 7 June 1894, the same month that Wilde was allegedly entertaining Freddie Atkins at dinner. Although the only extant copy of the play exhibits no blue-pencilling by the Lord Chamberlain's Office, the authors, according to Addison Bright in *The Theatre*, complained that the play as performed was "a mangled and mutilated version of the first four acts ... scene after scene ruined by cuts, omissions, impoverishment and slipshod" rehearsals.[21] Whatever the degree of mangling, the basic story remained.

Claud Price, an urbane and resourceful scoundrel of thirty-one, is blackmailing a married woman in high society who had once been his mistress; he is also cultivating a contempt for the world in Hyacinth Halford Dangar, the twenty-four-year old with whom he is infatuated. Hal (Hyacinth is an ancestral name, which only Claud uses) has already been practicing extortion on his college friends for some time and with some success. When he is exposed and rebuked by a family council and faced with exile to New Zealand, Hal briefly contemplates suicide, but a note from Claud arrives, inviting the disciple to join him in Paris: "I don't want to triumph without you, my pupil, soon to be my equal. Come. We understand each other now, and the World."[22]

The Times, which found the play "sordid and repulsive," described Hal as a "foolish youth" and Claud's influence over him as "sinister"; it noted that their "game appears to be perfectly well understood by the society in which they move, and which, nevertheless, tolerates them."[23] The dialogue portrays Claud as a drawing-room spell-binder, his "soothing ... voice" (26) uttering "long hypnotic speeches" (39); a young lady tells him: "The sound of your voice makes simply the old gurgling impression upon me, putting my senses to sleep" (39). *The Blackmailers* was written just at the time that Svengali, George Du Maurier's striking depiction of the degenerate Jew as mesmerist in *Trilby* (1894), was taking hold of the popular imagination. The conflation of Jew, artist, and sexual outsider was not unfamiliar, and, given Raffalovich's antecedents, might have triggered an unconscious shock of recognition. Claud, his origins obscure, also comes across as a tuppence-colored version of the romantic criminal, a loner who seeks a kindred spirit and finally finds him in the promising ephebe he molds into his weapon against society.

The English playwright Neil Bartlett perceptively equates the pair with Vautrin and Lucien de Rubempré in Balzac's *Les Illusions perdues* (1837) and *Les Splendeurs et misères des courtisanes* (1869).[24] The avowed intention of Gray and Raffalovich was to "trace the makings and downward career of a scoundrel," and Claud Price was seen by the critics as a "loathly object, played with due artistic loathsomeness" (*Theatre*, 1 July 1894, 37–38; *Lovesick*, 55). But it is clear that, like Balzac, the English authors had more fellow feeling for their scoundrels than for their respectable characters. Balzac's picaresque couple are not so well-matched: Lucien returns Vautrin's affection only on the level of filial gratitude, whereas Hal sets out to emulate his mentor's criminality and outdoes him in callousness (Prince Hal to Claud's Falstaff). The endurance of this kind of relationship as a homosexual trope is shown by its recent revival in the 1991 film *My Own Private Idaho*. On the one hand, Claud combines Vautrin's Olympian contempt for society with Svengali's skulking caddishness, but his own peculiar integrity prevents him from taking £2,000 to release Hal from his clutches. On the other hand, the disciple does betray his preceptor for money; Hal's rebellion against society is motivated less by love than by hatred of his family, a grotesque cartoon of an upper middle-class clan: the pillars of society are caricatured as domineering matrons, dotards, and mannish spinsters. The symbiosis between Claud and Hal turns out to be more adhesive and more vital than the claims of the traditional family.

I do not mean to suggest that Gray and Raffalovich intended the play as a manifesto of proto-gay liberation; they knew that the public at large would consider the behavior of Claud and Hal to be despicable, however eloquently their motives were declaimed. But Gray and Raffalovich were accustomed to pitching their literary works at a coterie audience. Since a phalanx of ephebes in green carnations had made itself conspicuous on the opening night of Gray's English translation of Théodore de Banville's *Le Baiser* at the Royalty Theatre on 5 March 1892, it may be conjectured that similar special interest groups turned out for events rumored to be meaningful for them. The audience of the Prince of Wales Theatre was moneyed, fashionable, and abreast of cultural trends; a contingent of artistic and sexually sympathetic acquaintances would have convened to see a one-shot performance of a work by Gray and Raffalovich. Such a group may well have heard of Wilde's Hyacinthus letter, copies of which were going the rounds, and may have gossiped about possible blackmail levied against the celebrity.

Elements in *The Blackmailers* bear a strong resemblance to similar plot points in a play which had run successfully the previous year, Wilde's *A Woman of No Importance*, begun in August 1892 – in particular, the attempts of Mrs. Arbuthnot to keep her son Gerald protected from the influence of the dangerous Lord Illingworth (who turns out to be his father). The homoerotic element in Wilde's play is submerged in the incestuous; but in a letter to Duncan Grant (2 June 1902), Lytton Strachey was not too wide of the mark in describing Illingworth as a "wicked Lord ... who has made up his mind to bugger one of the other guests – a handsome young man of twenty."[25]

Gray and Raffalovich, however, were copying not only Wilde's literary devices but his personal mannerisms as well. We know from Pierre Louÿs that Gray had felt suicidal when he was supplanted in Wilde's attentions by Douglas, and that, according to Ellmann, Raffalovich "denounced Wilde's intimacy with Douglas as vain and debauched" (369), perhaps with the age difference in mind. Ellen Moers credits Wilde's homosexuality with the "division of the *genus* dandy into two classes, the old and the young ... With the Lord Gorings and the Lord Henry Wottons, cynical, domineering, intellectual, essentially aristocratic, Wilde tried to identify himself. They are the Brummels of his world. Toward the Dorian Grays, the beautiful Narcissus boys, his attitude was distantly adoring and fearful."[26] Moers overlooks the ancient Greek pattern for this pairing, but it is certainly true that Wilde's contemporaries also pictured the pederastic relationship not as a union of equals and coevals, but as the unequal and hence unnatural coupling of

older man and youth. Wilde's association with Douglas certainly provided the model for the couple Esmé Amaranth and Lord Reggie Hastings in Robert Hichens' satirical novel *The Green Carnation* (1894),
which appeared the following September. Claud and Hal may thus be
seen as a scurrilous transposition of Oscar and Bosie into a nefarious
twosome. Certainly the in-crowd at the Prince of Wales's, used to reading between the lines, could easily break the code of *The Blackmailers.*

What kind of code? Claud – who has described himself as a "lonely
man; so lonely" (18) – confesses that "I don't feel so much alone since
we have met. I have been a lonely man. (*He pats Hyacinth's head very
lightly once or twice.*) ... When I met you you were on the verge of loneli-
ness. No one understood you" (29). Here the isolation of the romantic outlaw is diluted by a kind of self-pity that rings in the note of "all
the sad young men." Raffalovich in a later article on "uranists"
declared: "A man with this vice *withdraws* from himself, from the
human community ... He leads a life apart, in a confined corner, in a
brotherhood which recognizes one another by voice, by eye staring
straight ahead, by that singsong tone they all affect" (926). "Loneli-
ness" therefore is a code-word for sexual deviance, just as "stupidity" is
made a code-word for heterosexuality in a line spoken by Claud to Hal,
which the authors cut: "You are unfolding yourself, freeing yourself
from all the trammels of stupidity" (32). More ambiguous snatches of
dialogue lend themselves to interpretation. Hal soliloquizes: "Only
think of having to keep over your face, your gestures, to be acting
before one's nearest. Oh! that must be exciting, delightful, that must
be knowing that one lives" (11).

Ostensibly, this line relates to the victims of blackmail but can be read
as the homosexual's creed, the double game constantly played to avoid
detection. In Act 2, the ambiguity grows even stronger when Claud
backs Hal into a psychological corner:

> PRICE. You know what you are, Hyacinth, don't you?
> HAL. What am I? What do you mean?
> PRICE. You know the name by which this sort of transaction usually goes –
> even amongst the unprejudiced?
> HAL. No ... (*under PRICE's look he falters*) Yes.
> PRICE. And it is?
> HAL. Spare me! Spare me! Claud! (34)

After this hysterical build-up, Claud Price's line "Blackmail" is almost anticlimactic; since the coterie audience would have readily had "sod-omy" on its lips.

A year after *The Blackmailers* enjoyed its unique performance, the tri-als of Oscar Wilde would make even such an encoded and sublimated presentation impossible. Jeffrey Weeks calls the trials "labelling pro-cesses of a most explicit kind, drawing a clear line between acceptable and abhorrent behaviour,"[27] creating as never before a public image of the "homosexual" (a word that did not appear in English in print until 1897 and did not become common currency until the 1920s). As soon as the new type had become identified and defined, it was excluded from the dramatic gallery because of its "unspeakable" aspects.

V

But between *The Blackmailers* and the trials comes *The Importance of Being Earnest* (1895). Over the last few years there has been an effort to rein-vent this play as a founding document of modern homosexuality. Wilde is, of course, the likeliest candidate for "queering the canon"; Jonathan Dollimore has argued that Wilde's cult of anti-nature laid the founda-tion for a contemporary gay sensibility, and Neil Bartlett has traced the continuum of gay life in London from Wilde's time to our own.[28] The ambiguous nature of Bunburying, best pursued in town under an assumed name, has also enjoyed considerable interpretation, in the light of Wilde's own deceptions. As he wrote in June 1894 to his fellow boy-fancier George Ives: "I am charmed to see you are at the Albany – I am off to the country till Monday; I have said I am going to Cambridge to see you – but I am really going to see the young Domitian, who has taken to poetry" (*Complete Letters*, 592). The Albany Apartments, housing certain notorious gentlemen, is also Algernon Moncrieff's address. The cloakroom at Victoria Station has been suggested to be not a left-luggage hall, but a place of assignation, possibly a coded term for "the gents." "Earnest" and "Cecily" have been claimed as proto-gay slang.[29] I suspect that some future issue of *Modern Language Notes* is bound to fea-ture a disquisition on the not-very-covert significance of "cucumber sandwiches."

The contemporary stage has occasionally attempted to hold the encrypted messages up to the light, though, like the cultural critics, it too regards transvestitism as shorthand for same-sex relations. The tradi-tion of casting a man as Lady Bracknell goes back at least to 1977 when

Lionel Hamilton, a sometime pantomime dame who was playing Canon Chasuble at the Northampton Rep, took over the part from an indisposed Freda Jackson.[30] The same season Jonathan Hyde played a fearsome Aunt Augusta at the Glasgow Citizens' Theatre. As if following Camille Paglia's advice that all the female roles in *Earnest* be taken by female impersonators,[31] an eccentric rendition of Miss Prism and Lady Bracknell by the drag duo of Dr. Evadne Hinge and Dame Hilda Bracket in 1987 used the excuse that the other actresses were held up at Victoria Station (the Brighton Line) to usurp the roles of Cecily and Gwendolen as well. In the English Touring Theatre's one-hundredth anniversary production of *Earnest*, however, the director Nicholas Wright supercharged the transvestism by entrusting his Lady Bracknell to Bette Bourne, the husky-voiced founder of the radical-drag-clown troupe Bloolips.

Bloolips, founded in 1977 as a spin-off of the Gay Liberation Front, has been devoted to staging surrealistic musicals whose political message is transmitted by means of outrageous sight gags and outlandish innuendo. Bossy Bette, as Bourne is known in the company, was last seen in the United States as Blanche DuBois in *Belle Reprieve* (1991), a deconstruction of Williams created in collaboration with the lesbian team Split Britches. To cast Bourne as Lady Bracknell was a deliberate act of subversion, implying that *Earnest* is essentially a high camp exercise, not unlike Bloolips' recent confection, a Roman holiday about Hadrian and Antinous called *Get Hur.*

Algernon, in this English Touring Company production, came across as what one reviewer called "spritely, decidedly queenish"[32] and greeted Jack with a kiss on the lips. The kiss was not an original innovation. It seems to have made a debut in Galway in 1987 and was first seen in London in Nicholas Hytner's production at the Aldwych in March 1993. According to Stokes, the critics on that occasion either chose to ignore it or expressed relief that this promised exploration of the "gay sub-text" was abandoned once the ladies appeared, missing the point that physical affection between men does not exclude the love of women. It didn't in Wilde's case.[33]

Those first-nighters who did register Algy's osculatory salute assumed that his servant Lane must have been a man of more than usual discretion. Which is precisely the difficulty. Two men exchanging kisses in greeting, a common enough custom in Restoration comedy where it is invariably condemned by the unfashionable and by ladies, is too blatant in a late-Victorian context to be anything other than anachronistic. Lane may be so discreet a butler that he deliberately fails to register his master's choice of piano pieces, but even so, in Wilde's day the masters would have indulged themselves *pas devant les domestiques*. Men of the rank of Algernon and Jack would have rented discreet, servantless *garçonnières* for the purpose, if they did not frequent male brothels. Wilde's use of grand hotels and even his home in Tite Street for his trysts, his outrageous fumbling and fondling of boys in restaurants and cafés, were idiosyncratic, foolhardy, and full of risks, as the testimony at his trials revealed. But it goes against the grain of *Earnest* to spell out its ambiguities.

"[A] play about deception – clever ways of lying to get what and who you need to survive" is how the gay Chinese-American playwright Chay Yew describes the play.[34] Whether or not Wilde deliberately served up in-jokes that would be caviar to the general, keeping secrets certainly constitutes the soul of *Earnest*. Information of one's intimate life is valuable property to be hoarded and carefully meted out. No men ever mention their brothers, Gwendolen reminds us. She herself is expected to learn of her engagement through third parties; Algy learns of his through Cecily's diary entries, which contain, she says, "the wonderful secrets of my life."[35] The play's paper trail is a long, winding one: besides the two young women's diaries, other repositories of vital secrets are Lady Bracknell's tablets, Miss Prism's mislaid manuscript, the birth and medical certificates which guarantee Cecily's respectability, the first-class ticket for Worthing that provided Jack a surname, and Jack's calling card. Jack's loss of his cigarette case, engraved with another piece of covert information, impels him to write frantic letters to Scotland Yard. The inscriptions of name, birth, and love ties must be kept from general knowledge, at all costs.

"I know that there are men with horrible secrets in their lives – men who have done some shameful thing, and who in some critical moment have to pay for it, by doing some other act of shame. – oh ! don't tell me you are such as they are!"[36] This speech of Lady Chiltern's in *An Ideal Husband* (1895) sums up quite neatly the whole ethos of society melodrama: into a nutshell it packs horror, shame, the need for expiation, and the literally unspeakable nature of the fact ("Don't tell me! such as they!"). The hyperbolic rhetoric expresses a deep anxiety that society and social roles rest on friable foundations, and the least fissure in the surface will bring on utter collapse.

What is striking about *Earnest*, in contrast, is that all this baggage, like

Miss Prism's handbag, is mislaid or else shunted on to a siding. Letters are among the few personal items that do not incriminate: the only letters of consequence are the billets-doux bound up in blue ribbon that Cecily wrote to herself in the guise of Ernest. The woman with a past in this Utopia is not a *femme fatale*, but a prim and maidenly governess. The guilty secret is one which may lose Jack Gwendolen's hand, but not his position in society; a true hero of farce, he agonizes over consequences that are ultimately immaterial. Jack's putative brother, like the protagonists of *The Blackmailers*, may be a Paris-dwelling scapegrace threatened with exile to the Antipodes; but he is also a fiction, a figment of Jack's imagination. At the "critical moment," Jack is not only Ernest in earnest, but turns out to be of competent lineage to merit Gwendolen.

If the conventional guilty secrets of melodrama are evacuated of meaning by Wilde's nonsense, his own hidden life may seep through, both in the cryptic clues alluded to by modern critics and especially in the dandy Algernon. Algy, who regularly mocks Jack's overburdened conscience, is his true brother (whether or not he is also what the Germans called a *warme Bruder*): id to his ego, his Bunburying a more guilt-free version of Jack's hole-in-corner subterfuges. Algy's *savoir-vivre* enables him to bring off his social effractions with ease, while Jack invariably comes to grief whene'er he practices to deceive. In his teasing and wheedling, his prestidigitation of confidences, Algy is the closest thing to a blackmailer in this play – and consequently, the closest thing to a denizen of the Victorian subculture. His glancing comment that the lower orders "have absolutely no sense of their moral responsibility" opens a small window onto the real demi-monde of Wilde's adolescent exploiters. Algy's insouciance seems to parallel Oscar's sailing too near the wind.

There is a paradox here as intriguing as any Wilde conveyed in an epigram. At a time when his reputation and career were relatively secure, his plays dwelt, in rather conventional fashion, with fears of exposure, vulnerability to blackmail, reputations at the mercy of sinister revelations. Yet when he himself was skirting danger, ever more embroiled with blackmailers, approaching the imminent disclosure of his peccadilloes – a disclosure which was to be quite as cataclysmic as any feared by his characters – he writes a comedy whose protagonists engage in the most harmless of deceits, which when exposed turn out to be the salutary truth. The play's happy ending, its heroes' extrication from their suggestive imbroglios, is wishful thinking. It poignantly bespeaks its author's hope that one may have one's muffins and eat them too.

Notes

1 Richard Ellmann, *Oscar Wilde* (New York: Hamish Hamilton, 1987), fig. 49; further page reference appears in parentheses.
2 Norman Page, *An Oscar Wilde Chronology* (Boston: G.K. Hall, 1991).
3 Elaine Showalter, *Sexual Anarchy: Gender and Culture at the Fin de Siècle* (New York: Viking, 1990), 156. Celebrities usually had no difficulty in being photographed in fancy dress. The fifth Marquis of Anglesey, who danced in music halls in London and Europe, was extensively photographed in drag; see Christopher Simon Sykes, *The Visitors' Book. A Family Album* (New York: G.P. Putnam's Sons, 1978), 138–48.
4 Marjorie Garber, *Vested Interests: Cross Dressing and Cultural Anxiety* (New York: Routledge, 1992), 339, 342–43. A logical extension of the Lacanian formula would be "if I can't have a boy scout, I can dress as a boy scout."
5 John Stokes, "Wilde Shot," *London Review of Books*, 27 February 1992. This was reported to a wider public in the *Evening Standard*, 26 February1992, 8.
6 Merlin Holland. "Wilde as Salomé?" *Times Literary Supplement*, 22 July 1994, 14.
7 Elaine Showalter, "It's Still Salomé," *Times Literary Supplement*, 2 September 1994, 13; Emily Nussbaum, "The Portrait of a Lady," *Lingua Franca*, July-Aug. 1996, 15–16.
8 Alan Sinfield, *The Wilde Century: Effeminacy, Oscar Wilde and the Queer Moment* (New York: Columbia University Press, 1994), 6.
9 For a fuller exploration of this genre in Europe, see Laurence Senelick, "The Homosexual as Villain and Victim in Fin-de-Siècle Drama," *Journal of the History of Sexuality* 4 (1993), 201–29.
10 Louis Canler, *Mémoires de Canler, ancien chef du Service du sûreté*, ed. Jacques Brenner (Paris: Mercure de France, 1968), 321; my translation.
11 Labouchère had originally asked for only one years' imprisonment; it was the Attorney General who stiffened the penalty. For British law on the matter, see H. Montgomery Hyde, *The Love that Dared Not Speak Its Name: A Candid History of Homosexuality in Britain* (Boston: Little, Brown, 1970), 77, 90–91, 134–36.
12 For more on the subject and samples of blackmail letters, see Laurence Senelick, ed., *Lovesick: Modernist Plays of Same-Sex Love, 1894–1925* (London: Routledge, 1999), 3–5, 97–99.
13 *Teleny. A Novel Attributed to Oscar Wilde*, ed. Winston Leyland (San Francisco: Gay Sunshine Press, 1984), 98–99.
14 Quoted in Marc André Raffalovich, "Les groupes uranistes à Paris et à Berlin," *Archives de l'anthropologie criminelle* 19 (1904), 926; my translation; further page reference appears in parentheses.

15 Ed Cohen's exegesis of the trials, *Talk on the Wilde Side: Toward a Genealogy of a Discourse on Male Sexualities* (New York: Routledge, 1993), fails to place the testimony about blackmail in a specific historical context.

16 J.M. Stuart-Young, *Osrac, the Self-Sufficient* (London: Hermes Press, 1905), 11.

17 Timothy d'Arch Smith, *Love in Earnest. Some Notes on the Lives and Writings of English "Uranian" Poets from 1889 to 1930* (London: Routledge and Kegan Paul, 1970), 209–10.

18 [Anonymous,] *The Shame of Oscar Wilde* (Paris: n.p., 1906), 52–53.

19 Oscar Wilde, "To Lord Alfred Douglas," in *The Complete Letters*, ed. Merlin Holland and Rupert Hart-Davis (London: Fourth Estate, 2000), 559; further page references appear in parentheses.

20 André Raffalovich, "A propos du syndicat des uranistes," *Archives de l'anthropologie criminelle* 20 (1905), 285; my translation.

21 [Addison Bright,] "The Blackmailers," *Theatre* (1 July 1894), 37–38, reprinted in Senelick, ed., *Lovesick*, 56.

22 John Gray and Marc-André Raffalovich, *The Blackmailers*, in Senelick, ed., *Lovesick*, 52; further page references appear in parentheses. The text in this edition is based on the typescript submitted to the Lord Chamberlain's Office and held in the Manuscript Division of the British Library.

23 Quoted in Brocard Sewell, ed., *Two Friends: John Gray and André Raffalovich* (Aylesworth: St Albert's Press, 1963), 20–21, and Senelick, ed., *Lovesick*, 56.

24 Neil Bartlett, *Who Was That Man? A Present for Mr. Oscar Wilde* (London: Serpent's Tail, 1988), 122.

25 Quoted in Michael Holroyd, *Lytton Strachey* (London: Book Club Associates, 1973), 357–58.

26 Ellen Moers, *The Dandy: Brummel to Beerbohm* (New York: Viking Press, 1960), 306.

27 Jeffrey Weeks, *Sex, Politics and Society: The Regulation of Sexuality since 1800* (London: Longman, 1981), 103.

28 Jonathan Dollimore, *Sexual Dissidence: Augustine to Wilde, Freud to Foucault* (Oxford: Clarendon Press, 1991), 64–73, 307–28; Bartlett, *Who Was That Man?*

29 It was Timothy d'Arch Smith who first tried to trace a connection between John Gambril Nicholson's volume of Uranian poetry *Love in Earnest* and Wilde's work; see d'Arch Smith, *Love in Earnest*, xvii–xix.

30 "Lionel Steps In," unidentified clipping, David Cheshire collection.

31 Camille Paglia, *Sexual Personae. Art and Decadence from Nefertiti to Emily Dickinson* (New Haven, CT: Yale University Press, 1990), 535.

32 Robert Gore-Langton, "Importance of Being Outed," *Daily Telegraph*, 28 March 1995.

33 John Stokes, "Wilde Interpretations," *Modern Drama* 37 (1994), 166.

34 Steven Drukman, "Chay Yew: The Importance of Being Verbal," *American Theatre* 12 (1995), 60.

35 Wilde, *The Importance of Being Earnest: A Trivial Comedy for Serious People*, ed. Russell Jackson (London: Benn, 1980), 42.

36 Wilde, *An Ideal Husband*, in *Two Society Comedies*, ed. Russell Jackson and Ian Small (London: Benn, 1983), 172.

PART III

WILDE CONTEXTS

chapter eight

Wilde's *The Woman's World* and the Culture of Aesthetic Philanthropy

DIANA MALTZ

I

In *The Picture of Dorian Gray*, in reply to the grave observation that "the East End is a very important problem," Lord Henry Wotton states, "Quite so. It is the problem of slavery, and we try to solve it by amusing the slaves."[1] In the early pages of the 1891 edition of the novel, Aunt Agatha has enlisted Dorian to play piano duets with her in Whitechapel. Lord Henry refers to such amusements as "rational recreations," a phrase the Victorians invented to describe the efforts of the upper and middle classes to disseminate culture to the poor for free. Oscar Wilde thus begins the novel with a critique of art philanthropy, the unique appropriation of aestheticism to serve social, ethical ends. Wilde, being Wilde, would paraphrase his own idea a year later in "The Soul of Man under Socialism" (1891) when he censures "a very advanced school" who "try to solve the problem of poverty ... by amusing the poor."[2] This chapter considers Wilde's pleas for individualism and socialism, and his disdain for the sins of charity, in light of one phase of his literary production, his editorship of *The Woman's World* from 1887 through 1889 – that is, the years immediately preceding *Dorian Gray* and "The Soul of Man."

The philanthropic project of bringing art to the poor, or as Ian Fletcher has termed it, "'missionary' aestheticism," was itself a sprawling subculture.[3] Disciples of John Ruskin, missionary aesthetes believed that exposure to art and to bourgeois manners would "elevate" the poor and inculcate habits of self-regulation. They argued that to live an aesthetic life in a practical sense demanded commitments to organized movements. These aesthetes worked accordingly to provide free concerts,

playgrounds, and public gardens in working-class neighborhoods, lobbied for extended museum and gallery hours on Sundays, and encouraged artists to open their studios to the poor. While the mainstream
middle-class press lampooned them as effeminate men and flighty girls,
dandies assuming postures of idleness also derided them as hopelessly
practical, unimaginative, and tedious. Hearing of Dorian's work prior to
meeting him, Lord Henry imagined "a creature with spectacles and lank
hair, horribly freckled and tramping about on huge feet" (17). He
rejoices in missing dinner with his aunt for "the whole conversation
would have been about the feeding of the poor and the necessity for
model lodging houses ... It was charming to have escaped all that!" (16).

    Yet "all that" is precisely what Wilde as editor sought to include in *The
Woman's World*. Wilde recognized that his magazine was catering to a
middle-class female readership whose opportunities for entering the
public sphere had been dominated by volunteerism. Around the time
this new journal appeared, economic crises among underemployed and
sweated laborers of London's East End were visible on the streets – in
socialist marches through the wealthy West End in 1886, in the police
repression of working-class demonstrators on Bloody Sunday in 1887,
and in the dramatic strikes of dock-workers and match-girls in 1888 and
1889. Far from retreating into domestic seclusion, middle-class women
established female university settlements in East London so that they
could live among the poor. They contributed to Walter Besant's cultural
center, the People's Palace, founded in 1887, and some worked as inves-
tigators for Charles Booth's massive social survey, *Life and Labour of the
People of London* (1889–1903), tracing the root causes of urban poverty.
By the late 1880s, that dauntless organizer Octavia Hill, who had devised
the role of lady rent collector as a means of supervising and regulating
poor families, had systematized visitation into an efficient network that
included female settlement house workers, sanitary inspectors, district
nurses, and poor law guardians.

    Holding to Wilde's promise to address "everything that is likely to be
of interest to Englishwomen," *The Woman's World* featured essays not
only on middle-class women's aspirations towards university education
and professional employment. It also discussed the struggles of poor
needle-women, Irish weavers, French lace-makers, London dressmakers,
and those temporary female laborers who took whatever work was sea-
sonally available: makers of matchboxes, jam, and fans. Writers such as
Harriette Brooke Davies, Clementina Black, and Ellen Joyce penetrated
sweatshops and calculated the difficulties of living by piecework: it was

"slavery on 3–6 shillings a week," semi-starvation, insufficient clothing, unhealthy air. They explained for their readers the elementary economics of the division of labor, the problem of a glutted workforce of cheap foreign labor, the need to eliminate sweating and the middleman, and the need to teach women how to combine into unions and cooperatives. In her essay, "The Children of a Great City," Lady Jeune refers to the cry of homeless children. This was no doubt a play on the title of Andrew Mearns's sensationalistic pamphlet of four years before, "The Bitter Cry of Outcast London," whose notorious accounts of the hungry and homeless mobilized armies of philanthropic men and women.[4]

Recent scholarship has examined Wilde's relationship to New Women and early feminism.[5] Among the feminists from whom Wilde solicited articles, such as Millicent Fawcett, Florence Lady Harburton, Lady Jeune, and Eveline Countess of Portsmouth, were those who also lobbied to improve the lives of the poor, such as trades-unionists Edith Simcox and Clementina Black, as well as social activists who were especially committed to bringing art to the working classes. As I have argued elsewhere, the most practical programs for the reform of the workers accommodated, and even promoted, a strain of practical aestheticism.[6] Tenement reformer Octavia Hill wanted her tenants to be clean, quiet, and orderly, but she taught them flower arranging, as well as encouraging garden competitions between them. Besides Hill, central missionary aesthetes of the 1880s included well-known figures in areas of creative and political life: Samuel Barnett and Henrietta Barnett (founders of the Toynbee Hall university settlement); G. F. Watts and Walter Crane (whose respective works adorned Toynbee Hall and Hill's model village); and the Earl of Meath and Lady Meath (leaders of the Open Spaces movement). This community underpins the first volume of *The Woman's World*, from Walter Crane's illustration in the second issue to Wilde's commendation in his editor's notes of student sonnets inspired by a Watts painting.[7] In this column Wilde also praises the work of the Popular Musical Union, a society providing free concerts in the East End whose treasurer was Samuel Barnett.[8]

Talia Schaffer has argued that by placing his name on the cover of *The Woman's World*, and then soliciting articles on the history of the shoe, the fan, and the bonnet, Wilde sought to legitimize these objects as works of art in themselves.[9] He thus expanded the definition of aestheticism to include the so-called lower arts of the home such as embroidery, lace-making, and clothing design, arts with which women had familiar quotidian experience. I extend Schaffer's thesis in a new direction. In his lectures in America in 1882 and 1883, Wilde – though he did not adopt John Ruskin and William Morris' emphasis on enhancing one's life through imaginative labor – insisted upon an environment of beautiful things as a precondition for elevated consciousness. In this way, he extended Morris' proposal that to live an aesthetic life, one needed clean air and water, unadulterated food, sufficient leisure, gratifying work, and a pleasant place to do such work. If we can judge by the article on needle-women that he accepted from Clementina Black, Wilde may be said to have adopted, or at least approved, a socialist definition of aestheticism. Black laments the monotony and scrimping of the needle-woman's life: "How much resistance of temptations to spend a Sunday out, to take the omnibus instead of walking home, to buy a new silk handkerchief or a bunch of primroses, do these savings represent!" [10] Here Black argues for a life of universally accessible sensuous experience. With articles on the material struggles of East Enders, Wilde lends conscience to the aesthetic magazine and aestheticizes the social reform journal. Although an article on, say, pit women may be no different from that in an issue of *Nineteenth Century*, by featuring it in *The Woman's World* Wilde reveals that its concerns are aesthetic ones.[11]

In an effort to combat poverty, various contributors to *The Woman's World* advocate artistic cooperatives. Irishwomen suffering from the latest wave of famine are provided work through subsidized English programs that teach them the local crafts of spinning, knitting, and dying that their grandmothers had known. Dorothea Roberts, a businesswoman who commissions the weaver's work, justifies the project as a model of discriminative philanthropy (self-help) and a "good educational and civilising influence."[12] Like the impoverished Irishwomen, fallen gentlewomen left widowed and without means can find work through home crafts: one essay praises the Working Ladies' Guild, a group which discreetly channels fine sewing work to ladies in their homes. Conscious of the reader's question – "How will you make this scheme pay?" – proponents of the Guild emphasized that it was not only a philanthropic venture but also a solvent cooperative: "we have never been in debt."[13] It is as close as missionary aesthetes came to a visionary feminist economics in which working women could live their lives as art.

Contributors to *The Woman's World* were at their best when they broached the cultural difficulties of communicating across class boundaries. This was an aesthetic issue of a different order. Harriette Brooke Davies claims that female philanthropists are put off by the girls' manners because they assume that coarse language implies vice:

They assume the girls are "wicked" because they are rude, ungracious, ungrateful, frequently untruthful, and entirely devoid of conventionality; while they, not unnaturally, regard ladies who have nothing to do but go about asking questions, with envy and some suspicion. The lady's ways are not as the factory girl's ways; her accent and dress create amusement, which is generally expressed with the utmost freedom; but rudeness which proceeds from ignorance, not ill-feeling, should not be confounded with wickedness. In too many instances a lesson on morals is severely given when a lesson on manners, gently offered, would prove of more real value.[14]

Davies alternately defends working girls accused of wickedness by turning to their conditions and saying, yes, "the frightful struggle for existence in the East End is doing much to barbarise people" (66): all the more reason to pity and aid, rather than condemn them. Henrietta Barnett also encourages the act of social conciliation with working people through her essay, "The Uses of a Drawing Room." Looking at the absence of domestic pleasures in a working household, Barnett urges her readers to host "At Homes" so that the poor might have access to music, lively conversation, games, and good food. Drawing on her years of experience as a minister's wife in Whitechapel (and as an activist there in her own right), she knows the initial distrust of the poor towards the wealthy. Following a day at a country estate, one poor man can only imagine that his host "had some snug hole in the Company, or why should he do it?"[15] The blindness, however, is not all on the side of the poor, and Barnett expresses grief and rage at common assumptions among the wealthy that the poor are less sensitive to pain and beauty. She recoils at lines she has heard such as: "Very sad, shocking, but then they don't feel things as we do ... I know they often lose their children, but then the poor like to have funerals" and "It certainly is an infernal row, but I suppose they will think it music" (290–91). Sensitive to poor visitors' pride, she reminds would-be hosts that piling their plates with food is likely to embarrass them.

Barnett's aim for cross-class mutual understanding is heartfelt, yet she also occasionally laughs at working people's faux pas, such as their ignorance at the term "RSVP," and mistaken stabs at defining it. She describes another instance in which a shoemaker brings his book of seaweeds with him as a conversation piece:

[S]tanding gravely in the doorway, which he completely blocked before all the in-coming guests, he commenced to open a long roll of cardboard on which had been pressed many-hued seaweeds dried in fantastic shapes. All over the room went the helpful man, showing his treasure to dull ladies, or any one whom he saw silent, learning finally from a learned professor something about seaweed classification and artistic arrangements. (292)

As Barnett sees it, the shoemaker is not only bumbling but also in need of instruction about his own hobby: both points indicate her condescension toward him. The meeting with the learned professor also implies a greater guidance at work. Such friendships that Barnett would cultivate between rich and poor are politically motivated; she anchors her essay in reports of impending class warfare, and claims that these "At Homes" necessarily prevent social unrest. Aggrandizing in its recitation of laborers' gratitude for these parties, her essay flatters the women who would sponsor them.

Barnett's observation that "manners are caught, not taught" demonstrates how missionary aesthetes, including those writing for *The Woman's World*, were strikingly paternalistic (292). They rarely challenged the economic status quo. Few were socialists, and even those who were urged wealthier and more educated classes to bestow an aesthetic and aestheticizing influence on the lives of laborers. Their faith in "personal influence" through friendships with the poor betrays their desire for control over them. Although slum reformer Octavia Hill did not contribute to *The Woman's World* (we have no evidence that Wilde solicited an article from her), her work is cited repeatedly by others for its powerful influence on the poor. "One grain of example is worth a pound of precept," an essayist claims, "one neat, orderly house in a sordid, uncleanly, neglected 'row' of twelve, does more to stimulate neatness and order than a dozen lectures on 'the beauty of order.'"[16] Encouraging educated women to work as teachers, Theresa, Countess of Shrewsbury reasons that "the refinement and culture of their life and manners would do more to raise and refine the life of the masses than any other agency which could be employed."[17]

Most of the contributors to *The Woman's World* adhered to the tenets of the Charity Organization Society, a clearinghouse founded to discourage indiscriminate almsgiving by distinguishing deserving recipients of charity from non-deserving, and they sustained the COS's explicit judgment of the poor. In her *The Woman's World* essay, Lady Jeune remarks:

The lives of needy men and women may be full of misery, distress; poverty

– hard to bear, harder still to struggle against; but somehow a vague belief exists that they are more or less the victims of their own actions; that drink, improvidence, and their many attendant consequences, have been the cause of the abject conditions under which they exist; and while pity is not lessened towards them, their condition forces on the minds of those who strive to alleviate the sadness of their lives the conviction, melancholy though it be, that nothing can be done, in any real degree, to repair the mischief which their own follies and weaknesses have brought on them. (27)

Jeune's essay explains how philanthropic machinery works to give the children of the poor the guidance that their inept, often drunken, parents can not provide, and to offer a refuge from those parents. Ideally, social reformers can instill a strong desire among the young for "lives higher, purer and happier than those of the people they see around them" (27). After-school playrooms "humanize and tame" children, make them "cleaner" and "better behaved" (256–57). Lady Jeune sanctifies trips to the country through Ruskinian rhetoric: "We can make the sky bigger to children, and the realisation of that fact on earth is perhaps the foretaste and symbol of the largeness and glory of the unseen world" (258).

Essayist Blanche Medhurst recalls how Raphael and van Eyck used their art to bring home lessons of mother love and child love to illiterate peasants. Calling for playgrounds and open spaces, she surveys the specimen of the slum child, who anticipates Thomas Hardy's Father Time in *Jude the Obscure* (1894): "the squalid pitiful *old* child of the people ... who cannot play, who is never young, because he is born old, who is not beautiful, but who is rickety and sickly for lack of fresh air, fresh water, good food and exercise."[18] This sentiment would seem like Morris were it not for the judgment that follows it: she detects in the eye of this boy "the evil light of premature cunning" (510). She uses this fear to justify the establishment of urban parks and assures her readers that lady volunteers have already begun teaching playground games which "[refine] and [elevate] the manners, the ways, the very tones and voices of the children" (511). M.C. Wentworth also recalls Morris in her piece on the educational Home Arts and Industries Association, when she records the testimony of a pupil: "[A] workman who spends his days among machinery alleges that his wood-carving in the evening keeps him from degenerating into a machine himself."[19] Yet she also falls short of Morris' socialist aesthetic: the fact that she commends her workman for

pursuing woodcarving in the evening as a hobby rather than demanding his opportunity to do it as a vocation shows her a philanthropist
intent on providing palliatives to an unpleasant industrial life. The adult
classes that were offered by the Home Arts and Industries Association in
wood-carving, clay modeling, china mosaic, and Venetian bent-ironwork
sought to act as improving rational recreations – a staple in the missionary aesthetic agenda.

In a review of a biography of educator Mary Carpenter in his editor's
notes of *The Woman's World*, Wilde briefly characterizes one woman's
aesthetic mission as naïve:

> There is something a little pathetic in the attempt to civilise the rough
> street-boy by means of the refining influence of ferns and fossils, and it is
> difficult to help feeling that Miss Carpenter rather over-estimated the value
> of elementary education. The poor are not to be fed upon facts. Even
> Shakespeare and the Pyramids are not sufficient; nor is there much use in
> giving them the results of culture, unless we also give them those condi-
> tions under which culture can be realised.[20]

The last sentence anticipates Wilde's developed critique of economics
in "The Soul of Man" four years later. In that essay, Wilde censures not
only cultural paternalism but the economic inequality that sustains it. By
way of a subversive strategy, he applauds those "educated men who live
in the East-End ... coming forward and imploring the community to
restrain its altruistic impulses of charity, benevolence and the like ... on
the ground that such charity degrades and demoralizes" (275). Given
that he appropriates their jargon, one would expect him to continue as
philanthropists do, by condemning the indiscriminate almsgiving that
pauperizes the unemployed. Yet Wilde shifts into an explanation not of
how charitable gifts degrade their recipient, but of how they degrade
their bestower. He further denies that palliatives are sufficient responses
to poverty: "It is immoral to use private property in order to alleviate the
horrible evils that result from the institution of private property" (275).

One wonders how long these retorts were brewing in Wilde, and
whether he simply ran the articles of Jeune, Medhurst, Wentworth, Barnett, and others because he was conscious of his commercial responsibility to appeal to bourgeois women active in, or at least sympathetic to,
charitable work. Wilde rejected their paternalism and the prevailing culture of philanthropy: a culture that demanded that one subject oneself
daily to the overcrowding, the cacophony and the general anti-aesthetic

of the slums. Ironically, while lady visitors were, in historian Anne Summers' words, supposed to "grace the homes of the poor ... exuding a wonderful and mysterious influence without abandoning an essentially passive role," charitable work itself was tedious and depressing.[21] Lady rent collectors, for instance, may have taught flower arranging and planned maypole dances for slum children, but they found their central responsibilities of rent collecting and hunting down tenants' references taxing and unpleasant. Beatrice Potter Webb's sister, Kate, who devoted six years to collecting rents in one of the roughest courts in the East End, complained that the life, with its scrupulous accounting of rents each week, made her feel "like a bit of lifeless perpetually moving machinery."[22] This is a far cry from Wilde's aesthetic ideal of living in accordance with the demands of one's nature. In the second half of this chapter, I examine some rifts in the fabric of *The Woman's World*, since some articles unwittingly reveal the voyeurism that motivates philanthropy, while others protest the culture of good works as a threat to individualism.

II

Under Wilde's editorship, *The Woman's World* embodies the tensions between Ruskinian ethical aesthetics and Paterian decadence – those postures of escapism espoused by Wilde's Lord Henry Wotton and occasionally by Wilde himself. In her two-part essay on the Russian painter and diarist Marie Bashkirtseff, for example, Mathilde Blind might have celebrated Bashkirtseff for the same reasons that the young painter was beloved by English aesthetes. As a consumptive, Bashkirtseff had lived a Paterian life, eager to get as many pulsations as she could into a given moment. "[E]ven from my decease," wrote Bashkirtseff, "I shall manage to extract some exquisite and delightful sensations."[23] Yet in her *The Woman's World* essay, Blind judges this sentiment as frivolous and chooses instead to narrate Bashkirtseff's life as a morality tale, one that depicts an awakening of conscience like Siddhartha's. "[T]he sights of Paris in the nineteenth century could hardly fail to perplex a sensitive artist to whom the poetry of the street revealed itself one day as an inspiration" (454). Blind recounts how Bashkirtseff, after reading Zola's fiction, seeks out dark alleyways and street arabs; in Spain, the painter discovers Velasquez' painting and tours the prisons where convicts worked as slaves.

If Mathilde Blind's essay resembles any other Victorian text, it is

Ruskin's "Two Boyhoods" (1860), which praises Turner for his depiction of common life in all its squalor, a vision relieved only by Turner's
extraordinary compassion for the poor. Compare Blind on Bashkirtseff's temperament: "Her primitive, and in many respects untutored
nature, must have felt occult sympathies with what is oppressed and
downtrodden on earth."[24] As a feminist, Blind attributes Bashkirtseff's
sensibility to her sex, claiming that women are becoming "the interpret-
ers and champions of the social and humanitarian movement of our
time" (356). One might agree seeing the realism of Bashkirtseff's street
paintings (figure 8), but Blind downplays the more fabulous and sensational aspects of Bashkirtseff's life that actually monopolize her diary
entries: her love affairs, her desperate vitality, her striking moods, and
her childishness. The painter never left these behind, never truly transcended them, but Blind wants to claim her as a model of conscience, as
Ruskin the moralist had claimed Turner.

   Poverty, the prime fascination for the slummer, provoked either disci-
plined action in the form of charity or the passive spectatorship of the
dilettante flâneur. (The term "slumming," by the way, encompassed
both practices: it was defined in 1884 as visiting the slums not only
"for charitable or philanthropic purpose" but also "out of curiosity,
especially as a fashionable pursuit.")[25] Male aesthete Dorian Gray is
chastened for going "down into the depths" and for dragging his com-
panions down with him (118). For the record, some women went to the
East End for the same thrills: "I should like to go where there is condensed misery," one told a reformer.[26] University settlement workers
emphatically distinguished their commitment to living among the poor
from the occasional slumming of society men and ladies. They despised
social slumming for its invasiveness into the domestic lives of the poor.
One East End settler, Arthur Pillans Laurie, recalled: "After a good dinner, a crowd of men and women in evening dress would be personally
conducted through the worst slums known, prying into people's homes
and behaving in an intolerable manner."[27] Yet in a stunning confession,
the slum settler and writer Henry Nevinson admitted that his "shamed
sympathy" or middle-class guilt not only coexisted with but also was
manifested by a less noble and less understandable "attraction of repul-
sion" – in Nevinson's case, the journalistic desire to track down and
record "things at their worst."[28] Nevinson thus collapsed the line
between settler and slummer. In other instances, settlers like Olive
Schreiner and Stephen Hobhouse (Beatrice Webb's nephew) played at
poverty, living in decrepit lodgings and eating off newspapers rather

8 Marie Bashkirtseff, "The Meeting" (1884), Musée D'Orsay.

than tablecloths in order to approximate the lives of the poor.[29] Such behavior was not the opposite of aestheticism but a variation on it, another consciously designed lifestyle. (We might call it "ascetic aestheticism.") This development reveals a movement from the application of the aesthetic design (such as lilies and sunflowers) and the reading of Ruskin in the slums to the aestheticizing of the slums themselves. If such "ascetic aestheticism" has a haunting familiarity about it, then perhaps we can attribute its emergence to that part of the settler that is also the slummer – in other words, the flâneur in the philanthropist.

The Woman's World claimed a role in responsible activism against the ills of poverty; at the same time, however, it was complicit in satisfying a public greedy to hear of and view squalor. In its coverage of the struggles of the poor, the magazine repeatedly blurs the boundary between charitable concern and voyeurism. Even Bashkirtseff in Blind's powerfully sympathetic essay approaches the part of a slummer seeking the thrill of "condensed misery":

> Her sentiment for [the convicts of Granada] is a strange mixture of womanly compassion with artistic enjoyment. These picturesque criminals with their wild heads, and shifty expressions, and unstudied attitudes, drive her almost crazy with the longing to paint them ... Some of her critics asked in astonishment why this rich young Russian girl, delicately nurtured and beautiful, should go out of her way to represent on canvas some of the saddest, even ugliest scenes of city life; the waifs and strays of the streets, the loafer, the homeless tramp furtively snatching a moment's oblivion by the wayside. And she herself would have failed fully to account for her choice. Obscure instincts, deeper than the reasons she assigns, were probably at work within her. (356)

Blind then turns to her theories of universal sympathy in women, eliding the point that Bashkirtseff might have been partially motivated by a nostalgie de la boue. Wilde himself was interested in this attraction to the ugly. Writing in his editorial column on W.E. Henley's hospital poems, he argued: "while echo or mirror can repeat for us a beautiful thing, to artistically render a thing that is ugly requires the most exquisite alchemy of form, the most subtle magic of transformation," thus claiming that anything in life was worthy of artistic representation.[30] Yet just as Blind commends Bashkirtseff for her Turner-like compassion, Wilde, surveying Henley's realistic verses on amputees and burn victims in the "In Hospital" series (1875), returns to a Ruskinian aesthetic instead of a formalistic one when he extols the "strong humane personality" of the poet behind the poems (109).

Other sources in *The Woman's World* open up new questions about authorial responsibility regarding the representation of the poor. Dorothy Tennant's illustrations for Mary Jeune's essay "The Children of a Great City" aestheticize street urchins either as cherubic (see figure 9 for a child resembling John Millais's famous "Bubbles" [1886]) or as pubescently handsome and bare-chested, or with rags falling in Grecian folds (figure 10). It is ironic that Jeune's article, which extols the efforts of London charities including Dr. Barnardo's Homes, should inadvertently echo Thomas Barnardo's notorious aesthetic exploitation of the poor (in his case, through staged photographs; see figure 11). Like Barnardo, Tennant posed street urchins in rags, in her studio, with props. Encountering these images, the reader unexpectedly occupies the place of voyeur, straddling the line between earnest sympathizer and suspect slummer, and in a troubling way, savoring the beauty of another's abject misery.

In this regard, the representation of the poor in Wilde's *The Woman's World* did not differ from that in other slumming- and social-reform minded publications of 1870s and 1880s, for instance, Gustave Doré and Blanchard Jerrold's *London: A Pilgrimage* (1872) in which Doré substituted muscular male nudes for the scrawny, emaciated indigents in the communal workhouse bath (figure 12).[31] Such misrepresentations of impoverished people might be called "Decadent" in that they are not "disinterested" in a Kantian sense but instead satisfy the tastes of the spectator. In "The Soul of Man," Wilde derides the artist who works to please the public and to avoid accusations of "morbidity," and one might answer the sentimentality of Tennant's work with Wilde's statement that "Wealthy people are, as a class, better than impoverished people, more moral, more intellectual, more well-behaved." "There is only one class in the community that thinks more about money than the rich," he adds, "and that is the poor. The poor can think of nothing else. That is the misery of being poor" (289).

A more obvious brand of Decadence marked by Pater's ideal "intensity" and Wilde's ideal idleness makes fleeting appearances throughout *The Woman's World*. We see playful moments of irreverence and rebellion. Ever aware of the popular postures of aestheticism, some contributors toyed with stereotypes, and even fed them. One begins her essay on Japanese fan design: "Stern moralists are suspiciously unanimous today in taunting the rest of us with a craving after novelty. 'A morbid craving'

9 Dorothy Tennant, "A Garret," *The Woman's World* 1 (1887–88), 256.

10 Dorothy Tennant, "In the Cold," *The Woman's World* 1 (1887–88), 254.

11 A Barnardo Boy, *c.*1888, Barnardo Photographic Archives.

12 Gustave Doré, "A House of Refuge – In the Bath," in Doré and
Blanchard Jerrold, *London: A Pilgrimage* (London: Grant, 1872), 144.

they are fond of calling it."[32] And what aesthetic publication would be complete without a variation on Pater's *La Gioconda*, here Helen Mary Tiraud's meditation on the Sphinx:

> Time and space have passed away to him; the sun of yesterday and the sun of the morrow are to him as ever-present day. Hidden in the great natural limestone rock, he had waited perhaps for ages, longing that the veil which bound those deep-set eyes should be torn away, that he might look for the dawn ... [L]ooking at [those eyes,] we feel that they will watch through endless ages.[33]

More than one essay complains of frenzy within reformist circles. The active lifestyle of philanthropy appears to have engendered in its observers a resistant Paterian desire to stand back, to stretch the moment, to examine it thoroughly. In a piece titled simply "Hurry," Janet E. Hogarth laments, "Truly this might be said to be the Age of Societies":

> [We] lose a vast amount of pleasure by not knowing how to take life lightly, and by being absolutely incapable of appreciating that greatest of all enjoyments commonly called "doing nothing," but as interpreted by the initiated, "dreaming." After all, in spite of its paradox, there is a great deal to be said for the poet's "Why should he do anything? Is it not enough to exist beautifully?" or to pass from the fanciful to the sublime, for Mr. Pater's notion of the complete self-surrender of an artistic nature to the pleasurable influences of the moment, of the realization of the fulness of many-sided life, as indeed a counsel of Perfection.[34]

In another article, we learn of the proposal at an Oxford Ladies' College for a "Society for the Cultivation of Graceful Leisure" – a society for doing nothing, for "existing beautifully" – which is vetoed out of existence by the more straitlaced student majority.[35] But the most iconoclastic, subversive, and complex entry is M.R. Lacey's "A Plea for the Indifferent":

> Most people are in such deadly earnest nowadays! ... [They] fill their speeches, their essays, their sermons, their talk, with the duty of working for Others (with a very large round O of solemnity) until we begin to wonder who the Others may be, and to hope that there are enough to go around. Women are much more bitten with this earnest mood then men. Was there ever such an age as ours for societies, guilds, federations? Some

of them the women have all to themselves, and there are very few to which they are not admitted. The Post-office floods the country with papers headed by mysterious initials, notices of meetings of the F.O.O.O., summonses to the committee of the A.V.S., agenda for the next business meeting of the W.L.F., voting papers for officers of the S.R.N.C. Many women spend their lives at committee meetings. If anything is to be preserved, if Opposition to Oppression is to be Organized, if society is to be saved from dissolution, or the Nineteenth Century in general to be Regenerated, the women must meet and talk about it, and resolve themselves into an association ...

There are a few unlucky people, even among the women, who cannot go with the strong tide that is setting towards excitement and earnestness, and noise, and talk, and altruism. It is sad for them that their lot is cast on days like these. Holy hands of horror are lifted when they are seen stretched at their ease by the wayside of life, listening with amazement or contempt to the hasty footfalls and the clamorous confusion of the struggling throng. But this is the least of their troubles. Grave moral dangers threaten them, whose presence they realize far more intensely and painfully than do the philanthropists who label them "selfish" and loftily pass on.[36]

In making these comments, M.R. Lacey does not fear for the Indifferentist's salvation, but she does feel for the despair this solitary figure endures in isolation. One cannot be made to believe in social improvement if one believes it is futile. Lacey admits her own cynicism toward philanthropic organization: she sees meanness and folly and self-delusion among the reformers. "One can't get out of the way of facts," she writes (417). As a solution, Lacey suggests that rather than grow bitter, the Indifferentist learn to love and to laugh genially at the philanthropists. Yet complexly and ambiguously, she feels the compulsion to claim the Indifferentist as a contributor of indirect charity – in fact, of aesthetic charity. By love and laughter,

[a]ngularities may be smoothed down, noise a little quieted, eccentrics tamed, the life of the real workers made generally more comfortable. That may be worth doing, if one loves the workers, and does not merely look upon them as Others. So perhaps, after all, the indifferentists find the Others sooner than the committee-women. But, of course, it is the committee-women who keep the world going. (418)

Clearly, the closing sentence that commends the "committee-women"

exhibits a degree of sarcasm, perhaps of that genial laughter she has recommended. But I am interested in the transition that has occurred in
the body of the essay, from a defense of indifference and idleness
("those stretched at their ease by the wayside of life") to a rewriting of
indifference into an alternative, individualized kind of social action.
Ultimately, Lacey is not opposed to good works per se, but to being told
which good works to do and how to do them. She thus accuses commit-
tees of mandating conformity. In this way, she anticipates Wilde's argument in "The Soul of Man" where he says that "Father Damien was
Christlike when he went out to live with the lepers ... he was not more
Christlike than Wagner when he realised his soul in music; or than Shelley when he realised his soul in song." " There is no one type for man,"
Wilde concluded (298). Nor for woman, Lacey seems to suggest.

Wilde did not write Lacey's article, but as editor he approved it for
publication, and he also chose where it would fall in the table of contents. Certainly, he would have seen the irony of sandwiching "A Plea for
the Indifferent" between essays commending the subsidizing of Irish
industries and the work of the Home Arts and Industries Association.

III

This chapter concludes with some observations about the social life of
aestheticism and returns finally to Wilde. As *The Woman's World* demonstrates, some of the most formalist of fin-de-siècle aesthetes participated
in a climate of social consciousness and reform. The symbolist poet
Arthur Symons' contribution to the journal, a poem entitled "Charity,"
reproaches hypocritical philanthropists for worrying about the souls of
the poor while letting them starve.[37] An essay in *The Woman's World* by
the female aesthete Ouida begins as a standard polemic against the
drabness of London architecture vis-à-vis that of cities on the Continent.
But it none the less develops into a missionary-aesthetic treatise on the
need for public art to relieve the dreary, dark lives of the poor.

> I am inclined to believe that the monotony of ugliness in the London
> streets ... affects the minds of those who live amongst it, and the sickly
> anaemia of the factory or the serving-girl becomes the dyspepsia and the
> boredom of the woman of fashion; and I believe that the hypochondria of
> English men and women is due much less to climate than it is to the
> absence of beauty about them in their daily lives, and to the unenjoying
> haste at which they live. The influences of beauty on the mind are never

sufficiently remembered or esteemed ... The pall of smoke which is drawn like a stifling curtain around London, shuts out loveliness and light, and mirth their sister. Society has a substitute for these in what is called Pleasure, but the streets, and the people in the streets, have no compensation for their darkness.[38]

With its attention to the sensory experience of the poor, it is a piece that one might easily attribute to art-socialists like William Morris or Robert Blatchford, and indeed, passages of it would fit neatly into either *Justice* or the *Clarion* newspapers. Yet interestingly, Ouida uses the occasion of this diatribe to indulge in characteristically purple prose: "The same anxiety which would make one commit suicide in a back street off of Eaton Square, seems but a mote in the air as we glide through silver water to Venetian islets, or see the sunshine glisten through the gay green leaves of the PréCatalan or the rich vernal aisles of the Bois du Chambre" (484). She thus harnesses aestheticism and aesthetic literary style (an easy familiarity with the Continent, Paterian cadences, and sensuous descriptions) to the cause of civic reform.

In her important article on *The Woman's World*, Stephanie Green writes: "The 'New Woman' trod its pages wearing sensible shoes, but still elegantly clothed in a satin bodice, carrying her ostrich feather fan" (102). The alliance of the ostrich feather with sensible shoes represents the union of aestheticism with practical social work. Contributors to *The Woman's World* seem to have lived a double life – one is tempted to call it a kind of bunburying in reverse – where time away from the business of art is spent in respectable slum work. But to describe it as a dichotomy or duality denies the smooth way that the aesthetic life accommodated social work. For women like Lady Jeune, that "sort of amiable lion huntress," as Vernon Lee styles her,[39] the vase one painted or tapestry one wove went to an East End hospital or social hall. The aesthetic journal wanted to know what one's new association was doing for the poor. These were female aesthetes writing as social workers and reformers composing innovative prose. They were at home in the fashionable Grosvenor Gallery (which opened on New Bond Street in 1877) and if not at home then on familiar terms, statistically and personally, with East Enders. Novelist Frances Mabel Robinson and her sister, the respected poet A. Mary F. Robinson, had met Wilde along with the Brownings, George Moore, Henry James, William Rossetti, and John Addington Symonds in their parents' Gower Street salon. No doubt influenced by this aesthetic upbringing, Mary still went in for charitable work in the late 1880s. Writing at the same time, Frances also plays the moralist when in the midst of a rather dull *The Woman's World* essay, she balks at the cost of an expensive French fan in these terms: "A hundred pounds! What education it might bring to untaught aspiring talent – what pleasure to a hundred fanless, pretty girls!" [40] The meshing of social reform and art is epitomized in the figure of Lady Dilke, a contributor to *The Woman's World* who established herself as a trades union activist and an art critic.[41] At the time she was writing her essays for *The Woman's World*, Clementina Black was secretary of the Women's Provident and Protective League, a union founded to protect working-class women from sweated labor. Black is more remembered today as a trades unionist than as a novelist who for a time lived in Europe with the poet Amy Levy. But she was both. In their desire for a just distribution of pleasure in society, these women perpetuated Ruskin's ethical aesthetic, indeed taking up the reins at precisely the time when Ruskin retreated into silence and seclusion.

Most interesting, it seems, is Wilde's ambivalent accommodation of such missionary-aesthetic feelings and pursuits in his magazine. On the one hand, he had brought communities of reformers and artists together in print, intent on transforming *The Woman's World* into an inclusive journal of social and artistic issues. On the other hand, Wilde remained deeply suspicious of the climate of conscience of the 1880s, its potential for hypocrisy and for trivializing art. In the editorial column of *The Woman's World*, he even noted that literature had suffered through the recent fictional conceit of the hardworking East End curate as hero.[42] The unevenness of the journal's articles reflected Wilde's unease with philanthropy. While some essays responsibly documented the financial difficulties of poor working women, promoted unionism and inveighed against sweated labor,[43] others merely commended private philanthropy and perpetuated judgments about the non-deserving poor. The journal drew attention to the particular troubles of homeless and abused children but was none the less complicit in aestheticizing their misfortune through sentimental illustrations. It mocked philanthropic culture as a site of bourgeois constraint and conformity, and then promoted visitation. Thus it may not be an exaggeration to claim that the oppositional voices that Wilde encountered (and cultivated) in *The Woman's World* lay the groundwork for his thesis in "The Soul of Man." Moreover, it is fair to say that his essay's extended attacks on missionary aestheticism and discriminate almsgiving are replies that he permitted himself only once he became free of the magazine and his position as editor.

Notes

The research and writing of this essay were supported by an Ahmanson-Getty Postdoctoral Fellowship administered through the Center for Seventeenth- and Eighteenth- Century Studies at UCLA. I am grateful to the Ahmanson Foundation and the Center, the staff of UCLA's Clark Library, and Joseph Bristow for their generous assistance.

1 Oscar Wilde, *The Picture of Dorian Gray*, ed. Donald L. Lawler (New York: W.W. Norton, 1988), 36; further page references appear in parentheses. Lawler's edition reprints both the 1890 and 1891 texts of *Dorian Gray*. My quotations follow Lawler's reprinting of the 1891 text published in London by Ward, Lock and Company.
2 Oscar Wilde, "The Soul of Man under Socialism," in Wilde, *Works*, 14 vols. (London: Methuen, 1908–22), VIII, 274; further page references appear in parentheses.
3 Ian Fletcher, "Some Aspects of Aestheticism," in O.M. Brack, Jr., ed., *Twilight of Dawn: Studies of English Literature in Transition* (Tucson: University of Arizona Press, 1987), 24. Missionary aestheticism was the practical application of Ruskin's belief that exposure to art was inherently ennobling and beneficial to society. The founders of missionary-aesthetic societies were inspired by Ruskin, quoted him in their own writings, and often knew him personally. The Kyrle Society for the Diffusion of Beauty among the People was founded in 1875 by Miranda Hill and Octavia Hill, the latter a former art student under Ruskin who purchased her first properties in 1865 with money from Ruskin. Kyrle Society women provided the flowers that Hill's lady visitors brought to her working-class tenants. Galleries for the working classes and the promotional literature about them were saturated in Ruskinism. The Rev. Samuel Barnett and Henrietta Barnett frequently quoted Ruskin in catalogues for their free art exhibits in Whitechapel. The central room of William Rossiter's South London Art Gallery was named after Ruskin, and the Gallery's decorative symbol was inspired by a line in his writings. Ruskin himself was a direct and early participant in such ventures. His own schemes, like the thwarted building of the road at Ferry Hincksey in 1874, and his Guild of St. George (founded in 1874) motivated many young men to commit themselves to lives of both public service and cultural diffusion. Wilde famously joined the likes of Arnold Toynbee in building the road at Ferry Hincksey, and in the 1880s he was a visitor to the university settlement, Toynbee Hall, which the public associated with aesthetic tastes.
4 Mary Jeune, "The Children of a Great City," *The Woman's World* 1 (1887) 258;

further page references appear in parentheses. Andrew Mearns, "The Bitter Cry of Outcast London" (Boston: Cupples and Upham, 1883).

5 Anya Clayworth, "*The Woman's World*: Oscar Wilde as Editor," *Victorian Periodicals Review* 30 (1997), 84–101; and Stephanie Green, "Oscar Wilde's *The Woman's World*," *Victorian Periodicals Review* 30 (1997), 102–20 (further page reference appears in parentheses).

6 Diana Maltz, "Lessons in Sensuous Discontent: The Aesthetic Mission to the British Working Classes, 1870–1914," doctoral dissertation, Stanford University, 1997.

7 Walter Crane, "The Young Knight," *The Woman's World* 1 (1887), 77; Oscar Wilde, "Literary and Other Notes," *The Woman's World* 1 (1888), 184; further page references appear in parentheses.

8 Wilde, "Literary and Other Notes," *The Woman's World* 1 (1887–88), 136. As Helen Meller has argued in her study of the provincial governing elite in Victorian Bristol (*Leisure and the Changing City: 1870–1914* [London: Routledge and Kegan Paul, 1976], 76), central figures assumed roles of responsibility in various local societies. This is true of missionary-aesthetic work: Samuel Barnett was the initiator of the St. Jude's Free Easter Picture Exhibitions as well as the secretary of the Sunday Society for extending museum hours. Similar overlaps of interest and responsibility are borne out in the authorship and mutual admiration of essayists writing for *The Woman's World*. Blanche Medhurst's article on the development of public playgrounds for poor children praises the Earl of Meath for his work as chair of the Metropolitan Public Gardens Association; his wife and co-worker in the open spaces lobby also writes for the magazine, not on public parks but on the Ministering Children's League, a society administered by Blanche Medhurst.

9 Talia Schaffer, *The Forgotten Female Aesthetes: Literary Culture in Late-Victorian England* (Charlottesville, VA: University Press of Virginia, 2000), 2, 4, 82–3, 103, 105.

10 Clementina Black, "Something about Needle-women," *The Woman's World* 1 (1888), 303.

11 In the spring of 1887 Wilde began soliciting articles for *The Woman's World* through a form letter which he edited slightly as he drafted it to one female writer and then the next (see Ian Small, *Oscar Wilde Revalued : An Essay on New Materials and Methods of Research* [Greensboro, NC: ELT Press, 1993], 41–42; Clayworth, "*The Woman's World*," 91). Reiterating his main point that the journal would feature essays by women of culture and intellect, he added in a letter to Emily Thursfield, "would you care to do an article on pit women with illustrations?" While this essay was never produced in the magazine, Wilde refers to the plight of contemporary pit women twice in the first

volume. Several of Wilde's initial form letters about the magazine to women of literary and social standing are owned by the Clark Library.

12 Dorothea Roberts, "The Knitters of the Rosses," *The Woman's World* 1 (1888), 405.

13 Mary C. Tabor, "The Working Ladies' Guild," *The Woman's World* 1 (1888), 424. Cf. B.A. Cookson-Crackanthorpe's essay, "The Society of Lady Dressmakers," *The Woman's World* 1 (1888): "We are not a Society that asks for alms; we are strictly commercial and intend to 'survive' on the Darwinian principle" (374).

14 Harriette Brooke Davies, "Another Voice from the East End," *The Woman's World* 2 (1889), 66; further page references appear in parentheses.

15 Henrietta O. Barnett, "The Uses of a Drawing Room," *The Woman's World* 1 (1888), 290; further page references appear in parentheses.

16 Harriette Brooke Davies, "Culture versus Cookery," *The Woman's World* 1 (1888), 202. Cf. M.C. Wentworth, "The Home Arts and Industries Association," *The Woman's World* 1 (1888): "Just as Octavia Hill observes that the cleanliness of the staircase and passages in her tenements 'gradually invades the neighboring rooms,' so the introduction of a tasteful bracket or cupboard, carved by one of the inmates, distinctly tends to develop a pride in the condition of a cottage home" (419).

17 Theresa, Countess of Shrewsbury, "Our Girl Workers," *The Woman's World* 1 (1888), 155.

18 Blanche Medhurst, "Playgrounds and Open Spaces," *The Woman's World* 1 (1888), 510; further page references appear in parentheses.

19 M.C. Wentworth, "The Homes Arts and Industries Association," *The Woman's World* 1 (1888), 421.

20 Oscar Wilde, "Literary and Other Notes," *The Woman's World* 1 (1887), 83.

21 Anne Summers, "A Home from Home: Women's Philanthropic Work in the Nineteenth Century," in Sandra Burman, ed., *Fit Work for Women* (London: Croom Helm, 1979), 45.

22 Gillian Darley, *Octavia Hill: A Life* (London: Constable, 1990), 215.

23 Mathilde Blind, "Marie Bashkirtseff, the Russian Painter, Part 2," *The Woman's World* 1 (1888), 456; further page references appear in parentheses.

24 Mathilde Blind, "Marie Bashkirtseff, the Russian Painter, Part 1," *The Woman's World* 1 (1888), 356; further page references appear in parentheses.

25 Alison Adburgham, *A Punch History of Manners and Modes, 1841–1940* (London, Hutchinson, 1961), 143.

26 Octavia Hill, "Colour, Space and Music for the People," *Nineteenth Century* 15 (1884), 745. Gareth Stedman Jones referred to an "epidemic of slumming" in the 1880s (*Outcast London: A Study in the Relation between Classes in Victorian*

Society, [Oxford Clarendon Press, 1971], 285). Feminist scholars have described the emancipatory potential of slum work for middle-class women: see, for example, Martha Vicinus, *Independent Women: Work and Commuity for Single Women* (Chicago: University of Chicago Press, 1985), 220. Most recently, Seth Koven's research has critiqued slummers' attraction to squalor by excavating the homoerotic, cross-class dynamics underpinning slum visitation. On male homoeroticism in sensationalistic exposes of the poor wards, see Koven, "Hideous Enjoyments: Slumming, Sex, and the Houseless Poor in Victorian London" (unpublished essay). On female slumming and the erotics of dirt, see Koven, "Dirty Books," paper presented at the American Historical Association, 2001.

27 Arthur P. Laurie, *Pictures and Politics: A Book of Reminiscences* (London: International Publishing Co., 1934), 73, cited in Alan Crawford, *C.R. Ashbee: Architect, Designer, and Romantic Socialist* (New Haven, CT: Yale University Press, 1985), 24.

28 Henry W. Nevinson, *Changes and Chances* (London: Nisbet, 1923), 119– 21.

29 See Stephen Hobhouse, *Forty Years and An Epilogue: An Autobiography, 1881– 1951* (London: J. Clarke, 1951), 137.

30 Oscar Wilde, "A Note on Some Modern Poets," *The Woman's World* 2 (1888), 108; further page references appear in parentheses.

31 I am grateful to Seth Koven of Villanova University for introducing me to Doré's images in his excellent essay, "Hideous Enjoyments: Slumming, Sex and the Houseless Poor in Victorian London." For his work on Barnardo's representation of the poor, see "Dr. Barnardo's 'Artistic Fictions': Photography, Sexuality, and the Ragged Child in Victorian London," *Radical History Review* 69 (1997), 6–45.

32 J. W. Gleeson White, "The Kakémono Frame," *The Woman's World* 2 (1889), 614.

33 Helen Mary Tiraud, "The Great Sphinx," *The Woman's World* 2 (1888), 578–79.

34 Janet E. Hogarth, "Hurry," *The Woman's World* 2 (1889), 508. Both Janet E. Hogarth's "Hurry" and Helen Mary Tiraud's "The Great Sphinx" were published after Wilde's departure from the magazine in June 1889 (see *The Woman's World* 2 [1889], 578–79 and 574–79). This date, however, is approximate, and Wilde's involvement in the early production of these issues difficult to prove or disprove. This problem poses interesting questions for the reader: Did Wilde's influence continue to inform the style of the journal after he left? How much of this style can we actually attribute to Wilde individually? If anything, the journal's attention to class issues, particularly its

editorial reports of the match-girl strikes and meetings of female trades unions, intensifies in its third and final volume, under new editorship.

35 "The Oxford Ladies' Colleges by a Member of One of Them," *The Woman's World* 1 (1887), 33.

36 M. R. Lacey, "A Plea for the Indifferent," *The Woman's World* 1 (1888), 417; further page references appear in parentheses.

37 Arthur Symons, "Charity," *The Woman's World* 1 (1888), 499.

38 Ouida, "The Streets of London," *The Woman's World* 1 (1888), 484; further page references appear in parentheses.

39 Peter Gunn, *Vernon Lee; Violet Paget, 1856–1935* (London: Oxford University Press, 1964), 108.

40 F. Mabel Robinson, "Fans," *The Woman's World* 2 (1889), 119.

41 See Kali Israel, *Names and Stories: Emilia Dilke and Victorian Culture* (New York: Oxford University Press, 1999).

42 Oscar Wilde, "Literary Notes," *The Woman's World* 2 (1889), 279.

43 Harriette Brooke Davies, writing on casual female laborers, admits the impossibility of getting them to organize into unions, given their remoteness from one another's trades and their desperation for any wages. While she does not suggest boycotting outright, she ventures that if "public opinion were brought to bear on employers, if their sense of justice and humanity were aroused, they might take more interest in the real producers and less in the middle-man" ("Another Voice," 65). The idea seems to be to shame employers into sacrificing profits.

chapter nine

The Origins of the Aesthetic Novel:
Ouida, Wilde, and the Popular Romance

TALIA SCHAFFER

What we sometimes assume to be Wilde's voice par excellence *is really that of another, lost to memory, speaking through him.*

– Kerry Powell

When we think of the aesthetic novel today, Oscar Wilde's *The Picture of Dorian Gray* (1890, 1891) springs to mind, followed perhaps by Joris-Karl Huysmans' *A Rebours* (1884), Walter Pater's *Marius the Epicurean* (1885), and a few less well-known examples like Henry Harland's *The Cardinal's Snuff Box* (1900), John Meade Falkner's *The Lost Stradivarius* (1896), and Maurice Hewlett's *The Forest Lovers* (1898). These novels share certain distinctive characteristics that we have come to identify as the hallmarks of aesthetic fiction. They are written in a stylish epigrammatic or archaic discourse, the kind of "archaisms and argot" whose development Linda Dowling has described.[1] They are set in a fantasized locale, either an aristocratic establishment composed of rare and priceless artifacts, or a nostalgically idealized remote past. They center on a languid, often effete male dandy who searches for emotional fulfillment, rather than more concrete rewards such as political power or wealth. They have strong homoerotic undercurrents, for the dandy often has ambiguous but powerful bonds with other men. Finally, as you will have noticed from the list above, they are novels about men written by men.

In this chapter, however, I suggest a different kind of aesthetic history. The aesthetic novel was actually a form associated with women writers and women readers at the *fin de siècle*, and every one of the aesthetic novel's characteristics I have mentioned above derives from women's work. There was a strong tradition of women writing in aesthetic styles, including Lucas Malet (Mary St Leger Kingsley Harrison), Mary and Jane Findlater, Una Ashworth Taylor, Ella D'Arcy, Netta Syrett, Ella Hepworth Dixon, Vernon Lee (Violet Paget), John Oliver Hobbes (Pearl Mary Theresa Richard Craigie), Alice Meynell, Elizabeth Robins Pennell, Rosamund Marriott Watson, and Michael Field (Edith Cooper and Katherine Bradley). These writers inherited a genre that was already associated with women's writing, for the person who popularized the aesthetic novel was neither Wilde nor Pater but someone who seems much more unlikely: Ouida, Queen of the Circulating Libraries.

Today we might characterize the aesthetic novel as a rare, elite, and limited-edition artistic production. But in the Victorian era the aesthetic novel was seen primarily as a popular romance, and aesthetic writers maintained a tremendous amount of ambivalence toward their somewhat embarrassing precursor. While they borrowed Ouida's characters, conventions, dialogue styles, and narratives, later aesthetes also engineered changes designed to distance themselves from the circulating-library romance. Over ten years ago, Regenia Gagnier pointed out that "[j]ust as Wilde had dedicated his stories and tales to women of Society who would thereby ensure his reputation, he constructed the narrative of *Dorian Gray* from the standard elements of a certain genre of upper-class women's literature: art, psychology, sin, and luxury."[2] *Dorian Gray* is a pastiche of Ouidean elements, and *Dorian Gray*, the most famous of the aesthetic novels, carries the cumulative and complex traces of its history of negotiations with its genre.

Ouida's life, like her writing, was highly aesthetic. She wrote her novels in purple ink on large blue sheets of paper, while sitting in a huge bed in an enormous room shrouded in black velvet curtains and filled with candles.[3] She spent £100 to £200 a week on exotic flowers.[4] She demanded that Worth produce clothing that she designed herself, favoring pastel satin gowns and tiny bejeweled satin slippers. When she wrote a novel, however, she adopted her heroine's costume, so that when describing a peasant maiden Ouida could be found gazing rapturously at the dawn in a muslin gown with a blue sash.[5] Ouida felt strongly that "the correct morning dress of an English gentleman should consist of a coat and knickerbockers of violet velvet, a lace collar, and a wide-awake hat trimmed with ostrich plumes."[6] She collected art, painted, and served tea to her guests in priceless Capo di Monte china, and she flouted all convention by publicly pursuing men with whom she was in love. This sort of artistic and erotic self-assertion may have worked for male dandies, but it was much more controversial when a middle-class woman practiced it. Ouida's eccentric performances comported oddly with her notoriously unattractive body and hoarse voice, and both contemporary observers and subsequent biographers recorded the immense distaste that she generated.

Since Ouida and Wilde, however, shared a fervent love of self-dramatization, it is not surprising that during the 1880s the two writers had a useful personal and professional relationship. Wilde attended Ouida's parties at the Langham Hotel and invited Ouida to contribute articles to his magazine *The Woman's World*.[7] Ouida wrote four essays: "Apropos of a Dinner," "The Streets of London," "Field-Work for Women," and "War."[8] These wide-ranging interests reveal Ouida's social and political activities and fit into Wilde's project to make the magazine more serious. Wilde wrote an affectionate if critical review of Ouida's work for the *Pall Mall Gazette*, in which he gently poked fun at her "amazing romance."[9] Ouida's writing was evidently quite familiar to him, since he was able to recognize that *Guilderoy* (1889) had a plot derived from earlier novels. Ouida, in turn, publicly complimented Wilde by invoking him as a touchstone of taste in *Princess Napraxine* (1884).[10] Joseph Bristow's apt description of Wilde could apply to Ouida equally well: "His chosen style was, in the late 1870s and early 1880s, a daring mode of self-exhibition, concerned not only with turning out phrases that were eminently quotable in their capacity to shock, but also in transgressing dress codes to stage an alluring form of spectacle."[11] Both Wilde and Ouida were accused of pandering to a debased public taste by presenting superficial nonsense. Both were seen as pretenders whose national or class origins made them incompetent to describe the aristocratic English world that most interested them. Both were eager to present themselves as outrageous public spectacles; both despised middle-class English philistinism above everything. Both became infamous for their unconventional sexual appetites. And both were obsessed with preaching the gospel of art and inventing an imaginary realm of spectacular artistic excess in which they situated their most privileged characters.

Ouida's earliest novels, written in the 1860s, developed a new kind of dandy and popularized a particularly satisfying narrative for him. She did not invent the dandy, which has of course a much longer history. But she may have been the first writer to delineate the particular dandy identity that would come to be associated with the *fin de siècle*: a person primarily characterized by insouciant cynicism, outrageous flair, obtrusive apathy, and superb taste. Earlier silver-fork novels, such as Disraeli's

Vivian Grey (1826–27), Bulwer-Lytton's *Pelham* (1828), and Catherine Gore's *Cecil* (1845), depicted a quite different sort of dandy. In these novels, the dandy smothers strong political aspirations and intellectual might under his deplorably frivolous exterior. Melancholy and indolent by day, he secretly cons parliamentary reports by night. By the end of the novel, he bursts from his shell to assume his rightful place as a powerful force in national life. As Carol L. Bernstein asks: "[W]hy ... is political life eventually valorized, the world of luxury reduced to a setting for motifs of political responsibility, spiritual commitment and noblesse oblige?"[12] Such questions, however, cannot be asked of Ouida's novels. Her dandies, by contrast, focus on art and scholarship, maintaining their exquisite taste through the most grueling plot reversals. Generally they have to relinquish phenomenal wealth for a period of enforced exile, bankruptcy, and disgrace. During their banishment, the Ouidean dandies persist in a profound disdain for "the world," a category which includes politics, commerce, and journalism. They remain in an isolated, scenic, and pastoral landscape where they can study literary masterpieces. In this respect, where the silver-fork dandy novels tend to be Bildungsromans, showing the dandy's progress towards civic responsibility, Ouida's dandy novels have a more circular structure, in which the dandy loses paradise only to earn it back at last.

Ouida's first memorable version of the effete dandy figure appears in *Chandos* (1866). It focuses on the intense feelings between two epicurean dandies, one named Ernest, and the other named Jack, or, technically, John. As the novel begins, Ernest Chandos

> lay in idleness and ease, indolently smoking a narghilé from a great silver basin of rosewater. A stray sunbeam lingered here and there on some delicate bit of statuary, or jewelled tazze, or Cellini cup, in a chamber luxurious enough for an imperial bride's, with its hangings of violet velvet, its ceiling painted after Greuze, its walls hung with rich Old Masters.[13]

John Trevenna, Chandos's aide, is passionately attracted to his employer, but Trevenna's desire is poisoned with envy and twisted into internalized homophobia, so that the more he is attracted to Chandos, the more he works to punish him. In a typical scene, Chandos touches Trevenna's shoulder, leading Trevenna to muse: "No wonder the women are so fond of the caresses of those *mains blanches*; they are as white and as soft and as delicate as a girl's – curse him!" (I: 156). When the two men turn out to be half-brothers, their mutual loathing achieves the ring of classic tragedy, of Edmund and Edgar, Cain and Abel, Jacob and Esau, even Christ and Judas. Trevenna's vengeance forces Chandos to wander in poverty and suffering for decades. During this period we discover that Chandos has a passionate and pure love for a golden-haired aristocrat named Philippe d'Orvâle, who dies in Chandos's arms, saying, "do not suffer for me, *caro*. It is a fair fate, – a long life enjoyed, and a swift death by a bullet, with your eyes on mine to the last." "Oh God! – to lose you!" cries Chandos in anguish (III, 317). Fortunately, Chandos discovers that d'Orvâle has a daughter who looks exactly like him, so that the hero can channel his desires into an acceptably hetero-sexual and marital framework.

It should be clear why such a narrative would have attracted Wilde, as well as many other readers. *Chandos* takes the thrillingly forbidden topic of passion between two men and structures it according to the arche-typal narrative form of the brother-brother conflict. The story treats homoerotic desire, not as an unspeakable, unnatural sin, but rather as the fundamental material of classic tragedy which develops along preor-dained lines. At the same time, the reader can rely upon Ouida to trans-form the characters and plot into a reassuringly conventional love story. Chandos's period of exile punishes his desires and turns him from a golden-haired, fabulously wealthy, beautiful, opium-smoking, artistic lad into a sober, quiet, and mature patriarch. The reader's private pleasure in a heroically treated male-male romance subsides into public concur-rence in an orthodox resolution. And Ernest Chandos recovers his ancestral estate as a reward for achieving real "earnestness" (to use Wilde's term), successful masculinization and heterosexualization.

In her best-selling novel of 1867, *Under Two Flags*, Ouida built on this same basic structure, and by examining this novel in some detail we can begin to appreciate how Ouida accommodated homoerotic desires within the conventional romance. Like *Chandos*, *Under Two Flags* opens with the iconic Ouida scene: a gorgeous dandy lounging and smoking in a lavish room. The Hon. Bertie Cecil, "known generally in the Bri-gades as 'Beauty,'" reclines smoking upon "the softest of sofas" in a dressing-room with silken rose-colored hangings, bottles of perfume, sil-ver toiletries studded with turquoises, Paris novels, pink notes, embroi-dered velvet cigar pouches, all mingled with hunting paraphernalia in a "delicious confusion."[14] His closest friend is Philip, Marquis of Rocking-ham, nicknamed "The Seraph" and admired particularly for his mighty build and magnificent blond whiskers. Cecil is "inconceivably effemi-nate in every one of his habits," as Ouida explains (I: 111). When Bertie

Cecil's younger brother Berkeley forges Rockingham's name on a bill, Cecil magnanimously accepts the blame and flees England with his adoring servant Rake. The two men end up in Algeria, fighting in the French colonial army.

The flight to Algeria initially promises to enable two men in love to stay together, since Bertie's devoted servant Rake follows him there. In this respect it resembles her later novel, *Syrlin* (1890), which sends a young male couple off to find a happy home in Palestine. As Joseph A. Boone argues, the Middle East was seen as a kind of homoerotic paradise in the nineteenth century.[15] As soon as the men embark on their journey, Rake begins to express heretofore unspoken feelings:

> "Don't send me from you, sir, as you took mercy on me once!" Rake's voice shook a little towards the close of his harangue, and in the shadows of evening light, as the train plunged through the gathering gloom, his ruddy bright bronzed face looked very pale and wistful ... [Cecil's] voice was very low; the man's loyalty touched him keenly. "It was only for yourself, Rake, that I ever wished you to leave me." "God bless you, sir," said Rake, passionately. (I: 290–91)

Algerian life becomes a kind of fantasy fulfillment for Rake, who can share his master's tent, express utter fidelity, and refuse ever to leave him, all safely within the soldier's comradely code. Rake can also continue to exploit the erotic potential of the servant's role. He begs, for instance, to be allowed to divest Bertie of his uniform in the privacy of their tent (see II: 83). It is also significant of course that Ouida sends her two men to Algiers, a place that Boone points out was particularly well known for accommodating homosexual activities. (Algiers is also where Dorian and Lord Henry later share a house.)[16] Cecil remains carefully indifferent to Rake's devotion, only occasionally worrying that he cannot repay it with anything warmer than gratitude. But Rake finally manages to achieve his erotic apotheosis by dying on Cecil's lap, cradled in his arms, in what Ouida calls "a fidelity passing the fidelity of woman" (II: 409).

Meanwhile, Cecil acquires another unacceptable admirer: the cross-dressing, racially hybrid, and sexually adventurous Cigarette. Cigarette keeps her hair in a short boyish crop, wears an army uniform, sells wine, rides and shoots better than any man, identifies herself as a revolutionary, and sleeps with anyone she likes. As she encounters Cecil's grave old-world courtesy, however, she slowly begins to be ashamed of her lack of feminine modesty. She learns to blush and weep. She is forced to acknowledge the innate superiority of the British aristocracy. Eventually she sacrifices herself to preserve Cecil's life, happily dying in his lap too.

While the reader weeps over the martyrdom of these two working-class heroes, Cecil's erotic attention moves elsewhere. The Seraph unexpectedly shows up in Algeria, making Cecil feel "one forbidden longing" and an "anguish of desire [that] shook him now as strong winds shake a tree" (III: 82, 88). Algeria, however, has altered Bertie Cecil. The wild desert does not licence his unlawful passions but instead makes him articulate his heretofore implicit English moral code. It makes him bronzed, hardened, silent, and war-weary, giving "steel and strength to the indolence and languor of his nature" (II: 112). At heroic cost, he manages to repress his desire for the Seraph. Then he is rewarded when he meets the Seraph's identical sister, who is also – somewhat improbably – roaming around the army camp. With those unacceptable objects of desire, Rake and Cigarette, safely dead, Cecil is now free to marry his best friend's sisterly stand-in and move back to England, a sadder and wiser man, rewarded for his heterosexualization by retrieving his aristocratic status and his wealthy estates.

It is obvious how much *Under Two Flags* resembles *Chandos*. In both cases, the reader is encouraged to identify with a fantasy figure, the handsome languid dandy, and to invest strongly in a passionate relationship with the dandy's blond best friend. A period of prolonged suffering disciplines the dandy, allows the reader both the pleasures of sobbing over the dandy's sacrifices and the relief of knowing that he is turning into a more conventionally acceptable hero. The hero's inconveniently passionate male admirer conveniently dies. Reward comes when he marries the female version of his friend and moves back to his ancestral home.

But this basic plot also bears some resemblance to *Dorian Gray*, which begins with the instantly recognizable Ouidean opening scene, the dandy lazily smoking while sprawled in a luxurious private room: "From the corner of the divan of Persian saddlebags on which he was lying, smoking, as was his custom, innumerable cigarettes, Lord Henry Wotton could just catch the gleam of the honey-sweet and honey-coloured blossoms" (7). *Dorian Gray* also traces the fantasy life of a golden-haired hero of extraordinary personal beauty, whose close male friendships shape his life. *Dorian Gray* even has Dorian have an affair with his best friend's sister.

And yet what is also vividly obvious about *Dorian Gray* is how much it does *not* resemble the Ouidean model. We discover Dorian's affair with Lord Henry's sister, Lady Gwendolen, in a momentary comment, not the emotional culmination of the novel. (Basil remarks: "I know you and Harry are inseparable. Surely for that reason, if for none other, you should not have made his sister's name a by-word" (118).) Far from resolving Dorian's problematic desires, this affair makes one in a long catalogue of Dorian's sins. Not only does Wilde treat the relationship more casually, but he also reverses its didactic charge. Whereas Ouida would have made the sister purify Dorian, Wilde has Dorian corrupt Lady Gwendolen.

Similarly, Wilde borrows the plot of *Under Two Flags* when a minor character forges his friend's name on a bill and then asks his brother to pay it. In Ouida's hands, this is a betrayal of a sacred code that dooms the criminal to a lifetime of guilty misery and his heroic brother Bertie to dishonored exile. In Wilde's hands, it is treated as a convenient settlement. "Darlington is not going to do anything. My brother paid the bill at last," Adrian Singleton explains in the opium den. "'I don't care,' he added with a sigh. 'As long as one has this stuff, one doesn't want friends'" (144). Relegating this story to a subplot and dismissing it with a pragmatic solution, Wilde effortlessly punctures Ouida's vast drama of violated honor and superb martyrdom.

Just as Ouida disposes of Rake and Philippe d'Orvâle, Wilde kills off Basil Hallward; the man who cannot keep his adoration of the hero concealed must die. Wilde rewrote this scene, too. Whereas Ouida's sidekicks die from manly bullet wounds, and the hero endures an agony of remorseful grief thereafter, Dorian stabs Basil and then refuses to dwell on it. Whereas Ouida uses the death scene for a particularly erotically charged final confession, a unique scene when the long-repressed love can speak its name at last, Wilde has Basil admits his love in the most embarrassed, stilted way, while scolding Dorian and demanding (of all things) that he pray. Nor does this scene have any catharctic pleasure for the reader, since Basil has already told Lord Henry how he feels. In short, Wilde borrows the formal structure of the Ouidian convention of the frustrated lover's death, but cheekily reverses its meaning at every point. Whereas Ouida's death scenes show men's emotions wrought up to unbearable intensity, Wilde's death scene functions to prove how inadequate, how silly, how self-defeating, and how inarticulate men's emotional responses could be.

Nor does Dorian's lifelong training have the emotional meaning it has in Ouida's fiction. Dorian undergoes a discipline in suffering like any Ouidean dandy, but the whole point of the novel is that it fails to change him at all. He is not remotely purified by the experience. And whereas his predecessors Chandos and Cecil have to learn to do without their rosewater and narghiles and satin pillows, undergoing a brutal sensory deprivation, Dorian gets to keep it all. He may be hideously unrecognizeable in death, but he still has his priceless rings on.

In fact, *Dorian Gray* is a canny and deliberate reworking of the Ouidean romance. Wilde took the youthful hero's dandy paradise from Ouida, but wondered: what if he never had to leave it? Or, in Lord Henry's words, what if "one man were to live out his life fully and completely, were to give form to every feeling, expression to every thought, reality to every dream"? (20). Dorian is a Ouidean dandy who never has to undergo the self-inflicted discipline of heroic martyrdom, the physical torture of suffering, because he transfers all that onto the picture. Lord Henry quite explicitly argues that Dorian should never experience painful self-repression at all: "self-denial ... mars our lives. We are punished for our refusals. Every impulse that we strive to strangle broods in the mind, and poisons us." Dorian Gray is like a Ouida hero trapped in perpetual adolescence. Because maturation means, in Ouida's world, heterosexualization and masculization, Wilde kept his hero perpetually youthful. *Dorian Gray* is a Ouida novel frozen in volume one – and Wilde is clever enough to make his character fully aware that he is frozen in development, and to derive his psychological interest from that recognition.

Chandos and *Under Two Flags* are not the only Ouida narratives that influenced *Dorian Gray*. Ouida's "Afternoon" (1883) is a remarkable short play about a supercilious dandy named Earl L'Estrange, "this Ruskin of the drawing-room; this aesthetic of aesthetics," who has to be taught to respect women.[17] L'Estrange's friend and acolyte is a man named Aldred Dorian, whose home is described in the following stage directions: "Studio of Aldred Dorian. Tapestried Walls, Paintings, Marbles, Bronzes, Carved Chairs, Artistic Litter" (176). This Dorian achieves fame for his collections of antique tapestries, china, and silver, and he gives exquisite parties to the artistic elite. He is also a painter of portraits. Although Dorian determines to sell all his collections and flee abroad, his mentor ensures that he can never manage to escape his all-too-spectacular artistic home. It is hard to imagine that Aldred Dorian did not contribute to his namesake eight years later.

In her great novels of the 1880s, *Princess Napraxine* and *Othmar* (1885), Ouida introduced a new kind of dandy: an utterly self-possessed and cynical connoisseur whose greatest pleasure is the manipulation of others, who dispassionately regards other people's emotions as merely material to examine, and who is a superb psychologist able to explain every character's inner feelings better than the characters themselves. Interestingly, that cynical dandy is a woman, Princess Nadine Napraxine. Like her male predecessors, Princess Napraxine gets a magnificently gorgeous private room – her boudoir is furnished in ivory and embroidered silver satin (I: 359). But by creating a specifically female dandy, a "mondaine," to use Ouida's own term, Ouida accomplished two things (III: 16).

First, she produced a version of the New Woman more amenable to her own aesthetic mindset. The mondaine is no struggling working woman with short hair and a bicycle; she is a phenomenally wealthy and extraordinarily powerful arbiter of international taste. In each novel, the mondaine battles against a traditional angel in the house, a plot that enacted her readers' conflicted affiliations with mutually exclusive models of female identity at the turn of the twentieth century. Instead of endorsing either feminist New Women or traditional domestic angels, Ouida tried to construct new compromise formations. Her mondaines get chastened and her ingenues get educated. The mondaine novels resemble Ouida's early dandy novels, for both genres let readers enjoy a fantasized unconventional gender-bending character for several hundred pages before providing a conventional foil (or a conventional resolution) to provide virtuous satisfaction in the last volume.

Secondly, Ouida's mondaines use a particular kind of speech, an epigrammatic dialogue derived from silver-fork novels and ultimately from Restoration comedy. The mondaines' wit allows them to voice quite daring ideas, including opposition to the institution of marriage, dislike of work, and cynicism about love. It also functions as a way of deflecting the connoisseur's appraising eye. Men can hardly subject the mondaines to a leisurely male gaze when the women are forcing them to engage in spirited, fast-moving, intellectually challenging conversations. Ouida's women take control by moving the interaction to a verbal instead of a visual level. Inevitably, the men complain. As Othmar tells Princess Napraxine, "If you wish for men who can, whilst they adore you, sit and drink chocolate and talk epigrams, seek elsewhere; I am not one of them" (I: 363). In "Afternoon," one woman warns L'Estrange to stop treating women like collectibles. L'Estrange responds plaintively, "you are so witty, Princess, that it is impossible to keep up with you, and I do not want wit today" (226). In Ouida's novels, then, epigrammatic dia-

logue works specifically as women's self-defense against the connoisseur's manipulative appraisals.[18]

Dorian Gray has to be read not only in terms of Dorian's debt to the
1860s novels but also in terms of Lord Henry's debt to the 1880s novels.
Just as Dorian is a Ouidean dandy from the early period frozen in adolescence, Lord Henry is a Ouidean dandy of the late period with his
gender changed. Lord Henry's dispassionate psychological cruelty and
his remorseless wit are both very similar to Princess Napraxine's. But by
transmuting Princess Napraxine's personality into a man's, Wilde was
able to expand the dandy's role. Lord Henry is a free agent, perpetually
ready to poison youthful minds. He grows more dangerously independent as the novel continues, since he breaks with Basil and divorces his
wife. Ouida, however, felt the overwhelming pressure of the marriage
plot hemming in her female mondaine. Whereas Lord Henry gets
divorced, Princess Napraxine unwillingly gets married, commenting
sadly on her author's lack of imagination: "what a pity to have married
him! It had been commonplace, *banal*, stupid – anybody would have
done it. There had been a complete absence of originality in such a conclusion to their story."[19] Wilde also enhanced the male dandy's dangerous powers in another way. In *Dorian Gray*, it is the manipulative male
connoisseur, Lord Henry, who deploys epigrams. He appropriates the
language that had originally been mobilized against him, virtually eradi-
cating its usefulness as a female defense. Only one woman in *Dorian Gray*
(Gladys, the Duchess of Monmouth) manages to counteract Lord
Henry's wit with *bon mots* of her own, and Lord Henry resents this
Ouidean relic just as much as his precursors did: "her clever tongue gets
on one's nerves," he complains (166).

Dorian Gray's language reveals just how much Wilde learned from his
friend's novels. "Youth is genius," Ouida wrote (*Chandos*, III: 105).
"Youth! There is nothing like it," Lord Henry agrees. "It's absurd to
talk of the ignorance of youth. The only people to whose opinions I listen now with any respect are people much younger than myself" (164).
Ouida writes that "when we were young, our mere life was a poem"
(*Chandos*, III: 106), and Lord Henry tells the eternally young Dorian
that "your days are your sonnets" (165). Princess Napraxine "would
sacrifice [her] own life for an epigram" (*Othmar*, I: 63), someone
observes dourly – just as Dorian claims "you would sacrifice anybody,
Harry, for the sake of an epigram" (156).

Ouida and Wilde both used epigrams to puncture bourgeois preferences for duty, work, morality, and earnestness, and to offer a new gospel of pleasure, passions, and unconventional modes of self-fulfillment. "Let us be robbed of everything except our illusions," Ouida wrote (*Princess Napraxine*, III: 15). A priest asks Princess Napraxine, "Does your conscience never tell you that you have done any harm, Princess?" She replies, "Oh, very often – a great deal ... But it does not tell me that I ought not to have done it" (*Princess Napraxine*, II: 295). On the topic of work, Princess Napraxine advises: "To know how to do nothing is a great secret of health and of comfort; but you must not wait till you are fatigued to do nothing, or you cannot enjoy it" (*Princess Napraxine*, I: 43). "It is awfully hard work doing nothing," Algernon agrees in *Earnest*.[20] Ouida was also quite cynical about the literary industry: "Reviewers puff bad books, as ladies praise plain women" (*Chandos*, I: 90). She is particularly cutting about love: "love is best worked with egotism, as gold is worked with alloy" (*Othmar*, I: 23).

Ouida was bitterly suspicious of "good women," perhaps in part because she was so often seen as a "bad woman" herself. Wilde particularly liked *Guilderoy*'s description of "one of those admirably virtuous women who are more likely to turn men away from the paths of virtue than the wickedest of sirens" ("Ouida's New Novel," 496). He has Lord Henry expresses a similar opinion: "the only way a woman can ever reform a man is by boring him so completely that he loses all possible interest in life" (79). Nor did Ouida approve of women's dependence on men. "[M]ost women cannot understand that too much of themselves may bring about a wayward wish to have none of them" (*Othmar*, I: 15). "Those women who make themselves a statue of fidelity ... will soon be left alone on their pedestals" (*Othmar*, I: 65). Such lines resemble Lord Henry's carping misogyny. But Ouida could be quite as critical of men, complaining that "men always consider women unjust to them, when they fail to deify their weaknesses" (quoted in Wilde, "Ouida's New Novel," 498). And she could find humor in the public spectacle of a failed marriage: the Divorce Court is "the only Law Court where the robber cuts a better figure than the robbed" (*Under Two Flags*, I: 132).

To a modern reader these epigrams are eerily familiar. Their condensed and inverted structure sounds awfully Wildean. Wilde and the other aesthetes seem to have adopted Ouida's signature style completely enough to obscure the fact that she had developed it first. As Alice Meynell commented in 1895:

Things improbable at the first glance in connection with her are to be

traced to Ouida: amongst others the "epigram" ... Many and many a little
author to-day would perhaps become less frivolously cheerful on finding the most modern of his inversions in the decorated pages of his half-
forgotten Ouida. The *pose* itself need no longer be copied by author from
contemporary author, for it can be had, at no more than second-hand ...
from her.[21]

Meynell's comment shows that for contemporary authors, Ouida was
quite precisely "half-forgotten"; her "inversions" (both sexual and lin-
guistic) were remembered, but her authorship, her role in developing
them, was ignored, suppressed, reworked, or transformed by many of
the leading aesthetes of the next generation.

Recognizing Wilde's debt to Ouida allows us to understand why Wilde
occasionally inserts witty female characters into his plays and his novel –
women who have no plot function other than to exchange clever repar-
tee. These characters allude to the mondaine. We hear Ouida's voice,
for instance, when Lady Narborough informs Dorian that "there is no
pleasure in taking in a husband who never sees anything," and when
Gladys, the Duchess of Monmouth, says that "we women ... love with our
ears, just as you men love with your eyes" (135, 151). These moments
spark the readers' reflexive fondness for the Ouidean world, providing a
metonymic connection to a more popular tradition.

Wilde's famous description of the fictional "golden book" also
strengthens his connection to the Ouidean tradition. As most critics
have noted, the golden book that poisons Dorian is based on both *A
Rebours* and *Marius the Epicurean*. But it also alludes to *Princess Napraxine*
and its sequel, *Othmar.* All of these novels satisfy Wilde's general description: "a psychological study" written in a "curious jewelled style," "without a plot, and with only one character" (97). However, Wilde's specific
plot summary – a beautiful young Parisian who came to dread the decay
of his beauty and power – describes *Othmar* perfectly, except that he has
turned Ouida's female main character into a man (97–99). The masculinization of Ouida's female prototypes is a pattern in *Dorian Gray*, as we
have seen with Lord Henry Wotton.

Virtually all of Ouida's 1880s novels have essentially the same plot.
"What is the story?" Wilde asked of *Guilderoy*. "Well, we must admit that
we have a faint suspicion that Ouida had told it to us before" ("Ouida's
New Novel," 495). In these romances, a sophisticated aristocrat falls in
love with a lovely, innocent peasant girl and marries her, but the mar-

riage makes both miserable, for she cannot adapt to his world and he is embarrassed by her faux pas. She usually kills herself. In 1894 Wilde proposed a play which would rewrite this plot. Here is the description that he gave to George Alexander: "A man of rank and fashion marries a simple sweet country girl ... and after a time he gets bored with her – but the woman takes a lover, becomes pregnant, and refuses to return to her husband. It is the husband who commits suicide" (*Complete Letters*, 599). This is a wonderful little *mise-en-abîme* of how Wilde borrowed Ouida's plots only to reverse their meaning and liberate the wrong characters.

Wilde wanted to affiliate himself with Ouida, to endorse her innovations, to inherit her popularity, and to trigger the complex emotional reactions that Ouidean language could produce in its avid readers. Wilde, however, also wanted to distance himself from Ouida's much-derided glaring cultural errors and hyper-romantic plots. Wilde's project, in short, was to build on Ouida's innovations but to transfer them to an almost all-male world in which dandyism and epigrammatic dialogue could become viable alternative models of *masculine* identity and behavior.

Wilde's debt to Ouida was obvious to his readers. Wilde's alterations, however, were as visible as his appropriations. Ouida's romance always end in redemptive marriage, but Wilde's treatment offers no marriage, no heterosexualization, and no masculinization. Ouida's epigrams protect women from objectification, but in Wilde's writings epigrams enable men to objectify others. Where Ouida's plots promote martyrdom, Wilde's endorse pleasure. Wilde took Ouida's cast-iron genre and spun it around to depict the reverse of the medal. He updated the Ouidean popular romance into a celebration of everything Ouida's novels opposed. No wonder that when *Dorian Gray* was published, Ouida's sole, wry comment was "that she *did* understand it."[22]

When Wilde reviewed *Guilderoy*, he gave it qualified praise, but worked to associate it with an earlier era of British literary history. "Ouida is the last of the romantics. She belongs to the school of Bulwer Lytton and George Sand," he wrote. "She tries to make passion, imagination, and poetry part of fiction. She still believes in heroes and in heroines. She is florid, and fervent and fanciful" ("Ouida's New Novel," 494–95). Although he immediately proceeds to give her credit for a contemporary interest in realism and psychological analysis, the opening of this review serves to separate himself from Ouida. He represents modernity, while she belongs to an outmoded past. The review also signals what he saw as the greatest difference between himself and his friend; it was indeed the feverish heroism of Ouida's fiction that Wilde worked to undo in *Dorian Gray*, published only a year after this review.

The other aesthetes had similarly complicated reactions to this somewhat inconvenient predecessor. They felt that she deserved admiration for her most aesthetic traits: her descriptions of beautiful scenery, her use of epigrams, and her sexually explicit, daring plots. But they derided her inadequacies in order to emphasize their own comparative sophistication. Like Wilde, Meynell, Max Beerbohm, and others acknowledged Ouida in a way that often showed their own ambivalence about her.

The aesthetes' ambivalent admiration is visible in "The Praises of Ouida," where Meynell deplores the fact that Ouida wastes her "rich vocabulary" and "admirable sense of place" in repetition, careless mediocrity, and sentimental conventions (6). An equally cautious endorsement appeared in 1895 in the *Yellow Book*, that famous manifesto of the Aesthetic Movement. G.S. Street admitted Ouida's vulgarity but praised the passion and vividness of her writing. But Max Beerbohm complained that "[i]t was a shy, self-conscious essay, written somewhat in the tone of a young man defending the moral character of a barmaid who has bewitched him."[23] He proceeded to demonstrate how Ouida *should* be praised, even going so far as to dedicate his book to her. He gave her credit for a particularly aesthetic achievement, claiming that "no writer was ever more finely endowed than Ouida with the love and knowledge of all kinds of beauty in art and nature" (112). Perhaps the most powerful acknowledgment of Ouida came from Lucas Malet, who wrote ambitious novels that one would imagine to be as far as possible from Ouida's racy popular romances. In "The Progress of Women in Literature," Malet calls Ouida one of the greatest living women writers.

> Yet it is impossible to deny her genius; and, genius being by no means a glut in the market just now, one bears with its faults in a tolerant spirit. As I say, this novelist's gifts are splendid. Her descriptive passages often run those of Mr. Ruskin as close as her pathetic passages run those of Mr. Bret Harte. One can hardly say more. And we owe her thanks for this also: that she has emancipated herself very completely [from] the tyranny of the Young Person.[24]

In other words, each one of these key aesthetic writers publicly stood up for Ouida's work, in spite of considerable public pressure to join the almost universal denunciations of Ouida in the critical press and significant dread that readers might condemn their own literature or literary taste. They did so because they realized that Ouida had helped form aesthetic prose, and that they were each personally indebted to her novels.

In her development of the *fin-de-siècle* dandy, epigrammatic dialogue, vivid descriptions of luxurious material culture, and homoerotic fantasies, Ouida offered elements that later writers would adapt for their own purposes. In her enormous popularity across all classes of the reading public, however, Ouida presented a problem for a movement whose participants often wanted to be a rarified and educated elite. Aesthetic writers found ways to be Ouidean without becoming Ouida. They picked up Ouida's characteristic conventions but set them in less melodramatic narratives.

I am not simply arguing that Ouida had a crucial influence on Wilde in particular and aesthetic writers in general. Such influence seems to me to be true from our necessarily retroactive perspective, in which we regard *Dorian Gray* as a significant work and search for its precursors. Yet we must remember that nobody read this way in 1891. Rather, Wilde must have appeared to be, to some extent, a derivative version of a far more powerful, prolific, and popular novelist, and to be struggling to differentiate himself from this much larger predecessor while nonetheless retaining the conventions that made her so successful. If we read *Dorian Gray* in this manner, then we fundamentally change how we see the gender and class dynamics of the aesthetic novel.

The aesthetic novel is easy to read as an Epicurean, aristocratic genre designed for elite male connoisseurs. Jonathan Freedman persuasively argues that Henry James's decision to move into this rarified market niche was the primary way that aestheticism informed modernism.[25] This move, I suggest, was a defensive attempt to distance oneself from an embarrassing and all too visible origin. In other words, the elements of the aesthetic novel, when not borrowed from Ouida, often constitute attempts to occlude the writer's connection to Ouida. The aesthetic novel was initially a recrudescence of popular romance, and its movement toward increasingly esoteric subjects, its courting of an elite readership, its fear of mass-marketing tactics, were all at least partly motivated by a flight from its most monstrously popular mother. Scholars have demonstrated that the aesthetic novel was influenced by many disparate sources, ranging from George Meredith to Charles Baudelaire. But one of the most extensive sources of aesthetic style, one of the most important, bestselling, and prolific authors of the nineteenth century, was the woman whose very visibility has made her so difficult to see.

Notes

1 Linda Dowling, *Language and Decadence in the Victorian Fin de Siècle* (Princeton, NJ: Princeton University Press, 1986), 144

2 Regenia Gagnier, *Idylls of the Marketplace: Oscar Wilde and the Victorian Public* (Stanford, CA: Stanford University Press, 1986), 66.

3 Yvonne Ffrench, *Ouida: A Study in Ostentation* (London: Cobden-Sanderson, 1938), 67; Eileen Bigland, *Ouida: The Passionate Victorian* (London: Jarrolds Publishers, 1950), 64–65.

4 Ffrench, *Ouida,*106.

5 These details are from Ffrench, *Ouida,* 73–74.

6 Bigland, *Ouida,* 99.

7 Wilde also mentioned Ouida approvingly in two letters. In late October 1887 he wrote to Mrs. Bernard Beere: "we have no *lionne* now but Ouida," and in June 1888 he declared to Harry Melvill, "Ouida has just sent me a clever article"; see Oscar Wilde, *The Complete Letters,* ed. Merlin Holland and Rupert Hart-Davis (London: Fourth Estate, 2000), 331, 352; further page reference appears in parentheses.

8 Ouida, *The Woman's World* 1 (1888), 193–94, 481–84, and 2 (1889), 171–73 and 339–42.

9 [Oscar Wilde,] "Ouida's New Novel," *Pall Mall Gazette,* 17 May 1889, 3, reprinted in Wilde, *Collected Works,* ed. Robert Ross, 14 vols. (London: Methuen, 1908), I: XIII: 495; further page references appear in parentheses.

10 Ouida, *Princess Napraxine,* 3 vols. (London: Chatto and Windus, 1884), I: 15; further volume and page references appear in parentheses.

11 Joseph Bristow, *Effeminate England: Homoerotic Writing after 1885* (New York: Columbia University Press, 1995), 20.

12 Carol L. Bernstein, *The Celebration of Scandal: Toward the Sublime in Victorian Urban Fiction* (University Park, PA: Pennsylvania State University Press, 1991), 118.

13 Ouida, *Chandos,* 3 vols. (London: Chapman and Hall, 1866), I: 14–15; further page volume and page references appear in parentheses.

14 Ouida, *Under Two Flags,* 3 vols. (London: Chapman and Hall, 1867), I: 3–4; further volume and page references appear in parentheses.

15 Joseph A. Boone, "Vacation Cruises: or, The Homoerotics of Orientalism," *PMLA* 110 (1995), 89–107.

16 Oscar Wilde, *The Picture of Dorian Gray: Authoritative Texts, Backgrounds, Reviews and Reactions, Criticism,* ed. Donald L. Lawler (New York: Norton, 1988) 110; further page references appear in parentheses.

17 Ouida, "Afternoon," in Ouida, *Frescoes, etc.: Dramatic Sketches* (London: Chatto and Windus, 1890), 164; further page references appear in parentheses.

18 For a more extensive reading of Ouida's work, see Talia Schaffer, *The Forgotten Female Aesthetes: Literary Culture in Late-Victorian England* (Charlottesville, VA: University Press of Virginia, 2000), 122–58.

19 Ouida, *Othmar*, 3 vols. (London: Chatto and Windus, 1885) I: 100; further volume and page references appear in parentheses.

20 Wilde, *The Importance of Being Earnest*, ed. Russell Jackson (London: Ernest Benn, 1980), 37.

21 Alice Meynell, "The Praises of Ouida," in *Pall Mall Gazette*, 16 August 1895, 4, reprinted in Meynell, *The Wares of Autolycus: Selected Literary Essays of Alice Meynell*, ed. P.M. Fraser (London: Oxford University Press, 1965), 8.

22 Richard Ellmann, *Oscar Wilde* (New York: Hamish Hamilton, 1987), 301.

23 Max Beerbohm, *More* (London: John Lane, The Bodley Head, 1899), 106.

24 Lucas Malet, "The Progress of Woman in Literature," *Universal Review* 2 (1888), 299.

25 Jonathan Freedman, *Professions of Taste: Henry James, British Aestheticism, and Commodity Culture* (Stanford, CA: Stanford University Press, 1990).

chapter ten

Oscar Wilde, New Women, and the Rhetoric of Effeminacy

LISA HAMILTON

Who or what, exactly, was the effeminate man in late-Victorian culture? Any discussion of the constitution and reception of effeminacy in the *fin de siècle* has necessarily centered on the figure of Oscar Wilde.[1] Wilde's body was reconfigured by representations in the popular press as the most recognizably effeminate man of the period, and Wilde himself was the author of numerous works that elaborately described effeminate men. But in focusing exclusively on Wilde and other male writers for a consideration of what it means to be effeminate, recent interpretations of this phenomenon analyze only those works whose authors appear to have understood and exploited effeminacy's potential as a coded representation of same-sex desire. These insider narratives include Wilde's *The Portrait of Mr. W.H.* (1889) and *The Picture of Dorian Gray* (1890, 1891), Robert Hichens' *The Green Carnation* (1894), stories such as John Francis Bloxam's "The Priest and the Acolyte" in the 1894 *Chameleon* magazine, and the pornographic novel *Teleny* (1893), which circulated privately throughout London and to which Wilde's name is often erroneously attached. Outside the homosexual subculture of the *fin de siècle,* however, effeminacy is ambiguously represented as a problematic form of heterosexuality, and an examination of the effeminate heterosexual provides a fuller picture of the *fin de siècle* and of one of its most puzzling cultural formations.

Many critics have argued that any widespread public understanding of effeminacy as encoding same-sex desire proves impossible until the conclusion of Wilde's trials in the spring of 1895. Such a stable "post-trial" construction of effeminacy, however, cannot be universally presumed. Moreover, the uses to which effeminacy was put before the trial – as the marker of many undesirable conditions besides, or in addition to, homosexuality – cannot be instantly transformed into a solely homosexual signification. Yet the conditions that effeminacy signified before the trials, generally relating to aristocratic licence, sexual deviance, "vice," or hereditary debilitation, also contributed to amplifying effeminacy's stereotypically negative associations once it became more stably identified as a signifier of same-sex desire in the subsequent decades.

In their novels from this period – *The Heavenly Twins* (1893), *The Beth Book* (1897), and *A Superfluous Woman* (1894) – New Women writers Sarah Grand and Emily Frances Brooke, who were contemporaries of Wilde, portray effeminate men as both physically and morally dangerous. Yet all of their effeminate men are firmly understood to be heterosexual; they are, in fact, what we might these days call "husband material." More curious still, the New Woman writers' physical descriptions of the effeminate man appear to be drawn directly from Wilde's writings and from those of his Decadent contemporaries. This heterosexualization of the effeminate man, both pre- and post-trial, is puzzling, but according to Joseph Bristow, their fluid conception of effeminacy is not out of line with Wilde's own ambiguous approach to the concept of effeminacy. Bristow argues that although Wilde's project was indeed an attempt "to make sexual desire between men as visible as possible," he had to do so in a way that would escape the punishments threatened by the Labouchère Amendment of 1885, which criminalized sexual relations between men. Moreover, as Bristow recognizes, Wilde also showed "a persistent interest in disclosing in public that sexual identities could not be so readily named" (45). Wilde, therefore, while painting many tantalizing portraits of effeminate dandies, pairs them with wives and mistresses. His deliberate vagueness about the meaning of effeminacy contributes to the ease with which the figure of the Decadent male dandy is appropriated and reused by New Women writers as a more general signifier of vice. Although Wilde's dandies and his effeminate men are deliberately left ambiguous in their sexual identities, this ambiguity in the hands of New Women writers produced the effeminate heterosexual, whose effeminacy signifies not same-sex desire but "vicious" and degenerate tendencies. And yet, when Sarah Grand decides to envision the ideal mate for the New Woman, that man looks suspiciously like the effeminate men these writers have spent so much time repudiating.

Much interesting work has been done on effeminacy in relation to the history of male same-sex desire, but the tendency has been to overread effeminacy as a stable signifier of homosexuality in the works of the nineteenth century and earlier periods. In this respect, Alan Sinfield's research has been tremendously useful because it carefully examines the historical representations of effeminacy in order to gauge its constantly shifting meanings over time. He starts by asking how Wilde's contemporaries viewed homosexuality, and he argues (quite correctly, I think) that before Wilde's 1895 trials there was no automatic association by the public of homosexuality with effeminacy. But, while Sinfield's argument unravels the automatic association between the two that we have retrospectively imposed, I think Sinfield does not go far enough. I want to unravel the automatic association of effeminacy and homosexuality even further by invoking the novels of Grand and Brooke that were written both before and after the trial. In doing so I will show that the concept of effeminacy is more capacious and unevenly developed than even Sinfield imagines. If before the trials, effeminacy signifies the "vice" that leads to the transmission of syphilis to women and thereby implies the heterosexual affinity, then it cannot be constructed as a stable signifier of same-sex desire. And if effeminacy continues, even after the trials, to represent these hetereosexualized modes of transmission to a fairly astute (and I might even argue, hostile) cultural critic such as Grand, then bifurcation of the representation of effeminacy into pre- and post-trial modes fails to capture the subtleties and even outright contradictions of *fin-de-siècle* effeminacy.

Effeminacy as Epithet

What did it mean to be effeminate? First of all, any attempt to define effeminacy becomes entangled in discussions of both dandyism and Decadence, two related phenomena. Among its many meanings, effeminacy referenced the aristocratic ethos of the eighteenth century, embodied by the effeminate and rakish nobleman. *Fin-de-siècle* dandy figures reinvigorated the ghostly spectacle of this effete aristocrat to shock and titillate the bourgeois class to which they belonged. Conversely, the bourgeoisie itself propagated the myth of the effeminate male as a way of critiquing those parts of society it considered insufficiently robust or non-productive. Effeminacy might also describe a man who was overidentified with so-called feminine concerns such as art, music, or poetry, or might signify the dandy figure's complicated relationship to female beauty, as the dandy desires feminine beauty as much as, or more than, he desires women themselves.[2] And the statement "Déjà les décadents, précurseurs de la société future ... L'homme s'affine, se féminisé, se divinise"[3] was affixed to the first issue of Anatole Baju's publication *Le Déca-dent* in 1886; it argued that to become feminized was not degenerate but "divine."

The many descriptions of "decadent" bodies in both French and English literature of the *fin de siècle* articulated a concrete, physicalized effeminacy and constructed the effeminate male body as one of the key symbols of Decadence. In their habitual mode of transvaluation, Decadents valued their own cultural exquisiteness – their "art-for-art's sake" philosophy – which placed their cultural production outside the emphatically bourgeois, productive, and therefore "masculine" Victorian sphere.[4] James Eli Adams's study of the figure of the dandy emphasizes the extent to which the figure of the intellectual is itself a feminized one, since he stands outside the productive economy of the robust nineteenth-century culture.[5] Along with their appropriation of femininity as a paradox of weakness and divinity, Decadent writers espoused an aristocratic, anti-bourgeois attitude arising out of what Ellen Moers calls their general abhorrence of "uniformity, mediocrity and vulgarity."[6]

Contemporary reviews were critical of the "unmanliness" and the "effeminate frivolity" of *The Picture of Dorian Gray*, for example, a response which made clear that Dorian's life was interpreted as unnatural and rejected as antithetical to public morals and the ideal of Victorian robustness.[7] There is evidence that the effeminacy of Decadent writing also signified same-sex desire for some readers. As part of his scathing (pre-trial) assessment of Wilde and his contemporaries in the first English translation of *Degeneration* (1895), Max Nordau condemned the art of the Decadents by linking it to an implied homosexuality.

> Mere sensuality passes as commonplace, and only finds admission when disguised as something unnatural and degenerate ... Elegant titillation only begins where normal sexual relations leave off ... Vice looks to Sodom and Lesbos ... for its embodiments. (13)

Nordau's reading of Wilde in particular leads him to make this assertion. But while "unnatural" and "degenerate" appear to be vague condemnations (although, as we will see, Hichens' *The Green Carnation* uses unnatural to imply homosexuality), the reference to Sodom and Lesbos leaves no doubt that Nordau was reading Wilde and other Decadents in the "insider" mode because it suited his critique of Victorian art as degenerate to do so. Yet it also must be noted that in a book filled with detailed charges against the immorality of nineteenth-century art, this particular charge is made only once, obliquely.

The *Evening News* condemned Wilde after his 1895 trial by asserting that "England has tolerated the man Wilde for too long ... he is a social pest, a centre of intellectual corruption ... who attacked all the wholesome, manly, simple ideals of English life."[8] During and after the 1895 trials, conservative critics and an anxious public began the process of interpreting the spectacle of the feminized male not as the symbol of a liberating philosophical position (as the Decadents would have it[9]) but as a real pathological threat to the health and robustness of the body politic – or, as in the syphilitic metaphor used by the prosecutor in the Wilde trial to describe the defendant's sexual practices, "a sore which cannot fail in time to corrupt and taint it all."[10] The prosecutor's elision of the details of Wilde's sexual practices and its replacement with the syphilitic metaphor indicates the degree to which vice was interchangeable in the *fin-de-siècle* mind: effeminacy, on this model, can easily represent heterosexual vice (the transmission of syphilis between prostitutes, men, and their wives) and homosexual vice (same-sex desire that could remain nameless because "vice" suffices as a descriptive term). Wilde's effeminacy was thereby confusingly reinterpreted as a hallmark of vice both heterosexual and homosexual.

Oscar Wilde: Author of Effeminates and Effeminate Author

Wilde's complex relationship to effeminacy manifests itself in his aphorisms, plays, and essays, as well as *The Picture of Dorian Gray*. Among Wilde's unpublished aphorisms are several that address the relative effeminacy and manliness of men and women. In describing a period in which the New Woman was beginning to make her presence felt through her violation of traditional sex roles, Wilde observes that "[m]anliness has become quite effeminate. Only women are manly nowadays." He attempts another variation on this theme when he writes: "I like manliness in women. Women are so manly that manliness looks effeminate in men."[11] The sleight of hand that produces manliness as an "effeminate" or woman-identified trait releases men from the obligation to be manly by redefining it out of existence. A stable definition of manliness remains impossible because it has been rendered indistinguishable from effeminacy.

Wilde's slipperiness on the subject of effeminacy matches his coy perspective on heterosexuality. His male characters also maintain an ambiguous relationship to heterosexuality. As another of his unpublished aphorisms observes, "leading a double life is the only proper preparation for a marriage."[12] The theme of doubleness and leading a double life that resonates with secrecy makes Wilde's writing susceptible to interpretations of how it encodes same-sex desire. Such coding has been commonly deciphered by queer theorists and other attentive readers. Yet Wilde is engaged more in a paradoxical exercise of mystification and provocative deconstruction of apparently stable categories than an exposé of *fin-de-siècle* homosexuality. Wilde's inversion of the concepts of manliness and effeminacy illustrates the much-discussed deconstructive bent of his aphorisms – his collapse of binary oppositions and the resulting deflation of truisms. In the same manner, then, marriage and a double life become oppositional concepts, just as they do for Lord Henry Wotton in *The Picture of Dorian Gray* and for Algernon and Jack in *The Importance of Being Earnest* (1895). The secret lives of Dorian, Lord Henry, Algernon, and Jack are set up in opposition to heterosexual liaisons, but do not by themselves constitute a concrete articulation of same-sex desire.

Effeminacy and Wilde's Public Image

In the *Star* newspaper's coverage of Wilde's trials, one reporter remarked about Oscar Wilde's physical presence that he was "a man whom no-one who once saw him would be likely to forget."[13] Wilde's public presence invited public attention, criticism, and controversy from the time that he was an undergraduate at Oxford, and one of the most common forms that the critique of him assumed was the cartoon or caricature. While many representations of Wilde's body highlighted what were thought to be his feminine features and physique, others evoke the conception of effeminacy as an association with women and art. In one such illustration, Wilde is portrayed in an intimate clinch with a female admirer, and the caption reads: "The sympathetic nature of Modern Poetry can be better realized in Private than in Public lectures" (figure 13).[14] This cartoon, lampooning a moment in Wilde's 1882 tour of America, represents both his heterosexuality and his effeminacy, and links the two together in a critique of his over-association with all things feminine. Another caricature of Wilde's lecture tour of North America presents before and after sketches of Wilde that suggest the bracing, manly effect that contact with North America has had on the infamous aesthete (figures 14 and 15).[15] Wilde's feminine figure and his

The sympathetic nature of Modern Poetry can be realized in Private than in Public

13 Caricature from a set of three first published at Oxford, 1881–82.

14 Caricature from "Our Oscar," *Sporting Dramatic*, 21 July 1883.

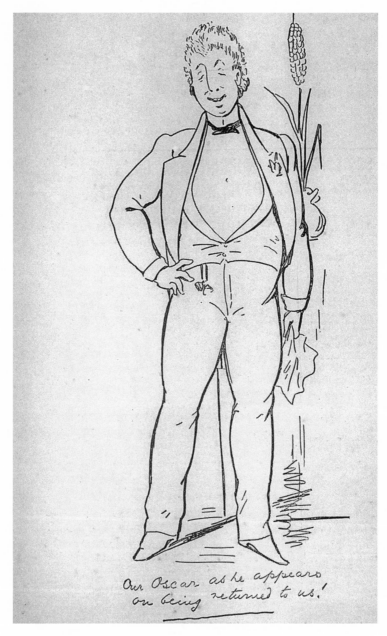

15 Caricature from "Our Oscar," *Sporting Dramatic*, 21 July 1883.

mincing pose are transformed into bulging, muscular thighs and a broad chest, and the lily – symbol of art-for-art's sake – has been transformed into a stalk of corn, a more utilitarian (and phallic) plant.

Other caricatures of Wilde from the same period emphasize an imagined femininity of his waist and hips, and exaggerate his lips, eyelashes, and long curling hair, while placing him in the midst of flowers (especially lilies and sunflowers), china, and drawing-room culture. These pre-trial depictions read Wilde's effeminacy in traditional ways, associating him with women's concerns and, especially in the before-and-after-America sketches, with the debility of an old and effete culture. Wilde, for his part, chose to ignore these depictions of himself, remarking in an 1882 letter to the manager of his American tour, Colonel Morse, that "I regard all caricature and satire as absolutely beneath notice."[16]

Edgar Charles Beall's *The Life Sexual* (1905) reuses two of the famous Napoleon Sarony studio photographs of Wilde taken for the American tour and affixes captions to them that urge readers to "Note the Femininity in All the Features" (figure 16) and "Note the Femininity in the Pose" (figure 17).[17] Retrospectively, the culture thought it could see in Wilde the effeminacy that indicated perversion, or more concretely, "inversion." A contemporary handwritten manuscript about Wilde entitled "Sexual Perversion"[18] endorses the very theories of inversion that Wilde himself often resisted. The writer explicitly agrees with Otto Weininger's *Sex and Character* (1905) in asserting that "no individual is entirely male or entirely female" (2) and that there are those in whom the parts of male and female are so equal as to have produced an individual whose sex appears to have been decided by chance. Such is the condition, the author concludes, of "effeminate men and masculine women" (3). He explains the concept of inversion by stating:

> Extreme cases are well known in which an individual, physically male, appears to be psychically entirely female. Such men delight to garb themselves in feminine raiment and to associate as a woman among women; in the way of a woman they seek to attract the attention of men, and they appear to experience all the sensations that are peculiar to the female sex. (3)

The author of "Sexual Perversion" postulates that there are other possible reasons for male homosexuality, including "criminal tendenc[ies]," "mental disease," and "intemperance" (4, 5) – all of which seek novel sensations. This post-trial assessment of Wilde as a figure of pathology

OSCAR WILDE—Note Femininity in All the Features

16 Studio photograph of Oscar Wilde by Napoleon Sarony, January 1882,
reproduced with caption in Edgar Charles Beall, *The Life Sexual*
(New York: Vim, 1905), facing 174.

OSCAR WILDE—Note the Femininity in the Pose

17 Studio photograph of Oscar Wilde by Napoleon Sarony, January 1882,
reproduced with caption in Edgar Charles Beall, *The Life Sexual*
(New York: Vim, 1905), facing 176.

builds on his putative effeminacy and constructs a model of the male homosexual as partaking in a host of pathological symptoms –"Intemperance with regard to eating should be included with the abuse of alcohol" (5). I single out the anonymous author's emphasis on excess because it is also a notorious attribute of the eighteenth-century effeminate aristocrat and the nineteenth-century degenerate. The stereotypes associated with effeminacy persist in the sexological analysis offered in this manuscript, and they are the traits that will persistently identify the effeminate and vice-ridden man, whether homosexual or heterosexual.

At his trial Wilde was confronted with a copy of the magazine *The Chameleon*, an 1894 publication to which he had contributed the collection of aphorisms, "Phrases and Philosophies for the Use of the Young."[19] Wilde was held morally accountable by prosecutors for the provocative story called "The Priest and the Acolyte," in which the priest Ronald Heatherington relates his unholy passion for his fourteen-year-old acolyte, a boy with "soft scarlet lips" and a "shy treble."[20] Censure of their sexual relationship drives Ronald and the boy to a double suicide. The feminine appearance and description of the child (soft curls, etc.) mirror those of the melancholic youth in the piece which precedes the story, "Two Loves," Lord Alfred Douglas's poem where he famously coined the phrase "the Love that dare not speak its name."[21] *The Chameleon*'s surprisingly forthright descriptions of same-sex desire utilize effeminacy as a key descriptive trope: for example, the figure representing homosexual love in "Two Loves" has cheeks like "pallid lilies" and "lips / Like poppies" (27–28). But the manipulation of effeminate images produces a more subversive effect in Douglas's poem than Heatherington's somewhat conventional (and perhaps even stereotypical) uses of effeminate tropes.

In "Two Loves," the reader is drawn into the poem by a guide whose overtures to an ostensibly male reader/viewer contradict the negativity and dejectedness of the figure of the "Love that dare not speak its name." This guiding figure is a naked youth with "wind-tossed hair" (27) entwined with purple flowers; he has wine-red lips, kisses the lips of the onlooker, feeds him grapes, and directs his gaze to the pageant of heterosexual love and its pale, homosexual counterpart. It is notable that all of the poem's figures are male, and that the melancholic youth is almost an afterthought in this all-male paradise. The figure of heterosexual Love may sing "of pretty maids / And joyous love of comely girl and boy" (27). But such comely figures are not found in the poem. In their place, the guide reveals the naked guide, the titillated reader, and the two "Loves," both beautiful men, frolicking in a pastoral setting.

Instead of presenting "sweet" (27) women with "lips / Like poppies," the poem conjures an exclusively male world in which the several meanings of effeminacy are referenced, including an over-identification with women and art, as well as an identification of the male subject as feminized and as a work of art. Although Douglas may pretend to wag his finger about the "Love that dare not speak its name," in his poem this personified Love is celebrated through its attention to male beauty and effeminacy, and through its simultaneous parody and exclusion of heterosexual coupling.

The pornographic novel *Teleny* portrays the homosexual underground of London as populated with a wide variety of homosexual types, but effeminacy represents only one possible persona. There is transvestitism, fleetingly, but it exists mainly on the fringes of a society that celebrated masculine virility and sexual prowess. The overused stereotype of the effeminate man who represents all homosexual men that emerged in the twentieth century is scarcely to be found here, suggesting that the lopsided portrayal of the equivalence of effeminacy and same-sex desire emanated from the desire of the culture to mark out difference as recognizable. In recycling effeminacy yet again, in reusing the signs of "vice" that marked eighteenth-century aristocrats and nineteenth-century degenerates, the culture thereby created an overdetermined set of traits that the healthy, right-minded population should avoid. Yet that is not to say that "Two Loves," "The Priest and the Acolyte," and *Teleny* in the 1890s held a monopoly on how the effeminate man should be construed in terms of types of homosexual preference. Effeminacy in this decade was not necessarily or exclusively inflected with a homoerotic charge. What remains largely obscured from the critical debate on effeminacy during this period is how the effeminate man might be a potential or actual husband, if of a singularly hazardous kind.

Marrying the Effeminate Man

Wilde was not the only *fin-de-siècle* writer whose conception of effeminacy remained tantalizingly vague. Contemporary accounts of effeminacy mixed aristocratic and homosexual meanings. Hichens' *The Green Carnation* provides an example of the marriage prospects of the Decadent artist from the Decadent point of view. It also provides a valuable account of the reading of the body of the effeminate man by a woman who is confused about what his effeminacy signifies. Hichens' account of the effeminate man is most interesting for its construction of an insider/outsider set of perspectives: those who are privy to the possible significations of effeminacy watch a woman who is an outsider trying to decipher its signs.

The Green Carnation is a thinly veiled roman-à-clef about the relationship between Wilde and Lord Alfred Douglas. Douglas appears as Reggie Hastings, a beautiful, effeminate young nobleman who has fallen under the spell of Esmé Amarinth, a Wildean dandy figure. Hastings is being put forward by a female relative as a prospective suitor of a widow, and the rather thin plot follows the development of their tepid courtship. What remains significant in the novel's construction of the effeminate heterosexual is the problem that Hastings poses for the widowed Lady Locke as a potential husband.

Wilde's life and art are doubly referenced here in the representation of Hastings and Amarinth as figures that closely resemble Dorian Gray and Lord Henry Wotton. The novel draws heavily on the themes of Dorian Gray, while also purporting to reveal something about Wilde and Douglas, one year before the trial that made their relationship infamous. Lady Locke perceives Hastings as an interesting and even sexually attractive partner, but there is something dangerous about him that she has difficulty naming. One day, however, she overhears Hastings in the garden speaking with her son Tommy, who is interested in the green carnations that Hastings and Amarinth habitually wear. Lady Locke hears Hastings tell the boy that the green carnation "has the supreme merit of being perfectly unnatural. To be unnatural is often to be great."[22] Reggie, of whom it is said that he "worships the abnormal," appears to be speaking in code here in his repetition of the word "unnatural," whose connotations are slowly becoming clear to both Lady Locke and the reader. While Reggie's effeminate bearing has not put off Lady Locke from finding him attractive (and indeed has provided something of a welcome contrast to her first husband, a soldier), this conversation unsettles Lady Locke and she refuses Reggie's diffidently offered proposal of marriage. While she harbors feelings for this "tired, unnatural boy," she none the less finds that his speech has opened her eyes and "shown her in a flash the influence that a mere pose may have upon others who are not posing" (160).

The transmission of influence from an older, more experienced man to a younger impressionable man that provided one of the central themes of Dorian Gray is emphasized here in the fictionalized portrait of the Wilde-Douglas friendship, and in the exchange between Hastings and Lady Locke's young son. Lady Locke, whether she realizes it or not, recognizes that the unusual kind of friendship that exists between Amarinth and Hastings might exist between Hastings and Tommy. Here she reacts not to protect herself but to defend the traditional family structure and the morals of her child. And while Lady Locke cannot quite understand what it is about Amarinth and Hastings that bothers her, she senses his essential unsuitability to be her husband. This novel reveals that Lady Locke and many others in her society could remain unaware of the possible meaning of the homosexual signifiers associated with Reggie, even to the point of finding the men thus described sexually attractive. While readers are, from a position of retrospective understanding, in on the joke of trying to marry off Reggie, the picture painted of *fin-de-siècle* culture is an ambiguous one in which the effeminate man might still be desirable as a husband.

New Women and the Effeminate Heterosexual

The bogey of the effeminate eighteenth-century aristocrat – the all-purpose villain whose behavior informed that of many a nineteenth-century dandy – is revived by New Women writers who drew explicit connections between their nineteenth-century novels about syphilitic husbands and eighteenth-century novels like Samuel Richardson's *Clarissa* (1747–48), in which women are sexually victimized by men. In appropriating the theme of victimhood at the hands of callous aristocrats, such novels also import the descriptions of hereditary weakness and vice-ridden debilitation associated with this aristocratic model of effeminacy. Their villains are decayed noblemen whose effeminacy is signaled through their use of makeup, their clothing, and their enervated and feminized bodies.[23]

This reception and redeployment of the concept of effeminacy by the New Women writers emphasized the sexual awareness of women in the face of the spread of syphilis. Grand and Brooke represent what we might consider to be a conservative strain of early feminism that arose out of the sexual purity campaigns in defense of marriage and motherhood. (Although Grand and Brooke in many ways represent the politics of sexual purity shared by many other New Women writers, these two authors embody a different kind of feminism from that of novelist Mona Caird, whose influential thinking about marriage and sexuality, to our eyes at least, looks more radical.) Brooke's *A Superfluous Woman* relates the tragedy of a pure young woman choosing a vice-ridden and syphilitic aristocratic husband who has "vile eyes" and "heavily scented apparel." Both Brooke and Grand want to educate women to recognize the signs of degeneracy by drawing their attention to physical markings they cobbled together out of the degeneration theories of Nordau, Cesare Lombroso, and other *fin-de-siècle* cultural critics, as well as out of Wilde's works themselves. Grand's *The Heavenly Twins* describes the syphilitic man as weakened, enervated, and effeminate, while her 1897 novel *The Beth Book* expands the warnings about syphilitic men to more general warnings about the dangerous kinds of art produced by Decadent writers and their imitators. It is only by reading Grand's two books together that one can see the development of the metaphor of infection as it is applied first to the actual physical danger of syphilis and then to the abstract danger of the "art-for-art's sake" movement.

Grand's novels written before and after the Wilde trials do not alter their view of the effeminate man in any significant way. After the trial, many critics have argued, *Dorian Gray* was widely reread as an account of male homosexuality. The New Women novels rely not only on Wilde's detailed descriptions of effeminate men like Dorian but also a Dorian Gray-like scenario of deceptive appearances that signal male vice. In New Women's accounts, the Dorian figure is beautiful, but closer examination reveals the signs of vice that signify their potential as carriers of syphilis. These books expose the fact that one might have known that the beautiful man was in fact dangerous because of his rose-red lips and his hereditary effeminacy.

Grand and Brooke also transformed the rhetoric of effeminacy to some degree by engaging in a discussion of evolutionary effemination. By that, I mean that they argued that effeminate men were part of a class of degenerates who were failing to progress according to contemporary notions of evolutionary theory. In her nonfiction essays, Grand translates physical shortcomings into abstract qualities that denote male inability to adapt to the progressive improvement of the human race, and she argues that conservative men who oppose progress are "effeminated by position of nature."[24] Although to contemporary eyes Grand's anxiety about gender behavior is more in line with conservative critiques of dandies and New Women such as those found in *Punch*, Grand articulates an entire discourse of political and social progressivism based upon the relative evolutionary positions of effeminate men and New Women. By deflecting all criticism back onto a perceived crisis of masculinity among males, she sidesteps the frequent charge of excessive masculinity on the part of women. Grand diagnoses the ills of her society by arguing that "the trouble is not because women are mannish, but because men grow ever more effeminate." Insufficiently masculine men cannot play their proper role as husbands, and the whole structure of society is thereby thrown out of balance. Effeminacy therefore appears unnatural but it has been stripped of any of its homosexual signification, and instead stands for something "unnatural" and "vice-ridden" in both an evolutionary and degenerationist sense and an eighteenth-century sense – thus marking the effeminate man as a kind of throwback. Although Grand and Brooke adapt Wildean figurations of the effeminate man for their purposes, they do not retain any hint of a coded assignment of homosexuality to effeminacy. In fact, effeminacy is even portrayed as a quality often attractive to women (the exception to that emerges in Brooke's book, where Lord Heriot is portrayed as revolting, and the heroine Jessamine is "naturally" attracted to a healthy peasant).

The uneven development of the association of effeminacy, vice, and homosexuality is paralleled by the uneven development of radical politics at the *fin-de-siècle*. Grand and those like her disapprove of Decadence because it is a deliberately retrogressive movement; it was, however, also considered simultaneously "modern," as Lady Locke senses. Yet the paradox of the Decadent sensibility – that one must go back in order to progress – is not appreciated by Grand and some of the other New Women. It is one shared by many critics of today who place Wilde and Decadence at the very start of the Modernist sensibility, but this association would have unsettled Grand and Brooke because their vision of progress was strikingly different; it was pragmatic instead of artistic and intellectual, moral instead of relativist, political instead of playful. For example, *The Green Carnation* pokes fun at the earnestness of works by Grand and Mrs. Humphry Ward, who was not herself a New Woman but was actively and earnestly involved in other political movements – anti-suffrage in her case. Hichens' drawing of the lines in this way pits aesthetic concerns against political ones, despite the great differences between writers like Grand and Ward. This phenomenon highlights the difficulty of separating *fin-de-siècle* politics into conservative or radical camps, since there are at least three different positions that could be taken, if not more. Teresa Magnum proposes that what she calls "the ethical aesthetics of the New Woman" should replace the usual pejorative charge of didacticism that stigmatized politically motivated writing.[25] I like this term because it admits the extent to which there is a conscious set of both moral and artistic considerations driving the work of writers such as Grand, and even hints at their susceptibility to "aesthetic" ways of approaching the world. Grand's conclusion to *The Beth*

Book attempts to mediate between aesthetics and ethics by proposing a quasi-Decadent, or perhaps even a reformed Decadent, as a partner for the New Woman. He is neither a virile athlete nor what Grand would have considered an amoral Decadent aesthete, but he combines the fantasy of the "best" parts of both. This fantasy is still necessarily heterosexualized.

In her post-trial novel, *The Beth Book*, Grand expands the scope of the connection between effeminacy, Decadent writers, and danger to women. Whereas the effeminate man first posed a threat to the physical health of women, he now poses a threat to the health of their art and to their morals. The writer Beth's attraction to the dandy figure Alfred Cayley Pounce is dangerous because Pounce represents both physical and artistic degeneracy. Grand's descriptions of Pounce as a very young man are quite similar to those which designate the misleading features of *Dorian Gray* and of the dangerous husbands in *The Heavenly Twins* and *A Superfluous Woman*: Pounce has "well-shaped feet and long, delicate, nervous hands. His face was shaved clean ... so that his somewhat shallow complexion looked smooth to effeminacy" (257). Pounce has "refined" features and "china-blue eyes," and Grand remarks that "every inch of him was a joy" to Beth, thus alerting women to the danger of their own sexual desire for such men (257–58). As Pounce ages, however, he degenerates into "an old-looking young man" whose body is stooped and nearing nervous collapse, and Grand assigns Pounce the stereotypically negative feminized traits of hysteria and conceit (484). Beth appears to understand the danger that Pounce poses: he represents Decadence (with a capital D) that is as much a stylistic threat to her emerging literary talent as syphilis might be to her body. Beth has been taught earlier in the novel by one of her literary mentors to recognize bad literature as both French literature and Decadent literature:

> If France is to be judged by the tendency of its literature and art at present, one would suppose it to be dominated and doomed to destruction by a gang of lascivious authors and artists who are sapping the manhood of the country and degrading the womanhood by idealizing self-indulgence and mean intrigue. The man or woman who lives low, or even thinks low, in that sense of the word, will tend always to descend still lower in times of trial. (398)

Beth has therefore learned to spurn "art for art's sake" in favor of "art for man's sake" because, as another of Grand's characters declares, "the work of art for art's sake and style for style's sake end on the shelf much respected, while their authors end in the asylum, the prison, and the premature grave" (500). This unmistakable reference to the fates of Wilde and other Decadent writers classifies Pounce as one of them and links him to the Decadent privileging of style over moral or political content. Grand's descriptions of his body alert the reader to the dangers of Pounce's Decadence, and the literary and political threat that this Decadence poses to the New Woman is deliberately described in the same terms as the bodily threat that the syphilitic poses to his wife.

But Grand's New Woman has difficulty escaping her attraction to the Decadent man. Beth's ideal man Arthur (and I think of course that the Britishness of his name is quite significant because it emphasizes that he is not French) is physically similar to both Alfred Cayley Pounce and to the Keatsian Romantic prototype of the artist which was in many ways appropriated and transformed by Decadent writers into the pale and sickly aesthete. Beth's lover Arthur is described as "refined," "delicate," "tall," "slim," "ethereal," and "consecrated to death by some insidious slow disease from which there is no escape" (535). This ideal man that Grand's novel promotes is significantly not the vigorous masculine type that Grand's non-fiction essays hail as the savior of civilization, but a more moderate and unusual man – refined but "virile" – whose description is mediated through the very effeminacy that she claims to disdain. The reasons that the New Women embraced (both literally and metaphorically) the figure of the effeminate man as both an all-purpose villain and a problematic object of desire would include, I think, their own desire to escape the charge of excessive masculinity with which the figure of the New Woman was often tarred. In seeking to shift the focus away from the charge of excess masculinity in women and onto a crisis of masculinity in men, the New Women reformulate the terms of the critique used against them and portray the effeminate as the weaker partner in a binaristic gender structure. Grand's position in particular is inherently unstable, in that it both repudiates and desires the effeminate man and constructs effeminacy as both sexually and morally attractive and sexually and morally dangerous.

The assumption that Wilde's contemporaries immediately understood and accepted the implications of his trial when evaluating the concept of effeminacy, then, is to impose retrospectively an anachronistic and unsustainable coherence upon a complex cultural phenomenon. Grand, as her diatribes against the Decadent artist expose, was reading Wilde's dandyism as a *heterosexual* threat both before and after the trial.

Moreover, the effeminate man, despite Grand's calls for increased masculinity, still constitutes an object of desire, however perverse that may
seem. Grand's notable exception is not one that proves the rule, but
instead calls into question the wisdom of making a rule at all.

This chapter has interrogated whether there is such a thing as effeminacy that can be discussed or referred to with any sense of ontological
certainty. And it has revealed that the problem of effeminacy is a subset
of a larger problem of assigning contemporary political valuations to
fin-de-siècle political formations. The question of who or what is radical
and who or what is conservative is often clouded by our desire to align
the two *fin-de-siècles* and privilege what we consider radical. Both Decadents and New Women, in their manipulation of effeminacy and in
their politics as a whole, have progressive and regressive elements that
make their work complex and therefore not easily or immediately
categorizable.

Notes

1 The most important of these include James Eli Adams, *Dandies and Desert
   Saints: Styles of Victorian Masculinity* (Ithaca, NY: Cornell University Press,
   1995); Joseph Bristow, *Effeminate England: Homoerotic Writing after 1885* (New
   York: Columbia University Press, 1995), further page references in paren-
   theses; Richard Dellamora, *Masculine Desire: The Sexual Politics of Victorian
   Aestheticism* (Chapel Hill, NC: University of North Carolina Press, 1990);
   Linda Dowling, *Hellenism and Homosexuality in Victorian Oxford* (Ithaca, NY:
   Cornell University Press, 1994), further page references in parentheses;
   Jessica Feldman, *Gender on the Divide: The Dandy in Modernist Literature*
   (Ithaca, NY: Cornell University Press, 1993); and Alan Sinfield, *The Wilde
   Century: Effeminacy, Oscar Wilde, and the Queer Moment* (New York: Columbia
   University Press, 1994), further page references in parentheses.
2 A.J.A. Symons' analysis of Oscar Wilde in an unpublished manuscript "Oscar
   Wilde in America" (Clark Library, manuscript Wilde S988M3 081, 193–?)
   includes a discussion of Wilde's "feminine sensibility" and his "womanly"
   liking for luxurious fabrics (f.22). Symons direly notes that this "feminine"
   appreciation of beautiful objects was subsequently transferred to the bodies
   of young men.
3 Pierre Vareilles, "Le progrès," in Anatole Baju, ed, *Le Décadent*, 1 (1886),
   cited in Barbara Spackman, *Decadent Genealogies: The Rhetoric of Sickness from
   Baudelaire to D'Annunzio* (Ithaca, NY: Cornell University Press, 1989), 5.

Spackman translates this passage as follows: "Precursors of future society, the decadents are already quite close to the ideal type of perfection ... Man becomes more refined, more feminine, more divine."

4 See the chapter "Anarchy and Physical Culture" in Bruce Haley, *The Healthy Body and Victorian Culture* (Cambridge, MA: Harvard University Press, 1978) for an interesting discussion of the longstanding tension between manliness and effeminacy in Victorian culture; Haley considers Matthew Arnold's *Culture and Anarchy* (1869) and its robust-minded critics, who read Arnold's call for "sweetness and light" as "effeminate" (174).

5 See Adams, *Dandies and Desert Saints*. Adams' conclusions suggest the extent to which the identification of social and economic utility and masculinity are equivalent, and charts the attempts by writers such as Thomas Carlyle to reconcile intellectuality and masculine identity by reconfiguring masculinity itself, a project which exposes masculinity as a constructed and performative (and therefore "feminized") identity, traits which it shares with the hated figure of the dandy. Studies like Adams' deconstruct binaries of gender that the Victorians were so clearly anxious to naturalize, but the paradox of the representation of the Decadent male (*by* the Decadent male) is the extent to which it simultaneously reinforces and questions such gendered stereotypes. By reaffirming the body of the female as symbolic "other," they both challenged social conventions of masculinity and reinforced through celebration the stereotype of female weakness, decorativeness, and economic marginality. This double movement is confusingly both progressive and regressive, highlighting the difficulties of assigning modern political terminology to this complex cultural maneuver; however, the retention of many of degenerationism's original and troubling implications is the logical result of a discourse being reused but not thoroughly reformulated.

6 Ellen Moers, *The Dandy: Brummell to Beerbohm* (Lincoln, NB: University of Nebraska Press, 1978), 264. Moers's study was first published in 1960.

7 Rita Felski, "The Counter-Discourse of the Feminine in Three Texts by Wilde, Huysmans, and Sacher-Masoch," *PMLA* 106 (1991), 1098, and Regenia Gagnier, *Idylls of the Marketplace: Oscar Wilde and the Victorian Public* (Stanford, CA: Stanford University Press, 1986), 59.

8 *Evening News*, 27 May 1895, 1.

9 Linda Dowling observes that Walter Pater and his Oxonian disciples had developed, after Plato and Socrates, a revised theory of effeminacy which argued that, as the robust population of Victorian England was not in danger if some citizens did not contribute to its increasing size, a higher form of procreation, "spiritual procreancy," was available to educated men; essentially, they withdrew themselves from a man's role in the reproductive

economy of Victorian Britain. This kind of theorizing allows Wilde to argue at his trial that his relationship with Alfred Douglas was one "such as Plato made the very basis of his philosophy" (*Hellenism and Homosexuality in Victorian Oxford*, 1).

10 H. Montgomery Hyde, *The Trials of Oscar Wilde*, 2nd ed. (New York: Dover), 213.

11 These aphorisms are taken from one of Wilde's notebooks held in the Clark Library ([Phrases, Aphorisms, and Fragments of Verse] Wilde 672 1M3 P576 [189–] Bound), penultimate leaf.

12 Wilde, [Phrases, Aphorisms, and Fragments of Verse], eight pages from end of notebook.

13 *Star*, 6 April 1895, in Clark Library, Wilde uncatalogued rare 1895–1914 news cuttings of three trials Bound Boxed, 27.

14 This caricature is the last in a set of three photographs that were originally published at Oxford, 1881–82. It comes from an album assembled by Christopher Millard and held at the William Andrews Clark Memorial Library: Wildeiana 7.18b.

15 These two caricatures belong to a set of four that appeared under the heading "Our Oscar," *Sporting Dramatic*, 21 July 1883. They are taken from an album assembled by Christopher Millard and held at the William Andrews Clark Memorial Library: Wildeiana 7.6a and b.

16 Wide, "To Colonel W.F. Morse," late June 1882, in *The Complete Letters of Oscar Wilde*, ed. Merlin Holland and Rupert Hart-Davis (London: Fourth Estate, 2000), 174.

17 Edgar Charles Beall, *The Life Sexual: A Study of the Philosophy, Physiology, Science, Art, and Hygiene of Love* (New York: Vim, 1905), facing 174.

18 "Sexual Perversion," f2; further folio numbers appear in parentheses. "Sexual Perversion" is an unsigned manuscript held at the Clark Library (Wilde uncataloged drawer 12f). Its provenance is unclear but the language it uses, the concepts it espouses, and the people and events to which it refers place it in the first decade of the twentieth century, around the same time as the figures from Beall's *The Life Sexual.*

19 Wilde, "Phrases and Philosophies for the Use of the Young," *The Chameleon* 1 (1894), 1–3.

20 John Francis Bloxam, "The Priest and the Acolyte," *The Chameleon* 1 (1894), 30.

21 Lord Alfred Douglas, "Two Loves," *The Chameleon* 1 (1894), 28; further page references appear in parentheses.

22 [Robert Hichens,] *The Green Carnation*, The Pioneer Series (London: William Heinemann, 1894), 130; further page references appear in parentheses.

23 See my article, "New Women and 'Old' Men: Gendering Degeneration," in
   Talia Schaffer and Kathy Alexis Psomiades, eds., *Women and British Aestheticism* (Charlottesville, VA: University Press of Virginia, 1999), 62–80, for a
   fuller discussion of the problem in Brooke's and Grand's fiction.
24 Sarah Grand, "The New Aspects of the Woman Question," *North American
   Review* 158 (1894), 274–75.
25 Teresa Magnum, "Style Wars of the 1890s: The New Woman and the Decadent," in Nikki Lee Manos and Meri-Jane Rochelson, eds., *Transforming
   Genres: New Approaches to British Fiction of the 1890s* (New York: St. Martin's
   Press, 1994), 49.

chapter eleven

Oscar Wilde and Jesus Christ

STEPHEN ARATA

As my title indicates, the topic of this chapter is Oscar Wilde and Jesus Christ, but I would like to begin with a few words about Lord Byron. Shortly after Easter 1816 Byron left England never to return, bringing to a close what a recent biographer justly calls his *annus horribilis*. The scandalous rumors – some true, others fabricated, all exquisitely titillating – surrounding Byron's conduct during his brief marriage to and very public separation from Annabella Milbanke left him with few friends and even fewer defenders.[1] "I was accused," he wrote later, "of every monstrous vice by public rumour, – and private rancour ... I felt that, If what was whispered and muttered and murmured was true – I was unfit for England, – if false – England was unfit for me."[2] Once abroad, Byron, being Byron, further increased his notoriety by feeding off it. In Cantos III and IV of *Childe Harold's Pilgrimage* (1816–18) he offered to his public a darker, more terrible version of the poetic persona that had won him fame in Cantos I and II in 1812. In the poem's most openly autobiographical passage, stanzas 130–37 of Canto IV, the speaker awakens the goddess Nemesis to help avenge the egregious wrongs done to him. Do not mistake me, he cautions us. It is not that I am guiltless. It is that I am being punished by those whose guilt far exceeds my own. Through my own "faults," he writes, I "have incurr'd / ... the wound / I bleed withal, and, had it been conferr'd / With a just weapon, it had flowed unbound."[3] Seeking retribution, the poet finds that the sole weapon at his disposal is words. And so we get the magnificent invective of stanzas 134 and 135. Here is the key part for my purposes:

> But in this page a record will I seek.
> Not in the air shall these my words disperse,

Though I be ashes; a far hour shall wreak
The deep prophetic fullness of this verse,
And pile on human heads the mountain of my curse!

That curse shall be Forgiveness. (1202–07)

The "forgiveness curse" is a quintessentially Byronic gesture. It rivets our attention on the transcendent sufferings of the poet – "Have I not had my brain seared, my heart riven, / Hopes sapp'd, name blighted, Life's life lied away?" (1211–12) – while also serving to damn further the very objects of his ostensible forgiveness. The passage concludes with Byron's bold assertion that "something unearthly" (1230) within him will survive even his death and – this is the climax of the episode – that this something will finally, inexplicably, be the agent of love and perhaps even of forgiveness.

But I have lived, and have not lived in vain:
My mind may lose its force, my blood its fire,
And my frame perish even in conquering pain,
But there is that within me which shall tire
Torture and Time, and breathe when I expire;
Something unearthly, which they deem not of,
Like the remembered tone of a mute lyre,
Shall on their softened spirits sink, and move
In hearts all rocky now the late remorse of love. (1225–34)

Oscar Wilde liked to say that one's ancestry could be traced through books as well as through blood.[4] In this special sense, Byron is Wilde's ancestor. It is not merely that his life-plot – self-creation, fame, self-promotion, sexual impropriety, scandal, disgrace, exile, self-justification, early death, posthumous notoriety – bears an intriguing if finally superficial resemblance to Byron's. (I remain, however, fascinated, as Wilde himself was, by the way that he seemed continually to be reenacting other people's lives, even afterlives, in his own.) It is also not simply that Byron's forgiveness curse finds its far-off echo in the damning absolution bestowed on Alfred Douglas in the long letter that Wilde composed to Douglas during the last months of his imprisonment in early 1897.[5] Byron is a precursor to Wilde in Wilde's highly idiosyncratic use of that term, a figure to be imitated precisely because he is, literally, inimitable.

Along with other controversial nineteenth-century figures such as Percy Bysshe Shelley, Charles Baudelaire, Paul Verlaine, Robert Browning, and Prince Peter Kropotkin, Byron belongs to Wilde's select confraternity of those who, as he puts it in "The Soul of Man under Socialism" (1891), have been able "to realise their personality more or less completely."[6] Like the others, Byron in Wilde's view created himself out of his own imagination and thus became, to lift a phrase from his prison letter to Douglas, "the fulfilment of a prophecy."[7] But Byron can claim membership in an even more select group within this distinguished brotherhood, namely those who have been compelled by circumstance to realize their personality in opposition to the dominant culture. "*Most personalities have been obliged to be rebels,*" Wilde writes emphatically in "The Soul of Man under Socialism," since the development of their individuality entails rejecting or subverting social norms (297). For Wilde the path of the rebel is heroic, though the rebel personality is inevitably "wounded, or worried, or maimed, or [put] in danger" by the very "*friction*" of opposition (297–98). "Byron was never able to give us what he might have given us," Wilde writes, because his personality "was terribly wasted in its battle with the stupidity, and hypocrisy, and Philistinism of the English" (298). The rebel inevitably pays for his rebellion not only by being imprisoned (like Verlaine and Kropotkin), exiled (like Shelley and Byron), or ostracized (like Baudelaire and Swinburne), but also by failing to achieve what Wilde calls the perfection or full expression of the self. By the mid-1890s Wilde – imprisoned, exiled, ostracized – had reason to fear that his own personality had suffered a similar wounding.

Yet even within this brotherhood of the maimed, Byron occupies a special place. In his prison letter to Douglas, Wilde famously claimed for himself the distinction of one who "stood in symbolic relations to the art and culture of [his] age." Less often remembered is the fact that he then goes on to accord to Byron the same honor. Wilde compares himself to Byron ostensibly in order to highlight an important difference. "Byron," he writes, "was a symbolic figure, but his relations were to the passion of his age and its weariness of passion. Mine were to something more noble, more permanent, of more vital issue, of larger scope" (*Complete Letters*, 729). Within two paragraphs of this claim, however, Wilde implicitly underlines his affinity with rather than his difference from Byron. "Tired of being on the heights I deliberately went to the depths in the search for new sensations. What the paradox was to me in the sphere of thought, perversity became to me in the sphere of passion.

Desire, at the end, was a malady, or a madness, or both" (730). Thus he too, Wilde seems here to acknowledge, could be said to stand in symbolic relation both to the passion and to the weariness of passion of his age. Yet these lines serve finally to point toward another, perhaps richer, way to articulate the distinction between the respective situations of Byron and Wilde than the one Wilde begins with. That distinction turns on the different valences of the pseudo-synonyms "passion" and "desire." It is no accident that in this section of his prison manuscript a discussion of passion modulates into a meditation on desire. The change in fact occurs in the sentences I just quoted, where passion is the final word of one sentence, desire the initial word of the next. In that transition we can discern one sign of a larger shift from a Romanticist to a post-Romanticist relation to feeling. By the 1890s desire had long since become a central term within the discourses of clinical psychology. As Sigmund Freud's work shows most clearly, the modern study of emotion circles inescapably around the question – and it always is a question – of desire, with its diverse and highly charged affects and vicissitudes. To speak, however, of passion, as Wilde does with increasing frequency in his later writings, is to invoke older though no less familiar discursive structures regarding the feelings. Passion for Wilde almost invariably connotes a fullness, self-sufficiency, or self-identity of feeling that seemed to many nearly impossible to achieve in the modern world. In that sense passion is the very antithesis of desire, which, as all theorists of psychology from the 1870s to the present have insisted, is defined and driven by lack. In *Byron and the Victorians* (1995), Andrew Elfenbein argues that in the last quarter of the nineteenth century the name Byron came to stand for and to some extent authorize a certain range of illicit desires, including but not limited to same-sex desire.[8] But Byron could also be said to stand, in a word, for passion, for fully self-sufficient and transformative emotion of a kind that the late Victorians associated with Romanticism. By linking himself to Byron, Wilde is in effect giving yet another name to the love that imprisoned him.

Through his discussion of passion, moreover, Wilde links both himself and Byron to the figure of Jesus Christ. In Wilde's cosmology, Christ, like Byron and like Wilde himself, is a figure that stands in symbolic relation to his own age. He is thus an important Wildean precursor. Moreover, any inquiry into Wilde's use of the term "passion" must take into account both the literary and the theological contexts in which that term operates. Especially in his prison letter to Douglas, Wilde's empathy with Christ is thoroughly informed by his understanding of Christ's passion, which in turn is thoroughly informed by – though far from identical with – his notion of Romantic passion. In many respects it is easier to see what is at issue in Wilde's use of Byron, which is one reason I began with him. Byron does not show up often in Wilde's writings, but when he appears it is usually at intense, well-illuminated moments.[9] Christ by comparison is well nigh ubiquitous in Wilde's canon. Yet it is, oddly, that very visibility that has made assessment difficult. Critics have always acknowledged Christ's importance to Wilde, but the exact nature of the importance has not been adequately explored.

One problem is that we have not sufficiently historicized Jesus. That is to say, we have as yet not fully accounted for the range of meanings and values attached to the figure of Christ in the Victorian *fin de siècle*, nor for the range of potential uses – personal, political, aesthetic – to which those meanings and values could be put. It is safe to say that Jesus enjoyed something of a vogue in the nineteenth century. One index of this popularity is the sheer number of *Lebenen Jesu* that the era produced. Writing in the *Contemporary Review* in January 1900, James Stalker noted that "no characteristic of the theology of the second half of the nineteenth century has been more outstanding than its preoccupation with the life of Christ."[10] Stalker is referring both to the vast numbers of "Lives of Christ" published between 1850 and 1900 as well as to the popularity and influence of some of them. Works in English such as J.R. Seeley's *Ecce Homo* (1865), F.W. Farrar's *The Life of Christ* (1874), and Alfred Edersheim's *Life and Times of Jesus the Messiah* (1883) were bestsellers. Meanwhile, more controversial works from abroad – most notably, David Strauss's *Das Leben Jesu* (1835), Ernest Renan's *Vie de Jésus* (1863), and the many studies that they spawned – continued to be reprinted and to sell briskly in translation right through the end of the century. As the names of Strauss and Renan suggest, and as Stalker himself indicates, the scholarly study of the life of Christ was anything but a dusty or merely pedantic affair. It was by way of the figure of Jesus that some of the more pressing intellectual problems of the century – problems often existing at the intensely charged intersection of faith, politics, and scholarship – were most clearly articulated. Victorian "Lives of Christ" were always frankly and forthrightly "interested"; their ideological commitments were always clearly on display.

By the 1890s there were, in effect, many different Christs, and to invoke him was necessarily to bring into play a complex array of political and theological controversies. That depth of field is usually flattened out in contemporary Wilde criticism, with the result that we often do not see with as much clarity as we might what precisely is at stake when Wilde brings Christ on stage. Most accounts of Wilde's interest in Jesus, for instance, link it, explicitly or implicitly, to his lifelong fascination with Roman Catholicism. In such accounts, both Christ and Catholicism are then usually discussed in the context of a highly generalized portrait of late-century Decadence. This conflation is perfectly understandable, given Wilde's close connection (both personal and temperamental) to a tradition of French Decadent Catholicism, beginning with Charles Baudelaire and Jules Barbey d'Aurevilly and running through Paul Verlaine, Villiers de L'Isle-Adam, and, most notoriously, Joris-Karl Huysmans; given, too, how Christ-centric were the many converts to Rome within the more flaccid tradition of English Decadence. But even in the 1890s Catholicism and Decadence were hardly the synonyms they have often since been made out to be, and neither Catholicism nor Decadence provides us with an historical context in itself sufficient to account for the range of meanings and values inhering in the figure of Christ. With Wilde especially, it is important at least provisionally to dissociate Christ from these particular late-century discourses. Wilde was well read in classical and contemporary philosophy, theology, and aesthetics.[11] He would have been aware of the implications of the controversies swirling around not just the Higher Criticism but more specifically those surrounding the historical study of the life of Jesus. Wilde's Christ differs in important ways from the Christ of *fin-de-siècle* Decadence. While we can certainly find examples of a "decadent" Christ in Wilde's work, mostly in the early poetry, in the end that is not a model that gets us very far. Instead, we need to become more attuned to the range of meanings that came to be attached to the figure of Christ and were thus available for Wilde's use.

Interestingly, one familiar set of meanings Wilde consistently neglects or refuses to invoke involves Christ's sexuality. As Leo Steinberg demonstrates in *The Sexuality of Christ* (1983), from the Renaissance onward the physicality of Jesus – God incarnate – has been a key tenet of Christian theology as well as an inescapable fact of Christian art. What Steinberg calls the humanation of Christ by Renaissance artists and theologians alike – an insistence on his dual nature, fully divine yet also fully human – was inseparable from an intense if sometimes troubled awareness of Jesus's body as the site of, among other things, erotic desire.[12] The same dynamic operates in the nineteenth century, though with a difference.

Whereas Renaissance art generally focuses on Christ's own sexual potency as a clear sign of his status as redeemer and regenerator of the world, in the nineteenth century the emphasis switches, so that the body of Christ becomes an *incitement* to desire on the part of the believer. The more spectacular examples of this erotic are to be found, again, in the French Decadent tradition. I am thinking in particular of Huysmans' meditations on the erotics of sadism. In his novel *A Rebours* (1884), Huysmans calls sadism a "strange and ill-defined condition" that "cannot in fact arise in the mind of an unbeliever," since in its pure sense it is a form of sacrilege directed, ultimately, at the body of Christ.[13]

In England the eros of Christ generally takes milder forms. Hilary Fraser correctly notes that one distinguishing feature of popular theological writing in late-Victorian Britain was an intense interest in "the humanity and physicality of Christ."[14] Matthew Arnold's portrait of Jesus in *Literature and Dogma* (1871) emphasizes not just what Arnold calls the "sweet reasonableness" of the Messiah's character but also the comeliness of his figure.[15] In Thomas Hughes's *The Manliness of Christ* (1880) Christ, as Hughes's title suggests, is portrayed as both forceful in character and athletic in physique.[16] Walter Pater too is quite alive to Christ's physical beauty. In his novel *Marius the Epicurean* (1885) the attraction of Christianity is shown to be intimately bound up with an awareness of Christ as one who is as lovely as any Greek or Roman god. "All influence reached Marius ... through the medium of sense," Pater's narrator tells us; Marius's faith, like Pater's own, begins in sensuality.[17] So too does that of Gerard Manley Hopkins. "There met in Jesus Christ all things that can make man lovely and loveable. In his body he was most beautiful," Hopkins writes in a sermon he preached in 1879. Hopkins enumerates at some length the different features of Christ's "strong, healthy, and beautiful" body. "I leave it to you, brethren," he concludes, "to picture him, in whom the fulness of the godhead dwelt bodily, in his bearing how majestic, how strong and yet how lovely and lissome in his limbs, in his look how earnest, grave but kind ... for myself I make no secret I look forward with eager desire to seeing the matchless beauty of Christ's body in the heavenly light."[18]

If we search hard enough, we can find moments in Wilde's work where Christ is similarly eroticized. The image of the suffering, crucified Christ in his poem "Humanitad" is, as Patricia Clements has pointed out, deeply indebted to Baudelaire,[19] while in "Quia Multum Amavi" the speaker forthrightly compares his passion for his beloved to that of a priest for the Eucharist:

Dear Heart, I think the young impassioned priest
  When first he takes from out the hidden shrine
His God imprisoned in the Eucharist,
  And eats the bread, and drinks the dreadful wine,

Feels not such awful wonder as I felt
  When first my smitten eyes beat full on thee.[20]

The point to emphasize about such moments, though, is precisely their scarcity in Wilde's oeuvre. Generally speaking, his Jesus is an oddly disembodied figure. Counterintuitive though it may seem, the fact is that Wilde seldom avails himself of the vocabularies of decadence, eroticism, or even of physical beauty when he writes of Christ. It cannot be that he was unaware of these traditions. If Wilde conspicuously refuses to activate certain contemporary discourses regarding Christ and sexual desire, that fact alone suggests that he has other ends in mind. Indeed, an overlooked but finally more relevant context for understanding Wilde's depictions of Christ is a political one.

Here we must acknowledge the enormous importance of Renan's *Vie de Jésus*, specifically for Wilde but also for the later nineteenth century as a whole. Wilde's admiration for Renan's work was lifelong, deep, and, as far as the word can be made to apply to Wilde, sincere. With typical hyperbole, Wilde writes in "The Critic as Artist" that "the nineteenth century is a turning point in history simply on account of the work of two men, Darwin and Renan, the one the critic of the Book of Nature, the other the critic of the books of God."[21] Darwin and Renan are linked here because each can be said to have desacralized the world. Renan's Christ, like Strauss's before him, is fully human. In Renan's rendering, Jesus is the pious son of poor and obscure Galilean parents whose gentle religious temperament is decisively altered by his encounter with John the Baptist. The trajectory of Jesus's life is toward ever greater acceptance of John's harsh, messianic, apocalyptic message until, believing finally that he is in fact the Messiah whose self-sacrifice will redeem the world, Jesus allows himself to be captured and crucified by the Romans. The myth of the Resurrection Renan attributes to Mary Magdalen, while the task of crafting the supreme fiction of Christ's divinity is left to the compilers of the New Testament.[22] Like Strauss, Renan was harshly criticized not just for denying the divinity of Christ but for his overall insistence that the Bible be read as a set of historical documents rather than as divine revelation. Renan, though, is finally much less interested than Strauss had been in the simple task of debunking. To apply a wholly anachronistic vocabulary to their respective endeavors, we can say that where Strauss was primarily concerned to expose the false consciousness that both produced the Bible and continued to be produced by it, Renan is engaged in the more Wildean project of delineating the processes through which false consciousness produces "truth."

That project in turn is driven by Renan's desire to reclaim Christ as a vital cultural force. It is important to see that Renan humanizes Christ not in order to exorcize him from Western consciousness (which, it could be said, was one of Strauss's goals) but so as to make him relevant again to secular political thinking. Wilde was far from the only reader who found in Renan's narrative of Christ's life a kind of proto-socialist parable. As Daniel Pals has suggested, Renan's work became the basis for a range of "leftist" Christs promulgated by late-century theological and political thinkers.[23] Wilde's highly idiosyncratic contribution to this genre is "The Soul of Man under Socialism." In that essay Jesus is brought forward as the very prototype of the modern radical thinker, whose deceptively simple yet ultimately subversive message – "Be thyself" (298) – can serve, Wilde insists, as the ground for both personal salvation (again, in a wholly secular sense) and social renewal. This aspect of the essay has been well-studied, and I do not propose to pursue it here, except to observe that Wilde's depiction of Jesus as politically engaged rebel did not strike contemporary reviewers as at all unusual – which is not to deny that many found it objectionable. In other words, while Wilde's version of socialism was seen as idiosyncratic, his vision of Christ was not. It fitted securely within a tradition that could be traced back to Renan himself, for whom Jesus was "a man of the people" who effected not just a spiritual or moral revolution but a political one as well. Christianity, Renan argued, "was the first triumph of the Revolution, the victory of public opinion, the advent of the simple of heart, the inauguration of the beautiful as understood by the people. Jesus thus opened in the aristocratic societies of antiquity the breach through which all shall pass."[24] For Wilde, the terms of the revolution may have been different, but Christ's role as catalyst and exemplar is the same for him as it had been for Renan.

As many critics have noted, there are clear continuities between "The Soul of Man" and Wilde's prison letter to Douglas, most notably in their shared depiction of Christ as "the supreme individualist" and the type of the Romantic artist. In the latter work especially, Wilde insists on the "poetry" of Christ. "He is just like a work of art himself" (487). "His entire life ... is the most wonderful of poems" (477), while the reenactment of that life's final tragedy in the Mass is the most splendid of artistic rituals and "the supreme office of the Church" (478). Indeed, wherever there is great art, claims Wilde, "there, somehow, and under some form, is Christ, or the soul of Christ" (482).[25]

Yet the meditations on Jesus that occupy much of the epistle to Alfred Douglas also mark significant changes in the nature of Wilde's interest in Christ. Or, instead of "interest in," perhaps we should say "identification with." What is most immediately apparent in the prison letter is Wilde's insistence that we see in his trial and imprisonment a reenactment of Christ's last days. At times, Wilde's mapping of his own situation on to that of Christ is nearly complete. Many otherwise sympathetic readers, from James Joyce at the turn of the century through W.H. Auden in the 1950s to Jonathan Dollimore in the 1990s, have found this identification a discomforting, not to say fatuous, sign that Wilde had succumbed entirely to narcissism or self-pity, or both.[26]

Yet it is worth thinking again about Wilde's motives. Having identified his own story with Christ's, Wilde stresses an important difference between the two. The narrative arc of Jesus's life has a "sublimity of tragic effect" (478) unequaled in Western history or literature, Wilde writes, while "everything about" his own situation "has been hideous, mean, repellent, lacking in style" (490). Its squalor appalls; the absence of aesthetic form threatens to deprive his narrative of meaning. "Form, which is the birth of passion, is also the death of pain," Wilde had written in "The Critic as Artist" (1890),[27] and now the intensely felt formlessness of his prison life serves to augment his suffering. If in his prison letter Wilde offers himself as Christ's double, it is a doubling much like the one Wilde describes in a parable he told André Gide in the early 1890s. After the crucifixion, Joseph of Arimathaea encounters a young man weeping and, assuming that he is mourning Christ's death, attempts to comfort him.

> But the young man answered: "Oh! that's not why I am weeping. I'm weeping because I too have performed miracles! I too have restored sight to the blind, I have healed paralytics and I have raised up the dead. I too have withered the barren fig-tree and I have changed water into wine ... And men have not crucified me."[28]

In Wilde's view, the crucifixion confers meaning retrospectively on all

Christ's actions by binding those actions into a narrative whole. This is one reason why Wilde insists on calling the Gospels a tragedy: like the Greek tragedians, the evangelists understood that to redeem suffering one must give it form. By contrast, the weeping man of the parable, like Wilde himself in prison, finds himself in a plot without a resolution. And without a crucifixion there can be no resurrection, even a figurative one. "I am quite conscious of the fact," Wilde wrote to Robert Ross during the months before his release from Reading Gaol, "that when the end [of my imprisonment] *does* come I shall return an unwelcome visitant to a world that does not want me; a *revenant*, as the French say ... Horrible as are the dead when they rise from their tombs, the living who come out from tombs are more horrible still" (*Complete Letters*, 669).

The letters that Wilde wrote during the prison years continually return to his worry that his suffering will prove to have been pointless, precisely because it resists being given meaningful form. As a result, Wilde fears that he will walk as a revenant among the living, his own life-plot unconcluded and unredeemed. The prison letter to Douglas constitutes Wilde's most sustained effort to forestall that event. In effect, this long epistle is Wilde's attempt to write his own secular Gospel, by which I mean that like the New Testament it strives to translate the all-too-human passion of a particular exemplary individual into a textual event.[29] It is only through being transformed into text that his life can assume what Wilde considered to be its appropriate form, namely the form of tragedy. In the process, Wilde implicitly rewrites his aphorism from "The Critic as Artist." No longer is it sufficient to say that form is the death of pain. According to the Wilde of the prison manuscript, pain is the form of art.

Here again Renan's example is uppermost in Wilde's mind. The translation of Christ into text is precisely what Renan found most troubling about the New Testament. In his *Vie de Jésus* he undertakes the impossible task (in full knowledge of its impossibility) of trying to see Christ independently of the writings about him. Careful textual scholar that he was, impassioned lover of the Gospels that he was, Renan nevertheless strives, as Edward Said notes, to present Jesus "*as he could have existed* were it not for the intervening and authoritatively Christian text of the Gospels."[30] For Renan, Jesus's power lay in his originality, which Renan figures as a resistance to representation, a resistance to textuality. So extraordinary were Jesus's life and teachings that they could not be adequately conveyed through writing. Indeed, Renan makes much of the fact that Christ left no texts of his own, nor did he oversee or even encourage attempts by his disciples to codify his teachings. It is important to recognize, says Renan, that Christianity was originally inseparable from the person of Christ, which is to say inseparable from his spoken words as well as from the specific events of his life. Wilde made this same point in conversation with Robert Sherard: "It was by the voice he [i.e. Christ] found expression – that's what the voice is for, but few can find it by that medium, and none in the manner born of Christ."[31] In his life of Jesus, as in his later work on the apostles, Renan devotes considerable energy to tracing the processes by which this living, breathing, speaking man is translated, over the next two centuries, into increasingly authoritative texts that – while ensuring the continuity of Christianity – inevitably also diminish, dissemble, distort, and rigidify.

In his prison manuscript Wilde is unburdened by the yearning for presence that drives Renan's efforts to recover an authentic, historical Jesus, one not mediated by the intervening texts of the New Testament. Wilde's Christ is thoroughly enmeshed in the kind of textuality that Renan had described. Jesus is in Wilde's conception no longer a person at all (and not a God, either: Wilde entertains no doubts on that score)[32] but an artwork, a self-created one at that. Wilde's discussion of Christ takes place under the twin signs of sorrow and passion – passion in its older theological sense of suffering. To be defined by sorrow and passion is according to Wilde to be identical with yourself, to have no depth, no interiority, and no history. It is, strictly speaking, to be inhuman. It is to make yourself into what Wilde terms, oxymoronically, an incarnate image. And it is precisely as an incarnate image that Christ continues to exert power over the contemporary world. Such power, Wilde claims, is finally indistinguishable from the power of an ideal art. "[F]eeling, with the artistic nature of one to whom Sorrow and Suffering were modes through which he could realise his conception of the Beautiful, that an idea is of no value till it becomes incarnate and is made an image, [Jesus made] of himself the image of the Man of Sorrows" (*Complete Letters*, 746). In order for his prison letter to function as a secular gospel, Wilde must first translate himself into an incarnate image, an image of the Man of Sorrows. This is another way of saying that he must strive to give both his life and his writing the form of suffering. "Perhaps there may come into my art also," he writes, "no less than into my life, a still deeper note, one of greater unity of passion" (755). Unity of passion displaces the multiplicities of desire and appetite – "appetite without distinction, desire without limit and formless greed" (726) – that, according to Wilde, marked his former life and continues to mark the life of Alfred Douglas. This unity likewise supplants the truth of masks: indeed, one of the more intriguing features of this text is Wilde's insistence that the mask, arguably the central image of his writing prior to 1895, must be stripped away before "the dynamic forces of life" can "become incarnate" (753). If, as Wilde reiterates throughout the letter, Douglas is guilty of the supreme vice, "shallowness," the cure is not "depth" but "realisation." To realize oneself is to become self-identical and thus to refashion oneself as an incarnate image. Whatever is realized is right.

In remaking himself into the image of the Man of Sorrows, Wilde was negotiating in complex ways with the public identity that he had taken such care to craft over the previous two decades. That identity had always been enmeshed in the idea of "presence." Indeed, if there was one thing everyone knew about Wilde in 1880s and 1890s, it was precisely that he was a textless original. His full "meaning" somehow inhered in his person. How many testimonies from Wilde's contemporaries do we have of this one essential truth: that truly to know Wilde one had to experience him, had to hear him speak, see him act? The much-quoted saying about Wilde putting his genius into his life and only his talent into his work is very much to the point here.[33] We are continually told by those who knew Wilde that to read about him or even to read his works is a poor, not to say misleading, substitute for the real thing. Significantly, throughout most of this century, the "facts" of Wilde's life have been transmitted primarily by way of anecdote, personal reminiscence, gossip, legend, second-hand report, tall tale, apocryphal story scattered through innumerable memoirs, autobiographies, histories, essays, and newspaper articles. This situation has really changed only in the past decade or so, with the appearance of scholarly biographies by Richard Ellmann and Richard Pine.[34] The only comparable figure, in this respect, is Byron. Anyone who has done research on Wilde has had the experience of coming upon the same anecdote multiple times, each version slightly different from the others, sometimes related by "witnesses" who could not have been at the original event. This kind of writing accumulates around many literary figures, especially those writers who lived in the memoir-mad century that stretches from 1850 to 1950, but with Wilde the process is especially marked. It is also, and this is the important point, fundamental to our understanding of him, even more so perhaps than his own writings are.

Wilde of course was well aware of this aspect of his reputation and took care to nurture the impression that he had to be seen and heard to be appreciated. But he was equally aware of the corollary point: that his status as a textless original depended entirely on textuality, on the continued dissemination through print of a figure called "Oscar Wilde." With characteristic insouciance, even before his trial and imprisonment Wilde was not above seeing his situation as a profane version of Christ's. "Every time my name is mentioned in a paper," Frank Harris says Wilde said to him, "I write at once to admit that I am the Messiah ... The journalist is my 'John the Baptist.'"[35] And, we might add, the memoirist is his disciple. When, to take only one example, William Butler Yeats in his autobiography anointed Wilde as the greatest talker of the age, he confirmed Wilde's identity as the period's pre-eminent textless original while also acknowledging the dependence of that identity on the continued production of texts.[36]

In the twentieth century the process by which "Oscar Wilde" passed from the oral to the textual bears intriguing similarities to the process described by Renan in relation to the life of Christ. According to Renan, for the first century after Jesus's death the various documents recording his life and discourses were not treated as sacred texts closed to further development. Instead they remained permeable. New stories, anecdotes, information were freely added to the record, as were emendations and elaborations of existing material. Renan traces the slow process by which these fluid accounts solidified into authoritative texts. As Said notes, Renan "imagines the texts as first continuing, then replacing, then displacing a textless original" (217). In the beginning, Jesus's life "was the common spiritual property of friends and apostles; no one document contained his life complete. Each version in its own way continued his life, gently and silently replacing a previous version with a 'fuller' one ... Authority appears, or begins, when this process of silent replacement stops. *The authority of a text, according to Renan, is tied to the realization that a text has outlived whomever participated in its original making*" (217, italics in original). Wilde was aware of this dynamic in relation both to the gospels and to their secular analogs. As the records of his conversation as well as his own letters indicate, the twin examples of Christ and Byron were very much in his mind from the early 1890s onward.[37] By then Byron had passed into Renan's final stage. All the many and diverse texts – not just those by Byron but also and especially those about him – that together produced the figure "Byron" had by the last decades of the century outlived their originators. This is a significant moment in the reception history of any public figure, but especially for those like Byron or Wilde whose meaning or significance seems bound inextricably to their presence.

This context can help illuminate the vexed question of Wilde's motivations in writing his prison letter to Douglas. James Winchell, intriguingly, has called that letter an act of auto-hagiography.[38] As I suggested earlier, though, it makes more sense to see it as Wilde's attempt to write a gospel of his own. Among other things, Wilde hoped that such a document would counter the spurious "official" version of his later life, "one no less grotesque than venomous," being circulated by Douglas's father. "That version has now actually passed into serious history," Wilde complains. "It is quoted, believed, and chronicled: the preacher has taken it for his text, and the moralist for his barren theme" (*Complete Letters*, 719). In its place he offers the text of his letter to Douglas, a letter which, as John Albert has suggested, performs the traditional office of sacred writings by providing "material for the monastic exercise of *lectio* that leads to meditation, prayer, and contemplation."[39] Moreover, like the New Testament, Wilde's text aspires to function as what Said calls the sign of "a communal guilt and redemption" (210). In both texts a living "presence is transmuted into or sacrificed for words," a sacrifice that "makes possible the presence of an apostolic community forever stained with guilt" (210–11). To read the prison manuscript in this way is not to deny the multiple contradictions and tensions of this text: the tension between, for instance, Wilde's insistence on the specificity of his situation and his desire to generalize his experiences into parables; or between his depictions of the pain that degrades and the suffering that transfigures him; or, most notably, between his struggle to forgive Alfred Douglas as a gesture of Christian meekness and humility and his impulse to turn that forgiveness into a forgiveness curse. Despite these often jarring dissonances, the reception history of this text in all its various forms in the twentieth century provides ample evidence that a secular "apostolic community" quickly formed around the figure of the suffering and martyred Wilde, a body of readers who found and continue to find in Wilde's texts and in his life the occasion for a communal guilt and redemption.

Notes

1 See Phyllis Grosskurth, *Byron: The Flawed Angel* (Boston: Houghton Mifflin, 1997), 229. Byron and Milbanke married in January 1815. The following year was marked by financial difficulties and much erratic behavior by both parties; the couple were legally separated before the end of 1815. At some

point during this time Byron began an affair with his half-sister Augusta. The subsequent scandal was the most immediate cause of his departure from England in April 1816.

2 George Gordon Byron, *The Complete Miscellaneous Prose,* ed. Andrew Nicholson (Oxford: Clarendon Press, 1991), 95.

3 George Gordon Byron, *Childe Harold's Pilgrimage,* IV, lines 1190–92, in *Byron,* ed. Jerome J. McGann (Oxford: Oxford University Press, 1986); further line references to this poem appear in parentheses.

4 "Yet one had ancestors in literature, as well as in one's own race, nearer perhaps in type and temperament, many of them, and certainly with an influence of which one was more absolutely conscious": Oscar Wilde, *The Picture of Dorian Gray: Authoritative Texts, Backgrounds, Reviews and Reactions, Criticism,* ed. Donald L. Lawler (New York: W.W. Norton, 1988), 113.

5 When Robert Ross published slightly different abridged versions of this letter in 1905 and 1908, he titled it *De Profundis.* Since then, scholars have invariably called the letter by this title, a practice that, as Ian Small demonstrates in his contribution to the present volume (86–100), obscures the complex textual history of Wilde's letter. I have thus followed Small's practice of referring to the document Wilde wrote (which was first reproduced in Oscar Wilde, *Letters,* ed. Rupert Hart-Davis [London: Rupert Hart-Davis, 1962], 423–511) to Douglas as his prison letter or prison manuscript, in order to distinguish it from Ross's published versions.

6 "The Soul of Man under Socialism," *The Fortnightly Review* n.s. 49 (1891), 292; further page references appear in parentheses.

7 Wilde, "To Lord Alfred Douglas," January-March 1897, *The Complete Letters,* ed. Merlin Holland and Rupert Hart-Davis (London: Fourth Estate, 2000), 747; further page references appear in parentheses. See *Complete Letters,* 683, for a brief account of the letter's composition and earlier, partial publication.

8 Andrew Elfenbein, *Byron and the Victorians* (Cambridge: Cambridge University Press, 1995). Elfenbein is among the few critics to have written on Wilde's interest in Byron: see 229–38. But see also G. Wilson Knight's stimulating remarks on Wilde, Byron, and Christ in *The Christian Renaissance* (New York: W.W. Norton, 1962), especially 287–338.

9 Byron plays a key part in "Ravenna" (1878), for instance, a poem that Wilde consistently placed at or near the front of editions of his poems.

10 James Stalker, "Our Present Knowledge of the Life of Christ," *Contemporary Review* 77 (1900), 124.

11 See, for instance, Michael S. Helfand and Philip E. Smith II, eds., *Oscar Wilde's Oxford Notebooks: A Portrait of Mind in the Making* (Oxford: Oxford University Press, 1989).

12 Leo Steinberg, *The Sexuality of Christ in Renaissance Art and in Modern Oblivion*, second edition (Chicago: University of Chicago Press, 1983). Steinberg introduces the term "humanation" on 11.

13 J.K. Huysmans, *Against Nature [A Rebours]*, trans. Robert Baldick ([1884] Harmondsworth: Penguin, 1959), 162.

14 Hilary Fraser, *Beauty and Belief: Aesthetics and Religion in Victorian Literature* (Cambridge: Cambridge University Press, 1986), 219.

15 Matthew Arnold, *Literature and Dogma: An Essay Towards a Better Apprehension of the Bible* in Matthew Arnold: *Dissent and Dogma*, in *The Complete Prose Works of Matthew Arnold*, ed. R. H. Super, 11 vols. (Ann Arbor: University of Michigan Press, 1960–77), VI: esp. 217–21.

16 "Christ's whole life on earth was the assertion and example of true manliness": Thomas Hughes, *The Manliness of Christ* (Boston: Houghton, Osgood, 1880), 67.

17 Walter Pater, *Marius the Epicurean: His Sensations and Ideas*, ed. Michael Levy ([1885] Harmondsworth: Penguin, 1985), 166.

18 Gerard Manley Hopkins, *The Sermons and Devotional Writings*, ed. Christopher Devlin, SJ (London: Oxford University Press, 1959), 35–36.

19 Patricia Clements, *Baudelaire and the English Tradition* (Princeton, NJ: Princeton University Press, 1985), 172–73.

20 Oscar Wilde, "Quia Multum Amavi," in *Poems, Collected Works*, 14 vols, ed. Robert Ross (London: Methuen, 1908), IX: 199.

21 Wilde, "The Critic as Artist," *Collected Works*, VIII: 222.

22 Wilde has Renan in mind when he writes of Mary Magdalen in his "Sonnet: On the Massacre of the Christians in Bulgaria": "And was thy Rising only dreamed by Her / Whose love of thee for all her sin atones?" (*Collected Works*, IX: 34.)

23 Daniel Pals, *The Victorian "Lives" of Jesus* (San Antonio, TX: Trinity University Press, 1982), especially 59–124.

24 Ernest Renan, *The Life of Jesus*, trans. Charles Edwin Wilbour (New York: Carleton, 1864), 361.

25 What Wilde actually writes is that Christ is palpable "wherever there is a romantic movement in Art" (482). But Wilde includes under that heading everything he considers worthwhile in art, from Arthurian tales and Provençal poetry to Shakespeare's plays, Thomas Chatterton's verse, and the diverse works of the English Romantic poets.

26 See James Joyce, "Oscar Wilde: The Poet of 'Salomé'" (1909), in *The Critical Writings of James Joyce*, ed. Richard Ellmann and Ellsworth Mason (Ithaca: Cornell University Press, 1989), 201–05; W. H. Auden, "An Improbable Life," in *Oscar Wilde: A Collection of Critical Essays*, ed. Richard Ellmann (Englewood

Cliffs, NJ: Prentice-Hall, 1969), 116–37; Jonathan Dollimore, *Sexual Dissidence: Augustine to Wilde, Freud to Foucault* (Oxford: Clarendon Press, 1991), 95–97.

27 Wilde, "The Critic as Artist," *Collected Works*, VIII: 208.

28 E. H. Mikhail, ed., *Oscar Wilde: Interviews and Recollections*, 2 vols. (London: Macmillan, 1979), II: 292.

29 In calling Wilde's prison letter a secular gospel, I am mindful of Ian Small's cautions regarding the generic complexities of this text – or rather, texts, since the letter exists in several distinct versions, each keyed, as Small points out, to a different imagined audience and thus operating under a different generic sign. (Though Small does not mention it, a similar argument can be made about other of Wilde's texts, most notably his fairy tales.) The version I consider here is the typescript Small labels A4 (see this volume, 94). Like Small, I am persuaded that Wilde intended the letter *in this form* to be read not as private correspondence but as a public document addressed to Douglas.

30 Edward Said, *Beginnings: Intention and Method*, 2nd ed. (New York: Columbia University Press, 1985), 219. The italics in the quotation are Said's. Subsequent page references to this book are given parenthetically in the text. My subsequent discussion of Renan draws on Said's suggestive remarks, which also apply in interesting ways to Wilde's situation.

31 Robert Sherard, *The Life of Oscar Wilde* (London: T. Werner Laurie, 1906), 379.

32 See, for instance, Sherard, *Life of Oscar Wilde*: "'The divinity of Christ,' said [Wilde], 'in its generally accepted sense, I, of course, do not believe'" (380).

33 According to André Gide, Wilde once said to him: "C'est que j'ai mis mon génie dans ma vie; je n'ai mis que mon talent dans mes œuvre": *Letters*, ed. Hart-Davis, ix.

34 Richard Ellmann, *Oscar Wilde* (London: Hamish Hamilton, 1987); Richard Pine, *The Thief of Reason: Oscar Wilde and Modern Ireland* (Dublin: Gill and Macmillan, 1995). This is not to diminish the importance of earlier memoirs and biographical sketches such as those by Robert Sherard, Bernard Shaw, Frank Harris, Hesketh Pearson, and even Alfred Douglas himself, but only to point out that Wilde's afterlife has moved into a new phase.

35 Frank Harris, *Oscar Wilde: His Life and Confessions* (New York: Printed and published by the author, 1916), 104.

36 See *Autobiographies*, ed. William H. O'Donnell and Douglas N. Archibald, *The Collected Works of W.B. Yeats*, 14 vols. (New York: Scribner, 1989–2000), III: 124. On the importance of speech and oral narrative to Wilde's self-construction, see Deirdre Toomey's stimulating essay, "The Story-Teller at

Fault: Oscar Wilde and Irish Orality," in Jerusha McCormack, ed. *Wilde the Irishman* (New Haven, CT: Yale University Press, 1998), 24–35.

37 The conjunction is implicit in "Sebastian Melmoth," the pseudonym Wilde adopted in the late 1890s, which gestures both towards Saint Sebastian the early Christian martyr and towards the Byronic title character of *Melmoth the Wanderer* (1820), the Gothic novel written by Wilde's ancestor Charles Maturin.

38 James Winchell, "Wilde and Huysmans: Autonomy, Reference, and the Myth of Expiation," in Regenia Gagnier, ed., *Critical Essays on Oscar Wilde* (New York: G.K. Hall, 1991), 236.

39 John Albert, "The Christ of Oscar Wilde," in Gagnier, ed., *Critical Essays on Oscar Wilde*, 241. Albert's remains the most intriguing essay on Wilde in general and *De Profundis* in particular. Albert is not an academic critic, not even a "general reader." He's a Trappist monk, bound by vows of monasticism, meditation, and silence, who is drawn to Wilde's works, he tells us, not for "literary" reasons but for spiritual renewal.

PART IV

WILDE LEGACIES

chapter twelve

Oscar Wilde's Legacies to *Clarion* and *New Age* Socialist Aestheticism

ANN ARDIS

The best thing for everybody now is to forget all about Oscar Wilde, his perpetual postings, his aesthetical teachings and his theatrical productions. Let him go into silence, and be heard from no more.

– The Echo 1895[1]

This chapter focuses on Oscar Wilde's intricate "travels" into two central but critically neglected venues of early twentieth-century British socialist debate about art and politics, the *Clarion* (1891–1935) and the *New Age* (1894–1934). By Oscar Wilde I mean not the man himself, whose many travels included his humiliating train journey from Reading Gaol to Clapham Junction and then his migration incognito through France and Italy before his penurious death in Paris in 1900. I mean rather the figure of the sexually transgressive *fin-de-siècle* artist whose reproduction and/or erasure played such an important role in shaping British discourses about art in the early twentieth century.[2] As critics such as Jonathan Freedman and Eve Kosofsky Sedgwick have noted, Wilde both does and does not figure in modernist mappings of literary history, haunting the modernist imaginary as an ambiguously gendered father figure whose paternity was extremely dangerous to claim.[3] I will show in this essay how, in an equally ambivalent manner, Wilde both does and does not figure in early twentieth-century British socialist debates about art and culture. These debates had a wider provenance than we typically recognize at the turn of our own century. Yet they were cast into what Raymond Williams calls "the wide margins of the century"[4] not only by modernism's hegemony but also by the dominance of economic models of culture in left social theory in Britain until at least the early 1960s. Understanding Wilde's legacies to early twentieth-century socialist aestheticism and his "ghosting" from it – that is, the denial or (as Terry Castle puts it) "de-realization"[5] of his impact on this particular vein of British political and aesthetic theory – therefore involves a re-mapping of modern cultural history.

I. The Counter-Public Sphere of British Socialism at the Turn of the Twentieth Century

In his well-known study of national identity, Benedict Anderson claims that newspapers created and sustained a sense of Britishness in the eighteenth and nineteenth centuries.[6] To read the *Clarion* and the *New Age*, however, is to appreciate how the bourgeois public sphere underwent considerable fracturing at the turn of the twentieth century. Such fracturing occurred not only because of new developments in the newspaper publishing industry but also through the emergence of a counter-public sphere of British socialism and the influence and example of radical social democratic movements on the Continent. Rather than consolidating a newly literate populace, the rapidly expanding newspaper industry was commonly viewed as both fragmenting the public sphere into special-interest sub-markets and coterie cultures and dumbing itself down to the lowest common denominator of mass spectacle, inspiring "terror" in the likes of Matthew Arnold in the process.[7]

Within this context, the *Clarion* and the *New Age* were key venues of public debate about radical democratic alternatives to capitalism, individualism, and the English class system. Scholars tend to remember the *New Age* mainly as a vehicle for the presentation of modernist art and manifestos. Yet the journal editors' eclectic reading habits and tastes, both politically and artistically, and their practice of excerpting material from other publications, enabled its readers to keep abreast of conservative as well as socialist debates about literature, politics, and the arts. The *New Age* is thus an invaluable source of information about both the British newspaper industry and the internecine disputes among British socialists during this era. The journal covers large-circulation "dominant" culture newspapers and periodicals (such as the *Times*, the *Spectator*, and the *Daily Mail*), as well as mid-range and small-circulation regional and special-interest political and literary weeklies and monthlies (such as the *New Statesman*, the *Christian World*, the *Liverpool Courier*, the *Glebe*, the *English Review*, and the *Clarion*).[8]

Several other basic facts that mark important distinctions between the *Clarion* and the *New Age* are worth noting. In 1900, when the Independent Labour Party had a mere six thousand members, two to three thousand Clarion socialists attended meetings of the Clarion Vocal Union, and the weekly *Clarion* enjoyed a circulation of about fifty thousand. [9] The *New Age*'s circulation was never that large, with a fifteen-year average slightly over three thousand. Columns by the editor, A.R. Orage, dating from the mid-1910s suggest both a certain sense of relief at securing funding sufficient to maintain a print run of about two thousand copies and pride in maintaining the relatively low cost to subscribers of sixpence an issue.[10]

In *British Socialists and the Politics of Popular Culture, 1880–1914* (1990), Chris Waters has scrupulously researched and documented the history of the *Clarion* and the Clarion Movement. Jane Marcus's introduction to *The Young Rebecca* (1982), a collection of Rebecca West's early *Clarion* writings, is another invaluable source of information about Robert Blatchford's penny weekly.[11] But it remains the case that Guild Socialism has earned little more than passing reference in recent scholarship. I need therefore to outline the main tenets of this movement before considering these two periodicals' unique contribution to an emergent socialist counter-public sphere in Britain.

Guild Socialists were opposed to the narrowly class-based politics of the Labour Party and other socialists. Although half of the funding for the *New Age* was provided by George Bernard Shaw when Orage and Holbrook Jackson first took it over in 1907, the journal quickly outgrew its Fabian Art League support. Soon it featured Shaw and H.G. Wells, along with Beatrice Potter Webb and Sidney Webb, in a series of political caricatures that provide visual reinforcement of the verbal critiques offered in the journal's regular columns.[12] The *New Age* took particular issue with the Webbs, who believed in the gradual transformation of a capitalist economy through the nationalization of industry and the development of the bureaucratic, and heavily centralized, infrastructures of a modern welfare state. By contrast, as Wallace Martin observes, Guild Socialists wanted to "free workers from the unrelieved tedium of mass production and restore a sense of craftsmanship which would make labour satisfying and its products beautiful."[13] Unlike French Syndicalists, British Guild Socialists did not envisage the disappearance of the state. Instead, they proposed that citizens would elect a state government – one that would, according to Martin, "regulate the guilds, enact national legislation, and conduct international affairs"[14] – in order to create a form of society that would be a genuine alternative to either capitalist commodity culture or State socialism.

I have mentioned that the *New Age* has been described as a vehicle for the presentation of modernist literature and art. Certainly, it is possible to characterize the journal in this way, given the famous manifestos redacted from its pages: for example, in Herbert Read's collection of T.E. Hulme's essays, *Further Speculations* (1954), the Clarendon Press's edition of *The Collected Writings of T.E. Hulme* (1994), and T.S. Eliot's *Literary Essays of Ezra Pound* (1968). Yet to read the journal cover to cover, year after year, leaves one with a very different impression. Every article or letter to the editor or sample of modernist writing or art featured in its pages is counter-balanced by a parody, critique, or counter-manifesto. In the process, following the *Clarion*'s lead, the *New Age* contends that the arts are a key means of transforming bourgeois culture.

In an editorial titled "Journals Insurgent," for example, Orage offers a usefully detailed explanation of the *New Age*'s commitment to reviewing "politics, literature, and art" (the phrasing of the journal's subtitle). In his view, these are not discontiguous fields of activity but interconnected aspects of a single, organic culture. "Not the least of the revolutionary journal's troubles," Orage writes, "is the difficulty to drive into the minds of its readers that life is not composed of water-tight compartments."[15] Although "it is quite usual for many so-called revolutionary journals to assume that the economic struggle can be maintained without affecting the canons that govern the writing of books, the painting of pictures, the preaching of sermons, and even the fabric and texture of religion," "we are under no such delusions."

Hence the *New Age*, unlike the *New Statesman*, the official journal of Fabian Socialism, gives itself literary and artistic as well as political work to do. In other words, the journal conceptualizes its participation in debate about literature, art, and culture as part and parcel of its political work. Specifically, Orage argues that

> the literary work of the revolutionary journal, whether creative or critical, must cut across all modern canons of conduct, of literature, or of art. *It is our experience that reviews and critiques so inspired hurt far more than our analysis of the wage-system, our attacks on the political parties or our advocacy of monopoly labour.* But we know in fact as well as in reason that the economic emancipation of the workers is a dream until its conception has entered into and coloured and changed the minds and hearts of all who minister to our reason and imagination. (emphasis added)

In two key respects the *New Age* carefully distances itself from the *Clarion*. Letters to the editor in 1913 criticize the *Clarion* for providing no opportunity "for 'living' discussion or controversy" because it is not willing to serve as a clearing house for new socialist ideas such as those espoused by the *New Age*.[16] The *Clarion*'s dependence for its livelihood on the sale of advertisements, and particularly the sale of patent-medicine advertisements, also made it a subject of regular ridicule in the *New Age*. In July 1915, for example, "Current Cant" mocks the worry that Julia Dawson, a regular contributor to the *Clarion*'s "Women's Column," expresses regarding the fate of the journal: "What lives if the 'Clarion' dies?" [17] A month later, "Readers and Writers" notes with triumph that the *New Age* continues to thrive without advertisements, alluding indirectly to the withdrawal of the *Clarion* from circulation: "that final divorce between publicism and advertisement which so many of you have long desired" has finally been achieved. "The pillmakers having gone, let them never come back. Let them spread their nets in the dailies, those breeding-places of wild geese. But let us weeklies abjure them and trust to the public even if we perish of it."[18] Insofar as the *New Age* never paid its contributors and was funded solely by subscriptions and anonymous patronage, the journal prided itself on functioning as a Guild, an alternative to a capitalist wage labor system. Not only did Orage refuse to solicit advertisements, he also apologized very grandly and publicly to his readers when a single advertisement for Allen Upward's *The Divine Mystery* appeared in the 5 February 1914 issue. Orage promised that this "breach in the good manners of THE NEW AGE" would never happen again.[19]

In spite of these obvious points of disagreement on socialist politics and editorial policy, the *Clarion* and the *New Age* stand together behind the idea that a revolutionary socialist journal's treatment of the arts is even more effective politically than political commentary per se because literature and art "chang[e] the minds and hearts of readers, minister to reason *and* imagination." Montague Blatchford, a frequent contributor to the *Clarion* under the pseudonym "Mont Blong," writes: "To have a Democracy we must have Democrats, to have Socialism we must have Socialists; and as such can only be made by persuasion and not by force, it is not to force but to persuasion we must betake ourselves – and that is, I consider, just where the *Clarion* proves its usefulness."[20] In another editorial justifying the cultural work of the Clarion movement, he observes: "there are thousands of good people, members of the Independent Labour Party, the Social Democratic Federation, and other

Socialist bodies, who honestly believe that what they call 'the cause' is actually weakened and is in danger of being slain by the *Clarion* and all its works!" These same people view the *Clarion* as "too mild and too amusing; it does not sufficiently belaud the toilers, nor denounce with sufficient bitterness everybody else. It is argued that the Clarion cyclists and their meets, the Vocal Unions and their concerts, weaken 'the cause' by drawing men away from 'the work.'" But "[w]hat is 'the cause,' then?" he goes on to ask. "Humanity!" is his answer.

> What is "the work"? The breaking down of class privileges, the removal of obstructions to human progress, the raising of the economic, social, and moral condition of the people; and to provide by political and educational means for their freedom and enjoyment. *To transform, in fact, the drudges of what we call civilisation into brave, honest, kindly, wise, and happy human beings.* Can such a cause be weakened by the *Clarion*, or such work be hindered by its cyclists or its singers? Let us consider.[21] (emphasis added)

Of course Blatchford is not really interested in simply "considering" the matter. Rather, he and the *Clarion* are committed, as are *New Age* Guild Socialists, to refuting other turn-of-the-century British socialists' – specifically, Fabian Socialists' and Independent Labour Party socialists' – exclusive focus on political reform. To understand fully *Clarion* and *New Age* socialists' joint commitment to the integration of the arts into a radical agenda of social change, it remains vital to consider their debts to late nineteenth-century socialist writings about art and art's role in culture.

II. The Legacies of Ruskin, Morris, and Wilde to the *Clarion* and the *New Age*

Blatchford's eulogy for John Ruskin in 1900 suggests how important Ruskin's legacy was to early twentieth-century socialist aestheticians writing for both the *Clarion* and the *New Age*. "There seems to be little connection between art and political economy," he notes:

> [Y]et Ruskin showed that truth and beauty are the essentials of both. He taught many men to see and appreciate the beauty of nature, of sound art, and of sound economy, who never even knew where to look for either until he taught them. He saw that our competitive commercial system was a bad one, and told the students in one of his Oxford lectures that neither sound art, politics, property, or religion could exist in England until we resolved

that the streets which are the habitation of the poor and the playgrounds of their children, shall be made living examples of all that is decent, orderly, beautiful, and pure.[22]

A second important source of early twentieth-century socialist aestheticians' commitment to an organic theory of culture and their belief in art's central role as a vehicle of social change is, of course, William Morris. In 1900 Blatchford described Morris as a man known better "as a maker of wallpaper than as a poet, outside Socialist ranks." Even among socialists, his writings "are not widely read."[23] An article praising Morris ends with the following quotation, which expresses a commitment to the beautification of working-class homes and environments that distinguishes the *Clarion*'s agenda from that of other socialist movements and periodicals of the time:

My hope is that people will some day learn something of art, and so long for more, and will find, as I have, that there is no getting it save by the general acknowledgement of the right of every man to have fit work to do in a beautiful home. Therein lies all that is indestructible of the pleasure of life; no man need ask for more than that, no man should be granted less; and if he falls short of it, it is through waste and injustice that he is kept out of his birthright ... [E]very one of the things that goes to make up the surroundings among which we live must either be beautiful or ugly, either elevating or degrading to us, either a [torment] and [burden] to the maker of it, or a pleasure and solace to him.[24]

Although Blatchford himself does not claim Wilde as a third important precursor in this regard, the points of connection between his characterization of Morris's interests and Wildean aestheticism, specifically the political agenda Wilde presents in "The Soul of Man under Socialism" (1891), need to be acknowledged. I am thinking here of both Blatchford's and Wilde's emphasis on individual happiness and self-actualization as centerpieces of a socialist political platform.[25] Guild Socialists writing for the *New Age* in the 1910s will have choice words to say about how Wilde and Morris turned socialist collectivism astray in emphasizing the individual's pleasure in the production of beautiful objects. As I mentioned earlier, they will offer equally choice words about the *Clarion*'s participation in capitalist commodity culture and a wage economy through its sale of advertisements and its payments to contributors. And they will distance themselves from all manner of "intellectual decadence" in the 1910s – whether this term is used to refer to Wilde specifi-cally, 1890s aestheticism more generally, Fabian Socialism, or the British modernist avant-garde.[26] Yet both the *Clarion* and the *New Age* are more indebted than they admit to a tradition of British aestheticism that, as Freedman has explained, was always already political.

In other words, I am drawing attention to the Wildean motifs that – in spite of either the thundering silence or the explicit and typically hostile disavowals of Wilde elsewhere in both periodicals – recur through key platform statements such as the following:

> Of the "movements" which aspire to modify the social order, that which aims at instituting National Guilds is the most inclusively human, and appeals most completely to the whole gamut of Nature's finest faculties. It is scientific, but it always subordinates science – whether it be economics or sociology – to art, to the great art of living. We need to realise that econom-ics alone, and that even science in general, is quite unequal to the task of controlling the destinies of man. To live, or rather, to live well, is an art. This is as true of human society as of the individual. The government of man is more than a science; it is an art, based not on economics but on phi-losophy, and the building of an ideal, well-ordered society, such as Social-ists dream of, is emphatically a work of art ... The new order of society, if it is to be attained at all, calls for imagination, courage, devotion, and high-spirited allegiance to its great ideals. It is in that spirit that some of us see in National Guilds the mould of a new civilisation. The mark of that new fra-ternal civilisation will not be a false and impossible equality, but fair play and freedom in the fellowship of the Guilds. The Guilds will raise and expand the standard of life for the whole of their members. Leisure and plenty, culture and fine character will no longer be buried out of bounds for the many, as at present. To work for the coming of the Guilds is to work for the re-establishment of fellowship in the world of Labour. It is to work not merely for a new economic system, but for the humanising influences that would be liberated thereby.[27]

Note the general dynamic here: when Wilde is mentioned explicitly in the *New Age*, he is characterized negatively. In countless editorials, Ramiro De Maetzu stresses over and over again that both Wilde and Morris "went wrong" in dreaming of turning society into "a corporation of artists who ... discover their joy in the production of beautiful things." "You cannot make workmen happy by utilising their energies in the pro-duction of beautiful things," he insists, arguing that the production of beautiful things in a capitalist commodity culture is harnessed inevitably to "the service of luxury, vice, and decoration."[28]

Significantly, Wilde also figures centrally in the *New Age*'s exposé of the modernist avant-garde's "decadence" in an entry of "Current Cant" devoted almost exclusively to a review of the first issue of *Blast*.[29] Yet de Maetzu's essays echo so strongly certain ideas in "The Soul of Man under Socialism" that certain questions immediately arise. Why is there this pattern of disassociation from Wilde? Why does the *New Age* present overt critiques of "intellectual decadence" at the same time as it borrows voraciously, both thematically *and* formally,[30] from Wilde?

A comment of Montague Blatchford's begins to offer an explanation. In response to concerns expressed by his socialist comrades about the "effeminacy" of the arts, he writes:

> Some prefer study, or art, or music; why should we call them effeminate? Have the intellectually-gifted to be compelled to take violent physical exercise, or the physically-vigorous to be condemned to intellectual or imaginative amusement for which nature never fitted them; or have both to be crammed into a severe conventional mould to suit the crochets of some purblind old lady of the masculine gender?
>
> No, there is a great amount of natural aptitude, as well as a great deal of human nature in most people, and whether in work or play, those will be the happiest and the best who make the wisest use of their capacities. I like to see people happy at their work and merry at their play, and the only thing we have to consider is how they may become so.[31]

The association of intellectuality with effeminacy that Blatchford describes turns a Wildean interest in the decorative arts into "women's work" in the *Clarion*. Even if Blatchford (as editor of the *Clarion*) refuses to treat the study of art and music as "effeminate," what Kathy Alexis Psomiades has termed life-style aestheticism will be pursued almost exclusively in the "Women's Column" by female *Clarion* socialists such as Julia Dawson and Rebecca West.[32] The following essay of Dawson's is a good example of how she takes up a Wildean project as she urges her readers to understand how domestic style can be a vehicle for social transformation:

> A few days ago I was in a little, wee home. There was nothing pretentio[u]s about it anywhere, but it was more *pleasing* to the eye, I think, than any other house I had ever entered, large or small, because everything in it had

been bought with care an eye for beauty. The designs of the kitchen chairs and dresser had been as carefully selected as the furniture in any other rooms in the house; and the every-day teacups were of such quaint shape, in blue-and-white china, that the tea tasted far nicer in them than in any cups I had ever used.

It *does* make a difference. Tea out of any ugly thick earthenware vessel is fit only for mortals of the meanest order – the same tea out of delicate china, artistic in colour and design, is a drink fit for the gods ...

I'm *certain* a horse's load is lighter to draw when he is decorated for May Day, *certain* that a woman does not get half so tired walking when she is well dressed as when she wears what she doesn't like; and *certain* that any one can be happier and merrier with only one pretty thing in possession than with a cart-load of ugly things.[33]

By relegating life-style aestheticism to the *Clarion*'s "Women's Columns," does Blatchford thereby perhaps protect the journal as a whole from charges of intellectual effeminacy? It is one thing, it would seem, to defend a socialist's right to be interested in literature and the arts; it is quite another to theorize the design of kitchen chairs, tea pots, and the gendered habits of everyday life.

III. Refiguring the Wildean Aesthete: Blatchford's "Julie"

The turn-of-the-century British socialists' association of intellectuality with "effeminacy" and Wilde with "decadence" also strongly colors Blatchford's treatment of a Wildean dandy's relationship to his young working-class protégé in "Julie," a novel that he serialized in the *Clarion* during May to November of 1900. I want to offer a close reading of this little-known narrative in order to suggest how Blatchford responds to the homophobic panic sparked by Wilde's trials without ever mentioning Wilde explicitly. This narrative is less well-known to today's readers than Blatchford's *Merrie England* (1894), a series of letters addressed to John Smith of Oldham, a "typical" workman, which Jane Marcus describes as "one of the most successful pieces of propaganda in the history of the British labour movement" (91). "Julie" sparked a great deal of response from readers in letters to the editor during its serialization, and there was a flurry of renewed interest when it was about to appear in hard cover in November 1900. "Julie" tells the story of a beautiful and musically gifted working-class girl who is "rescued" from the East End by Merton Guineagold, an elegant, elderly dandy, when he observes her response to an open-air concert. The following passage from the first instalment of the serial establishes Julie's musical genius and her fine, albeit untrained, aesthetic sensibility as she loses all sense of her shabby surroundings, transfixed and transformed as she is by the vocalist's performance:

> The crowd that drifted past the end of the quiet street was a crowd of shadows; the vast city of endless streets and fussy millions beyond and around her was a blank abstraction, like the maps at school. Julie was alone: alone with her own soul – alone in Space, with the spark of genius kindling, with her imagination roused, and her delicate aural nerves spreading to the harmony as flowers to the sun.[34]

When the music ends Julie is "no longer a genius and kinswoman to the gods." Nonetheless, Guineagold, who has watched Julie's transformation through her response to the performance, still knows that her "senses were shrewd and fine, ready, if tried, to discriminate the delicate degrees of flavour and aroma in old wines, choice fruits, costly cigarettes, and the still more subtle variations of colour and of tone in painting and in music."[35]

Blatchford's characterization of his heroine and her dandy rescuer involves a very complex set of assumptions about working-class environments and character, the innateness of aesthetic response, and the sensual (indeed, physiological, as well as the moral and aesthetic) components of the appeal of music, art, or fine wine. Note in particular that the emphasis Blatchford places on the importance of aesthetic responsiveness in an agenda of social change is as much a borrowing from Wilde as from Morris or social reformers such as Octavia Hill or Margaret McMillan. As an exciting new vein of feminist scholarship on Victorian aestheticism has richly demonstrated, nineteenth-century aesthetes typically associate the material (female) body with corruption, decay, and degeneration.[36] What Blatchford describes in "Julie," however, is a far more positive conceptualization of the body's role in aesthetic response. Julie's "little form" "thrill[s] with a dumb longing, an inarticulate joy" when for the first time she hears a really talented musician playing the piano. The music "sent the blood back to her heart and brought the tears into her eyes"; that is, its power is registered through the intensity of her physiological responses, not a more purely intellectualized and abstract response.[37]

One thinks here not only of Lord Henry Wotton's characterization of the physiology of aesthetic response in *The Picture of Dorian Gray* (1890,

1891) but also of Wilde's modeling of the individual's self-actualization in "The Soul of Man under Socialism":

> It will be a marvellous thing – the true personality of man – when we see it. It will grow naturally and simply, flower-like, or as a tree grows ... [Jesus] said to man: "You have a wonderful personality. Develop it. Be yourself. Don't imagine that your perfection lies in accumulating or possessing external things. Your affection is inside of you. If only you could realise that, you would not want to be rich. Ordinary riches can be stolen from a man. Real riches cannot. In the treasury-house of your soul, there are infinitely precious things, that may not be taken from you.[38]

Notably, though, Blatchford is very careful to make Julie's music, not Julie herself, the Body of Beauty in question. What Frederick S. Roden has described specifically as Dorian's eucharistic feast and more generally as Wilde's incarnationalist queer liberation theology is detached not only from same-sex desire but also from sexualized desire even of a heteronormative kind by Blatchford as he refigures the Platonic relationship between teacher and student in "Julie."[39] Julie's and Guineagold's responsiveness to music is fully sensual, transcendent *and* materialist at one and the same time. But their relationship is *not* sexual. And I think that we need to ask whether Blatchford's simultaneous desexualization and heterosexualization of a cross-class relationship that in so many other regards mirrors the patterning of the classic New Hellenist male-male partnership is overdetermined by the homophobic panic sparked by Wilde's trials and the "scandalous" revelations of his relationships with working-class men in 1895.

Blatchford's other significant rewriting of Wildean aesthetics in "Julie" takes place through his politicization of the aesthete. Guineagold is training Julie to play concerts in the West End. When Charlie Chigwin, an acquaintance from the old neighborhood, now the secretary of the Coal Porters' Union, challenges Julie to put her musical genius to political use, she convinces Guineagold to let her do so. "Think what you're doing," Chigwin urges her:

> What crushes the workers down? Nothing but the burden of the respectable and cultured classes who live on them. You are clever. You do what other clever workers do. You go over to the enemy and help to sit on the poor. You know our lives. You know our homes. You know our wrongs. Why

don't you be true and womanly? Come back to the poor? Take your weight off their bowed backs and weary arms. Give your talents to their dull lives. If you want to play, come into the filthy and wicked slums and play to the slaves and the broken wrecks of women and men. Give them some joy. Cast out pride and selfishness. Help your sisters. Let the rich find their own music. You belong to us, and to God.[40]

Guineagold's response picks up the same note of religious rhetoric in Chigwin's socialist challenge: "Do all the good you can, my dear, to *all* men," not just the people of the East End. "Music, dear Julie, is a divine thing. It is given to us for our own delight, and to give pleasure to others. If we have a gift or a guinea we should spend it freely – give our fellow creatures all the joy we can. Yes. You might play to them. God gave you genius. You know that, Julie."[41]

What happens next in the narrative, however, raises compelling questions about the transformational potentiality of aesthetic responsiveness, undermining severely the utopian optimism in this regard of "The Soul of Man under Socialism." This is the first of many street concerts that Julie plays in her old neighborhood. I want to call attention to Blatchford's very careful detailing of the crowd's changing responses to Julie's singing. In the following passage, we also hear the voice of her friend Fantine, another ex-East Ender whom Guineagold has "rescued" and trained as a concert musician:

Almost at the first stroke of the bow the Court awoke; before the first phrases of the first melody had melted on the breathless and greasy air the balconies were filled with half-dressed and dishevelled listeners; the pot-house had discharged itself, like a prison van, of a company strongly reminiscent of Black Maria society, and the entrances to the Dean were thronged with eager children. Fantine, with a hot blush on her handsome face, looked down under the searching and unabashed stare of this weird audience. Julie, with compressed lips, contracted brows, and eyes lighted by excitement played the old melodies and folk songs with an almost supernatural fervour, tenderness, and spirit. The crowd grew denser. In a few minutes the court was packed, the windows and balconies were crowded, and the children flocked so closely round the player that she had scarcely room to draw her bow.

Such a wild, motley, unwashed mob of ragamuffins Fantine had never before encountered. Yet she feared them less and less every moment. For

not a sound was heard save the music. Not a figure stirred. On all the faces
was a rapt, tense look, a strange kind of light, that never shone on sea or
land. The Dean was spellbound. The monkey-like freakish urchins, the
bemused sots from the tavern, the fierce-eyed corner wench, the rakehell
ruffian, the weary labourer, and the spent slattern, with sud-writhed arms
and bleary eyes, were for the first time transfigured out of themselves, surprised into a mood of mercy and romance, enticed into forgetfulness of
their iron-fisted, bargain-driving, loud-swearing, deep-drinking, drab-hued,
and dismal world, and sent a-wondering, happy and off their guard, into
moonlighted, flower-scented, and melodious realms of dream.[42]

To this point at least, Julie's and Fantine's music has transfigured her
working-class listeners, taken them out of their "drab-hued" world and
given them a glimpse of utopia – as she herself had been transported
out of herself on first hearing Fantine play. When Julie stops playing,
however, the "soft glances" quickly harden, unconscious smiles fade,
and "the glamour of outwards die[s] out and le[aves] harsh faces cold."
"A feeling of astonishment and curiosity held the audience mute," but
there is no applause. The court will not "resoun[d] to volleys of hand
clappings" until after Julie responds to "a young thief's" Cockney
request for "somefin to make our feet move" by playing a succession of
bright folk dances – mazurkas, German waltzes, Irish jigs, Scottish reels,
old English minuets, and modern Spanish cachucas – "stringing them
together in gay and varied sequence, and transmitting them all into
grace and poetry by her deftness and dainty perception." Finally, when
Fantine sings for Julie, "the ripe, full voice, of perfect culture and sovereign quality" "thrill[s]" and "[works] upon the grim visaged dull-eyed
drudges of Shantytown in a marvellous way." And in response to their
request for yet another encore, Julie offers to play the Paganini that she
performed at her first public concert several months before: "They shall
have my best," she tells her companion. "It is not too good for them."[43]

    There are at least two important aspects to this scene: the range of
music that Julie and Fantine play, from folk tunes to Paganini, as well as
the implied assumptions about what is or is not "too good for them";
and the characterization of music's ability to transfigure these working-
class listeners "out of themselves." What interests me most is Blatchford's characterization of the impermanence of this crowd's transfigura-
tion. As Waters has discussed in great detail, music was an important
component of British socialists' attempts to produce a politically pro-

gressive popular culture at the turn of the century. Blatchford's Clarion movement, with its city choirs and national choral concerts, as well as its Cinderella Clubs, its Cycling Clubs, and its Clarion vans, exemplifies this effort. Ultimately, however, the Clarion movement also epitomizes turn-of-the-century British socialism's failures in this regard. Not only was the "desire for a musical culture developed by workers themselves" "fraught with contradictions," as Waters has noted (103). Socialism's version of "rational leisure" and its continuation of a nineteenth-century tradition of working-class autodidacticism would ultimately have limited appeal in the face of increasing competition with emergent forms of mass entertainment such as popular film.

Again, though, I am interested in the questions that Blatchford raises about whether and how the self-actualization of the individual is related to the utopian socialist collective which Wilde models in "The Soul of Man under Socialism." Julie wants to give her working-class audience "her best"; she believes that they deserve to hear not only the Paganini she played at her first professional concert but also Fantine's "ripe, full voice, of perfect culture and sovereign quality." It is not at all clear from this scene, however, if the working-class audience values a "perfect" high culture music over a highly skilled rendition of folk music (i.e. "their" music). Moreover, bringing such music to Flowery Dean does not in fact work the kind of ethical and political miracles that her old acquaintance from the neighborhood had challenged Julie with providing. It does not relieve them of "the burden of the respectable and cultured classes who live on them," as he suggested on his first visit to Guineagold's home.[44] Nor does it turn out to be possible to "sing and play the devil out of" a drunken woman's heart, to sing her "back her hope, her womanhood, her chastity, and her reason."[45] What it offers instead is simply a moment of quiet wonder. Like Julie herself – the child who once sat squeezed into a window sill trying to hear the music from the pub down the street – the people of Flowery Dean who are drawn to the sound of her violin are "transfigured out of themselves" as they listen. Unlike Julie, however, they lack the musical talent, together with the opportunity to develop it, that would make a moment's experience of listening pleasure generate a new life. Instead, they are momentarily "surprised into a mood of mercy and romance, enticed into forgetfulness of their iron-fisted, bargain-driving, loud-swearing, deep-drinking, drab-hued, and dismal world, and sent a-wondering, happy and off their guard, into moonlighted, flower-scented, and melodious realms of dream." When the music stops, "the glamour of outwards die[s]" out as well, leaving "harsh faces cold" and "soft glances" to harden quickly.

Is this, I would want to ask, a eugenically inflected and very sobering response to the high-flung religious rhetoric of "The Soul of Man under Socialism" regarding the socially transformative potentialities of aesthetic response? I do not have hard biographical evidence of Blatchford's reading to be able to prove that Blatchford had Wilde's writings in mind when writing "Julie." Nonetheless, I would like to insist on the importance of the larger pattern that I have been describing here: namely, the silence, the belligerent disavowals, and the illicit but nonetheless voracious borrowings from Wilde in early twentieth-century *Clarion* and *New Age* socialism.

The tradition of early twentieth-century British socialist aestheticism discussed in this essay was partially recuperated by Carolyn Steedman in her recent book on Margaret McMillan, *Childhood, Culture and Class in Britain: Margaret McMillan, 1860–1931* (1990). Yet the movement has proved curiously absent from other important recent studies of turn-of-the-century British socialism and socialist popular culture such as Waters' *British Socialism and the Politics of Popular Culture*, Tom Steele's *Alfred Orage and the Leeds Arts Club* (1990), and Pamela Fox's *Class Fictions* (1994).[46] Amazingly, Steele's study of Orage's earliest history with socialism and Waters' analysis of the Clarion Movement fail to mention Wilde or "The Soul of Man under Socialism." Fox's study reinforces standard associations of socialism with realism even while offering a very important kind of correction to and commentary on the gender politics of early British socialism. Feminist critics such as Julia Swindells have questioned the exclusion of gender from left social commentary. But what *else* is being left out, and why, we might well ask.[47] In ending with the following quotation from Arthur Ransome's 1912 biography of Wilde, I invite us to scrutizine carefully our own silences about Wilde, not simply those of early twentieth-century British socialists:

> Whether [Wilde's] writings are perfectly successful or not, they altered in some degree the course of literature of his time, and are still an active power when the wind has long blown away the dust of newspaper criticism with which they were received. It is already clear that Wilde has an historical importance too easily underestimated. His indirect influence is incalculable, for his attitude in writing gave literature new standards of valuation, and men are writing under their influence who would indignantly deny that their work was in any way dictated by Wilde.[48]

Notes

1 As quoted by Regenia Gagnier, *Idylls of the Marketplace : Oscar Wilde and the Victorian Public* (Stanford: Stanford University Press, 1986), 29.

2 I use "travel" thus in Edward Said's sense of the term, as a means of talking about how ideas circulate and are transformed through their circulation. See Edward W. Said, "Traveling Theory," in Said, *The World, the Text, and the Critic* (Cambridge, MA: Harvard University Press, 1983), 226–47. As Michel Foucault has suggested, silence is "less the absolute limit of discourse ... [than] an element that functions alongside the things said ... There is no binary division to be made between what one says and what one does not say." See Foucault, *The History of Sexuality – Volume One: An Introduction*, trans. Robert Hurley (New York: Vintage Books, 1980), 27. In focusing in this essay on the way Wilde's ideas and ideas about Wilde travel through British socialist discourse about aesthetics at the turn of the twentieth century, I must be as attentive to silences as to what is said about him and his writings.

3 Jonathan L. Freedman, *Professions of Taste: Henry James, British Aestheticism, and Commodity Culture* (Stanford: Stanford University Press, 1990); Eve Kosofsky Sedgwick, *Epistemology of the Closet* (Berkeley: University of California Press, 1990).

4 Raymond Williams, "Metropolitan Perceptions and the Emergence of Modernism," in *The Politics of Modernism: Against the New Conformists* (London and New York: Verso, 1996), 62.

5 Ghosting and derealization are Terry Castle's terms, as used throughout *The Apparitional Lesbian: Female Homosexuality and Modern Culture* (New York: Columbia University Press, 1993).

6 Benedict Anderson, *Imagined Communities: Reflections on the Origin and Spread of Nationalism* (London: Verso, 1983).

7 This is Laurel Brake's phrasing in "The Deaths of Heroes: Pater, Symonds, and the Discourse of the Press in the Mid-1890s," unpublished paper presented at the conference on Sexual Controversies of the Fin de Siècle, William Andrews Clark Memorial Library, 15 May 1999.

8 "Current Cant" and "Press Cuttings" are two regularly featured columns consisting, respectively, of very short (one-sentence or paragraph-length) quotations from other periodicals. The frequency with which Orage's "Readers and Writers" columns refer and respond to articles in other publications also registers the journal's sense of commitment to providing an overview of the periodical press. See Ann Ardis, *Modernism and Cultural Conflict, 1880–1922* (Cambridge: Cambridge University Press, 2002), 143–72, for further discussion of the *New Age.*

9 Martin Pugh, *The Tories and the People, 1880–1935* (Oxford: Blackwell, 1985, 2), as quoted by Chris Waters, *British Socialists and the Politics of Popular Culture, 1884–1914* (Manchester: Manchester University Press, 1990), 2; further page reference appears in parentheses.

10 See Wallace Martin, *The New Age under Orage: Chapters in English Cultural History* (Manchester University Press; New York: Barnes & Noble, 1967), 10; and "Readers and Writers," *New Age*, 30 April 1914, 816, and 7 May 1914, 14.

11 Jane Marcus, *The Young Rebecca: Writings of Rebecca West, 1911–17* (London: Macmillan in association with Virago Press, 1982); further page reference appears in parentheses.

12 See "Tom Titt" (Jan de Junosza Rosciszewski)'s brilliant cartoons of Shaw, *New Age*, 5 June 1913, 160, and 12 March 1914, 608; of the Webbs, 10 April 1913, back cover; and of Wells, 29 May 1913, 128.

13 Martin, *The New Age under Orage*, 206.

14 Martin, *The New Age under Orage*, 209.

15 A.R. Orage, "Journals Insurgent," *New Age*, 7 August 1913, 415; further quotations appear on this page.

16 *New Age*, 23 October 1913, 773.

17 "Current Cant," *New Age*, 8 July 1915, 237.

18 Orage, "Readers and Writers," *New Age*, August 12, 1915, 357.

19 Orage, "Readers and Writers," *New Age*, February 19, 1914, 499. See also Orage's general critique of modern newspapers' reliance on advertising, "Readers and Writers," *New Age*, 15 January 1914, 339.

20 "Mont Blong" (Montague Blatchford), *Clarion*, 3 November 1900, 353.

21 Blatchford, *Clarion*, 8 December 1900 393.

22 Blatchford, *Clarion*, 27 January 1900, 25.

23 Blatchford, *Clarion*, 13 January 1900, 1.

24 Blatchford, *Clarion*, 4 August 1900, 250. The last sentence of this quotation is from Morris' "Art and Plutocracy," a lecture he delivered at University College, Oxford in 1883. See *The Collected Works of William Morris*, ed. May Morris, 24 vols. (London: Longmans, Green, 1915), XXIII, 165. Blatchford seems to have taken some liberties with Morris' work here, quoting from more than one source without acknowledging them appropriately. I would like to thank Florence Boos for help in identifying this quotation.

25 As Freedman notes, Wilde "undertakes the project of uniting aestheticism and socialism by arguing that the freedom the former preaches in the purely 'aesthetic' realm ought to be realized in the political realm as well" (*Professions of Taste*, 12); "socialism is to be desired because it is the inevitable fulfillment of the central assumptions of its seeming antagonist, bourgeois individualism" (73). Orage is quite careful to distance the *New Age* from

Wilde upon occasions such as the publication of Methuen's edition of his selected prose in 1914 ("Strange how this man lasts!" is his comment in "Readers and Writers" that week, *New Age* 6 April 1914, 755). Nonetheless, this Wildean argument for a socialist individualism appears frequently in the *New Age*. See, for example, A.J. Penty's impassioned conclusion to his series on "Art and Luxury": "Social reform means ultimately personal reform ... If we are content to living as a nation of Philistines, indifferent alike to poetry, religion, ideas, and art, worshipping vulgar success, wasting our precious gifts in sordid speculative enterprises and our leisure in senseless luxury[, and] dissipation ... then no power on earth can save us. We shall continue to wallow in the troughs of commercialism, and no solution of our problems is possible, though every voice in the land should demand it. Unless individually we are prepared to live for the truth and to make sacrifices for it, society will remain as at present at the mercy of the speculator, the hustler, the mountebank, and the adventurer" (*New Age*, 11 September 1913, 573). In spite of Orage's distancing remarks in April 1914 regarding Methuen's publication of Wilde's selected prose, it should also be noted that the *New Age* published a full-page reproduction of Jacob Epstein's controversial design for Wilde's tomb at Père Lachaise in June 1912 at the very height of the controversy regarding Epstein's depiction of Wilde's exposed genitalia. See Martin, *The New Age under Orage*, 186, and the *New Age* 6 June, 1912, photographic supplement.

26 See, for example, Ramiro De Maetzu's critique of Wilde and Gautier in "On Art and Luxury," *New Age*, 15 April 1914, 640. On 1890s decadence more generally, see the critique of *Blast*, 31 July 1913, 395. *Blast*'s "idea," Orage notes, was to "repeat the office of the 'Yellow Book,'" which was to "collect contemporary decadence and make a school of it." He is quick to refute the value of this enterprise: "There is no life in decadence, however, nowadays; its future is past." The *New Age*'s "'idea,'" by contrast, is "brilliant commonsense ... Only those writers belong to the new age and have a future before them who can write sense. I emphasize both the writing and the sense" (395).

27 From the Bristol *Venture*, quoted in the *New Age*, 9 September 1915, 464.

28 De Maetzu, "Not Happiness, But ..." *New Age*, 8 July 1915, 224; "On Art and Luxury," *New Age*, 15 April 1915, 640.

29 "Current Cant," *New Age*, 23 July 1914, 268.

30 I have emphasized the intellectual debts of early twentieth-century socialist aesthetes to Wilde here, but an equally good argument could be made for the formal borrowings, especially given the prominence of Wildean dialogue-type essays in the *New Age*.

31 "Mont Blong" [Montague Blatchford], "Seasonable Rejoicings," *Clarion*, 15 December 1900, 402.

32 Kathy Alexis Psomiades, *Beauty's Body: Femininity and Representation in British Aestheticism* (Stanford, CA: Stanford University Press, 1997).

33 Julia Dawson, *Clarion*, 15 December 1900, 398.

34 Blatchford, "Julie," *Clarion*, 12 May 1900, 149.

35 Blatchford, "Julie," *Clarion*, 19 May 1900, 160.

36 See, for example, Rita Felski, *The Gender of Modernity* (Cambridge, MA: Harvard University Press, 1995), 91–114; Talia Schaffer and Kathy Alexis Psomiades, eds., *Women and British Aestheticism* (Charlottesville: University Press of Virginia, 1999); Schaffer, *The Forgotten Female Aesthetes: Literary Culture in Late-Victorian England* (Charlottesville: University Press of Virginia, 2000); and Linda Hughes, "A Female Aesthete at the Helm: *Sylvia's Journal* and 'Graham R. Tomson,' 1893–1894," *Victorian Periodicals Review* 29 (1996), 173–92.

37 Blatchford, "Julie," *Clarion*, 2 June 1900, 173.

38 Oscar Wilde, "The Soul of Man under Socialism," in Wilde, *Collected Works*, ed. Robert Ross, 14 vols. (London: Methuen, 1908), VIII, 287, 288–89.

39 Frederick S. Roden, "Queer Theologies at the Fin de Siècle and Beyond," unpublished paper presented at the conference on Sexual Controversies of the Fin de Siècle, William Andrews Clark Memorial Library, 15 May 1999.

40 Blatchford, "Julie," *Clarion*, 30 June 1900, 206.

41 Blatchford, "Julie," *Clarion*, 7 July 1900, 214.

42 Blatchford, "Julie," *Clarion*, 21 July 1900, 229.

43 Blatchford, "Julie," *Clarion*, 21 July 1900, 230.

44 Blatchford, "Julie," *Clarion*, 30 June 1900, 206.

45 Blatchford, "Julie," *Clarion*, 21 July 1900, 229.

46 Carolyn Steedman, *Childhood, Culture and Class in Britain: Margaret McMillan, 1860–1931* (London: Virago Press, 1990); Pamela Fox, *Class Fictions: Shame and Resistance in the British Working-Class Novel, 1890–1945* (Durham, NC: Duke University Press, 1994); Tom Steele, *Alfred Orage and the Leeds Arts Club 1893–1923* (Aldershot: Scolar Press, 1990).

47 Julia Swindells and Lisa Jardine, *What's Left? Women in Culture and the Labour Movement* (London, New York: Routledge, 1990).

48 Arthur Ransome, *Oscar Wilde: A Critical Study* (London: Methuen, 1917), 20–21. Ransome's biography first appeared in 1912.

chapter thirteen

Salomé in China:
The Aesthetic Art of Dying

XIAOYI ZHOU

I

From the early part of the twentieth century, Chinese intellectuals regarded Oscar Wilde as a leading representative of the British Aesthetic Movement. Wilde's forceful propounding of the principles of art for art's sake and life for art's sake made him a popular and influential figure among the leading writers and critics of the May Fourth generation – a generation associated with the Chinese enlightenment cultural movement at the turn of the twentieth century.[1] They regarded Wilde as an apostle of art, and a spokesperson of the idea of artistic autonomy. His works were repeatedly translated into Chinese and his plays frequently appeared on the Chinese stage. Many Chinese writers were attracted to Wilde's uncompromising aestheticism, and they produced works in the aestheticist style. As we shall see below, this aesthetic style expressed particular social meanings for the Chinese intellectuals of this generation. They used Wilde's aestheticism as a powerful weapon against traditional Confucian ideology. Among Wilde's most prominent Chinese supporters were Tian Han (1898–1968), Hong Shen (1894–1955), Guo Moruo (1892–1978) and Bai Wei (1894–1987), all influential shapers of modern Chinese drama. Their works – Tian Han's *The Death of an Actress* (1927), Guo Moruo's *Wang Zhaojun* (1924), and Bai Wei's *Linli* (1926) – all reflected the influence of Wilde in terms of the aestheticist idea of life for art's sake as well as in their dramatic structure.[2] Hong Shen's adaptation of Wilde's *Lady Windermere's Fan* (1924) also aroused interest among Chinese audiences. The names of personae are changed to common Chinese names; and the details of the play are also adapted to Chinese custom and convention.

The earliest known Chinese translation of Wilde's work is "The Happy Prince," which appeared in *Collected Foreign Short Stories*, a volume published in Tokyo in 1909.[3] Zhou Zuoren, one of the most influential critics and essayists of the time, translated Wilde's story into elegant classical Chinese. In his introduction, Zhou maintains that the key to Wilde's aestheticism is to "transform life into an art." Zhou must have been well aware of Wilde's eccentric personal style in the early 1880s, and he regards this image of Wilde as typifying the aesthete. He describes Wilde in the following manner: "He himself practised it by wearing eccentric clothes of an extraordinary shape and walking down in the street with a sunflower in hand."[4] From Zhou's perspective, therefore, Wilde was an artist driven to transcend ordinary life and ascend to the kingdom of art. Thus Wilde was initially introduced into China as an apostle of pure art and a practitioner of a new way of life, a way in which life was lived as a work of art. And it was Wilde's own self-created image as the aesthete par excellence, as much as his works of literary creation, which inspired such an avid following among Chinese intellectuals. It must, however, also be remembered that at this time there was a tendency among the Chinese writers of the May Fourth period to construct attractive images of Western artists for their own social and political interests. We come across similar examples in their adaptations and translations of works by Byron, Shelley, Whitman, Hardy, Ibsen, and Hugo.[5] Wilde is one of the most important links in this chain of Western intellectual hero-sages perfected in modern Chinese culture.

Soon after Chinese readers encountered Wilde's fairy tales and drama, there was a wave of literary and critical interest in Wilde. What the famous novelist and critic Mao Dun called an "aesthetic vogue" was current in Chinese intellectual life, and Wilde was one of its iconic figures.[6] This evaluation was based in the conception of Wilde as a theatrical personality and aestheticist martyr.[7] All of Wilde's major works were repeatedly translated and subjected to lively critical debate. By the end of the 1940s at least ten people had translated Wilde's fairy tales. Moreover, there were seven full translations of *Lady Windermere's Fan* and *Salomé* (plus one plot summary). There were also four Chinese translations of *An Ideal Husband* and two of *The Picture of Dorian Gray* (plus one plot summary). In addition, translators produced editions of *A Woman of No Importance*, *De Profundis*, *The Importance of Being Earnest* and *The Ballad of Reading Gaol*.[8] The sheer quantity of these publications demonstrates how large Wilde's

Chinese readership had grown during this time. The influence of this "aesthetic vogue" was exemplified by the enthusiastic Chinese reception of *Lady Windermere's Fan*, which was first performed in Shanghai from April to July of 1924. The gifted director and playwright Hong Shen, who was a graduate in drama from Harvard University, translated it and made many changes of his own. As a consequence, *Lady Windermere's Fan* became well known to Shanghai audiences.[9] Thereafter, the Peicheng Girl's Boarding School again performed the drama at Shanghai in 1930.[10] Mao Dun noted that at the time even *A Doll's House* by Henrik Ibsen, one of the most venerated foreign playwrights in China, could not rival *Lady Windermere's Fan* in popularity.[11]

It should be noted that the earliest Chinese figures to introduce Wilde and aestheticism were Shanghai writers. This was the region where aestheticism and Decadence became most popular and influential. Although Wilde's plays were also performed in Tianjin and Chengdu, their impact there was far less than in Shanghai. Ninety percent of the Chinese translations of Wilde's works were published in Shanghai by a constellation of over a dozen publishing houses; and nearly all of the translations of his poems, children's stories, and critical essays appeared in magazines and papers published in that city. So why was it that Wilde's aestheticism only became so predominant among Shanghai writers? Part of the explanation must surely lie in geographic factors. Shanghai was closer to Japan and generally more exposed to cosmopolitan cultural influences. Many of the major writers who lived in Shanghai and were exponents of Wilde's art and ideas, such as Lu Xun, Zhou Zuoren, Guo Moruo, Tian Han, and Yu Dafu, had studied in Japan. They were the first to import Wilde, aestheticism, and Decadence into China, and their natural port of entry was Shanghai.

It is therefore not surprising to discover that another play by Wilde exerted a major, perhaps even greater, influence on modern Chinese theatre in Shanghai. The work in question is *Salomé*. For Chinese writers, the biblical figure of Salomé expressed the aestheticist principle that life should be transformed into an intensive, artistic moment. In this way, Chinese critics emphasized the passionate and rebellious nature of the protagonist. "Salomé is a feverish nightmare which expresses a kind of degradation."[12] As we shall see below, this rebellious image of both Salomé and Wilde accompany a radical cultural stance, which is central to a key development in Chinese modernity. Namely, these images reinforce the responsibility of Chinese writers to propose a critique of traditional social conventions. Wilde as both an artist and a personality served this purpose well and was transformed into its artistic ideal.

This chapter explores the reception of *Salomé* within a specific Chinese cultural context. Within this context, a western post-enlightenment and romantic woman is misread and transformed in an image that embodies enlightenment and modernity. In order to explain the remarkable impact that *Salomé* had on Chinese cultural life, I need to outline the history of the translation and performance of the play in China. Further, I will illuminate the ways in which Chinese writers and critics debated the challenging sexual and religious themes of a controversial play – one banned by the British state – whose Symbolist style had already made serious demands on English and French readers.

The 1920s witnessed an extraordinary amount of interest in *Salomé*. In 1920 the first translation of the play was serialized in *Juewu* (*Awakening*), the literary supplement of *Mingguo Daily*, which displayed a particular interest in Wilde's works. Apart from *Salomé*, it also published fourteen poems by Wilde in translation between 1920 and 1923, *De Profundis* in 1922, and a long essay, "An Introduction to Wilde" (also in 1922) by Zhang Wentian. Zhang characterized *Salomé* as a sensual play that stresses transient and physical pleasures. Intrigued by the questions about sensuality and sexuality raised by the play's dramatic ending, Chinese readers became increasingly enthusiastic about *Salomé* after it first appeared in the newspaper supplement. In 1920 Tian Han, one of the founders of modern Chinese drama, completed his famous translation of *Salomé* in Japan where he studied between 1916 and 1922. His acclaimed translation appeared in one of the leading journals of the May Fourth Period, *Shaonian Zhongguo* (*Juvenile China*) in 1921. Two years later the Zhonghua Shuju Publishing House in Shanghai reprinted this translation, together with sixteen of Aubrey Beardsley's illustrations for the 1894 first edition.

Wilde's drama and the aesthetic theory he espoused exercised an enormous influence on Tian Han's theatrical practice. During his residence in Japan, Tian Han visited Hakuson Kuriyagawa, a Japanese professor and critic, who frequently wrote on Wilde and modern European literary life. Tian Han was also an enthusiastic reader of Arthur Symons's *The Symbolist Movement in Literature*.[13] He frequently

went to see *Lady Windermere's Fan* and *Salomé* when they were performed on the stage in Tokyo.[14] His attachment to Wilde was so profound that he used *De Profundis* as a textbook to teach his spouse
English.[15] In an essay on the work of Charles Baudelaire, he recalls
that aestheticism had transformed his literary outlook: "The direction
of my studies has dramatically shifted to the aristocratic current of literature, to [Edgar] Allan Poe, Oscar Wilde, and Paul Verlaine. My own
attitude towards art and creation has become a transcendental one."[16]
Wilde's drama and aesthetic theory exercised an enormous influence
on Tian Han's theatrical practice. From the early 1920s onward, Tian
Han was devising a scheme to introduce Wilde's writings to Chinese
readers. In particular, he wished to stage *Salomé* in China.[17] He realized his ambition in 1929.

Tian Han's version is clear and unadorned, retaining the distinctive
poetic flavor of the original. Later, his version of *Salomé* became a classic
in translation reprinted (though sometimes polished in language
according to contemporary usage) again and again from the 1920s to
the 1980s. Nevertheless, other writers translated *Salomé* into Chinese,
though none of them improves on Tian Han's version. Thus, other
translations do not seem to have been prompted by the sense that previous versions were unacceptable. Tian Han's translation is complete and
better than the first one in terms of language and style. For example,
stylistically Xu Baoyan's 1927 translation is somewhat clumsy. In 1937
the Qiming publishing house in Shanghai again published a translation
of the play by Shen Peiqiu and Wang Hongsheng. These multiple publications of *Salomé* certainly contributed to Wilde's popularity and large
readership at that time, especially in Shanghai.

According to recent studies of the origin and early development of
modern Chinese drama, the New Drama Comrades Association, a theater group founded in Tokyo in 1907, staged *Salomé* at the Spring Willow
Theatre in Shanghai around 1914.[18] According to one Japanese scholar,
Salomé was "distinctly popular among the Japanese" at the end of the
Meiji period (1855–1911) and then throughout the Taisho period
(1912–25).[19] The first Japanese translation of *Salomé* appeared in 1907,
initially as a plot summary and then as a complete version by Mori
Ohgai. Other writers translated it again around 1909, and a foreign theatrical troupe, Allan Wilkie and Company, gave the first performance
on the Japanese stage at Yokohama in 1912. The following year it was
performed by a local Japanese theatrical group, Geijutsuza, and it

proved extremely popular with audiences. *Salomé* was subsequently widely staged in Japan, mostly in Tokyo. According to the Japanese critic's estimates, there were more than 120 productions of the play in the Taisho period.[20] Little wonder, then, that Japan experienced "Salomé-fever" at this time: "Among young ladies an Oriental hair-style called *Salomé-Maki* came into favor."[21] As he observes, "For about 12 years in the Taisho Period (between 1914 and 1926), fourteen actresses played their own Salomé under various kinds of directors, and made a 'Salomé-Boom' in dress-fashions and in hair-styles."[22] Thus in both Japan and China the propagation and reception of Wilde's works remained implicated in emerging currents of urban consumerism and fashion. Wilde's themes of art and artifice both embodied and commented on this emergent aspect of Chinese urban culture.

The Spring Willow Theatrical Group did not perform *Salomé* during its Tokyo period. The only foreign plays that it staged in Japan were *A Doll's House* and an adaptation of Harriet Beecher Stowe's *Uncle Tom's Cabin*. But in this cultural milieu, the group was strongly influenced by Wilde's aestheticism. When the chief members of the Spring Willow Theatrical Group, Lu Jingruo and Ouyang Yuqian, returned to China, they founded New Drama Comrades Association (1912–15) in Shanghai and renamed the Moudeli Theatre as the Spring Willow Theatre: the venue for the first Chinese production of *Salomé*.[23] The Spring Willow Theatrical Group introduced Western-inspired theatrical settings, performance techniques, and dramatic organization into China, and these methods were entirely novel to local audiences who were reared on Peking and other local operas. The western drama was called "spoken drama" as opposed to traditional Chinese theater.[24]

Nineteen twenty-nine was the year of *Salomé*. The Nanguo Theatrical Group performed the play in Nanjing and Shanghai, and its performances were tremendously successful and widely reported. Shi Jihan described the premiere on 6 July 1929: "There were only three hundred seats in the theater, but the people who came to see the play numbered more than four hundred."[25] The large crowd made the theater almost unbearably stuffy and noisy. While on the first day tickets cost sixty pence, the manager raised the price to one silver dollar for the second performance – to the outrage of audiences.[26] Nevertheless, the Nanguo Theatrical Group's staging of Wilde's drama was popular and critically acclaimed for its performance (figure 18).[27]

The 1929 performance and translation of *Salomé* inspired debate

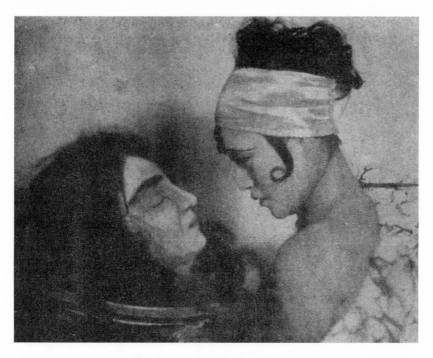

18 "Salomé and the Head of John the Baptist." *Liangyou*
[*The Young Companion*] 40 (1929), 20.

about the autonomy of art and life for art's sake among modern Chinese writers and critics. Not only did the ornate and aestheticist style and language of the play, which was entirely new and exotic, attract Chinese audiences. The story itself, focused on a passionate and strong-willed woman obsessed with kissing the dead mouth of John the Baptist, had a compelling power over Chinese audiences for several decades. This image remained potent for Chinese audiences not only because of its sexuality but also because the protagonist was seen as a symbol of an artist who performed in an aestheticist way of dying.[28] For Chinese artists, the most significant aspect of *Salomé* was that it embodied the aestheticist principle that life should be transformed into an intense artistic act. As Yuan Changying, a well-known drama critic of the day, pointed out: "In terms of its art and beauty, *Salomé* is a masterpiece and a representative work in Aestheticism in drama, as *The Picture of Dorian Gray* is in fiction and Baudelaire's *Les fleurs du mal* in poetry." Even Wilde's other social comedies "cannot represent what he adumbrated, namely, aestheticism with the principle of art for art's sake and beauty as religion. *Salomé*, only *Salomé*, written under the atmosphere of decadent literature which prevailed in Paris, embodies his artistic style."[29] Although Yuan Changying's remark is obviously a rather generalized judgment of Wilde's drama, it exemplifies how modern Chinese intellectuals evaluated Wilde's contribution to a European intellectual movement that sought to transform life into art.

II

After its appearance in Chinese translation, *Salomé* inspired a great many imitations. In particular, the climactic scene of the play, in which Salomé kisses the severed head of John only to be murdered by Herod's men, was a startling artistic revelation for many Chinese writers. A prominent example of the art it inspired is Guo Morou's *Wang Zhaojun* (1924). In this play, Han Yuan Di holds up the severed head of Mao Yanshou and repeatedly kisses its cheeks to savor the beautiful Wang Zhaojun's remaining fragrance.[30] Similarly, *Salomé* directly inspired Wang Tongzhao's *Victory after Death* (1922). The male protagonist is an artist very much in the vein of Basil Hallward in *The Picture of Dorian Gray*, and like Basil he functions as a symbol of the belief that art transcends life. The female protagonist is an idealized embodiment of love. At the end of the drama she casts aside all convention and kisses the bloodied lips of the artist – an obvious echo of the penultimate scene in *Salomé*.[31] This moment also represents a triumph over death, suggesting that beauty and love can transcend the limits of mortality.

Works such as these were numerous at the time. And they all shared a concern with the association of love and beauty with death. In other words, they all suggest that love is such a compelling emotional force and artistic topic because of its bonds with the forces of deathly destruction. For instance, Bai Wei's poetic drama *Linli* (1926) contains the following lines: "Limitless loving beauty and joy must perish on the ruby lips of the lover."[32] Likewise, a character in Yuan Changying's *The Peacock Flies Southeast* (1929) declares: "I am willing to die kissing you on the bone-scorching sun."[33] In his play *The Voice of the Ancient Pool* (1928), Tian Han also addresses the ways in which beauty connects with death, this time through an act of suicide. In order to hear again the sound of someone's voice, one of the characters presses his lips against the surface of an ancient pool, and then throws himself into the pool, taking his life.[34]

Some of these writers were so enraptured by *Salomé* that they did not stop at applying its ideas and actions in their artistic works; they also acted it out in their own lives. Bai Wei wrote to his lover: "If you don't kill me, I will kill you. I must kill you! I am Salomé; I'm more venomous than Salomé. Lover, lover, I must love you!"[35] Thus, echoing Wilde's call to make one's life a work of art, these Chinese artists used their own lives to reenact the aesthetic way of death dramatized in *Salomé*. The intellectual wellsprings for this ideal, of course, lay in the criticism of Walter Pater, itself a vital current in the formation of British aestheticism. It is well known that Wilde placed his own writings in a complex dialogue with Pater's *The Renaissance* (1873), among other works. In Pater's famous words: "For art comes to you, proposing frankly to give nothing but the highest quality to your moments as they pass, and simply for those moments' sake." And "To burn always with this hard, gem-like flame, to maintain this ecstasy, is success in life."[36]

Pater, too, was an influential figure among Chinese intellectuals in the 1920s, particularly revered by that group of artists who advocated art for art's sake. Guo Moruo was among the first to introduce Pater to Chinese audiences. In 1923 he published an essay, "On the Criticism of Walter Pater," that introduced and extolled Pater's ideas on art.[37] At this same time the preface and conclusion of Pater's *The Renaissance* was also translated into Chinese. Between 1922 and 1931 many other works by Pater, including "On Style" (1929), were also translated, and there were many volumes of essays explicating and promoting Pater's ideas. Chinese intellectuals at the time described Pater's understanding of life and art as "instantism" (*chana zhuyi*).[38] The popularity of *Salomé* among Chinese artists at this time was also an expression of the quest for immortal beauty in the passing instants of time that Pater championed. Judging from their various imitations of *Salomé*, these artists fully embraced Pater's belief that art was the sole immortal instant amid a continually fluctuating world. Writers such as Zhou Zuoren and Zhu Ziqing discussed and praised this pursuit of sensory ultimates in the present. Their prose writings were themselves attempts to extract the "instantist" moments of life and art in prosaic events and objects.

Instantism represented, above all, a conception of time at odds with conventional views of history as a linear development. It valorized the present and negated the past and the future. In other words, the present instant was the anchor to experience, including artistic experience. In instantism the present became a static vista, one in which the experience of the moment became the critical horizon. And this experience of the present was accessible through the senses of sight and hearing. Hence the corporeal body and the objects of experience were upheld as the vessels of aesthetic pleasure. Fredric Jameson's observations about the schizophrenic's experience of the world are increasingly relevant here. Jameson contends that as "temporal continuities break down, the experience of the present becomes powerfully, overwhelmingly vivid and 'material'": "the world comes before the schizophrenic with heightened intensity, bearing a mysterious and oppressive charge of affect, glowing with hallucinatory energy."[39] In precisely this way, *Salomé*'s wild act of kissing the severed head becomes intelligible: it represents an artistic embodiment of the schizophrenic experience of the world. Likewise, *Salomé*'s Chinese imitations, including Bai Wei's declaration to his lover, can be understood as intelligible artistic responses to a specific time and place. From the schizophrenic perspective, both the temporal rupture and the quest for the pleasure of the instant expressed in these works are reflections of a time when consumer culture was increasingly prevalent in everyday life. As we shall see below, the flowering of urban culture in Shanghai during the 1930s resulted in a certain style in literature.[40]

In the main, Western scholars have sought to interpret these concepts of a pure present and instantaneous pleasure from the perspectives of postmodernism and consumer society. As Jameson points out, "its formal features in many ways express the deeper logic of that particular social system" – namely, "the logic of consumer capitalism."[41] In other words, however noble and pure our experiences may be, and however full of beauty and aesthetic pleasure, they are ultimately also products of a commodified society and consumer culture.

Similarly, Regenia Gagnier relates Wilde to the Victorian public and consumer society in her ground-breaking book *Idylls of the Marketplace* (1986), and Rachel Bowlby examines Pater and Wilde from a consumerist point of view in her essay, "Promoting Dorian Gray" (1987). Bowlby argues that momentary pleasures unite "the interests of aesthete and consumer alike." She draws connections between the famous statement from the final paragraph of Pater's conclusion to *The Renaissance* and modern advertising techniques:

Art's representative offers his product with all the pseudo-artlessness of the professional salesman, including a personal touch "Art comes to you" – and proposing frankly its superior merits: "nothing but the highest quality" ... The final sentence of the "Conclusion" to *The Renaissance* is surely the last word in advertising technique. In its forceful promotion of the momentary personal pleasures promised by its object, it could be said to mark the beginning of modern consumer culture.[42]

I would argue that Bowlby's argument could also apply to the Chinese reception of *Salomé*. In the producers' and imitators' promotion of momentary pleasures as well as in the play's presentation of the aesthetic art of dying, the logic of consumer society emerges in a masked way.

There were, therefore, deeper social and cultural factors behind the blooming of Wildean thought in Shanghai. Aestheticism and Decadence represented not only currents of artistic sensibility but also a special lifestyle. And it was only possible to enact this lifestyle in a large, cosmopolitan metropolis such as Shanghai. During the 1920s and 1930s Shanghai was one of the largest commercial cities in Asia, renowned as the "Paris of the Orient."[43] The influx of domestic commerce and international capital since the early part of the century had made Shanghai a highly developed hub of commodity consumption and advertising. The level of advertising in Shanghai was by no means inferior to, say, London. Rather, the artistry and sophistication of the advertising showed that in Shanghai consumption and commercial imagery had already become artistic forms in their own right. The advertising current in Shanghai expressed a consumerist culture and lifestyle derived from Western sources and still alien to the rest of China. In this respect, two advertisements, one for bicycles, the other for cigarettes, are representative. Both carry elements of eroticism. Compared to more traditional advertisements that often featured Chinese women in traditional dress, they are quite untraditional, Western, and cosmopolitan. I believe that it was within this the commercialized setting that commodified imagery and art were conjoined, aestheticism and Decadence found a natural setting for their development. It was a place in which aestheticism and decadence could find a sympathetic reception among artists, writers, and audiences. And it was one in which Pater's instantism also resonated with people's experience of the flux of commercialized society. In other words, the experience of consumerist society could be aestheticized under the name of the ideas expressed by Pater, and thereby receive validation as an ideal lifestyle.

The bond between aestheticism and Decadence on the one hand, and consumerism and cosmopolitanism on the other hand, was most clearly expressed among a group of writers and artists less well known than Guo Moruo and Tian Han. These writers included Shao Xunmei, Zhang Kebiao, Ye Lingfeng, and Teng Gu. Their magazine was modeled on the *Yellow Book*, the journal established in London in 1894 that came before the public eye with striking illustrations by Aubrey Beardsley, the young artist whose artwork for Wilde's first edition of *Salomé* was sexually provocative. The Shanghai journal featured a yellow cover, and its contents also featured descriptions of a decadent and erotic world. Leo Ou-fan Lee has characterized Ye Lingfeng as a cosmopolitan "dandy" figure,[44] whose works are replete with descriptions of sensory experience. As a Decadent writer and artist, Ye Lingfeng became known as "China's Beardsley."[45] His pictures were extremely similar to Beardsley's, and in his novels he also imitated Beardsley's distinctive style. For example, one featured a description of a "powder room," lovingly detailing cosmetics, mirrors, and perfumes, much in the same vein as Beardsley's drawings. These literary images of Decadent lifestyles shared an intimate bond with Shanghai's urban culture. As Leo Ou-fan Lee points out, "The sources of the 'decadent' literature of China at this time lay in the fashions and the commercialization of literature after the May Fourth period."[46]

Wilde, in particular, appears repeatedly in the works of the Shanghai aesthetes. In Lin Weiyin's novel *The White Rose* (1929), the male and female protagonists devote an entire discussion to *Salomé* and its characters. He also claims to have seen the film version of Wilde's play: "Zhixi had enjoyed reading the script of *Salomé*. She would have liked to see it on stage, but had never had the opportunity. So she was delighted to now see it on the screen, and she viewed it with great attentiveness ... She felt that Salomé was truly great. She threw away everything for love; she even sacrificed the life of the one she loved for the sake of one kiss."[47] Here *Salomé* is not merely an insignificant detail within the life of the protagonists; "Salomé's kiss" has become an integral part of the thoughts and emotions of the protagonists, a representation of their worldview. Indeed, Wilde and his works were extremely popular among young people in urban China. As this scene suggests, the drama was discussed as if it was a fashionable commodity, one in which Wilde and Salomé become signs of value which circulate around the city. What is most astonishing is how Wilde's supreme aestheticist work becomes entwined with other products in a department store. Take, for example, the following description of a shop display in another Shanghai novel-ette of the 1930s:

> The neon lights lorded over them: delicate decorations, imitation diamond rings, cigarette cases, lighters, powder boxes, dancing shoes, stockings, chocolate assortments, wines from Berlin, the works of Wilde, penny dreadfuls, adventure stories, Parisian magazines, the *New Fashion Monthly*, *jiadang*, contraceptives, *gaotaikesi*, *shanderhengli*, Sana from the Berlin Hospital, British-made Everprotect.[48]

Wilde's name is thus evoked as a sign in a bright display window, nestled in a bright pile of other goods – a striking conjunction. This description figuratively erases the distinction between literature and life's commodities, so that Wilde's works achieve their value through commercial processes that are essentially no different from those that determine the value of cigarettes, chocolate, wine or fashion magazines. In other words, the image of high art does not prevent it from also becoming an object of consumption.

This lifestyle and its corresponding artistic temperament certainly reflect the social phenomenon of reification that Georg Lukács, Theodor Adorno, and Fredric Jameson have described. The Chinese absorption of *Salomé* lays bare a highly significant aspect of the reification that is evident in Wilde's original *Salomé*. The Chinese reception of Wilde's drama surpassed even the kind of visual reification that Jameson has analyzed in Joseph Conrad's works. Wilde's play, I contend, is even more palpably implicated in commodity culture. Although *Salomé* does not directly describe commercial commodities or urban life, it addresses the phenomenon of reification at an aesthetic level. One noticeable feature of the play is that the individual no longer exists as a self-contained and autonomous whole. Instead, the body is dismembered, and its component parts become isolated objects – objects of sensual desire and, further, aesthetic desire. The individual thus becomes totally reified and objectified. The soul is extinguished, so that only the reified corporeal body and its organs are subject to felt experience.

This idea comes into focus when we see how Salomé's concept of the body vanquishes Iokanaan's concept of the soul. It also appears in the numerous descriptions of the human body and organs that occur throughout the play. Indeed, the climax of the play that so stirred Chinese writers encapsulates perfectly how corporeal sensuality extinguishes the soul, just as it shows how the body and senses have been disassembled into objects, as if they were parts of a machine. In the 1929 staging of *Salomé*, this scene and the severed head received particular attention (Tian Han made the head himself). Chinese works inspired by *Salomé* not only copied this representation of how sensory feeling triumphed over the soul, they also praised and extolled the dismemberment of the body into its component parts. For example, in Xiang Peiliang's *Annen* (1926) the female protagonist's fingers and lips are described with hypersensitive acuteness as "the buds on a grapevine" and "ripened pomegranates."[49] Such descriptions obviously bear traces of *Salomé*, and they can be found in many other Chinese dramas of the time. Outwardly, this florid style appears to be a purely aesthetic device, but just as Jameson notes in describing Conrad's impressionism, it is also an "ideology of form." *Salomé*, too, becomes "the final consumable commodity ... the transformation of all these realities into style and the work of what we will call the impressionistic strategy of modernism whose function is to derealize the content and make it available for consumption on some purely aesthetic level."[50]

The crux of the issue does not lie in the relationship between aestheticism and consumer culture. (This is a topic that has been discussed at length in recent years.) Rather, it lies in the fact that Chinese proponents of aestheticism failed to express any awareness of the issues of reification and post-enlightenment objectification found in their aestheticist works and images. In China aestheticism became identified, at least in the works of authors such as Guo Moruo and Tian Han, with the campaigns against traditional Confucian culture and for "enlightenment" that followed in the wake of the May Fourth cultural movement. For such writers, the commodified relations and sensory reification behind aestheticism were supplanted by the relationship between modernity and tradition. This shift is illustrated in the subtle alterations in their changing representations of Salomé. In her Chinese incarnation she becomes a "new," modern woman who is willing to pay with her life for resisting tradition. Salomé represented the ideal of life for art's sake, and the courage to throw everything that one possesses into an act of rebellion. In the process, the urban cultural reality recedes into insignificance. Indeed, the relationship between art and commerce in the image of Salomé is not a simple one. The relationship between *Salomé* and social reality, in Louis Althusser's words, "is not one of identity but one of difference."[51] Althusser has provided a theoretical framework for analyzing the negative relationship between art and society, one that seeks out the social presence in art of absences and negations. In this way, we can discern the blindness of the aesthetes. For the Chinese aes-theticists, the adaptations of Salomé's sexuality became closely associated with their enlightenment project against traditional Confucian ideology, although it seems to us the investment there was in making sensuality into a series of bodily parts. Salomé's art of dying represented the way Chinese aesthetes experienced the modern world, as a place in which reality could be replaced by an aesthetic ideal.

But how was this blindness or the replacement of the material world made possible? One well-known example from modern Chinese literature helps to answer this question. In 1921 Guo Moruo published his collection of poems, *The Goddess*, which had a phenomenal impact on Chinese literary life and made him the most important poet of the May Fourth enlightenment generation. A representative work from *The Goddess* is "Nirvana of the Phoenixes," which cites the myth of the phoenix rising from the ashes and undergoing rebirth. The phoenix becomes a symbol of Chinese society at the time. In his words, "the poem symbolizes the rebirth of China, and also my own rebirth."[52] Guo Moruo and Tian Han both belonged to the Creation Society; they were intellectually akin. For Guo and Tian, the symbol of the phoenix came to reflect and shape their views of death and the present. Death, particularly as it was embodied in Salomé's aesthetic art of dying, implied above all rebirth. They incorporated the concepts of rebirth and of the future into the concept of time found in Pater's instantism. Thus the original notion of the present instant was reworked and expanded. Time, in this Chinese reworking of the concept, did not stop at the present point; it indicated the way to renewed futures. In addition, progressive enlightenment beliefs in historical progress, social development, and utopian futures became incorporated into the enveloping concept of rebirth, thereby becoming possible in material reality. The Chinese reimagining of Salomé through a phoenix-like image of rebirth was the most important outcome of the reception of Wilde's play. It made the aesthetic art of dying a part of Chinese aestheticist authors' rebellion against tradition, supporting their critique of the present, and advancing their quest for progressive enlightenment. In his appraisal of *Salomé*, Tian Han commented: "In this script the attitude of rebellion against society is most obvious." He explained a line from *Salomé* thus: "Art, using Wilde's means of expression, is a 'red blast of trumpets' to announce the arrival of a new era and to scare its enemies into retreat."[53] Elsewhere, he claimed: "Freedom and liberty loving masses! So you are also learning to pursue this love through this single-minded dauntless spirit!"[54]

19 "Miss Yu Shan, who Plays the Role of the Heroine in Wilde's 'Salomé,' presented by Nan Kuo Sheh," *Liangyou* [*The Young Companion*] 40 (1929), 20.

In conclusion, I would to like return to the final text that was used for the 1929 performance of *Salomé* to show how the Chinese aesthetes misused it as part of their enlightenment project. According to his memoirs, the famous painter Wu Zuroen designed the setting of the play for the Nanguo Theatrical Group. It was the first time that realist scenery had been used in a modern Chinese drama. The music used in Salomé's dance of the seven veils, a piece by Beethoven, was played by Xian Xinghai on the piano, and Wu Zuoren on the violin.[55] The success of *Salomé* was inseparable from the performance of Yu Shan, a rising star of the stage (see figure 19). Wang Yi'an recalls: "Madame Yu Shan, who won fame through her performance in *Salomé*, was physically beautiful and performed with vigour, and she won universal plaudits."[56] Subsequently Yu Shan also played Carmen. Clearly, she was extremely suited to playing rebellious roles. From these details, we can clearly see the director Tian Han's intentions. The realist scenery, Beethoven's music, and a passionate performance all combined to bring the rebellious force of Wilde's play to the fore. This rendition divested Salomé of her decadent eroticism. She assumed instead the primary role of a rebel and destroyer of tradition, one who embraced the future with revolutionary zeal.

Notes

1 "The 1911 Revolution overturned the Qing Dynasty and represented the beginning of what is thought of modern Chinese history. Yet the disintegration of the Qing Empire did not bring in it national strength or prosperity. Nor did the collapse of the old order lead to the establishment of new social ideals and norms ... These dark realities and the defeat of political revolution led people to embrace a solution in spiritual and cultural enlightenment. A feature of the enlightenment movement in modern Chinese history was the introduction of Western culture to reflect upon and criticise traditional Chinese culture. During the first decade of the New Culture Movement between 1915 and 1925 a large number of Western authors were introduced into China. Through translation, an array of Western intellectual and artistic fashions flooded into China. That aestheticism enjoyed a vogue in China was therefore not surprising". Xiaoyi Zhou, "Oscar Wilde: An Image of Artistic Self-Fashioning in Modern China: 1909–1949," in Hua Meng and Sukehiro Hirakawa, eds., *Images of Westerners in Chinese and Japanese Literature* (Amsterdam: Rodopi Press, 2000), 112. For more information on the May Fourth

Movement, see Márian Gálik, ed., *Interliterary and Intraliterary Aspect of the May Fourth Movement 1919 in China* (Bratislava: Slovak Academy of Sciences, 1990), Vera Schwartz, *The Chinese Enlightenment: Intellectuals and the Legacy of the May Fourth Movement of 1919* (Berkeley: University of California Press, 1986), Merle Goldman, ed., *Modern Chinese Literature in the May Fourth Era* (Cambridge: Harvard University Press, 1977), and Chow Tse-tsung, *The May Fourth Movement: Intellectual Revolution in Modern China* (Cambridge: Harvard University Press, 1960).

2 For details of Wilde's influence on modern Chinese writers, see Xiaoyi Zhou, "Oscar Wilde," 95–113.

3 It was translated again by Ba Jin in 1942, and later included in *The Happy Prince and Other Stories*, a collection of Wilde's fairy tales and prose poems, published by Shanghai Wenhua Publishing House in 1948. For an early account of other translations of Wilde's works in China, see Bonnie S. McDougall, *The Introduction of Western Literary Theories into Modern China 1919–1925* (Tokyo: Centre for East Asian Cultural Studies, 1971), 64–66. For a more detailed, up-to-date account of all Chinese translations of Wilde's works before 1949, see Xie Zhixi, *Mei de pianzhi* (*The Apex of Beauty*) (Shanghai: Shanghai Literature and Art Press, 1997), 17–22.

4 Zhou, Zuoren, "About the Authors," *Yuwai xiaoshuo ji* (*Collected Foreign Short Stories*), ed. and trans. Zhou Zuoren (Shanghai: Shanghai Qunyi Press, 1921), 1.

5 Leo Ou-fan Lee, *Xiandaixing de zhuiqiu* (*In Search of Modernity: Essays in Cultural Criticism*), ed. David Der-Wei Wang (Taipei: Rye Field Publishing Company, 1996), 275. Leo Ou-fan Lee argues that "Byron's translator was more fascinated by the legend of Byron than by the real Byron himself, and the legacy of Chinese Byroniana, begun by Su Man-shu, has perpetuated this English poet in the glittering image of the Byronic hero." It is also true in the cases of Wilde, Shelley, Whitman, Hardy, Ibsen, and Hugo. See Leo Ou-fan Lee, *The Romantic Generation of Modern Chinese Writers* (Cambridge: Harvard University Press, 1973), 74.

6 Mao Dun, *Mao Dun quanji* (*Complete Works of Mao Dun*), 41 vols. (Beijing: People's Literature Press, 1984–2001), XVIII: 410.

7 Wilde advocated making life an object of art and spreading the religion of beauty. "Through the elevation of the mundane world, life could be consecrated with idealism. Many Chinese critics such as Zhou Zuoren, Yu Dafu, Shao Xunmei all embraced this aspiration and attempted to live it out and spread it. The particular riches of Chinese aesthetic culture made this ideal even more refined and palpable, and it was expressed in dress, food, home furnishings and other aspects of lifestyle. The Chinese introduction to

Wilde's work, no doubt, initiated this trend of aesthetic culture." Xiaoyi Zhou, "Oscar Wilde: An Image of Artistic Self-Fashioning in Modern China: 1909–1949," 113.

8 For more information on the names of translators and dates of publication, see Zhou, "Oscar Wilde," 98.

9 The success of *Lady Windermere's Fan* in Shanghai encouraged the producers to put the play on stage in other cities throughout China. The Nankai theatrical troupe produced it in Tianjin on 2 and 3 May 1925, on 22 December 1927, and on 10 May 1929. See *Nankai Drama Movement: A Collection of Documents 1923–1949*, eds. Cui Guoliang et al (Tianjin: Nankai University Press, 1993), 177, 196, 251. The Sichuan Theatre Association staged it in Chengdu in 1926. See Sun Xiaofang, *Sichuan's Drama Movement during the Sino-Japanese Wars* (Chengdu: Sichuan University Press, 1989), 3. *Lady Windermere's Fan* was again staged in Tianjin by The Chinese Travelling Theatrical Group from 27 June to 3 July, and then from 9 to 21 October 1935. See *Collected Documents for Chinese Drama*, ed. Institute of Drama, Chinese Academy of Art (Beijing: Culture and Art Press, 1987), I, 183–85. Hong Shen's production was regarded as a model by these followers.

10 See Wang Lieyao, "Wilde and Modern Chinese Literature," *Heilongjiang jiaoyuxueyuan xuebao (Journal of Heilongjiang Educational Institute)* 3 (1988), 29.

11 For details of Mao Dun's comments on *Lady Windermere's Fan*, see Xiaoyi Zhou, "Oscar Wilde: An Image of Artistic Self-Fashioning in Modern China: 1909–1949," 99. For a brief account of Ibsen's influence in modern China, see Wang Jinghou, *May Fourth New Literature and Foreign Literature*, rev. ed. (Chengdu: Sichuan University Press, 1996), 207–23.

12 Shen, Zemin, "A Critical Introduction to Wilde," *Xiaoshuo yuebao (Short Story Monthly)* 12: 5 (1921), 11.

13 Dong Jian, *Life of Tian Han* (Beijing: Beijing October Press of Literature and Art), 106.

14 Dong Jian, *Life of Tian Han*, 177.

15 See, Zhu Shoutong, "Aestheticism in Tian Han's Early Drama," *Literary Review* 4 (1985), 93.

16 Tian Han, "A Centennial Memorial to Baudelaire, the Demonic Poet," *Shaonian Zhongguo (Juvenile China)*, 3: 4–5 (October/November 1921).

17 Tian Han discussed this plan with Guo Moruo in March 1920. See Dong Jian, *Life of Tian Han*, 163.

18 See Yuan Guoxing, *The Birth and Development of Chinese Drama* (Taipei: Wenjin Press, 1993), 219. A detailed record of this performance is not available in this book.

19 See Kimie Imura Lawlor, "Salomé in Japan: A Drama of Desire," in Earl

Miner, Toru Haga et al., eds., *Dramas of Desire; Visions of Beauty, Proceedings of the XIIIth Congress of the International Comparative Literature Association*, 6 vols. (Tokyo: International Comparative Literature Association, 1995), 2:40. For Wilde in Japan, see Jeff Nunokawa, "Oscar Wilde in Japan: Aestheticism, Orientalism, and the Derealization of the Homosexual," in Gary Y. Okihiro et al., eds., *Privileging Positions: The Sites of Asian American Studies* (Washington: Washington State University Press, 1995), 281–90.

20 Kimie Imura Lawlor, "Salomé in Japan: A Drama of Desire," 40.

21 Kimie Imura Lawlor, "Salomé in Japan: A Drama of Desire," 41.

22 Kimie Imura Lawlor, "Salomé in Japan: A Drama of Desire," 45, n19.

23 See Yuan Guoxing, *The Birth and Establishment of Chinese Drama* (Taipei: Wenjin Press, 1993), 219, 248. Yuan recorded that *Salomé* was performed by the theatrical group, but does not specify the date.

24 The traditional Chinese theater was dominated by musicals, Peking and other local operas in which singing is the most important part of performance. This situation changed after the introduction of Western drama to the Chinese theatre in the early twentieth century.

25 Shi Jihan, "Notes on the Plays Staged by the Nanguo Theatrical Group," *Xiju yu yishu (Drama and the Arts)* 1:4 (1929), 93.

26 See *Collected Documents for Chinese Drama*, ed. Institute of Drama, Chinese Academy of Art (Beijing: Culture and Art Press, 1987), I: 122. The original notice for this change as recorded by Tian Han reads: "As the weather is extremely hot, and the theatre is small and too crowded, it is not only the theatrical atmosphere cannot be created, and it is also harmful to the audience's health. We are sorry that we have to increase the price to the level of our first performance trip (one silver dollar)." See *Tian Han wenji (The Works of Tian Han)*, 16 vols. (Beijing: China's Drama Press, 1983–86), XIV: 344.

27 As we shall see below, some critics, including Wang Yi'an, liked the performance of Yu Shan, who performed Salomé with vigor and passion.

28 As Shen Zemin points out in his fine introduction to Wilde, "*Salomé* is the symbol of Wilde himself, Salomé's passion is Wilde's passion. In writing *Salomé*, Wilde is actually writing about himself." See Shen Zemin, "A Critical Introduction to Wilde," *Xiaoshuo yuebao (Short Story Monthly)*, 12: 5 (1921), 12.

29 Yuan Changying, "About *Salomé*," in *Collected Works of Yuan Changying* (Changsha: Hunan People's Publisher, 1985), 273.

30 Guo Moruo, *Guo Moruo juzuo quanji (Plays of Guo Moruo)*, ed., China's Drama Press (Beijing: China's Drama Press, 1982), 148.

31 Wang Tongzhao, *Victory After Death, Xaioshuo yuebao (Short Story Monthly)*, 13: 7 (1922), 32.

32 Bai Wei, *Linli* (Shanghai: Commercial Press, 1926), 96.

33 Yuan Changying, *The Peacock Flies Southeast and Other One-Act Plays* (Taipei: Taiwan Commercial Press, 1983), 55.

34 See Tian Han, *Tian Han wenji* (*The Works of Tian Han*) (Beijing: China's Drama Press, 1983), II: 41–43.

35 Bai Wei and Yang Sao, *Zuo ye* (*Last Night*) (Shijiazhuang: Hebei Jiaoyu chubanshe [Hebai Education Press], 1994), 20.

36 Walter Pater, *The Renaissance: Studies in Art and Poetry – The 1893 Text*, ed. Donald L. Hill (Berekeley CA: University of California Press, 1980), 180, 179.

37 See Xie Zhixi, *Mei de pianzhi*, 15–17.

38 *Chana zhuyi* (instantism) was coined by modern Chinese writers to summarize Pater's theory and describe an aestheticist way of being, which has a strong taste of Buddhism. For a Buddhist perspective of *Chana zhuyi* in modern Chinese literature, see Tan Guilin, "Yu Pingbo: Changeable Lire and *Chana zhuyi*," *Zhongguo xiandai wenxue yanjiu congkan* (*Studies in modern Chinese literature series*), 2 (1996), 137–42.

39 Fredric Jameson, "Postmodernism and Consumer Society," in Hal Foster, ed., *The Anti-Aesthetic: Essays on Postmodern Culture* (Washington, WA: Bay Press, 1983), 120.

40 See also Leo Ou-fan Lee, *Shanghai Modern: The Flowering of a New Urban Culture in China, 1930–1945* (Cambridge, MA: Harvard University Press, 1999), 3–120.

41 Fredric Jameson, *The Political Unconscious: Narrative as a Socially Symbolic Act* (Ithaca, NY: Cornell University Press, 1981), 125.

42 Rachel Bowlby, *Shopping with Freud* (London: Routledge, 1993), 23–4.

43 See Leo Ou-fan Lee, *Xiandaixing de zhuiqiu*, 161. Shanghai was also known as "the Paris of Asia": see Lee, *Shanghai Modern*, 3. Lee observes that Tokyo, Hong Kong, and Singapore cannot compare with Shanghai in prosperity in the 1930s.

44 Lee, *Shanghai Modern*, 257–65.

45 Ye Lingfeng, "Beardsley's Drawings," *Dushu suibi* (*Random Jottings on Reading*), 2 (Beijing: Sanlian Shudian, 1988), 296.

46 Lee, *Xiandaixing de zhuiqiu*, 217; my translation.

47 See Liu Qinwei, ed., *Zhongguo xiandai weimeizhuyi wenxue zuoping xuan* (*Selected Works of Modern Chinese Aestheticism*) (Guangzhou: Huacheng chubanshe, 1996), 367.

48 He Jin, "Zaoxing donglixue" ('Modeling Kinetics'), *Xiaoshuo* (*Novel*), 1 October 1934.

49 Xiang Peiliang, *Annen*, in Liu Qinwei, ed., *Zhongguo xiandai weimeizhuyi wenxue zuoping xuan*, 754–55.

50 Jameson, *The Political Unconscious*, 214–15.

51 Louis Althusser, "A Letter on Art in Reply to André Daspre" (1966), in Raman Selden, ed., *The Theory of Criticism from Plato to the Present: A Reader* (London: Longman, 1988), 459.

52 Guo Moruo, *Nushen* (*The Goddess*), ed., Sang Fengkang, (Changsha, Hunan renmin chubanshe [Hunan People's Publisher], 1983), 206.

53 Tian Han, *Tian Han Wenji*, XIV: 341. Wilde's text reads: "The red blasts of trumpets, that herald the approach of kings, and make afraid the enemy, are not so red" (Wilde, *Salomé*, in *Works*, ed. Robert Ross, 14 vols. [London: Methuen, 1908], II: 30).

54 Tian Han, *Tian Han Wenji*, XIV: 343.

55 Wu Zuoren, "Yi Nanguoshe de Tian Han he Xu Beihong" (A Memoir of Tian Han and Xu Beihong in the Nanguo Theatrical Group), in *Tian Han: Huiyi Tian Han zhuanji* (*Tian Han: A Collection of Memoirs*) (Beijing: Wenshi ziliao chubanshe, 1985), 76, 78.

56 Wang Yi'an, "Ji Tian Han" (*Remembering Tian Han*), in Bo Bin & Xu Jing-dong, eds., *Zhongguo dangdai wenxue yanjiu ziliao congshu: Tian Han zhuanji* (*Contemporary Chinese Literature Research Materials: Tian Han Volume*) (Nanjing: Jiangsu renmin chubanshe, 1984), 245.

Notes on the Contributors

ANN ARDIS is Professor of English at the University of Delaware. She is the author of *New Women, New Novels: Feminism and Early Modernism* (Rutgers University Press, 1990) and *Modernism and Cultural Conflict, 1880–1922* (Cambridge University Press, 2002). She is co-editor (with Bonnie Kime Scott) of *Virginia Woolf Turning the Centuries: Selected Papers from the Ninth Annual Conference on Virginia Woolf* (Pace University Press, 2000) and (with Leslie Lewis) *Women's "Experience" of Modernity, 1875–1945* (Johns Hopkins University Press, 2002).

STEPHEN ARATA is Associate Professor of English at the University of Virginia. He is the author of *Fictions of the Loss in the Victorian Fin de Siècle* (Cambridge University Press, 1996) and of a number of essays on nineteenth- and twentieth-century British literature and culture.

JOSEPH BRISTOW is Professor of English at the University of California, Los Angeles, where he served as Clark Professor during 1998–99. His books include *Effeminate England: Homoerotic Writing after 1885* (Columbia University Press, 1995) and *Sexuality*, New Critical Idiom (Routledge, 1997). Among his edited volumes are (with Isobel Armstrong) *Nineteenth-Century Women Poets: An Oxford Anthology* (Oxford University Press, 1996) and *The Cambridge Companion to Victorian Poetry* (Cambridge University Press, 2000).

JOSEPHINE M. GUY is Reader in English at the University of Nottingham. Her most recent books include *The Victorian Social-Problem Novel* (Macmillan, 1996) and (with Ian Small) *Oscar Wilde's Profession: Writing and the Culture Industry in the Late Nineteenth Century* (Oxford University Press, 2000). She has also edited *The Victorian Age: An Anthology of Sources and Documents* (Routledge, 1998).

LISA HAMILTON is a literary agent based in New York City. She received her doctorate in English from Harvard University in 1998. Her chapter was written while she held an Ahmanson-Getty Fellowship at the William Andrews Clark Memorial Library of the University of California, Los Angeles in 1999.

ELLIS HANSON teaches English literature and gay studies at Cornell University and is the author of *Decadence and Catholicism* (Harvard University Press, 1997).

DIANA MALTZ is Assistant Professor of English at Southern Oregon University. In 1999 she was an Ahmanson-Getty Fellow at the William Andrews Clark Memorial Library of the University of California, Los Angeles. She has published articles on Victorian poverty and aesthetics. During 2000–1, she held a postdoctoral fellowship at the Paul Mellon Centre for Studies in British Art and the Yale Center for British Art in order to complete a book on aestheticism's mission to the working classes.

KERRY POWELL is Professor of English at Miami University, Oxford, Ohio. His books include *Oscar Wilde and the Theatre of the 1890s* (Cambridge University Press, 1990) and *Women and Victorian Theatre* (Cambridge, 1997). He is editor of the forthcoming *Cambridge Companion to Victorian and Edwardian Theatre*, and a contributor to *Queen of Decadence*, a collection of essays on the Salomé legend forthcoming from the University of Chicago Press. He is a contributor to the *Cambridge Companion to Oscar Wilde* (Cambridge University Press, 1997).

PETER RABY lectures in drama and English at the University of Cambridge. He has written extensively on theater and is the editor of *The Cambridge Companion to Oscar Wilde* (Cambridge University Press, 1997). His recent books include a biography of Alfred Russel Wallace (Princeton University Press, 2001). He is the book-writer of the musical *The Three Musketeers*, which premiered at San Jose, California, in March 2001.

TALIA SCHAFFER is Assistant Professor of English Queens College, City University of New York. She is the author of *The Forgotten Female Aesthetes: Literary Culture in Late-Victorian England* (University Press of Virginia,

2000) and the co-editor (with Kathy A. Psomiades), of *Women and British Aestheticism* (University Press of Virginia, 1999). She has also published numerous articles on late-Victorian writers, including Lucas Malet, Charlotte Yonge, Alice Meynell, Thomas Hardy, Henry James, and Bram Stoker.

LAURENCE SENELICK is Fletcher Professor of Drama at Tufts University. His most recent books include *The Changing Room: Sex, Drag and Theatre* (Routledge, 2000), *Lovesick: Modernist Plays of Same-Sex Love, 1894–1925* (Routledge, 1999), and *The Chekhov Theatre: A Century of the Plays in Performance* (Cambridge University Press, 1997), which won the Barnard Hewitt Award of the American Society for Theatre Research. He is an advisory editor of the *Journal of the History of Sexuality, Sexuality & Culture,* and *Nineteenth-Century Theatre.* Currently, he is working on a study of the popular imagery of sexual deviance and a documentary history of Soviet theater.

IAN SMALL is Professor of English literature at the University of Birmingham. He is general editor of the Oxford English Texts edition of *The Complete Works of Oscar Wilde,* the first volume of which was published by Oxford University Press in 2000. His recent books include (with Josephine M. Guy) *Oscar Wilde's Profession: Writing and the Culture Industry in the Late Nineteenth Century* (Oxford University Press, 2000), and *Oscar Wilde: Recent Research* (ELT Press, 2000).

JOHN STOKES is Professor of English at the Kings College, University of London. He has written widely on the culture of the *fin de siècle.* Most recently, he is the author of *Oscar Wilde: Myths, Miracles and Imitations* (Cambridge University Press, 1996) and editor of *Eleanor Marx (1855–1898): Life – Work – Contacts* (Ashgate, 2000). Together with Russell Jackson he is editing Wilde's journalism for Oxford English Texts.

XIAOYI ZHOU is Professor of English Literature at Beijing University. He earned his doctorate at the University of Lancaster, UK, in 1993, and was Research Fellow at the University of Hong Kong between 1997 and 2000. He has published widely on English and comparative literature, literary theory, and cultural studies. He is the author of *Beyond Aestheticism: Oscar Wilde and Consumer Society* (Peking University Press, 1996), and *Aestheticism and Consumer Culture* (Peking University Press, 2002).

Index